FREE

ENTERPRISE

CITY

Free Enterprise City: Houston in Political-Economic Perspective

JOE R. FEAGIN

RUTGERS UNIVERSITY PRESS   New Brunswick and London

Library of Congress Cataloging-in-Publication Data
Feagin, Joe R.
Free enterprise city:Houston in political-economic perspective /
Joe R. Feagin.
p. cm.
Includes index.
ISBN 0-8135-1321-9   ISBN 0-8135-1322-7 (pbk.)
1. Houston Metropolitan Area (Tex.)—Economic conditions.
2. Houston Metropolitan Area (Tex.)—Social conditions.   3. Business
enterprises—Texas—Houston Metropolitan Area.   4. Business and
politics—Texas—Houston Metropolitan Area.   5. Urban policy—
Texas—Houston Metropolitan Area.   I. Title.
HC108.H8F43 1988
976.4'1411— dc19
87-38116
CIP
British Cataloging-in-Publication information available

CONTENTS

LIST OF FIGURES AND MAPS

LIST OF TABLES

PREFACE

This book is the result of a long process of data gathering and conceptual gestation. When I started researching Houston in the early 1980s, I had originally planned to prepare an article or two on the city and to document how local developers operated for a book I was working on at the time, one subsequently called *The Urban Real Estate Game*. However, discussions with a number of Houstonians in business and government and urban sociology colleagues led me to rethink these limited goals and to undertake a systematic analysis of the Houston metropolis—the city widely regarded by U.S. analysts in the 1970s and early 1980s as the leading free enterprise model of urban development. The more material I gathered on the city's political and economic history, the more I was stimulated to examine, in conference papers and articles, theoretical questions and concepts in the contemporary urban literature. Among these were the issues of development capital, urban hierarchy and convergence, uneven development, primary extraction economies, and the role of the state.

Later, as I exchanged research papers and information with European scholars, I was somewhat surprised to learn that the U.S. city called the "shining buckle of the Sunbelt" was also cited in Europe as the prototypical free enterprise model of successful city development by conservative analysts and political activists seeking to dismantle urban planning and other governmental regulatory systems there. These discussions placed Houston in the context of worldwide debates over the best public policies for metropolitan growth and development. They also inspired me to expand my research to examine the historical and contemporary contours of planning efforts in this free enterprise city, as well as the social consequences of Houston's rapid economic and population growth, expansion rarely interrupted between 1836 and the extended recession of the mid-1980s. The result of reflection on the European perspective on Houston was to broaden my analysis of the metropolis to include the range of political and economic issues explored in the present monograph, most of which was written in 1987–1988.

I am indebted to many people for their assistance in preparing this book. In the Notes I have listed interviews with numerous knowledgeable Houstonians, some of whom wished to remain anonymous; I appreciate their often detailed and candid assessments of Houston. From the beginning Gideon Sjoberg and Walter Firey, premier urban sociologists, allowed me to explore conceptual and methodological problems with them; they, and later Anthony Orum, gave me the benefit of their decades of insightful research on urban development.

I am indebted to several scholars who undertook a critical reading of early articles or portions of this manuscript in its various drafts: these included Robert Beauregard, Robert Fisher, Stephen Klineberg, Roger M. Olien,

Joseph A. Pratt, Nestor Rodriguez, Richard Child Hill, David Perry, Michael Harloe, Michael Parkinson, Mark Gottdiener, and Dennis Judd. Among the most helpful reviewers of the final draft were John Gilderbloom and the members of his Fall 1987 graduate seminar in urban sociology at the Unviersity of Houston. This book has also been strengthened by discussions over the years, in various formats, of urban development and allied issues with Manuel Castells, Charles Tilly, Susan and Norman Fainstein, Michael Peter Smith, and Robin Boyle. Significant research assistance was supplied at the University of Texas by then graduate students Nestor Rodriguez, Kelly Riddell, Beth Anne Shelton, and Steven Worden.

I would like to thank William S. Livingston, Graduate Dean of the University of Texas at Austin, for his intellectual and small grant support, through the University Research Institute, and S. Dale McLemore, chair of the Department of Sociology at the University of Texas, for his long-term intellectual support. I am indebted to Michael Harloe, editor, and Edward Arnold, Ltd., publisher, for permission to use in substantially revised form portions of two articles published in the *International Journal of Urban and Regional Research:* "The Social Costs of Houston's Growth," *International Journal of Urban and Regional Research* 9 (June 1985):164–185; and "The Secondary Circuit of Capital: Office Construction in Houston, Texas," *International Journal of Urban and Regional Research* 11 (June 1987):172–191. I am indebted to Clairece B. Feagin for proofreading and indexing assistance.

Austin, Texas
January 1988

FREE

ENTERPRISE

CITY

1

Introduction: Houston,

The Free Enterprise City

On April 21, 1836, General Sam Houston and his 900–soldier army defeated Mexico's General Santa Anna and his 1,200–soldier army in the brief but famous battle of San Jacinto, on the banks of the Buffalo Bayou in an area that is now on the east side of the Houston metropolis. A boosterish article in a 1960 issue of the Houston Chamber of Commerce magazine notes the subsequent events: "Hardly had the smoke of battle cleared when two New York real-estate men, brothers John K. and Augustus C. Allen, decided to establish a city at the headwaters of Buffalo Bayou—eighteen miles upstream from San Jacinto."[1] Soon thereafter, the Allen brothers named their real estate development project after the daring hero of the Texas revolution, General Sam Houston. Between 1845, the year the U.S. Congress offered statehood to the infant Republic of Texas, and the early 1980s, the population of this Sunbelt development project would grow from about two thousand people to more than three million from the beginning to the present.

A Free Enterprise Model for the World

By the late 1970s Houston had not only become one of the largest cities in the United States but had also achieved the status of a widely cited model of the positive consequences of a free enterprise, laissez-faire approach to urban development. Publications of conservative research institutes in the United States have held Houston up as a model for urban development, a model of relatively unrestrained free enterprise. In *Resolving the Housing Crisis,* a 1982 publication of the Pacific Institute for Urban Policy Research, Houston is noted as a model for solving housing problems in other cities; the emphasis is on reducing housing regulations and reorienting housing markets to free enterprise. And this particular analysis has been praised by such prominent housing policy analysts as George Sternlieb and Anthony Downs. Conservative think tanks such as the Adam Smith Institute in Great Britain have used the Houston case as a primary example of the economic prosperity that comes from an unrestrained "supply-side" approach to urban economic investment

1

and development. In fact, in an Adam Smith Institute book, *Town and Country Chaos,* Robert Jones extols the virtues of Houston's lack of governmental planning and public sector intervention in the local economy and uses the Houston case to argue against the strict city planning controls in British cities.[2]

Reportedly, from the mid-1970s to the early 1980s leading business and political figures in both the United States and Europe cited the unplanned free enterpise economy and philosophy of Houston as the reasons for the city's remarkable record of material progress. For a time, then, Houston was more than a place in urban space; it had become a symbol in a resurgent free enterprise ideology.

Often called the "free enterprise capital," the "oil capital of the world," and the "shining buckle of the Sunbelt," Houston has received modest attention from social science researchers. Indeed, in 1987 we know more—in terms of substantial social science research—about small cities such as Muncie and New Haven than we do about Houston, a city more than six times their size. There are remarkable gaps in the sizable literature on American cities. Particularly striking is the absence of theoretically informed, relatively comprehensive, in-depth analyses of major U.S. cities. Over the last decade or two some excellent additions to the city literature have been published: book-length analyses of limited aspects of a particular city's development, such as histories of key politicians and political movements (e.g., Michael J. McDonald and William B. Wheeler's research on Knoxville, Tennessee), general histories with little theoretical bite (e.g., Carol Hoffecker's book on Wilmington), important analyses of urban renewal (Clarence Stone's book on Atlanta), specialized books on small towns (Roger and Diana Olien's work on oil boom towns), and important edited collections of articles on particular cities (e.g., the articles in *Restructuring the City*).[3] There are also a growing number of general theoretical analyses of cities, such as the work of Manuel Castells, Mark Gottdiener, David Harvey, and Michael Peter Smith.

Social science research on urban matters will be substantially improved with the addition of two dozen empirically based, theoretically informed case studies of particular metropolitan areas in the United States. In her book on Cairo Janet Abu-Lughod has written one of very few in-depth, theoretically informed social science portraits of a world-class city. She notes in her preface that cities mean different things to different people. The tourist looks at the city and sees excitement. But the same city is barely noticeable to the person who follows life's daily routines; he or she "envisages neither its extent or form nor its links with past and future."[4] A historian may ignore its modernity for its past. Yet other social scientists may be attracted to its structure, ecology, social problems, or power elite. Therefore, in my analysis of Houston, I hope to provide a broad social science analysis of Houston which takes into account its political-economic structure and form, its actors and vicissitudes, its past and its future, all assessed from a critical perspective.

Three Basic Themes in Analyzing Houston

A city is many things: an arena for capitalistic investment and location decisions, a set of complex labor markets, a complicated land and built environment, a political milieu in which various classes contend for control of the state, and neighborhoods where individuals and households live. In this book I will emphasize the importance of investment decisions and the capitalistic economy, the local and national state, and the sociospatial layout of the city. I will opt for a multifaceted theoretical framework that views the city not only as an economic reality but also as a political and spatial reality. For the sake of discussion I will often dissect these dimensions separately, although they cannot in reality be disconnected because they are intimately intertwined. What appears relevant only to the state from one perspective will be economically relevant from another; the converse is also true. Moreover, the spatial dimension is constantly relevant in the delineation of political and economic matters.

More specifically, in the following chapters I will note recurrent themes in assessing the Houston case, including:

1   A serious consideration of a city's global context can illuminate an understanding of the economic development, economic decline, and sociospatial character of a particular city. In the Houston case the relevant global context is the capitalistic world market.

2   The development and structuring of "free enterprise" cities often depend upon the decisions of state officials operating at local, regional, and national levels. In the Houston case these officials have usually been drawn from and have worked in close association with the city's business community.

3   Without substantial public planning in the public interest, unrestrained free enterprise development in cities can generate massive social costs for local residents and communities. In the Houston case local residents have paid a heavy price for the low-tax, laissez-faire, free market approach of the city's business leadership.

The first theme emphasizes the importance of setting a city within its world context. Social science analysis in the United States has tended to analyze

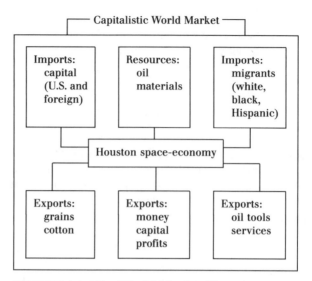

FIGURE 1.1. The World Market Context

social phenomena, including metropolitan development, within a regional or nation-state context. While it is probably the case that ignoring the global context of cities limits one's understanding of urban development in any historical period, neglecting the world context seems an egregious error in assessing a modern city. Most larger cities around the world have become more and more integrated into the global market of capitalism since the world wars. In the case of the Houston metropolitan area the relevant context for analysis is definitely this capitalistic world market. Selected dimensions of the global context are delineated in Figure 1.1.

This figure illustrates selected aspects of the flow of people, materials, and capital into and out of Houston for the period from the 1950s to the 1980s. The growth and development of Houston has involved the flow of domestic and foreign capital, primary resources and construction materials, and migrant labor *to* the city and the export of oil-related products, agricultural products, and money capital *out of* the city. Some of these factors have U.S. origins and destinations, but others have international sources and destinations. The actual entrance of Houston into the global market system began in the nineteenth century with the cotton trade between Houston and British cities. By the 1980s Houston was so well integrated into the world market that its severe economic recession was rooted in economic decisions of the international oil cartel and in the export problems caused by the high American dollar. The 1980s crash in oil prices brought substantial cutbacks in production and employee layoffs in the greater Houston area. Moreover, when the price of oil increased in 1987 selected sectors 'of the Houston economy rebounded to some extent. I will demonstrate in this book the fruitfulness of examining a major metropolitan area within the global context of modern capitalism.

A second major theme is that free enterprise cities are *not* in fact free market cities. Not only are such cities disproportionately shaped by decisions made by executives in a few large corporations in the relevant industries, but they are also substantially fashioned and formed by state intervention, often at the behest of business leaders. Figure 1.2 accents four governmental inputs essential to the development of the Houston political economy, one directed by Houston's business elite over the last half-century. The close relationship between the state and the business elite is one of the more revealing aspects of Houston's political-economic evolution. Here is the central importance of governmental infrastructure aid for projects desired by the local business community, such as federal money for highways and bridges, as well as substantial military-industrial aid for the burgeoning Houston petrochemical industry during World War II and later for the Johnson Space Center built in south Houston during the 1960s. The business elites, long in control of Houston's economy and government, aggressively sought this aid. This also provides examples of both local government aid for transport facilities, in the form of special bonds to expand local port facilities, and government officials working in coordination with the local business leadership to maintain a weak set of regulatory mechanisms for the city. Thus, Houston has become famous as the

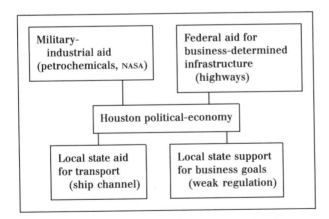

Figure 1.2. State Assistance and Involvement

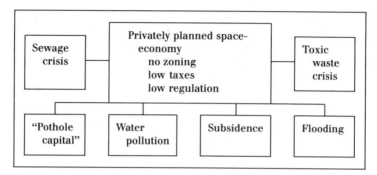

Figure 1.3. Social Costs of Growth

city with weak planning and no zoning. While Houston is often advertised as the premier free enterprise city, in reality the city's business leadership has regularly taken major governmental "handouts" for projects that support or create profit making in the city. Government action has in fact been opposed only for such activities as the provision of certain types of infrastructure for neighborhoods, the regulation of development with zoning or planning, the increase in taxation for many public services, and the assistance of poorer residents in the form of social welfare programs.

A third theme of this book relates to the unplanned character of Houston's remarkable growth and subsequent decline. Houston is indeed the unplanned city that many scholarly and popular writers have written about, but that relatively unplanned character, coupled with the aforementioned starvation of the public infrastructure, particularly for neighborhoods, and the low level of taxation, has brought massive social costs to the city's residents; the poorest Houstonians have often borne the heaviest burden. Houston has been celebrated by free market advocates the world over as the city where private enterprise has brought to the citizenry the unadulterated benefits of private development and private markets, without much in the way of major urban social problems. This rosy image of Houston is mythical, as Figure 1.3 indicates. Free enterprise Houston has a huge "laundry list" of urban problems, all of which have been either generated by or at least aggravated by the creation of a low-tax, business-oriented government and an emphasis on the "good business climate." Among these are major subsidence, flooding, water pollution, toxic waste, sewage, and street maintenance problems. While the residents in most U.S. cities have faced some of these difficulties, albeit to a variable degree, Houstonians have faced all of them, and more; indeed, most of these urban dilemmas have become worse over the last few decades.

A Descriptive Overview:
Population and Geography

Population Growth

Before examining the multifaceted economic, political, and spatial history of
the city of Houston, I will provide a brief demographic profile of the city over
the century and a half of its development. Table 1.1 shows the rapid growth
of the populations of the city and of the total metropolitan area. Between the
1850 census and the 1980 census the city grew from nearly 2,400 people to
almost 1.6 million, while the metropolitan area grew from 18,632 to nearly
three million. The Texas population grew more rapidly than Houston's until
the 1880s, but since that decade the city has grown faster than the state as a
whole. In 1880 Houston held only 1 percent of the Texas population, but by
the 1980s the Houston metropolitan area was the residence of more than
20 percent of the state's population. The average population growth per decade in the period between 1850 and 1980 was striking—an average increase
of 66 percent for the city and nearly 50 percent for the metropolitan area.
These rates of population growth, over so many decades, are probably the
most sustained for any city in North America.

Numerous analysts have emphasized Houston's rapid growth in the 1960s
and 1970s; the city gained about 30 percent in population in each of these
decades. Yet no analyst has noted that the most rapid growth in the city's history occurred in the years from 1920 to 1930, during which period the city
grew by more than 111 percent from 138,000 to 292,000 people. The surprisingly dramatic growth in this distant decade is just one of the tantalizing
demographic facts about Houston that begs for sociological explanation. With
the dramatic population increase Houston moved from the seventy-second
largest city in the United States in 1900 to the twenty-seventh largest in 1930.
By 1930 Houston was the second largest city in the South, second only to
New Orleans. Houston Chamber of Commerce officials excitedly proclaimed
Houston the "little New York of the South." Houston's population growth
continued even during the Great Depression—32 percent over that troubled
decade. From 1930 to 1940 only Washington, D.C., among the nation's major
cities had more rapid population growth than Houston. Real estate statistics
reflected a similar growth pattern.

The city's rapid rate of growth persisted until the 1980s. By 1940 the city
had grown to 384,000, with nearly 647,000 in the metropolitan area. Prior to
the 1960s few U.S. observers predicted that Houston would become a major city. Yet in the 1950s the London *Times* speculated that the United States

TABLE 1.1.

Houston's Population Growth: 1850–1990

| YEAR | City (Incorporated Area) | | |
	Population	Numerical Growth	Percentage Growth
1850	2,396		
		2,449	102.0
1860	4,845		
		4,537	93.6
1870	9,382		
		7,131	76.0
1880	16,513		
		11,044	67.0
1890	27,557		
		17,076	61.9
1900	44,633		
		34,167	76.5
1910	78,800		
		59,476	75.5
1920	138,276		
		154,076	111.4
1930	292,352		
		92,162	31.5
1940	384,514		
		211,649	55.0
1950	596,163		
		342,056	57.4
1960	938,219		
		295,286	31.5
1970	1,233,505		
		360,581	29.2
1980	1,594,086		
		294,016	18.4
1990 (projected)	1,888,102		

YEAR	Metropolitan Area Population	Numerical Growth	Percentage Growth
1850	18,632		
		16,809	90.2
1860	35,441		
		13,545	38.2
1870	48,986		
		22,330	45.6
1880	71,316		
		14,908	20.9
1890	86,224		
		48,376	56.1
1900	134,600		
		51,054	37.9
1910	185,654		
		86,821	46.8
1920	272,475		
		204,095	74.9
1930	456,570		
		190,299	41.7
1940	646,869		
		300,631	46.5
1950	947,500		
		482,894	51.0
1960	1,430,394		
		568,922	39.8
1970	1,999,316		
		906,034	45.3
1980	2,905,350		
		1,040,050	35.7
1990	3,945,400		

SOURCE: U.S. Bureau of the Census; Houston Chamber of Commerce, "Houston Data Sketch," 1981.
NOTE: The metropolitan area figures for the years prior to 1950 and the 1990 data are estimates.

would soon be organized around four great cities—New York, Chicago, Los Angeles, and Houston.[5] This prediction was not far off the mark. By 1970 Houston was a major metropolis. The city population and metropolitan population figures were 1.2 million and 2 million respectively. Between April 1970 and April 1980 an average of 1,300 people a week were added to the Harris County population. From 1975 to 1980, Houston grew at an average annual rate of 4.7 percent a year, the highest rate of growth for major U.S. cities. By 1980 the incorporated city of Houston had nearly 1.6 million people, and by 1983 Houston had surpassed Philadelphia to become the fourth largest city in the nation. By 1980 the Houston metropolitan area (M S A) was nearly 3 million. In the mid-1980s the U.S. Office of Management and the Budget defined a larger statistical unit than the traditional metropolitan area— a unit called the Houston-Galveston-Brazoria Consolidated Metropolitan Area (C M S A), a seven-county unit which encompasses most of the labor market and regional production for the greater Houston area. In 1984 there were 3.4 million people and 1.9 million workers in this Houston C M S A area.[6]

However, this 1970–1980 growth was very uneven. The resident population declined significantly in the downtown business district, from 3,719 people in 1970 to a twentieth-century low of only 2,145 in 1980. There was also a population decrease in the central city area (that within the Loop 610; see Map 1.2). The population within the central city area decreased from 570,394 to 524,345, a decline of 8 percent. Beyond Loop 610 there were very large population and percentage increases. The population in the adjacent ring increased by 48 percent, while that in the outlying sector of Harris County grew by 156 percent. By 1980 most of Houston's population resided outside the central city area, miles from the 1838 city limits.[7]

A Slowing of Growth

The data in Table 1.1 include the 1990 projections, made about 1980: about 1.9 million for the city and about 3.9 million for the metropolitan area. Because of the economic downturn in the mid-1980s these projections may be on the high side. The prosperity of the 1850–1980 period ended abruptly in the mid-1980s. As I will document in subsequent chapters, the city's economy went into a major tailspin and unemployment, bankruptcies, mortgage foreclosures, and despair hit an all-time high for the city that had missed most previous economic difficulties. During the U.S. recession of 1981–1982, a number of people migrated to Texas cities from other parts of the country in a quest for a decent job. But by 1983–1984 it had become clear to many of these "Snowbirds," as they were called by native Houstonians, that such a decision was a mistake. In 1982 there was a net immigration of 417,000 people entering Texas; by 1986 this had dropped to fewer than 5,000 people. And in the case of Houston, there was probably an actual loss of population. Although city population losses have not, as of 1987, been documented by an official census, some experts estimated the net loss at a few thousand for some years during the 1983–1987 period. By the late 1980s the outmigration, some experts suggested, had slowed to the point that the city's population had stabilized or even begun to grow slowly.

The Geographical Area of Houston

Map 1.1 indicates the extent of the city limits in 1840, a few years after the city's founding, and in 1927, nearly a century later. The city limits in 1840 were shaped like a large box encompassing what is now the downtown, an area just under nine square miles in size. A series of annexations, especially in

MAP 1.1. Houston City Limits, 1840 and 1927

SOURCE: Rice Center, "Northwest Area," *Area Profile 2* (Houston: Rice Center, 1986), p. 1. By permission of Rice Center. "Houston Map (1927)," Houston Metropolitan Research Center, Houston Public Library

MAP 1.2. Houston City Limits, 1986
SOURCE: See Map 1.1.

the years from 1900 to 1927, resulted in a much expanded Houson, several times the size of the original. In 1948 the city council annexed enough land outside its seventy-six-square-mile area to double its size, completely surrounding the small outlying cities of West University, Galena Park, and Pasadena. Since then a number of annexations have continued to expand the size of the city. Map 1.2 delineates the 1986 city limits, altogether an area of more than 500 square miles covering a large portion of Harris County. Because of the aggressive annexation policy most of the densely population areas of Harris County, the principal county in the metropolitan area, fall within the official city limits. About 60 percent of the metropolitan population also falls within the city limits, one of the highest proportions for major cities in the United States.[8]

The Structure of This Book

Chapter 2 provides a theoretical overview of mainstream approaches to the city in the United States, followed by a review of critical power-conflict perspectives on the city. I examine theories of convergence and of capitalistic development and emphasize the importance of examining cities—particularly Sunbelt cities—within a global context. Chapters 3 and 4 focus on the political-economic history of Houston over the last century, with particular attention to major periods of corporate investment and industrial change and to the intertwining of economic developments and state intervention into the economy. Chapter 5 probes the role of actors and agency in urban development by examining the historical development of the business elites in Houston over a century and a half; I emphasize the shifting composition and influence of these powerful coalitions as well as their role in promoting the city. Chapter 6 reviews the close relationship between the business elites and the governmental agencies. Houston has long had a local government willing to provide aid for business-oriented development and to maintain low property taxes. I will also scrutinize the impact of the laissez-faire approach on public planning and the absence of zoning.

Chapter 7 focuses on the secondary circuit of capital investment and the consequent built environment of Houston, including the residential subdivisions, multiple-use projects, and office towers. This chapter builds on earlier chapters and examines in depth the role of developers in creating the sociospatial layout that is modern Houston. Chapter 8 breaks new ground in looking at a range of social costs of Houston's growth against the backdrop of theoretical work on the social costs of private enterprise, and I explore the failure of local government to deal adequately with these diverse costs of urban growth. Chapter 9 extends Chapter 8, dealing with the costs of Houston's growth that have been imposed on the city's minority populations. The chapter also concerns a range of minority-related issues—race discrimination, provision of services, and minority politics and protest. Chapter 10 examines selected examples of business leadership and citizen response to Houston's social and environmental problems and provides a summary and conclusion for the book.

2

| Theories of Urban Development

The recent history of urban analysis in the United States has been dominated by a paradigmatic conflict between the market-centered approaches of mainstream social scientists and the political-economy and other "critical" perspectives that have developed in the work of such analysts as Manuel Castells, David Harvey, and Mark Gottdiener. In this theoretical chapter we will examine the mainstream market-centered approach, particularly the ecological perspective, and then proceed to a full examination of the critical approaches.

The Mainstream Ecological Paradigm

The Historical Background

Mainstream social scientists have long dominated the sociological and geographical debates on cities in the United States. During the 1920s and 1930s there was a major burst of energy and activity in urban sociology and ecology at the University of Chicago. There ecological researchers such as Robert Park and Ernest W. Burgess drew on nineteenth-century theorists, especially Herbert Spencer, in crafting an ecological framework for viewing urban life and urban development. Park and Burgess derived their concept of competitive, market-tested relations in part from the Spencerian tradition; competition "invariably tends to create an impersonal social order in which each individual, being free to pursue his own profit . . . invariably contributes . . . to the common welfare."[1] These social scientists viewed individualistic and group competition in urban markets as resulting in natural regularities in land use patterns and thus as generative of a social map of concentric zones. In the decades that followed, however, most ecologists have been more interested in urban demographic trends than in zoning mapping and allied spatial issues. For most mainstream urban ecologists and many other mainstream urban sociologists the processes of competition, conflict, and accommodation still take place, as Scott Greer has noted, within a "framework of rules approximately the same as those advocated by Herbert Spencer—with room for social evolution, enterprise, and the survival of those most fit to survive."[2]

A string of important books and articles published between the 1940s and the 1970s established the dominance of the ecological paradigm in urban sociology and in other social science disciplines in the United States. Although there have been a few dissenters, such as William Form, since the 1950s the ecologists in sociology, geography, and economics have dominated much discussion of cities in textbooks and journals in the United States.[3] Breaking with the earlier Chicago sociologists' concern about space, these contemporary urbanists emphasize demographic analysis and typically focus on population trends, such as migration flows and urban deconcentration, and on statistical distributions, especially those based on data drawn from the U.S. Bureau of the Census, in analyzing community development and adjustment. Amos Hawley, one of the most prominent of the mainstream theorists, has written many important analyses of ecological issues since the 1940s. In Hawley's theoretically oriented analysis, as well as in the analysis of less theoretically oriented ecologists, a central problem for inquiry is how a population organizes itself in adapting to a changing environment.[4] There is an underlying concern with subsistence, symbiosis, and equilibrium within a market-centered system, such as that of a metropolitan area. The urban political-economic system is not assessed in terms of its basic capitalistic and state institutions, economic structures, investment processes, inequalities, or conflicts. Indeed, the capitalistic system seems to be accepted as the "best of all possible" political-economic worlds. In a review article, "Spatial Processes," for *The Handbook of Modern Sociology* urban ecologists Parker Frisbie and John Kasarda have noted that mainstream urbanists do not share the view of the critical analysts that the flaws and contradictions of capitalism underlie contemporary urban structure and process.[5]

Although the ecological paradigm was sharply criticized and challenged in European scholarly circles by the late 1960s and early 1970s, it remained strong and rarely challenged in the United States until the late 1970s. One purpose of this book is to provide a sustained critique of the analyses of mainstream ecologists and similar mainstream urban scholars. Their arguments and assumptions generally include an uncritical acceptance of a self-regulating market system viewed as operating for the public good, a technological determinism, an emphasis on regional convergence and the filtering of growth down urban hierarchies, a neglect of the role of the state, a downplaying of inequality and conflict, and a macrostructural approach deemphasizing human agency.

Elements of the Dominant Ecological Paradigm

Many urban social scientists, and especially the ecologists, accept the capitalistic market system and its pervasive processes of capital accumulation uncritically. For example, urban sociologist John Kasarda has written of profit-seeking entrepreneurs operating in self-regulating markets as a wise guiding force in city development. Capitalists follow the beneficent profit logic of a competitive free market system which develops "good business climates" such as those in Sunbelt cities—"business climates" with low taxes, limited public services, low wages, and probusiness governments.[6] Individualized competition is a key idea for mainstream analysts. Thus, Janet Abu-Lughod argues that "traditionally, large cities have evolved as the aggregate product of thousands or even millions of individual decisions coordinated loosely, if at all, through the operation" of subconsensual processes.[7]

In their summary article for *The Handbook of Modern Sociology*, Frisbie and Kasarda seem willing to go beyond the traditional ecological approach and to carry on a dialogue with researchers doing the new critical work in the urban social sciences. But their review of the critical urban work is rather cursory, and they explicitly regard the ecological approach in sociology, geography, and economics as the "dominant (and arguably, the only) general theory of urban form and process that has been generative of systematic, empirically verifiable models."[8] Instead of a serious consideration of the full significance of the critical urban work in the United States and Europe, they provide a brief summary of the work of a few critical analysts, with the explicit goal of showing direct parallels to ecological research. For the most part, their lengthy article provides the reader with a review of mainstream research on urban demographic trends and statistical patterns. What little theoretical discourse there is dredges up the mainstream ideas of technological and communications determinism, centrifugal and centripetal forces, segregation, competition, individual motivation to compete, and rank-size city hierarchies. For example, they discuss competition for central city land sites in terms of transport accessibility and of better uses driving out lesser uses in terms of ability to pay. And the decentralizing suburbanization process in metropolitan areas, which ecological analysts such as Frisbie and Kasarda argue goes back to at least 1900, is viewed as reflecting the desires of individual American homeowners for affordable housing in a better physical environment, as expressed within a free market system. Neglected here is the issue of how the homeownership values of Americans are generated; slighted too are the institutional framework of real estate capitalism, the circuits of investment and the agent-investors, and the supportive governmental structure.

Generally, urban ecologists and similar mainstream urbanists analyze cities at an aggregate or macrostructural level. Yet for all their concern with markets and competition, the conventional researchers do not provide any serious in-depth analysis of the concrete institutional and structural aspects of the capitalistic market system. In addition, the powerful agents operating within this system receive little conceptual or empirical attention. Although competition among profit-seeking entrepreneurs and investors is recognized as important to market-driven cities, these capitalistic actors are neither researched nor analyzed in depth.[9]

The Emphasis on Technology

Mainstream ecologists and numerous other social scientists view the functional complexity of cities as substantially determined by developments in transportation and communication technologies, technologies whose political-economic contexts, histories, and possible technological alternatives are not examined in any detail. Changes in urban development and form are often explained in terms of some type of technological transformation, including shifts in water, rail, and automobile transport systems. Waterborne commerce favors port and river cities, while auto, train, and truck technologies facilitate the location of cities apart from water systems.

In a 1980 article Kasarda viewed the rapid growth of Sunbelt cities substantially in terms of technological developments, such as auto transport and highway systems, as well as in terms of the better business climate of Sunbelt cities. In *Urban Society*, Hawley looked at the relocation of industry from the industrial heartland to hinterland areas, also explaining decentralization substantially in terms of technological changes in transport and communication. In addition, in their summary article on urban processes Frisbie and Kasarda discuss population trends in urban development. Their fragmentary theoretical analysis utilizes technological and communications variables to explain urban expansion, particularly suburbanization. Although they are careful to note that urban expansion is not "solely determined" by improvement in transport and communication technologies, their predominant emphasis on these technologies suggests a theoretical preoccupation that disregards as important the role of the state and the actions of investors.[10]

Transport and communication technologies are important in urban centralization and decentralization. However, the political-economic history and decision-making context that resulted in the dominance of one type of transport, such as that of automobiles, over another, such as rail mass transit, cannot be ignored. This point has been well-documented in the work of Bradford Snell on the role of General Motors in the destruction of urban mass transit systems. Snell's work, together with the more recent research of Glenn Yago and J. Allen Whitt, documents the role of particular capitalistic actors in shaping auto-centered transport systems in the United States.[11] Furthermore, the role of government is often slighted in conventional discussions of such topics as metropolitan deconcentration and suburbanization. Federal intervention in the form of subsidies of home mortgages, highways, oil production, and decentralized airports significantly encouraged urban deconcentration by reducing the cost of decentralized suburban development. Urban processes such as suburbanization are not the natural result of automobile technology and free market forces but rather the result of intentional actions by powerful economic and governmental actors seeking particular goals in specific socio-historical settings.

Lack of Concern with Space and the Built Environment

In the 1920s and 1930s the Chicago school of urban sociology pioneered in the analysis of urban spatial growth. At the heart of the concerns of ecologists like McKenzie, Park, and Burgess was the tie between the spatial layout of cities and certain aspects of human social organization. In his 1925 paper, "The Growth of the City," Burgess emphasized population growth. As cities grow in population, they become segregated in spatial terms; thus, for Burgess, population growth and migration were critical environmental factors shaping how cities are organized.[12] Moreover, in a remarkable 1926 article, "The Scope of Human Ecology," McKenzie accented the actual built environment of cities: "All the more fixed aspects of human habitation, the buildings, roads, and centers of association, tend to become spatially distributed in accordance with forces operating in a particular area at a particular level of culture. In society, physical structure and cultural characteristics are parts of one complex."[13] For McKenzie the ecological forces lying behind the spatial distribution of "buildings, roads, and centers of association" specifically include geographical, political, cultural, and economic forces.

Yet since the classical period urban ecologists and many other mainstream analysts in the United States have given little serious attention to the fixed aspects of human habitation in cities—to the built environment of houses, malls, and office buildings. Analysts have largely ignored the role of differentiated capitalistic economic forces and specific corporate organizations in shaping particular types of urban spatial forms, such as large complexes of office towers, or of urban spatial distributions, such as the deconcentrated metropolitan areas described so well in their demographic reports. Indeed, mainstream urban ecological analysis since the Chicago school's heyday has moved away from a concern with many spatial aspects of cities to a focus on the demographic issues, including the migration and population segregation issues emphasized by Burgess. Population movements to and from central cities and suburbs, residential segregation patterns, and patterns of occupational distribution occupy much of the ecologists' attention. This neglect of built environment and other spatial issues can be seen in Berry and Kasarda's *Contemporary Urban Ecology,* in the overview book *Sociological Human Ecology* edited by Micklin and Choldin, in Choldin's prominent textbook *Cities and Suburbs,* and in the review article on "Spatial Processes" by Frisbie and Kasarda.[14]

An Emphasis on Convergence and Filtering

In the literature on the growth of Sunbelt and Frostbelt cities mainstream theories of city development espoused by ecologists, certain urban economists, and other mainstream social scientists often take the form of "convergence" theories. Convergence theories have emphasized that Sunbelt cities are catching up economically with northern cities; this convergence is part of an equilibrating tendency in U.S. society. For example, Williamson developed a thorough-going convergence theory; in his view a sharp and "increasing North-South dualism is typical of early development stages, while regional convergence is typical of the more mature stages of national growth and development." [15] These convergence theorists emphasize the regional disparities in an early stage of urban growth and convergence later on as regions mature. Terms such as "filtering" and "trickle down" have been used by mainstream scholars to describe the diffusion of urban growth from one region to another; a key aspect lies in labor markets, with higher-priced markets in cities higher up in the urban hierarchy leading firms to migrate to cheaper markets in cities in other regions.[16] The imagery is one of economic change being transmitted in order from higher to lower centers within a national urban hierarchy. Berry and Kasarda discuss this heartland-hinterland filtering on a national scale and suggest a threshold population of about one million as necessary for cities in peripheral regions to grow on their own, to be "self-generated metropolitan areas." [17] As I will show in Chapter 3 and 4, this hierarchical filtering is not an accurate view of certain U.S. cities, including Houston, which have developed within a global investment context.

Moreover, if one examines the ecological and demographic literatures on cities in the 1950s and 1960s, one will find that the economic and political significance of Sunbelt cities like Houston was poorly appreciated. For example, writing in the 1950s, Vance and Smith suggest that southern metropolises are "unremarkable cities. Human ecologists and students of urbanism have had little reason to study them." [18] They suggest that Sunbelt cities, though growing, are of regional importance. Vance and Smith developed an index of metropolitan economic function, encompassing such variables as wholesale sales and bank clearings, and therefore ranked Houston as a "third order" metropolitan area. The inadequacy of this evaluation, which among other things disregards the international context of Houston, will be demonstrated in subsequent chapters.

The Mainstream Approach to the State

Mainstream urban sociologists have given limited attention to the role of government in buttressing the capitalistic processes of urban development. For example, urban scholars such as Berry and Kasarda briefly note that in market-directed societies, particularly the United States, the role of the state has been primarily "limited to combating crises that threaten the societal mainstream," that state involvement tends to be incremental, and that state actions dealing with the "social consequences of laissez-faire urbanization" are "ineffective in most cases."[19] Mainstream urbanists tend to express a bias in favor of laissez-faire government, particularly in regard to intervention in self-regulating markets. Thus, in analyzing the rise of Sunbelt cities in the 1970s some mainstream theorists dissected not only the "good business climate" of Sunbelt cities but also the "bad business climate" of Frostbelt cities. Discussions of "bad" climates usually encompassed the idea that state intervention—particularly in the form of high-quality social services and high-level taxes—has had negative consequences for the health of Frostbelt cities.

Beyond these brief references, government generally is not an important subject for mainstream ecologists; this can be seen in the analyses of leading theorist Amos Hawley. In his central work, *Urban Society,* Hawley devoted little attention to the role of the state in city growth. Neither the 1984 analyses of urban and regional trends in the edited collection *Sociological Human Ecology* nor the textbook *Cities and Suburbs* included a significant discussion of the role of the state in urban development. The review article of Frisbie and Kasarda does recognize that the critical urban theorists have criticized mainstream research for dismissing the role of the state in urban development, but Frisbie and Kasarda themselves slight the role of the state in their own detailed assessments of urban evolution. I focus here primarily on social scientists adopting the ecological model. Some political scientists among contemporary urbanists have given considerable attention to the state, and I will assess those discussions later.

Policy and Mainstream Analysis

Frisbie and Kasarda also assert that inappropriate biases (and an "activistic orientation") are apparent in the new critical urban analysis. Yet all social science reflects the values and interests of the researchers, and this is definitely true of the mainstream urbanists. Mainstream analysis places an emphasis on capitalistic markets as the beneficent institutions driving urban development; this leads to not only an overly economistic theory but also a blindness to the normative character of ecological theory itself and of the implicit and explicit policy prescriptions of ecological analysts. Thus, ecological analysis tends to be conservative in social justice terms; this conventional analysis tends to see contemporary city patterns as inevitable, efficient, and neutral.

The work of mainstream ecologists has, particularly in the 1970s and 1980s, been used to buttress the existing urban system with its built-in social injustices. A 1980 report sponsored by the Carter administration suggested that the federal government should look with favor on business-generated growth in Sunbelt cities, even to the point of forswearing governmental intervention and thus letting northern cities stagnate and die.[21] Prepared by the President's Commission for a National Agenda for the Eighties, this report called on the federal government to refrain from assisting the declining cities of the north. Markets are given a central deterministic role in driving urban development. Not only are capitalistic markets seen as beneficent in this broadly accepted presidential framework for urban policymaking, but they are also seen as far more important than politics, the state, and even dominant multinational corporations in determining urban growth and decline. This market-knows-best view of the Frostbelt-Sunbelt shift in capital investment and of urban growth more generally drew on the work of urban ecologists. Thus, in some of Kasarda's work, accelerating the profit seeking of capitalist entrepreneurs appears to be a policy option for urban development: "An Urban Policy apropos northern cities should be well informed by the favorable business climate that has fostered so much recent economic development in the South."[22]

In addition, the omissions in mainstream ecological research reveal a conservative bias. Mainstream social science analysis has not dealt adequately with such critical factors in urban development as power and resource inequality, class and class conflict, vested capitalist interests operating in space, and pro−real estate government subsidy programs. To take one important example, in the volume *Sociological Human Ecology* ecologists and demographers reviewed the question of how humans survive in a changing social environment, including cities, but they did so without significantly discussing inequality, power, conflict or poverty, or the state.[23]

Critical Perspectives on City Development

The Critical Urban Paradigm

In the 1970–1980 decade the dominance of an urban social science rooted in ecological concepts linked ultimately to the ideas of Herbert Spencer and Social Darwinism was challenged by a "critical" paradigm influenced by a reading of Marx, Weber, and more recent European theorists such as Henri Lefebvre, David Harvey, and Manuel Castells. By the late 1960s and the early 1970s, a number of European social scientists had published critical assessments of the mainstream urban paradigm. Particularly important were the late 1960s articles of Manuel Castells, published in English by British sociologist C. G. Pickvance in his pioneering volume *Urban Sociology,* as well as Castells's book *The Urban Question.* Also important were David Harvey's critical articles collected in his 1973 *Social Justice and the City* and Henri Lefebvre's 1970 *La révolution urbaine.*[24]

Interestingly, both David Harvey and Manuel Castells moved from European universities to U.S. universities in the 1970s; in the United States they continued to have a stimulating effect on the new urban work. Several critical paradigm issues are central to David Harvey's analyses in two important books he published in the mid-1980s while he was teaching in the United States, *The Urbanization of Capital* and *Consciousness and the Urban Experience.*[25] In these books Harvey asks, "Can we derive a theoretical and historical understanding of the urban process under capitalism out of a study of the supposed laws of motion of a capitalist mode of production?" He answers, "yes." Understanding the logic of capitalistic production and investment flows is essential to understanding cities. And in a similarly ground-breaking book, *The City and the Grassroots,* Manuel Castells, teaching at the University of California, called for refocusing urban analysis so that it centers on the endless historical struggle between antagonistic social actors, on the social processes of urbanites constructing and reconstructing their environments and lives within capitalistic economic and political structures.[26]

In the late 1970s and early 1980s critical urban research blossomed in the United States. Influenced by the work of Harvey, Castells, and Lefebvre, many U.S. scholars began to flesh out a critical paradigm accenting the importance of analyzing capitalism, investment flows, class conflict, the unequal distribution of resources, and the state in assessing urban life, space, structure, and change. For example, in his 1979 *The City and Social Theory* political scientist Michael P. Smith developed one of the first political-economic critiques of the mainstream ecological tradition in the United States and provided a stimulating analysis of the role of corporate capital and the activist state in shaping urban form.[27] By the late 1970s and early 1980s sophisticated work was being published by such critical observers of the urban scene as Norman and Susan Fainstein, Richard Child Hill, Mark Gottdiener, Michael Dear, Richard Walker, and Alan Whitt, to mention just a few. One of the most thorough and provocative assessments in this critical tradition is *The Social Production of Urban Space*, a 1985 book by U.S. sociologist Mark Gottdiener. In this volume Gottdiener recognizes the importance of Castells's and Harvey's critical work, but he criticizes both for giving too much attention to the logic of production and allied structural issues and too little attention to state institutions and the crucial urban actors. Influenced by the writings of Henri Lefebvre, Gottdiener emphasizes the importance of looking at both the means of production and the state in making sense of urban spatial development and discusses the necessity of assessing the role of particular capitalistic and community actors as well as institutions in the shaping of cities.[28] Gottdiener places space at the center of his analysis; space is as essential to the theoretical analysis of cities as are the concepts of class and capital.

Features of the Critical Paradigm

Although there is still much diversity among urban scholars who have developed this critical paradigm, and there are debates over the relative weight of economy, space, and the state, there is a rough consensus among many on basic concepts and arguments:

1   In the current historical period Western societies are fundamentally rooted in and shaped by their capitalistic means of production. These societies, organized along class and race lines, are structured in terms of social institutions responsive to the logic of the capital accumulation process.

2   The capitalistic class structure and the logic of the accumulation process articulate with space to generate sociospatial patterns of production, distribution, and consumption. This articulation of capitalism with space involves the creation and destruction of the land and built environments we term cities. Particularly important is the uneven development of sociospatial patterns. Competition of places for capital is widespread and aggressive, with business elites or "growth coalitions" operating to promote thousands of cities, regions, and nations.

3   The capital accumulation process is centered in corporations that, for the most part, calculate profit and loss at the firm level; this calculation results in major societal contradictions, such as massive social costs associated with

the rapid inflow of capital investment and accompanying growth in urban places, with capital disinvestment and community abandonment, and with overproduction and underproduction crises in the industrial and real estate sectors.

4   The state in modern capitalistic societies is linked, in historically shaped and fluctuating ways, to capitalists and the capital accumulation process. The local and national states play a crucial, albeit sometimes dysfunctional, role in fostering capital accumulation, in grappling with market contradictions and the social costs of growth, in mediating struggles between classes and fractions of classes, and in enhancing the legitimacy of the established political-economic system.

Issues of Structuralism and Voluntarism

Scholars working on the new urban paradigm differ in the degree in which they regard the actors within the economic and political frameworks to be a major theoretical or empirical concern. Thus, one weakness in the work of David Harvey, the earlier analyses of Manuel Castells, and the research of similar Marxist structuralists is the neglect of the particular actors whose concrete actions actually shape urban development at the everyday level. The "structurationist" theory of Anthony Giddens and others suggests that both agency and structure are important in the production of cities and of spatial phenomena more generally, although this perspective is not as yet well developed. Gottdiener has noted that spatial forms are contingent on the "dialectical articulation between action and structures." [29] Spatial forms are not some easy and inevitable translation of deep-lying structural forces. Because structural changes are processed through human actions taken under historical conditions, I want to add to my earlier points a fifth argument important in some of the critical analysis:

5   Specific economic and state forms do not develop inevitably out of structural necessity. They develop in a contingent manner as the result of the conscious actions taken by members of various classes, acting singly or in concert, under particular historical and structural circumstances.

Basic Paradigm Contrasts

The contrast of the critical paradigm with mainstream ecology and similar urban analysis is evident. From this critical perspective society is characterized by capitalistic contradictions and antagonistic class relations which generate change; this is contrary to the mainstream ecologists who claim a natural market-oriented equilibrium upset only by outside influences such as new technologies. In contrast to the mainstream tradition's neglect of the state I find in much critical research a heavy emphasis on the local, regional, and national state. United States and West European societies have seen the emergence of strong capitalism-conditioned states, which periodically intervene to solve crises in market functioning and capital accumulation as well as to mediate conflict. A fundamental inequality of power, of control over economic and political resources, is a central and contradiction-generating feature of capitalistic societies, and thus of their cities, and not an inevitable consequence of all societal organization, as some mainstream ecologists would have it. In addition, the critical urban approach emphasizes the point that no society is an island in time or space; it must be analyzed in light of its history and its position in a globalized capitalistic system.

Capitalism and the Shaping of Urban Space: Structural and Institutional Issues

I will now discuss selected theoretical ideas and issues that follow from these innovative critical analyses of cities. First, I will examine structural and institutional issues, especially those relating to the sociospatial impact of capital investment and capital flow on a global scale. Then I will explore the role of agency in these developmental matters.

The Institutional Structure of Capitalism: Capital and Labor Power

The relationship of capital to cities can be viewed in terms of the broad structural context—the economic institutions of capitalism, the capital investment features and circuits, and the interventionist state. A metropolis can be viewed as the result of the application of private capital to create a built environment of factories, offices, and warehouses, together with the application of public capital for the infrastructure of roads, sewer and water systems, and state buildings. This private and public capital is put to work by the labor power of a large mass of workers of various statuses and races. As the structuralist Harvey put it, "a city is an agglomeration of productive forces built by labor employed within a temporal process of circulation of capital." [30]

Cities and Corporations in a World Economic System

City places are not islands unto themselves; rather, they are greatly affected by capital investment flows within the regional, national, and international contexts. Viewing cities in a larger national or international context is an important idea that has gained currency in recent decades. For example, Peter Hall used the concept of *world cities* in his examination of the physical characteristics of major conurbations around the globe. [31] But his 1970s analyses did not, for the most part, raise the critical questions about linkages between the capitalist world system and particular cities. One interesting aspect worthy of more study in this regard is the specialization of cities that has developed as the world market system organized by capitalism has expanded. Early Chicago urbanist R. D. McKenzie was one of the first social scientists to develop the concept of urban specialization, which he saw in ecological terminology as "the natural outcome of competition under prevailing conditions of transportation and communication." [32] Today mainstream urban ecology uses terms such as *node* and *specialization*. For example, Poston discusses ecological research on cities as nodes, but as nodes in a regional and national hierarchy of cities. As conceptualized in urban ecology, the terms node and specialization are understood in a natural or technological sense rather than a political-economic context. [33]

It is perhaps an empirical commonplace to observe that cities in the world system have tended to specialize in certain types of economic activities. But we need to go beyond this insight to understand that cities are closely related to the dominant forms of organization in the world economy. The world of modern capitalism is both a worldwide net of corporations and a global network of cities. These multinational corporations have for decades dominated worldwide markets in manufactured commodities and financial instruments. Hymer argued that corporations have three different functional levels: day-to-day operations, field office management, and top management and planning. [34] The top management function is located in world-class cities, the field management function in national cities, and the day-to-day operations in lesser cities around the world. Within this global framework of modern capitalism there are world command cities such as New York, London, and Tokyo; these cities house the headquarters of leading industrial and financial corporations. Major organizational units in this web of capitalism are the large international banks and transnational corporations; the latter today account for most world trade outside the centrally planned socialist countries. The top thousand multinational corporations not only sit at the top of a pyramid of interrelated capitalistic firms of all sizes, but they also create a truly transnational economy, whose geographical nodes are the world's cities.

But most cities are not at the world command level; indeed cities occupy a variety of niches. Specialized command cities house the headquarters operations of particular industries, such as the auto companies in Detroit. At first glance other specialized cities, like Houston, appear to fit Hymer's category of the field office management city; Houston lacks leading oil firm headquarters facilities, but it has a high concentration of major operational subsidiaries and divisions of the major oil corporations. Yet as I will demonstrate in Chapter 4, this characterization of Houston would be inaccurate. The city is a specialized command city with substantial influence and economic ties beyond the regional or field office level. Cities with more limited spheres of economic and political influence include those metropolitan areas specializing in a a particular type of manufacturing production, such as steelmaking in Birmingham, Alabama. There are also state command cities like Washington, D.C. Many other cities are difficult to classify because of their diverse economic, dependent and independent, and state functions, such as Singapore, Mexico City, and Sao Paulo in developing countries. Nonetheless, virtually all cities are to some degree linked by the organizational web of transnational corporations, their facilities, subsidiaries, suppliers, and subcontractors.

As of the mid-1980s, only a few studies of U.S. cities had paid serious attention to the capitalistic world market context of urban growth and decline. Exceptions include the work of Richard Child Hill and Christopher Chase-Dunn.[35] Hill has emphasized the role of the global economy in shaping Detroit's economic decline. One key aspect of this decline is the auto company investment in global sourcing, in dispersed automobile production. The global sourcing strategy of the automobile multinationals has for some time threatened Detroit with disinvestment and unemployment. Hill links the internationalization of production to crises facing cities around the globe.

Other world cities deserve a similar contextual analysis. New York's economic base and labor shifts have been analyzed in a world context by researchers such as Saskia Sassen-Koob, but no social scientist has yet published a systematic, in-depth book on New York's historical development set against the larger international context. Soja, Morales, and Wolff have examined the contemporary restructuring of Los Angeles and its rise as an international banking center. Implicit in their analysis is the suggestion that a U.S. city's economic and demographic growth or decline hinges far more than ever before on investment decisions made in multinational corporations operating in a global spatial economy. Thus, it is not sufficient for U.S. researchers to analyze Sunbelt cities primarily against a backdrop of declining Frostbelt cities.[36]

Several Circuits of Capital Investment

It is increasingly evident that capital investment across the world market is important to the development and decline of major cities. Given the significance of capital investment in creating the geographical topology we call cities, it seems essential for urban analysts to do extensive research on the character and velocity of capital flows. Several circuits of capital have been distinguished in the political economy literature. The primary circuit of capital encompasses the investment of capital in manufacturing, circulation, and distribution operations. The exploitation of labor power in the primary circuit is a foundation of capitalistic profit. Markusen has developed a suggestive model of profit cycles and regional development. She has argued that the worldwide investment and disinvestment of capital in the primary circuit of manufacturing is substantially shaped by the oligopolistic character of a particular industry, as well as by the character of the labor struggle, competition, and profits at a particular stage in an industry's development. The acceleration of decline in investment return in a variety of manufacturing industries has resulted in a greater velocity of capital movement into and out of particular urban places, thereby increasing the problems of community adjustment.[37]

The secondary circuit of capital encompasses the flow of capital into the built environments of both production, including factories and office buildings, and consumption, including houses and sidewalks. The French urbanist Henri Lefebvre argued that the urban process is critical to the dynamics of modern capitalism and that capitalism has survived by the constant production and shaping of urban space.[38] The built environment of cities functions as the general precondition for the direct forces of production, as well as for the forces of consumption. But it also functions as a place for the investment of surplus capital, for the type of investment that enhances the value of property or finance capital whether or not there is any payoff for actual production or consumption.

In addition, David Harvey has defined a tertiary circuit of capital as the circuit of investment in science and technology and in social programs for the reproduction of labor power. Because of the difficulty individual capitalists have in making these types of investments, they are often made through the agency of the state.

The Secondary Circuit
of Capital Investment

Lefebvre has developed the concept of the secondary circuit of capital, a circuit parallel to that of primary production and one encompassing real estate investments as investments for profit:

> At times of depression capital flows in its [secondary circuit's] direction. At first it makes fabulous profits, but soon it gets bogged down. In their sector the "multiplier" effects are weak: there is little secondary activity. . . . Capital is immobilized in building. . . . It can happen that real estate speculation becomes the principal source, the almost exclusive place of the "formation of capital.". . .[39]

Mark Gottdiener has discussed the complexity of Lefebvre's secondary circuit. The spatial environment of cities includes both undeveloped land and developed land—that is, the built environment. But in addition to private development the developed land in metropolitan areas also includes the state-subsidized infrastructure of bridges, roads, and water systems. Broadly construed, then, the property sector of late capitalism encompasses the land and building markets, the various development and banking fractions of capital, and the state agencies providing the state-subsidized infrastructure essential to metropolitan development.[40]

David Harvey emphasizes the theme of the secondary circuit of capital. In his view there must be a surplus of capital in the primary circuit of production for capital to flow into the built environment. A major aspect of Harvey's argument about the secondary circuit is that in the built environment investment is often undertaken solely in a quest for the highest rate of return.[41] For Harvey the interventionist state is the institution typically involved in facilitating the transfer of capital to the secondary circuit. Individual capitalists have difficulty in switching capital from one circuit to another because fixed investments are long-lasting. A functioning capital market, banking institutions, and a state willing to back up the market are essential to the speedy flow of capital between primary and secondary circuits.

Although they have not used the language of primary and secondary capital circuits, several American analysts have linked capital investment to urban space. In 1975 Larry Sawers noted the impact of capitalistic investment: "urban form flows out of and must remain consistent with the basic economic structure of which it is a part."[42] Moreover, one of the few articles in the urban literature that ties the concrete aspects of urban form to specific corporate location decisions for one urban area is that by Saxenian on rapid corporate growth in the Silicon Valley.[43] Saxenian demonstrates the impact of high-tech production and investment changes on the physical geography of Santa Clara County, California, and shows how urban geography is very closely tied to investment decisions by particular coalitions of capitalists. Saxenian notes that previous researchers have dealt with the impact of capital restructuring on broad regional patterns, but "they failed to examine the impact of production on patterns of urban development *within* a region." In addition, a number of critical analysts have demonstrated the relationship between state intervention in central cities and the flow of private investment capital into those areas. A number of authors—including Michael P. Smith, Susan and Norman Fainstein, Richard C. Hill, and Dennis Judd—writing about U.S. cites in *Restructuring the City* address the issue of urban form within the state context; they show how state-subsidized redevelopment in central business districts is tied to investment restructuring in modern capitalism.[44]

Capitalism and the Shaping of Space: Agency and Actors

Powerful Capitalistic Actors in Cities

In making sense out of capital investment decisions, including decisions about space, we must look beyond this agglomeration of productive forces and the macrostructural processes of capital creation and circulation to the specific players and sets of players who activate these forces and shape the capital circuits. The principal decision makers in most urban settings in Western countries include the capitalistic investors and producers. Today industrial, commercial, financial, and real estate capitalism is organized around a complicated network of individual entrepreneurs and groups of corporate actors of varying sizes and with different functions. To take a relevant example, we delineate the character and complexity of the urban development sector in the following list:

1   Industrial and commercial location decisions
     Executives in industrial companies (industrial capital)
     Executives in commercial companies (commercial capital)

2   Development decisions
    Executives in development firms (development capital)
    Land speculators (development capital)
    Investor-landowners (development capital)
3   Financial decisions
    Executives in commercial banks (finance capital)
    Executives in savings associations (finance capital)
    Executives in insurance companies (finance capital)
    Executives in mortgage companies (finance capital)
4   Construction and design decisions
    Executives in construction firms (construction capital)
    Executives in architectural, engineering firms (construction capital)

The capitalistic players in the urban drama can be identified in terms of the decisions essential for urban growth, development, and decline. It is preferable to think in terms of decision categories because one actor, such as the chief executive of a particular real estate development firm, can be involved in decisions in several of these categories.[45] Note here the important fractions of capital involved in shaping the urban environment: (a) industrial and commercial capital; (b) development capital; (c) finance capital; and (d) construction capital.

First, industrial and commercial capital encompasses those individual entrepreneurs and corporate executives in commercial and industrial firms whose location decisions (for example, to locate in northern or Sunbelt city) often set the other actors into motion. From the beginning of U.S. cities to the present the location of corporate enterprises has been at the heart of urban development. There are stories of famous capitalists like John D. Rockefeller, who reportedly spent hours bent over a map of communities in the United States planning the location of oil refineries and other Standard Oil facilities in a precise military way. This planning has been true of various decisions of commercial and industrial capitalists both before Rockefeller and since. Control over strategic places confers great power over labor, markets, and resources—and thereby over patterns of urban and metropolitan development.

Second, development capital covers the developers and land speculators who buy, package, and develop land for use by industrial and other corporations. Development capitalists often take the lead in planning and directing large projects; they build for industrial and commercial capital and hire construction capital. Third, finance capital encompasses those executives at the helm of financial corporations who make the major loans for corporate location, construction, and land purchase. Several groups work within the finance capital sector: local and outside commercial banks have financed construction; insurance and mortgage companies have handled long-term loans. Finally, construction capital includes the various construction actors who actually construct a variety of small-scale and large-scale urban development projects.

The Scale of Corporate Organization

In the contemporary city the crucial actors are often the top executives of large integrated corporations. The multinational corporation is capitalism's most characteristic form in the late twentieth century. In the late 1800s and the early 1900s a new type of economic organization developed in the United States—the large corporation. The marketplace was increasingly organized in terms of the interests of the large corporation, not in terms of a free market of thousands of small competing firms. At first, various state governments passed laws severely regulating the new corporations as something dangerous. Corporations were viewed as artificial entities with no individual rights. Pressures from those who owned and ran the new corporations led to new legal doctrines legitimating these new organizations. In 1886 the U.S. Supreme Court ruled that the corporation was indeed an individual under the law and that under the fourteenth and fifteenth amendments to the constitution these corporations had the civil rights of individuals. This legal fiction, part of a created ideology sanctifying the corporation as a legitimate reality, thereby gave the corporations an extraordinarily broad range of power and influence.[46]

Executives in large industrial, commercial, banking, and real estate firms often make the critical decisions that shape metropolitan growth and deterioration. Real estate decisions are made not only by influential executives in local real estate companies but also by powerful heads of regional and national companies. Large corporations also cut across decision-making categories. One real estate corporation often encompasses a development subdivision, which not only develops projects but also engages in land speculation, a real estate brokerage subsidiary, and a construction subsidiary.

Concrete Actors as Linkage

The urban actors conspicuous in many cities, particularly the most powerful individuals and groups of individuals, often provide the concrete linkages between the dominant institutions. These actors and their decisions underscore the point that individuals provide the concrete nodal connections between the abstract institutional structures, such as "local and national economies" and "local and national states." Economic and political *structures* are very important to an analysis of metropolitan development. Yet the evolution of a specific city entails a complex tapestry of structured relationships held together by individuals, with the most influential agents playing the greatest role in binding together the structural realities of state and economy. Since concrete individuals and groups of individuals actually make city-relevant decisions, their own family and social histories, ideologies, desires for profit or control of "turf," institutional positions, and linkage to other individuals become highly relevant for the analysis of particular cities. Nonetheless, the importance of individuals in the urban drama should not be taken as a sign of the inconsequentiality of institutions and structures, for particular individuals in specific historical times are limited in the range of their possible actions and decisions by those structures and institutions.

Citizen Resistance to Capitalists' Actions

Investment-driven urbanization is paralleled by an urbanization of social relations—for example, the separation of workplace and home or the organization of mass consumption under a profit-oriented market system—and thus an urbanization of citizen consciousness. Workers rent and buy places to live within the urban framework created by the investors in the primary and secondary investment circuits. To persist capitalists must continuously convert family and community space into commodity space. Whole communities created by a large developer, or organized around a particular industry, may be defined as commodity space; particular neighborhoods may be singled out to be converted into investment space, as in gentrified housing areas in central city areas from New York to Houston and San Francisco. Capitalism shapes the basic patterns of economy and housing communities in cities, but, once the community relationships are well institutionalized, the relations are transformed "into complex codes of urban living that have their own significance and rigidities." [47] Critical to the health and progress of U.S. society have been basic social and cultural arrangements—including relatively stable neighborhoods and communities and dependable social relationships.

In most cities citizen movements periodically emerge to protect these stable neighborhood and community arrangements against destructive capital investments. The important actors on the local scene include ordinary residents who find themselves in conflict with the goals of the development and industrial capitalists. In *The City and the Grassroots* Castells argues that "any theory of the city must be, at its starting point, a theory of social conflict." [48] Castells argues that the most successful community-based resistance movements are those that articulate three goals: collective consumption, community culture, and political self-management. People struggle for a city organized

around human, family, and neighborhood concerns that go beyond capital accumulation and profitability. A central concern in much critical analysis of
urban conflict is the way in which households struggle to survive and thereby
force restructuring the political priorities of business and political elites.
However, as we will see in the case of Houston, the extent of citizen protest
and organization *varies greatly* from one city to another. Citizen protest is
neither inevitable nor necessarily progressive.

The State and City Growth

Selected Theories of the State

One argument of this book is that the economy and the state should be analyzed in tandem. In the following chapters I will frequently assess the economy of Houston in connection with the arrangements and actions of relevant
levels of the state. In the abstract world of theory it is easy to differenti-
ate between economic arrangements and the state. But in the real world of
the twentieth-century metropolis, the economy and the state are integrally
intertwined.

In the last decade some of the most creative theoretical debates in the social
sciences have raged over the relationship of the state to modern capitalism.
The conventional pluralist paradigm has long dominated the mainstream
analysis of government, including much analysis of local politics. From this
perspective national and local governments are shaped by multiple pressure
groups.[49] In effect, a competitive market in the political sphere is analogous to
the market in the economic sphere, one in which individual voters and an array of interest groups compete for influence in urban politics within a general
value consensus. Much debate over the character of the state in a capitalist
society stems ultimately from a critique of this pluralist perspective. Beyond
the pluralist perspective, theories of the state can be loosely grouped into four
general categories of argument: (1) instrumentalist, (2) structuralist, (3) class
struggle, and (4) independent state. Within each category there is a range of
argument about the state, but I will provide only a brief summary of essential points.

The instrumentalist viewpoint on the state, traced to Marx and Engels's
comment that the state is "a committee for managing the common affairs of
the whole bourgeoisie," sees the state as an instrument of class rule. The early

books of Miliband and Domhoff are instrumentalist critiques of the pluralist viewpoint and emphasize the specific ties between the ruling class and the state, particularly the movement into and out of the state's key positions on the part of members of the capitalistic class.[50] Miliband confronts the traditional pluralist theorists of the state with the reality of interpersonal connections between economic elites and the state; he is concerned with the organizational level, the concrete ways in which capitalists control the modern state.

Combining an individual-level analysis with a class-oriented viewpoint, Domhoff's work has demonstrated that individual capitalists and their close subordinates do in fact rule by serving in critical governmental positions. In their later work Miliband and Domhoff have rejected a crude one-to-one instrumentalism and have explicitly recognized the complexity of the web linking the state to capital. Domhoff accents networks and makes an important point about agency: classes and institutions are conceptual units, but "individuals are the basic elements for building networks that make up classes and that locate the institutions in sociological space." Similarly, J. Allen Whitt argues that his California data on powerful individuals active in five major political campaigns centered on transportation issues indicate that corporate board interlocks, memberships in elite clubs, and regular socializing ties bind together an effective and very real "governing capitalist class." [51]

The structuralist viewpoint emerged in part as a critique of the instrumentalist perspective. In his early work Nicos Poulantzas rejects instrumentalism and criticizes Miliband for assessing the state in terms of its specific actors, rather than in terms of its structurally determined position in a capitalistic society. Whatever their socioeconomic origins, the state managers must maintain the conditions for successful capital accumulation. State action, structurally constrained by the dominance of the capitalistic class, serves the particular needs of that class in opposition to an often antagonistic working class.[52] Moreover, the class struggle viewpoint has a variety of adherents, and some authors couple it with a structuralist view. As class struggle analysts see the matter, the state is regularly shaped by class conflict, reflecting both working-class and ruling-class pressures. Organized worker movements have gained control over some state bureaucracies. The later work of Poulantzas accents this aspect of state development, as does the work of Erik O. Wright and Manuel Castells.[53]

The independent state perspective emphasizes that state managers are relatively independent arbiters of class conflict and capitalistic contradictions. In his innovative analysis Block argues that Marxists should reject "the idea of a class-conscious ruling class" and accept the view that there is "a division of labor between those who accumulate capital and those who manage the state apparatus." As a rule, capitalists do not directly manage the state, which is under the direction of relatively autonomous "state managers." Block questions Domhoff's argument that the ruling class places representative members as state managers; those members of the ruling class who serve as state managers are "atypical of their class, since they are forced to look at the world from the perspective of state managers." [54] Theda Skocpol and her coauthors argue that state officials have organizational interests of their own; they and the bureaucratic agencies they control compete vigorously with one another. New policies are often shaped by independent government officials who are ahead of either grassroots or business demands. [55]

The Character of the Local State

One weakness of this state theory literature is that it generally accents the national state and neglects the local state, particularly urban governments. In sorting out the levels of the state, one can distinguish at least three: (a) the central state (federal government); (b) the regional state (for example, the state of New York); and (c) the local state (city or county government).

Some analysis of city government has in effect emphasized an independent state perspective for the local level. For example, in *The Contested City* John Mollenkopf looks at data on urban development, particularly for Boston and San Francisco. Mollenkopf argues that both the new neo-Marxist analysis and the older pluralist analysis are wrong: "This study rejects the two dominant traditions for explaining the structure of political power: the notion that some controlling 'power structure' or capitalist elite intervenes to determine what decisions are made, or, alternatively, that they result from the contention among private interest groups." Mollenkopf argues that successful progrowth coalitions depend primarily on the guiding presence of a political entrepreneur, "one who gathers and risks political capital or support in order to reshape politics and create new sources of power by establishing new programs." [56] To document his political entrepreneur theory Mollenkopf reviews the cases of Boston and San Francisco, where, he argues, four mayors and two prominent urban renewal administrators used their political skills, together with help from national political entrepreneurs, to build huge redevelopment programs. However, empirical data on U.S. cities and U.S. governmental agencies do not support Mollenkopf's independent state view. In Mollenkopf's two major examples, Boston and San Francisco, there is substantial evidence of small business elites initiating and guiding urban development. Political entrepreneurs are important and should not be neglected, but they are not independent forces. [57]

The instrumentalist and structuralist views of the state deserve more attention for the local level. The arguments of O'Connor, whose general theory of the state overlaps the structuralist and ,class struggle perspectives, and the writings of Dear and Clark, whose structuralist work accents the local state, are useful for analyzing cities.[58] O'Connor views the falling rate of profit in capitalistic economies such as that of the United States as tied to underproduction which results from working-class demands for social spending. The state intervenes to subsidize profit making and to pay the social expenses of keeping the state legitimate in the eyes of the working class. O'Connor distinguishes between "social investment (capital) expenditures," government expenditures which enhance the profitability of private corporations, "social consumption expenditures," government expenditures which enhance the value of labor power, and "social expenses," government expenditures which enhance societal survival or legitimization, such as for state police and welfare programs. Examples of social investment capital include local government expenditures for urban infrastructure projects subsidizing corporate development. In a manner similar to O'Connor, Dear and Clark view the state as supporting the capitalist system by (1) providing for the conditions of capital accumulation, (2) providing for the welfare of labor, and (3) exercising ideological control over labor. They make an important distinction between the local and the central state: The local state specializes in providing state services, state jobs, and certain types of construction; it enhances the legitimacy of the overall political-economic system. Dear and Clark develop a view of local governments as dependent on the central government and emphasize that the state changes in response to crises in capital accumulation.[59]

The localized interrelationships between the state, private capital, and cities have been emphasized by Molotch and Domhoff.[60] Molotch has analyzed local growth coalitions, the groups of land-interested capitalists working with government officials to boost growth. Domhoff has noted the close linkage between land-interested capitalists operating at the local level and those operating at the helm of national corporations, for the local growth coalition seeks outside investment for the locality and thus for its own prosperity. Theorists emphasizing agency have sometimes been criticized for an inadequate conceptualization of structure in their concern with powerful actors. One weakness in the instrumentalist view, as Dear and Clark see it, is its failure "to identify the logic whereby the elites themselves are constituent elements of a wider social order which is independent of specific institutions and personalities."[61] However, many structuralist approaches err in the opposite direction, by neglecting the mechanisms and actors which implement the dictates, such as capital accumulation, of the wider capitalistic social order. A combination of the two perspectives would seem preferable for future theoretical explorations.

Business Elites and Urban Growth Coalitions

Growth Coalitions and Growth Politics in Cities

The term "growth coalitions" has been used for those local groups that since the 1930s have linked the business elites and local state officials in a quest for local economic and population growth. Molotch brought the analysis of local growth coalitions to the attention of social scientists. Most cities have such a local coalition, typically composed of those local capitalists with fixed capital investments (e.g., developers) and local government officials, who work aggressively to sell the city, in competition with other cities, to corporations seeking plant, warehouse, and office locations. Coalitions engage in different types of growth politics at the local level. Todd Swanstrom's *The Crisis of Growth Politics* is a case study of "growth politics" in Cleveland, Ohio. By growth politics Swanstrom means the efforts by local government officials to enhance the economic attractiveness of cities for capitalist investors with mobile wealth. He distinguishes two types. In *conservative* growth politics the planning and implementation of economic growth are left primarily to the private sector; this type of politics also rejects redistributive policies benefiting ordinary urbanites below the upper-income level. Government is not especially important. *Liberal* growth politics, in contrast, is a balancing act, where local politicians have the power to furnish incentives for wealthy investors interested in growth and also provide some redistributive support by the state for the nonwealthy.[62] Substantial citizen movements and organizations seem required for a city to have liberal growth politics.

The Pervasive Ideology of Growth

The development of cities is more than a question of capital. Substantial theoretical attention has been given to legitimation and ideology in the neo-Marxist and neo-Weberian theoretical literatures. Lefebvre, for example, notes that corporate capitalists are not content with dominating capital flows or the state; capitalists press further and set themselves up "as a model of organization and administration for society in general."[63] The capitalists' views on political-economic growth and development are expected to become prevalent. Business leaders in local growth coalitions have usually espoused an aggressive version of the growth-and-profit ideology. From this perspective profit is linked to constantly renewed expansion and economic growth, measured in terms of jobs, production, and population. The ideology of growth—seen in business-subsidized billboards asserting that "growth means jobs"—is so pervasive in the United States that it is difficult to sustain media and public attention for an alternative view. The local or regional need for economic growth, according to a Boston Federal Reserve Bank booklet, is a common justification for profit seeking: "In a private enterprise system the hope for profits encourages new production, investment and economic growth." [64] Coupled with this viewpoint is often the expressed idea of laissez-faire government: governments should not intervene in economic matters lest they interfere with the natural order of the free market.

The Social Costs of Urban Growth under Modern Capitalism

Defining Social Costs

The corporations recruited by the growth coalitions to a city become a powerful force for its social and physical transformation. Growth in capitalist cities typically hinges on the investment decisions made by these footloose controllers of capital who calculate profit at the firm level. Social costs, defined here as negative consequences of for-profit production, are not fully paid for by an individual corporation but are shifted onto third parties, especially outside individuals and communities. [65] In capitalistic societies, generally speaking, investment and production decisions are made without a satisfactory accounting of societal consequences. Costs are calculated at the microeconomic level of the individual company in terms of its profits, its future net revenues, or its share of the market. Decision making by this criterion will seek to reduce internal corporate costs and thus usually ignore many social costs that can be displaced onto third persons. Many urban problems are created because decision making affecting whole communities is made at the level of individual firms seeking to maximize their interests. Gottdiener notes that "at a certain point in community development . . . trajectories of economic growth and the quality of life diverge." [66]

Cities are geological and physical environments into which corporate and other human action has intruded. The physical environment has its own regularities and laws—ground and surface water flows, air patterns, rainfall, and soil characteristics. If these environmental factors are ignored or neglected when profit-centered investment and production decisions are made, then the consequences of such decisions can be negative.[67] Within a given natural environment, the rate of economic and consequent population growth can also accentuate the negative social costs of that growth. There is significant variability in the velocity of capital movement into and out of manufacturing, real estate, and construction ventures. Thus, Bluestone and Harrison have noted that the impact of city growth is greatly shaped by capital velocity:

> How much expansion can be absorbed, and how quickly, depends on the dynamics of the people and the environment of the community involved. . . . With suitable planning and reasonable forecasts, new schools can be built, teachers hired, roadways, water, and sewage systems constructed, and job training. . . . But when the capital influx is totally unrestrained, the absorptive capacity of the social system can be quickly overwhelmed.[68]

A high velocity of capital investment can accentuate infrastructural problems, including water pollution, traffic congestion, and toxic waste disposal. In addition, many social costs of unrestrained corporate growth take a long time to appear in a community.

Why are urban-based corporations able to create environmental and other social problems by shifting the social costs of growth they generated onto other people? The answer lies in their greater economic and political power and in their dominance of the ideological debate. In a society with significant inequality in income and in the ability to make decisions about jobs and resources, the production and distribution decisions of executives heading corporations, particularly large firms, are hard for ordinary citizens to resist or change.

Social Costs and the Local Government Dilemma

In most cities the local government faces pressures from the citizenry to handle these social costs, as well as pressures from business leaders to assist and subsidize the location expenses of companies investing within the city boundaries. Local government is pressured to accelerate economic growth and to recruit corporations in manufacturing and other industries; the result is a broad array of usually expensive and unnecessary tax and other subsidies. Studies have shown that tax credits and tax-exempt bonds are available to industrial and development capitalists in most urban areas, so special subsidies have in most cases a mild effect on location and investment decisions. Local governments are pressured to provide parking facilities, tax abatements, public services, zoning permissions, or administrative assistance in finding federal grants and loans. North and South, government officials have played a role in downtown office development, providing money for services such as new roads and sewers, giving away public land by closing streets and by urban renewal projects, and constructing business-oriented projects such as convention centers and parking garages.[69]

In addition, local government faces demands from its citizenry to deal with general neighborhood service requirements and with the social costs and problems of growth. A local government makes "defensive expenditures" for such items as road, water, sewage, and toxic waste problems. The scale of defensive expenditures is affected by a general process of urban growth, but that scale has been extended since World War II by spatial centralization and high concentrations of office towers in many cities.[70] These expenditures accelerate as growth increases. The fiscal capacity of a governmental system can easily be overwhelmed.

When local governments operate to facilitate the location or expansion of high water use or pollution-causing firms or when they retreat from the planning and intervention necessary to deal with the broad service problems created by private investments in corporate facilities, they cooperate with investors who inflict social costs on the urban citizenry. Under pressure from business elites local government officials are often slow to respond to the total community costs of unrestrained capitalistic growth. In many cities, especially in the Sunbelt, business leaders want most governmental regulations and taxes kept to a minimum; business interests do not want to see too much local government attention paid to neighborhood services or even for some of the major infrastructural costs of corporate-generated growth. Certainly some defensive expenditures for roads and sewers are necessary, but often infrastructural expenditures are kept at a level to keep taxes down.

Too much action on roads, sewers, water systems, and toxic waste problems can be costly, and it can require increased individual and business taxes. Since the typical local growth coalition generally demands a "good business climate" with low taxes, then it follows that public services and defensive expenditures must be kept at a level consistent with corporate recruitment and firm-level profitability. Yet there is a fundamental contradiction in this demand, for the costs of growth often overwhelm the capacity of government to deal with growth given the available governmental revenues, particularly in those cities with the "best business climates." Infrastructure can sometimes be starved in the short run, but in the long run someone will have to pay for costs of growth. After a few years the social problems or the unrestrained growth costs will be even more costly to clean up, especially in terms of tax dollars. This is particularly the case if an industry has begun to disinvest in a particular urban or metropolitan location, a common occurrence in U.S. cities; future generations of taxpayers eventually pay much of the money cost of elite-led growth and decline. And in both the present and the future ordinary citizens pay many costs in terms of human suffering. The social costs of investment-spurred growth in a particular urban area are not borne equally by all citizens. Those living in certain areas, such as central cities, growth corridors, or near toxic waste dumps, bear more costs than others; lower-income residents seem to pay a disproportionate part of the cost.

Conclusion: Exploring Urban Concepts

In the following chapters I will explore the usefulness of these concepts and theoretical frameworks for a full understanding of the development of a major American city. Houston, the nation's fourth largest city, is a major metropolitan area in the international world economy. Thus, the city provides an interesting case study which can be employed to evaluate the utility and heuristic value of an array of conceptions and explanations in the mainstream ecological framework and in the critical power-conflict frameworks. Houston is a city that has been cited and discussed by policymakers in the United States and Europe as the model for privatized urban development and planning, for laissez-faire government, and for supply-side economic policies. A careful study of this "capital of the Sunbelt" can provide a useful whetstone not only for testing social science theories of the city but also for evaluating public planning and investment policies in regard to the modern city.

3

More than Oil:

Houston's Multisectored

Economy

To provide an understanding of the character and development of the metropolitan area of Houston I will begin with an in-depth analysis of the economic
and political history of the city from the foundation years in the 1830s to the
turbulent boom and bust years of the 1970s and 1980s. Sifting through this
history, I will trace the evolution of Houston from an agricultural marketing
and primary extraction economy to a more complex economy with agricultural marketing, primary resource extraction, refining, petrochemicals, and
other oil-related manufacturing as principal features. This unfolding process
is grounded in varieties of capital investment and accumulation. The earliest
investments were in commercial enterprises designed to market agricultural
supplies and products, as well as in urban real estate speculation. This economic activity gradually became organized as local commercial firms and
business service networks of law and banking firms, a business infrastructure
which provided the foundation for later investments in resource extraction,
railroads, manufacturing, and a variety of commercial and industrial operations. Understanding the cumulative aspects of capitalistic development can
help answer the question of why and how a city such as Houston becomes the
dominant center for a particular industry.

From the cotton trade of the nineteenth century to oil exploration, oil tools,
and oil services in the twentieth century Houston has long been a global city,
integrated into the world market system. Although an argument can be made
for Houston as a culturally provincial city prior to the 1960s, one can also
argue with considerable evidence for the city's essential openness to international trade and influence from the mid-nineteenth century. In this and the
next chapter I will offer evidence for the proposition that cities such as Houston should be assessed within the relevant international context, and not, as
some mainstream analysts would have it, primarily as part of some national
filtering-down process.

Important, too, in this chapter on the first century of Houston's political-
economic history is the recurrent intervention of local and federal governments in the Houston economy, usually at the behest of local business elites.
In no meaningful sense can the city's history be described as lacking signifi-

cant governmental intervention or involvement. Governmental action has been such a constant thread throughout the city's history that prevailing theories of the local state might be illuminated by a consideration of the theoretical hints in these Houston materials.

The Houston Economy and the State: An Overview

The Multisectored Economy

Much writing about the Houston metropolitan area has portrayed its economy as a petroleum monoculture. Such a view of the city and its surrounding geographical area is exaggerated, for the metropolitan economic structure is in reality a palimpsest with a number of layers or sectors built up over a century and half, each with its distinctive economic and state intervention characteristics. This complex reality can be seen in Table 3.1. Historically viewed, Houston's economic structure can be divided into seven major sectors. The first and oldest dimension of the Houston economy is agricultural production, marketing, and processing, particularly sugar, cotton, and grain operations. This agricultural sector became important during Houston's first decades, and it has remained so to the present. Certain products such as cotton had become somewhat less significant by the 1960s, but other agricultural products such as grains took up the slack. Food processing had become consequential by 1900. The agricultural boom stimulated the development of a number of business service establishments, including banks and law firms. The agricultural economy also demanded construction of port facilities and numerous railroads; the latter brought not only the first major industrial workshops to the city but also the first regional headquarters of a major national corporation.

The next major sector in the greater Houston economy is "primary commodity" production—not only oil and gas but also sulphur, water, lumber, lime, and salt. The proximity of east Texas forests and the Gulf was notable in the development of these industries. The owners of forested and mineral-rich lands in the Houston–Gulf Coast area played a major role in the area's early exploitation of extractive materials. Timber and sulphur were particularly important primary commodities produced in the late nineteenth and early twentieth centuries. Several prominent Houstonians, including John Henry Kirby and Jesse Jones, had entrepreneurial roots in timber and lumber businesses (see Chapter 5). Moreover, beginning at the turn of the century the lumber

TABLE   3.1.
Economic Sectors in the Houston Area:
Approximate Periods of Predominance

SECTORS	1840	1860	1880	1900	1920	1940	1960	1980
Agricultural production marketing, processing								
Cotton marketing, processing	───	───	───	───	───	───	───	
Other products			───	───	───	───	───	───
Food processing				───	───	───	───	───
Banking, business services		───	───	───	───	───	───	───
Railroad industry and port facilities			───	───	───	───	───	───
Primary commodity production								
Timber industries				───	───	───	───	
Mineral production (e.g., sulphur)				───	───	───	───	───
Oil and gas exploration and production				───	───	───	───	───
Processing and manufacturing								
Oil refining					───	───	───	───
Oil tools, services					───	───	───	───
Petrochemicals						───	───	───
Paper/printing industries				───	───	───	───	───
Medical services							───	───
Space-related industry							───	───

industry was linked to the emergence of papermaking and printing industries in the metropolitan area. Oil was not the first extracted resource to generate allied manufacturing industries.

After 1901 oil and gas gradually became the dominant extraction commodities. Over the next three decades the oil and gas business upstaged the other extraction industries, but the former have remained important to the present day, in part because they provide feedstocks for the oil-related manufacturing industries. As can be seen in Table 3.1, the petroleum sector is complex, encompassing oil exploration, refining, tools and services industries, and the petrochemical industry. The manufacturing and service sectors developed in tandem with or on the heels of the oil exploration and production efforts. Different subsectors in the oil sector have distinctive trajectories, with oil production and marketing dating back to the early 1900s. Oil-related manufacturing had joined this primary production by the 1920s, when prominent oil refining facilities and oil tools complexes were established in the greater Houston area. Petrochemical production became a major subsector in the 1940s. The refining and petrochemical industries have been among the most high-tech of U.S. industries. The most recently developed sectors of the Houston economy are the medical and space sectors, large parts of which have also been labeled high-tech. The medical and space sectors are perhaps the most significant new types of economic activity and growth arriving in the city since the 1950s.

In the last chapter I noted that in the early decades of the twentieth century the "free market" of thousands of competing firms was displaced by a market increasingly controlled by the interests and investment decisions of large corporations.[1] This trend can be seen in the Houston economy. In various periods after the 1890s large cotton, railroad, banking, aerospace, and oil-related firms have been central in the city's economic story.

Houston's Antistate Ideology

In Chapter 2 I discussed the importance of the state in social science analysis of urban areas. These theories deal with who controls the state and the state's actual functions and characteristics. In this chapter and the next I will primarily be concerned with the question of the supportive functions and subsidies of the local and federal states. In Chapter 5 I examine the issue of the control of local government in more detail. To those readers familiar with the role of local government in northern U.S. and European cities, the data that follow on governmental intervention and subsidization in the Houston case may not seem surprising. But the extraordinary character of state intervention in the Houston metropolis becomes clear when one considers the antistate intervention, "free enterprise" ideology propounded and advertised by the city's dominant business elite and its allied politicians since the nineteenth century. Houston's fame around the globe casts the city in the light of one that "made it" without significant governmental assistance. A local political scientist noted this traditional "we don't need federal aid" stance of Houston's business-rooted politicians: "For many years, Houston politicians boasted that their city's growing economy allowed it to refuse federal aid while other cities pleaded for more and more help."[2] For many decades the idea of federal aid for most urban uses has even been publicly attacked as "socialistic" by local business groups and political candidates. An advertisement for Houston by the local business elite in *Fortune* magazine accented the good business climate and the lack of government interference proclaimed from the 1840s to the 1980s: "Houston, by virtue of being in Texas, reaps the benefits of a state that has one of the best business climates in the nation. It is not just lukewarm to business, it is probusiness. It welcomes new ideas and people. There's little in the way of red tape. Free enterprise is still the gospel."[3] The idea of the good business climate entails the view that local governments should be reluctant to intervene in major projects of interest to the local business elite. Houston's business elite has fought successfully against local government regulation in such areas as land use control since the 1930s; often cited as illustrating the prominence of the free enterprise ideology is the absence of city zoning laws, a situation unique among major U.S. cities. But the rejection of certain types of governmental intervention has not meant a rejection of many other forms of such aid.

The Reality of State Subsidies

Economic historians sometimes make the distinction between governmental regulatory policies and governmental promotional policies in assessing the development of the state in the United States. In the Houston data which follow I will show the difference between these two features of local government. Promotional activities have been pushed, while regulation has, with one or two notable exceptions, been kept at a minimal level. In Chapter 2 I considered O'Connor's social investment expenditures, social consumption expenditures, and social expenses. I also examined the work of Dear and Clark, who view the state as supporting the capitalist system by providing for the conditions of capital accumulation and the welfare of labor and exercising ideological control over labor.

From the detailed information on Houston in this chapter I will demonstrate that social investment expenditures dominate while social consumption expenditures have been kept relatively low. These social investment expenditures include a number of different projects at the local government level: (1) business-desired infrastructure projects, such as the perennial ship channel dredging; and (2) state subsidies for business enterprises, such as market houses and convention centers. Ideological control has also been important, although much of that activity has not been carried out by state officials but rather through the private sector. The federal government has often buttressed local officials in the provision of social capital investments for the Houston metropolitan area. For example, in the early decades of the twentieth century substantial federal investment capital flowed into both the dredging of the ship channel and the infrastructure of roads, schools, and governmental buildings. Moreover, social capital expenditures are not the only form of state intervention relevant to the Houston story. Contrary to the Chamber of Commerce pronouncements about the lack of interest in regulation, in the 1930s Houston and other Texas oil executives actively pressured the federal government to intervene in the new East Texas oil fields to *regulate* the flow of oil.

Houston: An Agricultural Entrepôt

A Commercial Center: King Cotton

Houston began in the 1830s as a speculative real estate venture by two northern capitalists, J. K. Allen and A. C. Allen, in a swampy Gulf Coast area. As I will document in more detail in Chapter 5, the Allen brothers viewed their new town as rapidly becoming a commercial center for the Gulf Coast. Commercial capitalism dominated the city's early economic history. Within a few decades Houston had emerged as a regional marketing city dominated by a healthy commerce in agricultural products. Lumber, grain, and cotton commodities generated an important infrastructure of railroads, warehouses, cotton gins, and banks servicing the southeast Texas agricultural economy. The official seal of Houston has at its center a plow and a locomotive, truly accurate symbols for an urban economy originally based on agricultural marketing and on railroads.

In the 1830s and 1840s cotton farming began in the rich river bottoms of southern Texas. By 1840 perhaps 1,000 bales were being marketed through Houston's cotton traders. By the mid-1840s that figure had increased to 14,000 bales, and by 1860 to 115,000 bales. In the 1850s cotton and lumber were the major products exported through the modest port facilities. Cotton was brought in by oxcart and wagon from nearby slave plantations. Soon Houston's most important businesses were cotton firms. Cotton was sold to English buyers; in return European goods bought by local merchants were sold to Texans. Some cotton merchants functioned as bankers, loaning large sums of money to local planters before there were organized banks in the area. Not surprisingly, this cotton society had great inequalities in income and wealth. From the beginning Houston was class stratified, with a small wealthy elite, a large poverty-stricken population, and a substantial middle-income sector. In the 1850s black slaves labored at the worst jobs in the city. Between 1850 and 1860 the share of wealth held by the richest 10 percent of the population increased from just over half to more than two-thirds.[4]

Although the Civil War reduced this cotton trade, it generated a great commercial increase in food products and other goods needed for the Confederate cause. The 1860s brought devastation to many cities in the South, but the most destructive effects of the Civil War did not reach Houston. Instead, the war made Houston into a significant southern marketplace and brought new wealth to the local elite. After the war cotton again became the main product in trade. Cotton first put Houston on the international economic map; and the expansion of cotton processing and cotton marketing required an improved regional transport network. But cotton was not the only agricultural buttress of the Houston economy. By the 1840s there was significant sugar cane production in the greater Houston area, and the first sugar mill, run by slaves, was established in 1843. After the Civil War E. H. Cunningham bought up several of the major plantations and invested heavily in new buildings and machinery, putting together a company town called Sugar Land, an area which still exists. Cunningham developed his sugar empire in part with convict labor leased from the Texas prison system.[5]

Cotton, Railroads, and Banking

Major buttresses of the Houston area economy by the late nineteenth century were the railroads; in fact, there was a close connection between cotton and sugar marketing and the coming of principal railroads. The poor quality of the transportation infrastructure around Houston, especially the impassable roads, was a major concern of the local merchants, who encouraged and participated in railroad ventures. After several decades of railroad growth, by the mid-1880s Houston had become a leading railroad city in the Southwest. The first manufacturing plant, an iron foundry, had been established in Houston in the 1850s. Other foundries and railroad shops added between the 1850s and the 1880s laid the industrial basis for the location of major railroad facilities in the city. Colis P. Huntington made Houston the regional headquarters for his Southern Pacific Railroad. Southern Pacific brought large payrolls and decent paying blue- and white-collar jobs, and this increased the number of union workers.[6]

The dramatic growth in rail lines improved Houston's transport ties to the outside world. Cotton and sugar barons successfully expanded rail transit. By the 1890s cotton brokerage houses were handling millions of bales. The railroads stimulated the development of the timber and lumber industries because of the burgeoning demand for railroad ties and building materials. Indeed, Gulf Coast railroad executives actively promoted new agricultural production; they publicized new crops such as rice for planting on the fertile lands around Houston, for rice meant more produce to haul. By the late 1880s Houston's merchants were being joined by business leaders associated with railroads and other industrial enterprises, including new manufacturing plants processing cotton and lumber. In addition, government-subsidized work on the city's ship channel was improving Houston's status as a Gulf Coast port. Tonnage shipped out of the port increased significantly in the 1870s and 1880s.

The railroad executives, together with the entrepreneurs in the expanding cotton enterprises, created a demand for improved business services, including enterprises such as banks and law firms. Prior to the 1880s it was difficult for local merchants and manufacturers to borrow sufficient capital to expand. Most were heavily dependent on banking corporations outside Texas for whatever capital they could secure. However, with the cotton marketing and railroad expansion in the 1880s came an enhanced flow of local profits and outside investor capital, which could be drawn upon to create better local banking firms. Local banks not only brought improved loan opportunities for local enterprises but also put more currency in local circulation; prior to the 1930s these local, called "national," banks could issue their own currency. In the years from 1886 to 1905 five important new banks were organized in the city. Not surprisingly, most Houston bankers had begun their careers in the cotton business.[7]

By the early 1900s Houston was home for large cotton brokerage companies. The city had become the major railroad center in the Southwest, and there were a growing number of banking and manufacturing enterprises. The city had grown to 44,000 people, and the metropolitan area exceeded 130,000 in population.

The Role of Government in Subsidizing Private Enterprise

From Houston's earliest days government funds have been used to facilitate private profit making. The Allen brothers called on local and Texas governments to subsidize their profitable land speculation. Their success in getting the new Republic of Texas capital located in Houston guaranteed visibility for their new town. Moreover, their immediate successors in the local business elite used local government funds and bonds to pay for the road and utility projects they required.

By the 1860s the city council greatly increased its efforts to provide the infrastructure for development—grading and surfacing streets, building bridges, and franchising private companies for gas lighting and horse-cars. Perhaps most important, in 1866 the city council set aside a significant percentage of government revenues to dredge Buffalo Bayou, a major local waterway, in order to provide a better ship channel. But this expansion of government-subsidized infrastructure projects eventually created a fiscal crisis. In the mid-1860s three dozen of the wealthiest men in the city, including top business leaders and six of Houston's next seven mayors, called a meeting to discuss liquidating the growing municipal debt. Presiding over the meeting was George Goldwaithe, chief lawyer for the Texas Central Railroad. This business group prepared a blueprint for future governmental progress: (1) a retirement of the floating debt of $40,000 by the council; (2) the issuance of one million dollars in municipal government bonds for utility projects.

Whether Democratic or Reconstruction-Republican, the next several city administrations pursued this business-created plan. All administrations reflected the tremendous business commitment to growth; some of the city's business and political leaders envisioned Houston as the "Chicago of the South." Between the 1860s and the 1880s the basic foundation for the Houston business elite's approach to government was laid down; this approach persists to the present. Business leaders, operating through their associations and governmental agencies, intentionally neglected the needs of residential areas for utility and other public services; they focused their concern on the business corridors, particularly those between the railroad stations and the downtown market square. These business areas received many of the important paving, drainage, lighting, and horse-car transit projects, actions which in fact improved trade. The idea of the city's business elite was that the first priority of government should be promoting the expansion and profitability of the private sector.[8]

This close linkage of government to local economic interests had broader consequences than the neglect of residential areas. The business clique's decision to finance needed infrastructure with municipal bonds tethered the growing municipality even more securely to national networks of finance and banking. And this entailed a substantial dependence on outside financial markets for assistance in generating funds for the requisite local infrastructure. In the 1870s a nationwide depression brought an economic downturn to the city, and the local government was unable to collect $100,000 in delinquent taxes. For this reason, the municipal authorities were unable to pay local and national creditors. Consequently, Houston's municipal government, together with governments in other cities, went bankrupt. As a result of a major crisis in the U.S. economy, tied in part to irregularities and contradictions in the United States banking system, local municipalities found themselves in serious fiscal difficulties.

Oil Comes to Houston, 1901–1919

Primary Commodity Production: Before Oil

Before the dominance of oil and gas the Houston–Gulf Coast economy was dominated by trade, agriculture, and certain types of primary commodity production, especially the extraction of sulphur, salt, lime, and other minerals from the land and the cutting of timber. Primary commodity production differs from production in value-added manufacturing industries. Its sphere involves the extraction of natural resources; this can lead to realizing large profits on capital investments, often in excess of profits garnered by manufacturing enterprises. By 1900 the timber and lumber industry in east Texas produced a more valuable product than any other industry. Some timber was shipped by railroad for processing in Houston mills. Pratt notes that, "as with the regional offices of the railroads, these large lumbering operations helped create financial, administrative, and communications resources that were helpful in bringing to Houston the regional offices of other companies in other industries."[9]

Before oil became dominant other mineral industries along the Houston–Gulf Coast area played a considerable role in its prosperity. For example, the highly profitable sulphur industry was monopolized by a few Houston area firms. In 1891 a Standard Oil chemist, Herman Frasch, developed a special process to bring underground deposits of Gulf Coast sulphur to the surface. In 1903–1906 Frasch's Union Sulphur Company brought tons of sulphur to the surface; substantial profits were one result. In 1912 the Freeport Sulphur Company was created near Houston, and within four years it was producing 500,000 tons annually. World War I brought the Union and Freeport firms high profits. Texas Gulf Sulphur, created in Houston at the end of World War I with operations in Matagorda County, soon became the dominant sulphur firm. A handful of companies monopolized the production of this extraordinarily important mineral, a principal ingredient in sulphuric acid and a chemical crucial to making many manufactured products.[10] At the turn of the century the ownership of timber and mineral lands brought much wealth to Houstonians and much economic development to the area.

New Oil Fields and Houston's Economic Dominance

The discovery of oil ninety miles east of Houston in 1901 and subsequent discoveries closer to the city in the 1905–1919 period set the stage for Houston to become a major oil and gas exploration and production center. In 1905 the Humble field near Houston, a major Texas field over the next two decades, began producing oil. By 1919 three-quarters of Gulf Coast oil was coming from fields in the Houston area.[11]

Why and how did Houston become the oil capital of the Gulf Coast? In 1890, with a population of 27,000, Houston was only the eighteenth largest city in the South; it was smaller than its sister city Galveston, and much smaller than Dallas and San Antonio, two other Texas cities. However, Houston's major coastal competitors in the region, Galveston and Beaumont, confronted major barriers to development. Galveston was the dominant Texas port prior to 1900; the high freight rates charged by Galveston's entrepreneurs began an intensely competitive relationship between the cities and their ports. In 1900 Galveston's port and population were devastated by a hurricane; executives in oil-related and other companies became concerned with its exposed coastal location. Beaumont, although a town close to major oil fields, did not have the railroad and banking infrastructure that Houston had already developed as an important center of agricultural commerce. By the early 1900s Houston was the sheltered harbor closest to the ranches and cotton fields of the Midwest and the central South. By 1912 no less than seventeen railroads used the city as a rail hub. Texas was producing two-thirds of all cotton in the United States, much of which was shipped through Houston, which had six cotton-seed processing mills.[12] Contrary to mainstream theories of urban growth which see Sunbelt cities as bypassed until postwar decades by economic growth, Houston had emerged by the early 1900s as a principal agricultural marketing center integrated into the world market. And the developed infrastructure of port facilities, railroads, and banks actually created the infrastructure foundation for Houston's subsequent dominance as an oil center.

Soon after 1901 several oil companies that organized production in the new Texas oil fields began to move their headquarters to the greater Houston area. The new Texas Company (later Texaco) came to Houston in 1908. In 1916 the Gulf Company, newly born in the oil fields, moved to Houston; this oil company was controlled by Mellon interests in Pittsburgh. For a brief period many companies organizing production in the Texas oil fields were local companies, but in the next decade or so the Gulf Coast oil industry would move through this highly competitive stage to a stage of oligopoly capitalism, one increasingly dominated by the larger oil companies.

Moreover, investment decisions made in Detroit spurred investment by oil companies and transformed Houston into an oil capital. This long-distance, intercity relationship was not one of filtering, as some mainstream urban analysts might describe it, but rather of concomitant capital investment in two cities linked by manufacturing requirements for processed raw materials. The events taking place in Detroit in the decade prior to Houston's major growth boom in the 1920s involved auto industrialists such as Henry Ford, who with his brilliant engineers perfected the mass production of the automobile. Until auto production accelerated in the 1904–1919 period, crude oil had been used for kerosene, fuel oil, and lubricants. In 1899 only 3,700 autos were built in the United States, but by 1909 the figure had grown to 126,600, and by 1919 to an impressive 1.7 million. As a result, fuel usage dramatically increased in this period, to 2.7 billion gallons by 1919.[13] Moreover, coal had fueled the rise of U.S. industry in the nineteenth century, but by the 1910s and 1920s oil was beginning to replace coal as the fuel of choice. Growing gasoline and oil sales generated much capital which oil-related corporations invested in Houston–Gulf Coast production and manufacturing facilities.

By the 1910s and 1920s the Houston–Gulf Coast area had become one of the world's major extraction economies. And oil was only one of the products extracted. In 1910 a local periodical ran an article on "Houston, the Greatest Lumber City"; Houston was still an important center for the lumber industry. Robert Wood, a top executive at Sears, Roebuck noted that "within a 200-mile radius of Houston more wealth is taken from the soil than from any equivalent area on earth." [14]

Continuing Local and Federal Government Aid

Houston's oil boom was not just a matter of massive investment by private corporations. Again state involvement was essential. There was substantial scientific and research support for the oil firms. In the early decades of the oil industry the U.S. Geological Survey provided accurate geological data on oil fields and potential oil fields; not until 1913–1915 did most oil companies establish geological departments. In addition, the tilt in federal transportation subsidies away from rail transit to the automobile began in this era. In 1916 the federal government began subsidizing highways, and by 1919 total local and federal government expenditures for roads had reached $200 million.

These social capital investments not only subsidized Detroit's rapidly expanding auto industry, but they also stimulated demand for Gulf Coast oil for road surfacing materials and gasoline. In addition, U.S. entry into World War I spurred defense-related demand for vehicles and thus for oil products. In mid-1917 President Wilson set up the U.S. Fuel Administration, whose attempts to coordinate oil production for defense needs had the major effect of stabilizing competition, prices, and profits in the oil industry in ways illegal oil trusts could not.[15]

A major example of state aid for Houston can be seen in the extraordinary story of the construction and rehabilitation of the ship channel. In this early period the local business elite played an important role in facilitating corporate investment. In spite of their outspoken laissez-faire view of government and their free enterprise philosophy, local bankers, merchants, and other business leaders pressed for considerable federal governmental subsidies to improve port facilities. Under pressure from this local growth coalition, the U.S. Congress in 1902 appropriated about $1 million in public investment capital for local port development, but this federal largess was not sufficient. A few years later Houston capitalists met in the mayor's office to work out a plan for further subsidization. Their rather unique idea was to raise private funds to buy local government bonds in order to match the federal subsidy. The local business leadership proposed that a special governmental unit called a "navigation district" be created to issue bonds; the federal government was then expected to match the local funds. Since the city had no authority to issue bonds for port development projects outside its city limits, attorneys were sent to lobby the Texas legislature to pass a law providing for navigation districts. Both the scale of the local business elite's lobbying effort and the new state creation, the navigation district, were unprecedented in Texas; and the navigation district may have been, at the time, a unique governmental innovation generated by the Houston business elite. The navigation district could issue taxpayer-backed bonds to pay for port expansion, but the U.S. Congress still had to be lobbied effectively for matching funds. In 1910 Congress approved $1.25 million for deepening the Houston ship channel, reportedly the largest grant for such development purposes made by the federal government up to that time. Actually after 1902 the federal government played a central and recurrent facilitating role in the rise of this Gulf Coast city.[16]

A Leading U.S. Port

This federal assistance speeded the flow of cotton and other agricultural products through Hosuton. By the 1910s the ship channel was deep enough for large ships. In 1913–1914 cotton was still the ship channel's most important export cargo. Even though the tonnage dropped significantly during World War I, from 2 million tons in 1910 to 1.2 million in 1920, by 1920 Houston had become the largest spot cotton market in the world. Moreover, by the 1920s oil company and other local executives were arguing that the channel needed to be dredged even deeper in order to accommodate oil tankers, a sign that oil was beginning to compete with cotton as a chief export.[17]

We should underscore at this point the importance of the port of Houston in the rise of the city to business prominence. Throughout the history of the city of Houston we glimpse the recurring story of the port and ship channel. From the city's first decade the business leadership was centrally concerned with the development and expansion of *waterborne* commerce. For that reason these entrepreneurs worked to create, or bring, shipping lines to the city, to subsidize through the state the dredging of the channel and the creation of port facilities, to issue bonds for private participation in the port expansion, and to foster national and international trade through the port. Both at the outset and in subsequent decades distinguished Houston leaders were associated with the development of the city's premier port facilities.

From Primary Commodity Production to Processing Industries, 1919–1931

The Role of Big Companies in Houston

By the decade of the 1920s the larger oil corporations were beginning to dominate many sectors of the Texas oil industry; over the next two decades they consolidated their control. Numerous refineries and other oil-related facilities were built in the Houston area because of the wealth of necessary raw materials and the state-subsidized port facilities. Capital was invested in value-added manufacturing, which involved the processing of the oil and gas produced by the older extraction and production operations. The new jobs in oil-related plants and offices attracted workers from other parts of Texas and from other regions of the United States, thus fueling the city's dramatic 111 percent population increase during the 1920s.

Moreover, the character of the oil industry was changing. Inside and outside Texas the number of top corporate decision makers declined as certain sectors of the oil industry became more centralized. Executives in the headquarters buildings of leading oil companies and large banks—including many on the East Coast—made the broad strategical decisions about investing capital in many areas of the oil industry, although many East Coast decisions were based on the advice of operations executives in Texas. Although Standard Oil (now Exxon) had been split up in 1911, by the 1920s the former Standard companies, together with a handful of newer companies, were beginning to dominate oil production. By the late 1920s fully 70 percent of Texas production was in the hands of twenty larger companies. The large firms frequently moved into new fields and drove smaller companies out of business; they expanded vertically by adding subsidiaries dealing with all aspects of the business from research to marketing. Much strategic control over key sectors of the Texas industry was in the hands of East Coast executives in oil companies and financial institutions. However, much of this decision making about companywide investments was grounded in what experienced operations executives reported to the headquarters offices of the big companies. In addition, many top executives at companies like Standard Oil and the Texas Company had lived and worked in the Southwest for long periods of time. In this sense East Coast management was more than "East Coast" in experience and background, even though ownership was substantially eastern.[18]

Standard Oil and Texas

Standard Oil was expanding into the Texas oil fields by 1918. Standard executives began by courting a Houston-based company. The web of ties between Eastern finance capital, the major oil companies, and Houston firms can be seen in the story of Houston's Humble Oil and Refining Company, a company formed by Texas entrepreneurs in 1917. Cash poor, these entrepreneurs needed capital since the new company's assets were primarily existing leases and equipment. Loans from local banks were secured, but soon Humble Oil sought out New York banks for loans. Humble's independence, and its capital problems, did not last long. In 1919 Standard Oil bought a controlling share. In part to get around Texas laws intentionally restricting Standard Oil's activities, the giant petroleum firm allowed Humble's board of directors substantial operational independence. Yet Standard executives controlled the flow of much capital to Humble and thereby exerted broad influence over its development. As a result of this new relationship, between 1918 and 1929 the fixed assets of Humble increased from $13 million to $233 million.[19]

Soon the Humble Oil subsidiary had become the largest producer of crude oil in the United States. In the 1920s Humble erected a headquarters building in downtown Houston. Humble's huge Baytown refinery, just across the ship channel from the city of Houston, sharply increased its daily oil refining capacity from 10,000 barrels in 1921 to 125,000 barrels a decade later. In fact, by 1927 the ship channel had no fewer than eight refineries along it, with half the crude oil coming in by pipeline and half by train, barge, and tanker. This black liquid cargo reinforced the city's top port status.[20]

Allied Companies

The expansion of Standard and other major oil companies generated investment in allied companies in the Houston metropolitan area. By the late 1920s oil services and manufactured products critical to the oil industry were increasingly being provided by local firms. Howard R. Hughes started the Hughes Tool Company, a symbol of the rising importance of oil tool and supply corporations. Cameron Iron Works, soon a stellar oil field equipment company, was established by James Abercrombie. Principal gas and gas pipeline companies were set up in these years. Oil tools, well equipment, and other service companies were financed to a substantial degree by Texas capital; and, unlike the oil companies, most were not acquired by northern corporations before World War II.[21] Thus, one must be careful in evaluating the centralization and concentration of capital in the oil industry, for the dominance of the big companies in the area of production did not mean dominance in such areas as oil tools and services or indeed in the actual drilling of wells themselves, typically the province of independent "wildcatters."

There has been substantial debate among analysts of the oil industry as to whether there is indeed great concentration and centralization in and of the sectors of the oil industry, in the present or in the past. Some would suggest that the oil industry should not be seen as an oligopoly because it has not been as dominated by only three or four firms as the auto industry. Although the auto industry has been more concentrated, in terms of market control, in a few firms than has the oil industry, the oil industry is still dominated by a handful of giants among the thousands of oil companies. Most productive assets in the industry are held by two dozen firms, and profits flow disproportionately into their treasuries.

Manufacturing Growth in Houston

Houston's manufacturing base was modest in the early 1900s, but it did grow significantly between 1904 and 1929, as can be seen in the census figures in Table 3.2. These data are for the top four manufacturing industries in number of employees in 1929. The total number of manufacturing firms grew sharply,

TABLE   3.2.
Houston Manufacturing Sectors: 1904–1929

SECTORS	1904		1929	
	No. of Firms	Product Value	No. of Firms	Product Value
Bakery products	20	$447,000	46	$6,939,000
Metalworking	12	$215,000	17	$3,747,000
Machine shops (foundries)	13	$878,000	41	$22,216,000
Printing, publishing	33	$881,000	61	$9,173,000
Totals	78	$2,421,000	205	$42,075,000

SOURCES: Census Bureau, Department of Commerce, *Manufactures: 1904–1914* (Washington, D.C.: Government Printing Office, 1923), p. 25; Census Bureau, Department of Commerce, *Manufactures: 1929, Texas* (Washington, D.C.: Government Printing Office, 1932), p. 11. These are the top four industries in number of employees in 1929; in that year the coffee and bag industries ranked higher than metalworking in product value.

from 78 in 1904 to 205 in 1929, while the total value of the products of manufacturing increased dramatically, from $2.4 million to $42 million. The product and employment dominance of the foundries, machine shops, printing and metalworking plants, and large bakeries is quite clear. The growth in machine shops and metalworking plants was closely linked to the rise of the oil industry. By 1930 the Houston area was a growing but modest manufacturing center, with more than 429 manufacturing plants of all sizes, a significant number of which were directly or indirectly connected to the oil industry. However, manufacturing was not as dominant in Houston as in most other industrial cities. Even in this early period, Houston had a large cohort of clerical, managerial, and professional workers in a growing number of the stores, office buildings, and laboratory facilities in the area.

State Intervention

Government aid remained important in the prosperous decade of the 1920s. Subsidies for the highway system had reached a billion dollars by 1930, and state intervention continued to be a major factor in stabilizing and subsidizing the oil industry. Federal officials supported the expansion of oil firms; for example, between 1919 and 1924 U.S. government officials worked with executives of the major oil companies to begin the pursuit of oil supplies overseas, an effort precipitated by naval officers' concern about oil supplies. By the mid-1920s the new oil discoveries resulting from these cooperative efforts had contributed to the creation of a world oil glut. Moreover, President Calvin Coolidge set up the Federal Oil Conservation Board to study how the government could promote conservation and stability in the petroleum industry. Some oil-state politicians and oil executives supported government intervention because of this growing instability in the world oil market. In 1926 Congress approved a large tax deduction, called the "oil depletion allowance," to support the industry. A tariff on foreign oil was also imposed to protect the domestic industry.[22]

The Importance of King Cotton

Although oil was becoming a major part of the booming Gulf Coast economy in the 1910s and 1920s, it was not yet the dominant factor it would be later. Indeed, during the 1920s the value of cotton flowing through Texas markets was still twice the value of the oil produced. The firm of Anderson Clayton came to Houston in 1916, and by 1920 it was the largest cotton brokerage company in the world (see Chapter 5). Houston was the commercial funnel for cotton from an area which included Texas, Oklahoma, Arkansas, and Louisiana, an area whose farmers grew more than half the cotton crop of the United States and about one-third of the cotton crop in the world. Flowing through Houston, this cotton was bought and sold, conditioned for shipment, loaded onto ships, and carried down the ship channel.

Cotton exports continued to expand Houston's economic connections to other countries. Local banks were experienced in financing the expansion of local cotton firms. Houston's entrepreneurs were shipping cotton to European nations such as England, France, and Germany and to Asian countries such as China, Japan, and India. Foreign demand increased significantly; local facilities supplied the raw materials for textile factories around the globe. More than eighty Houston companies engaged in cotton marketing; there were twenty-two high-density compresses. Major facilities for handling and warehousing cotton were built on the ship channel and near railroads. Cotton exports through these facilities increased to 1.8 million bales in 1925–1926 and 2.7 million bales in 1931–1932. By 1930 Houston, the leading port in the export of cotton in the Americas, led all Southern ports in exports. Other agricultural products were consequential in the emergence of Houston as a major commercial entrepôt. Grain from Texas, the Midwest, and Canada flowed through the city's port facilities. It is also crucial to note the continuing importance of sugar cane and sugar refining in the greater Houston area. In the early decades of the twentieth century the Kempner family took control over much of the sugar refining in the Sugar Land area, under the name Imperial Sugar Co.[23]

Likewise, the agricultural and oil expansion spurred the development of banking in the Houston area. By the late nineteenth century the five national banks in the area had formed a clearinghouse. Between that time and 1920 bank deposits increased sharply from a few million dollars to $75 million; these deposits would grow again to $350 million by 1940. Nonetheless, Dallas won out in the intercity competition for the important Federal Reserve District bank in the years 1913–1914. This federal decision had the consequence of insuring that Houston would remain in second-place behind Dallas as the Southwest's financial center.

"The City the Depression Missed": Houston in the Troubled 1930s

Houston and the East Texas Oil Fields

The oil industry was not as affected as other industries by the crisis of the Great Depression. The demand for oil was one-third higher in 1932 than in 1927 in spite of the depression. This fact helps explain Houston's relative prosperity and the sobriquet "the city depression missed." [24] Between January 1932 and March 1933, the nadir of the depression, hundreds of companies opened for business in Houston, including dozens of oil-related firms. Shell Petroleum Corporation and Tide Water Oil Company transferred their headquarters to Houston.[25]

By the mid-1930s Houstonians were proudly labeling their city the "oil capital of the *world*." There was empirical support for this boastful assertion: half the world's oil production was then located within 600 miles of Houston, a city with 4,200 miles of pipelines linking it to hundreds of oil fields. Covering a large section of eastern Texas, the huge East Texas oil field—the world's largest—was developed in the early 1930s; by 1939 there were 26,000 wells there. At first, 80 percent of that field was in the hands of the smaller oil companies with just 20 percent in the hands of the biggest companies; however, by 1940 these proportions were reversed. The large firms had begun to buy out the smaller "independents" during the early 1930s period of unrestricted production and low prices. Concentration and centralization had proceeded apace in the Texas petroleum industry. Large companies with subsidiaries in Houston made many decisions about newly discovered fields. About three-quarters of the oil produced in the midcontinent area was controlled by companies tied to Houston, and nearly half of all Texas oil was shipped through the Port of Houston.[26]

The Processing and Refining of Oil

The Houston metropolitan area was becoming an oil refining and processing center, as well as an oil tools and services city. The oil industry was now the largest manufacturer in Texas; and the Houston area was the site for much of this manufacturing, including oil refining and chemical facilities. From the 1920s to the 1940s a series of technological innovations in refining facilitated an increase in the quantity and quality of gasoline extracted from crude oil. By 1941 the Gulf Coast was a dominant refining region, with more than one-third of total U.S. capacity. Houston led all cities around the world in the manufacture of oil tools, supplies, and well equipment. Pipelines carried oil and gas from Texas, Oklahoma, and Louisiana oil fields to Gulf Coast refineries and to tankers at the Port of Houston. Humble Oil's Baytown refinery was one of the largest in the world.[27]

By the end of the Great Depression Houston reportedly housed 1,200 oil companies and supply houses of all sizes; large oil facilities, from refineries to office skyscrapers, were the concrete embodiment of a continuing oil boom. A *Fortune* magazine feature article on Texas and its cities noted that "Without oil Houston would have been just another cotton town. Oil has transformed it into a concrete column soaring grotesquely from a productive substratum. . . . Take oil away and Houston's skyscrapers would be tenanted by ghosts."[28] A contemporary survey by the local Chamber of Commerce estimated that 62 percent of the city's working population more or less depended on oil-related industries.[29]

Manufacturing and the General Economy

A major concern among some business leaders in the 1930s was the lack of diversified manufacturing in their Gulf Coast city. Nonetheless, because of the growth in oil refining facilities and the early development of petrochemical processing operations, Houston's taste of the Great Depression was relatively brief. Indeed, most of the 1930s was a boom period. Much capital flowed into Houston real estate. Even in 1932 Houston saw $3 million of new buildings built; in 1937 about $25 million in building permits were taken out, placing Houston fifth among U.S. cities. In the 1920s and 1930s nearly $30 million in new homes were built in the wealthy River Oaks suburb of Houston. And in 1939 *Fortune* magazine editors noted that Houston "has been made by, and lives for, business. Whereas in San Antonio they will tell you about the Alamo, and in Dallas about the Little Theatre, in Houston they cite figures: $293,000,000 worth of bank deposits . . . 1,200 oil companies . . . 300 oil supply houses . . . 1,000,000 bales of cotton."[30] Boosterism on the part of the local business elite had become conspicuous in this decade.

Additional State Invervention: Dredging the Port

The Houston business elite continued to seek state capital investments in port expansion. Between 1918 and 1938 the U.S. government expended $56 million to dredge deepwater ports at twelve Texas coastal cities, including Houston. The state-assisted development of Houston's port facilities helped the city prosper during the depression. Houston ranked fourth among U.S. ports in total export tonnage by 1930. Sixty-five steamship lines served the metropolitan area, with most of these engaged in foreign trade.[31]

In addition to cotton and oil exports, grain shipments were considerable. Houston was still a major storage and shipping center for rice and other grains, as well as for lumber from east Texas. The depression had a mild negative effect on tonnage shipped through the port, with a reduction in 1931–1932. Yet the port did more business in 1933 than it had in any previous year. Cotton, lumber, and oil accounted for the increase in tonnage shipped—from 1.3 million tons in 1919 to 27 million tons in 1941. Houston was challenging New Orleans for the position of dominant Gulf Coast port and leading Southern metropolis. By 1941 Houston was the third largest port in total tonnage shipped, ranking behind only New York and Philadelphia.[32]

Other State Subsidies: Houston City Infrastructure

In spite of the dramatic economic growth much of Houston's public infrastructure of roads, sewers, and schools remained underdeveloped. Only in the 1920s did natural gas for most houses and motorized fire equipment come to the city. The essential public infrastructure was expanded greatly in the 1930s with substantial federal subsidies. The provision of large-scale governmental aid was facilitated by close ties between the business elite in Houston and in Texas generally and the federal government. Then Vice-President John Nance Garner had represented Texas for many years in the House of Representatives. Texan Sam Rayburn was the House majority leader and, later, Speaker of the House. Houstonian Jesse Jones, a banker at the center of Houston's "Suite 8F" crowd (see Chapter 5), became head of the Reconstruction Finance Corporation (R F C) in the early 1930s and later served as Roosevelt's Secretary of Commerce. Money from the (R F C), the National Recovery Administration (N R A), the Public Works Administration (P W A), and the Works Progress Administration (W P A) rebuilt Houston businesses and facilitated construction of major public buildings, roads, and utilities. For example, in 1934 the P W A gave Harris County $653,000 for road and sewer projects, while the Post Office Department announced a new post office project. Several million dollars were provided for improvements to the ship channel. From 1932 to 1941 an improved public infrastructure, with much of its development guided by the business elite, was built with millions in federal capital.[33]

State Intervention for the Oil Corporation

One of the most interesting examples of massive state intervention in the economy can be seen in the case of the newly discovered East Texas oil field, whose rapid development in the early 1930s had brought Houston-based and other petroleum companies into extreme price competition. So much oil was available that prices dropped to low levels (ten cents a barrel); the profits of big and little firms dropped sharply. The Texas Railroad Commission, the Texas oil regulation agency, put quotas on production in an attempt to end the price chaos. But many entrepreneurs defied the quotas, and much oil was pumped out at rates violating the prorationing regulations. There were threats to dynamite wells to slow production. In 1931 Governor Ross Sterling, a former chief executive of Humble Oil, sent a National Guard unit and Texas Rangers into the East Texas field; the Texas Railroad Commission quotas were enforced by martial law. Ironically, the oil companies had helped create the Texas Railroad Commission as a government agency designed to deal with unrestrained free enterprise activity.

By the early 1930s oil company executives were begging federal officials to set up a federal "czar" to assist in the enforcement of oil pumping quotas for the East Texas fields. As a result, in 1933 President Roosevelt issued an executive order banning the interstate shipment of oil pumped in violation of Texas prorationing laws; federal agents were sent to Texas to enforce the order. This governmental intervention and continuing federal support for pro-rationing among petroleum companies operated from the 1930s to the 1970s to protect the industry. Industry-demanded intervention kept oil prices up and stabilized the oil industry. Thus Houston-based oil companies prospered under federal protection from "excessive" competition.[34] In this case, the state assistance took the form of *regulation,* one type of state intervention in the economy often criticized by those asserting the free enterprise philosophy.

Oil, The Petrochemical Industry, and the State: The 1940s

The Continuing Dominance of Oil

In the 1940s the expansion of oil production and oil-related industries accelerated. Within a radius of 150 miles of Houston there were 185 producing oil fields. More than half of all U.S. oil flowed through the metropolitan economy. There were fourteen major refineries in the greater Houston area. In addition, much of the world's oil tool and services business was still centered there. In 1941 there were no fewer than thirty refineries from Corpus Christi to Houston and Beaumont. Texas had the nation's most productive oil field as well as half the proven oil reserves in the United States. The oil industry retained its favored position in this era of continued governmental intervention in the Sunbelt economy. For example, in the late 1930s the Roosevelt administration began an antitrust suit against twenty-two major oil companies, but it dropped the suit as World War II broke out. In spite of pressures from reformers, no serious attempt was made to impose direct federal control on the oil industry or to break up the large oil companies engaged in monopolization.[35]

Subsidizing a New Industry: Petrochemicals

The petrochemical industry was initially scattered in several places in the United States, including California, New Jersey, and Indiana. In the early 1930s the chemical/petrochemical industry in the Houston area was of modest proportions. By the late 1930s, however, there was a significant spurt in industrialization linked to the war effort. For obvious reasons the Houston metropolitan area became a center of petrochemical production. The ship channel, a major shipping avenue for oil and gas products, was thus a natural site for petrochemical production. A decisive influence was the concentration of refinery capacity in the Houston area, particularly the advanced cat-cracker facilities which broke up crude petroleum into gasoline, heavy oils, and gasses. Refinery by-products from making gasoline and heating oils became the feedstocks for the new petrochemical industry—a principal reason why petrochemical plants are located near oil refineries and owned by oil companies. A trinity of resources—iron ore, coke, and limestone—had brought the steel age to cities such as Pittsburgh. Cramer has noted that "it is the trilogy of resources that has brought in the petrochemical industry in the South—a trilogy of oil and gas, sulfur, and fresh water." [36] The Texas Gulf Coast had the resources necessary for the rapid expansion of the petrochemical plants, as well as both low-cost energy (for example, natural gas) to run the plants and the transport systems to export the products.

A decisive influence was federal government aid. It took major state subsidies for the petrochemical industry to develop into its modern form. By the 1940s the federal government had become a major source of investment capital for U.S. industry, including the oil and petrochemical industries. Although not one of the nation's largest cities at the time, Houston was sixth in the amount of federal capital invested in new manufacturing facilities in the United States. Jesse Jones, a key member of the Houston business elite and the Roosevelt administration, played a role in channeling a large amount of New Deal public capital to the Houston metropolitan area during this period. About $450 million dollars in federal capital expenditures poured into private and joint private-public manufacturing enterprises in the greater Houston area for war-related efforts. Much of this federal capital flowed to the oil and petrochemical industries for such facilities as those producing high octane aviation fuel and synthetic rubber. From crude oil and natural gas came alkylate for aviation gasoline, butadiene and styrene for synthetic rubber, toluene for explosives, ethylene, and acetylene.

In August 1940 a $500,000 toluene plant was announced for Houston, to be built near a Shell oil refinery, for national defense purposes. Five oil companies (Mobil, A R C O, Gulf, Texaco, and Pure Oil) with refineries in southeast Texas created a nonprofit corporation to generate butylene for synthetic rubber. A private corporation ran the plant, but the federal government paid for it, thus providing major capital for petrochemical development. There were dozens of major chemical plants scattered along the ship channel. Texas moved from tenth to sixth in the percentage of total U.S. chemical production in this brief wartime period. The Texas Gulf Coast region not only received much public investment capital but also garnered substantial private capital flowing into petrochemicals and other chemicals. Between 1939 and 1950 no less than $1 billion was invested in chemical plants in the area. The war period has been termed the period of the most rapid recapitalization of industry in U.S. history.[37]

Although the end of World War II brought major cutbacks in production to most chemical production areas in the United States, there were relatively few cutbacks on the Texas Gulf Coast, primarily because there was a substantial regional demand, once met by imported plastics and similar products, which could now be met by local petrochemical plants. The huge federal capital flows to the area had made possible the dramatic postwar growth in the petrochemical industry, which now became heavily involved in production of commercial products for private markets. The federal subsidy had helped create a major industry.[38] But this subsidization was not the only source of the federal underwriting of the petrochemical and oil refining sectors of American industry. Federal government *purchase* and *consumption* of the products of these industries was crucial to longrun profitability and prosperity. Heavy government military requirements would guarantee a permanent military-industrial complex long beyond the end of World War II. Interestingly, "big government" in the United States was not primarily created by the New Deal social programs of the 1930s but rather by the massive industrial and military buildups of World War II.

Creating Allied and Support Industries

In the 1940s transportation companies, including railroad, truck, pipeline, and shipping firms, emerged and expanded in Houston as a result of the growing oil and petrochemical complexes. So, too, did steel, metal fabrication, oil tools, and construction companies. The first major steel plant in the Southwest was a plant built by the American Rolling Mill Company (Armco) on the Houston ship channel; this new facility was constructed with a federal (R F C) loan of $12 million. It was soon expanded under the aegis of R F C executive Jesse Jones to become a $40-million facility. Given the World War II expansion, the Gulf Coast area was no longer dependent on importing the metals needed for oil and petrochemical production, for other manufacturing enterprises, and for the local construction industry.[39]

The Rise of the Natural Gas Industry and the Government Pipelines

In the earliest decades of the Texas oil industry much gas that surfaced with oil was flared off. Not until later was the value of the gas recognized. The rise of the petrochemical industry made gas a much more desirable product, particularly during World War II. Federal government investment during this war period also took the form of subsidies for gas and oil distribution. In the early 1940s the Roosevelt administration decided to build two major oil pipelines, called the "Big Inch" and the "Little Inch," to carry oil products from Texas to the east coast, at a government cost of $142 million. After the war the government pipelines were sold at a "fair market" price to a new Houston-based gas company, Texas Eastern; it used that government-created base to become a large multinational company. As I will document in Chapter 5, Texas Eastern was created by central figures in the Houston business elite. The rise of the natural gas industry after World War II was an important part of the Houston economic "miracle." Companies like Texas Eastern, Tenneco, and Transco were created as Houston-based, locally financed, and locally managed firms which came to monopolize much of the gas pipeline business in the United States. They became major players in the national marketing of natural gas. These Houston- and Texas-based corporations prospered by bringing gas to people in many states from California to New England.[40] The gas firms also represent an important sector of the oil and gas industry not controlled on the east coast; the gas industry is substantially controlled from the Houston metropolitan area.

Federal Aid: Summing Up

During the 1930–1945 period the range of federal aid for development in this city dominated by a free enterprise ideology was broad, ranging from aid for major public infrastructure projects to capital for the petrochemical companies to regulation of oil field competition. As Mollenkopf's analysis has made clear, massive federal aid to recapitalize U.S. industry during World War II was focused disproportionately on selected cities, with middle-sized Houston (population 385,000) ranking sixth nationally and first regionally in the absolute level of federal plant investment.[41] It is also important to note just how significant war periods are in the capitalization of major industries in the United States. Without the rapid infusion of federal capital assistance during the World War II period, as well as during the earlier World War I era and subsequent Korean and Viet Nam war periods, U.S. oil and petrochemical industries would not have grown as dramatically as they did.

Houston and the Global Economy: Trade
Builds Up in the 1940s

While the most dramatic economic developments of this decade were in petroleum, petrochemical, and allied industries and in the massive governmental subsidies for these industries, it would be misleading to suggest that the Houston economy had severed its connections to agriculture. Even in the mid-1940s the immediate area around Houston had 35,100 farms with 1.4 million acres in cultivation. Houston remained the leading U.S. cotton port. Exports dropped significantly to 300,000 bales shipped in 1940–1941, down from 2.5 million in the mid-1930s, but by 1945–1946 had increased to 850,872 bales. However, by 1946 cotton accounted for only 10 percent of exports through the Port of Houston, while oil accounted for 80 percent. At that time there were many oil fields within a hundred-mile radius of Houston. During the wartime and immediate postwar periods the oil and gas industry surpassed agriculture as Houston's dominant economic sector.[42]

Houston's international trade position was further enhanced by the expansion of shipping networks during and after World War II. After the war the docks at the Port of Houston loaded and unloaded ships from Great Britain, France, Belgium, Holland, Italy, Spain, India, Scandinavia, Greece, Australia, and China, as well as from Latin American countries. One signal of the expanding world horizon of some in this city's conservative business elite was the organization in 1944 of a branch of the internationalist Foreign Policy Association, in part at the request of W. L. Clayton, a leading executive in Houston's huge Anderson, Clayton conglomerate.[43]

There was not even a brief pause in Houston's dramatic economic expansion after the war. In March 1948 the *Houston Post* ran a frontpage headline, "The Great Deluge of Dollars," which proclaimed a new investment boom. The city government had begun a $200-million public works project. Hundreds of millions of dollars flowed into public and private construction projects, the latter including new downtown office buildings and department stores and a growing number of suburban subdivisions.[44]

The Postwar Boom in the Houston
Metropolitan Area: The 1950s

A "Third Order" Metropolis?

In Chapter 2 I suggested that some ecological literature on Sunbelt cities, particularly for the 1950s, misinterpreted the significance of cities such as Houston. For example, Vance and Smith argued that southern metropolises are "unremarkable cities. Human ecologists and students of urbanism have had little reason to study them." [45] These scholars developed an index of metropolitan economic function, encompassing the dimensions of wholesale sales, business service receipts, number of branch offices, retail sales, bank clearings, and value added by manufacturing. On the basis of its 1950 ranking on these dimensions among major U.S. cities, Houston was classified as a "third order" metropolis, a category below Atlanta and Dallas, which were labeled "second order" metropolitan areas and "regional capitals." [46] None of these cities was seen as having a sphere of influence beyond the region. These and similar evaluations of Houston's economic position on the national urban map in the decade of the 1950s and 1960s have seriously underestimated the city's importance. There is an element of truth in the demographic analysis: Houston was not a major banking and sales center in the 1950s, but Houston's port, petroleum, and petrochemical industries would qualify the city as having more than third order economic importance among the nation's cities in this postwar period.

The Oil-Fueled Postwar Boom: The 1950s

By the early 1950s the Houston economy was well into a long postwar boom fueled in part by the rising demand for petroleum products, such as asphalt and plastics, and by a significant flow of capital into the secondary circuit of real estate investments. Much of the demand came from consumers seeking to improve their lives with products for consumption after the austerity of the 1930s and 1940s. At least as important to this burgeoning demand was the growing military-industrial complex and its insatiable thirst for oil-related products. There was also heavy lobbying of the highway interests, the auto construction complex, for more asphalt roads. State aid for the oil and petrochemical companies during the 1930s and 1940s helped place them in a position to take advantage of this expanding demand. Between 1940 and the late 1960s, petrochemical and other chemical production in the Houston area went up 600 percent. Texas ranked second only to New Jersey in the total number of chemical plants. A growing number of truck, pipeline, and shipping companies had sprouted in and near Houston's oil and petrochemical complexes. There was continued growth in the number and size of oil tools and services, metal, and construction companies. Indeed, by the late 1950s Houston was adding a new manufacturing plant every two weeks.[47]

While in the mid-1950s the growth in tonnage shipped through the Port of Houston leveled off, the ports of Philadelphia and New Orleans increased their tonnage to the point that Houston dropped from second to fourth among U.S. ports. The response of the local business leadership was to seek renewed governmental aid and secure bond issues to cover a new and massive port facility expansion program. As I have shown, local and federal funds have been critical to the development of the port facilities for a century; federal and local governments spent at least $92 million from the late 1800s to the early 1960s in developing the Houston ship channel. In part as a result of this state-assisted refurbishment of the channel and port facilities, Houston's rank as a leading port had risen again to third position in the 1960s.[48]

The Federal Government and the Construction Boom

A major boom in residential and commercial construction was part of the 1950s dynamism. In the 1950s no fewer than 99,000 new homes were built, thus expanding suburbia in the Houston metropolitan area. As in other cities, this boom was substantially fueled by a massive infusion of federal funds for single-family housing, particularly the federal F H A and V A programs. The exploding Sunbelt cities got a large share of this new federal largess, and the Houston real estate community was quick to take advantage of these loan protection programs. Again the central role of the federal government in Houston's dramatic development is evident. Moreover, numerous commercial and office buildings were completed in this period, thereby creating new business activity centers outside the downtown area.[49]

Conclusion: A Global City Comes of Age

Sunbelt cities have been very important in the history of the United States, and as the much touted "capital of the Sunbelt" Houston is an important city to examine in some detail. The growth of this powerful city has been closely related to the expansion of the capitalistic political economy into every nook and cranny on the face of the globe. From the 1840s to the 1980s Houston prospered and grew. In this chapter I have discussed Houston's economy as a multilayered palimpsest built up over this century and a half. Beginning with agricultural production, marketing, and processing, the economy expanded in the 1870s and 1880s to encompass the heart of a major railroad network in the Southwest. "King Cotton," in effect, created Houston as a modern commercial city with a full range of transport, banking, and legal firms. The discovery of oil added a new economic sector to the local economy, substantially because of the infrastructure established during the agricultural commerce period. The oil and gas industry exfoliated an array of allied industries, the most important of which was the petrochemical industry.

Houston's economic history reveals a gradual evolution from an agricultural and primary extraction economy to a more complex economy including oil-related processing and manufacturing. In these historical materials there is considerable support for our argument that Houston has long been an international city which responds as much to the rhythms of the global economy as it does to the ups and downs of the United States economy. From the cotton trade of the nineteenth century to oil-related exporting in the twentieth century the Houston metropolitan area has been well connected to the world market. Moreover, this position in the world oil and agricultural economies has not come without substantial state assistance, not only in the form of a world-class military establishment keeping the world "safe" for profit making by U.S. companies but also in the form of major subsidies for the oil and petrochemical industries, and in the guise of large-scale federal expenditures for urban infrastructural facilities.

4

The Houston Economy

since the 1950s:

Prosperity and Decline

in a World Context

In the decades since 1960 the political economy of Houston has been buffeted by contradictions inherent in the capitalistic means of production. Local political-economic institutions are responsive to the logic of the capital accumulation process; this can be seen in the vicissitudes of capital flows into and out of industrial, commercial, and real estate enterprises in Houston. Between the late 1950s and the early 1980s there was a long period of prosperity, followed by a deep and unprecedented economic decline. In the last chapter I documented the gradual evolution of Houston from an agricultural marketing and extraction economy to a more complex economy with oil refining, petrochemicals, and other oil-related manufacturing. These oil-related industries remained at the heart of the Houston economy in the period of prosperity.

Capital Accumulation in the Oil Patch: Houston's Recent Decades

The era of prosperity was closely associated with the continuing expansion of Houston's ties to the world market system. The international connections of the city were to a substantial degree signaled by the growing trade through the Port of Houston; for example, the value of foreign trade through the Port of Houston increased tenfold between 1970 and 1980. By the decade of the 1960s Houston had evolved into the oil technology distribution center for many of the oil fields across the globe, and the city was to retain this international importance into the late 1980s. Houston had become an international oil city whose economic base was as much affected by world events as by national events. In this chapter and the next two chapters on the business elite and the state I will document how the city's economic trajectory has been shaped by corporate and governmental decisions made in national and international settings.

A Corporate Center

The history of Houston in the last third of the twentieth century is a history of large corporations. As I suggested in Chapter 3, by the early 1900s the large corporation had begun to dominate the United States and Sunbelt economic system. The large multinational corporation becomes ever more important to the Houston story in the last half of the twentieth century. One issue is the relationship between the multinational corporate structure and the location of the various parts of that structure in particular cities. In this chapter I will examine the relationship between corporate structure and the layout of the corporate subsidiaries in national and international space. For example, this issue is suggested in the common statement that Houston is the "oil capital of the world." In what sense, if any, is this true? How much corporate centralization exists in the metropolitan area? Houston is a center for consequential decision making in the oil industry, but the exact character of this decision making is a major topic for examination in this chapter.

Recent Decline

An important aspect of this chapter is the documentation of economic decline in the Houston–Gulf Coast area. In the 1980s there was a significant disinvestment of capital in the Houston metropolitan area, particularly in enterprises related to oil and gas, agricultural exporting, and real estate. Houston's oil and gas economy buttressed the city during all twentieth-century recessions until the 1980s. As late as 1982, national and regional evaluations of the Houston economy and population forecasts (see Chapter 1) were very optimistic, but this optimism had eroded by 1983–1984. The prosperity of the 1960s and 1970s was followed in the 1980s by the most serious economic downturn in Houston's twentieth-century history. Having experienced economic and population growth even during the Great Depression, neither Houston's leaders nor its citizenry were prepared for this devastating economic crisis. A massive economic downturn brought high levels of unemployment, bankruptcies, and corporate restructuring. Responding to the logic of the world investment circuits, Houstonians experienced a major swing from widely heralded prosperity and profitability to unprecedented unemployment and unprofitability. In this chapter I will examine the industrial and commercial aspects of these shifts in investment. In Chapter 7 I will assess how these fluctuations in the capital accumulation process articulate with space to generate sociospatial patterns of production, distribution, and consumption in Houston.

The Question of State Aid

The expressed "we don't need federal aid" stance of Houston's business community became ever more publicized in this period. In the last chapter I cited the recent statements of the business elite to the effect that Houston has a uniquely free enterprise economy with little governmental interference and intervention. The city's leadership has placed special emphasis on the cooperation of local government and the business leadership, as well as on the rejection of federal government assistance. In the last chapter I documented the extent to which Houston was the scene of, or beneficiary of, much intervention by the local, Texas, and federal governments in its first 120 years of development. In this and the next two chapters I will discuss the continuation of this critical state intervention on behalf of business.

O'Connor's concept of social investment capital expenditures, government expenditures which enhance the profitability of private corporations, remains relevant to these later decades. There is the continuing local government support for infrastructure projects, such as a new convention center discussed in this chapter and the diversification efforts of the Houston Economic Development Council discussed in Chapter 6. Federal capital expenditures have taken the form of assistance for military-industrial ventures, such as the N A S A spacecraft facility and space-related contracts for many private contractors. Some research programs in the Houston medical center complex are also federally funded. But direct expenditures are not the only method by which the state supports capital accumulation. Tax and regulatory practices help to buttress the profitability of Houston's oil and gas corporations. In this chapter I concentrate primarily on the support that came from the state of Texas and from the federal government in the form of taxation, protection, and pricing policies. For example, the Texas Railroad Commission, a governmental agency, has strongly supported the oil and gas industry by creating the pricing and other regulatory policies the industry desired. Moreover, federal tax policy has supported Houston's oil-related firms, largely through the tax loophole called the oil depletion allowance. The state, at all levels, remains important to the Houston economy in the late twentieth century.

The Postwar Boom Continues: 1960–1980

Economic Prosperity in Houston: An Overview

Between the mid-1960s and the early 1970s the Texas economy grew about one and a half times as fast as the national economy; from the 1970s to the early 1980s it grew about two and a half times as fast. Between 1970 and 1981 the number of jobs in Texas doubled, and Houston employment grew at a similarly expansive rate. From 1962 to 1980 the Houston area employment growth rate averaged 5.4 percent a year, compared to 2.8 percent for the United States as a whole. During recessions in the 1970s, the other major Texas metropolis, Dallas-Ft. Worth, suffered high unemployment rates because of its more diversified goods producing industries, including electronics and aerospace manufacturing. In 1973–1975 employment fell 6 percent in Dallas-Ft. Worth, but in Houston employment grew by 18 percent because of higher oil and gas prices.[1] As a result of this oil-related prosperity and accompanying population growth Houston became a major retailing center, ranking eighth among major cities in the early 1980s with $17.3 billion in retail sales and an annual growth rate of 13 percent, well above the national average. Bank deposits in metropolitan Houston increased from $7.2 billion in 1972 to $23.5 billion in 1981.[2]

For most of the twentieth century Texas and its cities have lagged behind the rest of the nation in personal income. In 1949 per capita personal income for Texans was only 93 percent of the national figure; and the relative position of Texans declined to 85 percent in 1965. Yet by 1980 per capita income had climbed to the national average—for the first time in history. By the late 1970s Houston was leading the nation's cities in improvements in per capita income. In 1981 the Houston metropolitan area had risen to the eleventh highest in per capita income and the third lowest in cost of living among the twenty-four largest U.S. cities.[3] Yet this prosperity was not equally distributed; Sunbelt cities have great extremes in wealth. In the late 1970s the richest 5 percent of people in the Sunbelt had a greater share of income (16.4 percent) than in any other region, while the poorest 20 percent had less (4.8 percent) than in any other region. This inequality in income is true for Houston, with its huge poverty populations and large minority ghettos and its golden suburbs. Not surprisingly, one study of 1985 per capita income reported that two of the five wealthiest suburban areas in the United States were in Houston, each with over $45,000 in income per resident.[4]

Some Texas analysts boast that income for Houstonians and other Texans is

TABLE   4.1.
Employment in Houston: 1950–1982

YEAR	Manufacturing		Nonmanufacturing		Total	
	No.	%	No.	%	No.	%
1950	59,200	25	180,000	75	239,200	100
1960	96,400	25	284,600	75	381,000	100
1970	145,600	23	500,700	77	646,300	100
1980	218,900	19	953,600	81	1,172,000	100
1982	254,000	16	1,329,400	84	1,583,400	100

not as dependent on government employment and transfer payments as that in other states. For example, a 1980s booklet from Houston's Texas Commerce Bank considers this a major virtue: "Compared with the national average, Texas personal income derives more from private employment, proprietorship and poverty, and less from government and transfer payments." [5]

Area Growth in Manufacturing

In the 1960s two thousand new manufacturing plants opened in Texas; in the 1970s that number was six to seven thousand. Manufacturing growth in 1975–1981 was the most rapid in the nation. In Texas and in Houston the major areas of industrial expansion were nonelectrical machinery, fabricated metal products, chemicals, and electrical equipment. By the late 1970s Houston was ranked, in terms of the value added by manufacturing, as the fourth largest manufacturing city, behind Chicago, Detroit, and Los Angeles.[6] The number of Houston's manufacturing and nonmanufacturing jobs was significantly augmented between 1950 and 1982 (see Table 4.1).[7] The number of manufacturing jobs increased from 59,200 in 1950 to 254,000 in 1982, while the number of nonmanufacturing jobs grew at an even faster rate.

Houston's Burgeoning Labor Force: 1940–1980

As shown in Table 4.2, since 1940 a large proportion of Houston's workers have been white-collar. In 1940 about 43 percent of Houstonians worked as

TABLE   4.2.
Occupational Distributions for Houston, Texas (City):
1940–1980 (in percentages)

WORK FORCE	1940	1950	1960	1970	1980
White Collar					
Managers, officials,					
proprietors	10.7	11.5	10.7	8.8	11.7
Professional, technical					
workers	8.2	10.3	13.4	16.5	16.8
Clerical workers	23.8	16.1	17.8	20.1	19.4
Sales workers	—a	8.6	8.7	9.0	11.0
Blue Collar					
Craftsworkers,					
supervisors	12.5	15.2	13.7	13.1	13.7
Operatives	15.0	15.3	14.8	13.5	10.9
Laborers	8.2	8.0	6.2	5.4	4.9
Service workers	11.2	10.2	10.0	11.1	10.2
Domestic household					
workers	10.3	4.9	4.5	2.4	0.8
TOTAL	99.9	100.0	99.8	99.9	99.4

Sources: U.S. Bureau of the Census, census tract manuals, and advance estimates for 1980.
Notes: The 1980 data are sample-based estimates for Houston. The new category of fishing, farming, and forestry is not included here (0.6%). The 1980 data are categorized as in earlier censuses, but they are approximations because of new census procedures. Numbers do not add to 100 because of approximations.
aSales workers are included in clerical workers.

managers, proprietors, professional and technical workers, clerical workers, or sales workers. The proportion in those occupations climbed to just over 50 percent by 1960 and to 59 percent in 1980. Most of this increase was in the sales and professional categories. The proportions in the manager-officials and clerical categories changed relatively little. It is interesting to compare Houston to the general urban population in the United States. In 1940 nearly 38 percent of all urban workers were in white-collar occupations; by 1950 the proportion had increased to 42 percent. Both in 1940 and 1950 the proportion of Houston's workers in white-collar jobs was well above the proportion for the United States as a whole. In 1970 the Houston figure was 54 percent, still above the national urban statistic of 50 percent. In contrast to its "hard hat" image, Houston has for several decades been more white-collar than blue-collar in its employment mix.[8] The Houston economy has long been occupationally diverse, with both large white-collar and blue-collar proletariats.

The detailed manufacturing and nonmanufacturing categories in Table 4.3 provide additional insight into the character of the workforce in the greater

TABLE   4.3.
Houston's Labor Force: 1981–1983 (in 1,000s)

WORKERS	1981	1983
Total employed	1,647.3	1,512.9
Total manufacturing	276.6	196.6
Lumber, furniture, stone workers	13.4	13.1
Primary, fabricated metal workers	51.9	29.1
Nonelectrical machinery workers	75.6	40.5
Electrical, instruments workers	25.7	15.6
Transportation equipment and other workers	9.4	6.3
Food workers	13.5	12.9
Apparel, textile, leather workers	1.7	1.3
Petroleum refining workers	18.7	17.0
Paper and printing workers	21.5	20.8
Chemical workers	37.7	34.3
Other nondurable manufacturing workers	7.5	5.8
Mining	116.4	99.0
Construction	150.7	133.3
Transportation, utilities	113.0	103.5
Trade	395.7	373.7
Finance, insurance, real estate	96.2	105.2
Government—federal	20.5	22.1
Government—state, local	151.9	160.7
Services and miscellaneous	315.9	318.8

SOURCE: Texas Employment Commission, "Labor Force Estimates," n.d.
NOTE: Figures are for the metropolitan area. Agricultural employees are excluded. The small discrepancy in totals with Table 4.4 results from different TEC definitions.

Houston metropolitan area in the turbulent 1980s. In both 1981 and 1983 the largest employment category was retail and wholesale trade. The second largest was "services and miscellaneous," a category whose major subdivisions were business service workers, health service workers, and hotel and restaurant workers. The third largest general category was manufacturing, which in 1983 encompassed the subcategories of nonelectrical machinery workers, chemical workers, and fabricated metal workers, many of whom are directly or indirectly associated with the petroleum industry. Paper and printing workers were also high in number, as were lumber and furniture workers; both of these groups rooted in Houston's long-term connections to east Texas forests. Much larger than the individual manufacturing categories are the broad categories of construction, transportation and utilities, finance, and local-state government. The size of these latter categories of employment indicate the complexity of Houston's economy, as well as the large numbers engaged in the circulation of capital in the forms of both transport of products and finance capital. The manufacturing base supports large sectors of other workers.

There is the related question of the multiplier effect of Houston's economic base in the energy sectors. A report by the Center for Public Policy at the University of Houston has estimated that 81 percent of Houston's economic and employment base is directly or indirectly related to the exploration-refining-chemicals industrial sector. Although this 81 percent figure may be exaggerated—the port and agriculture may be underplayed in this particular economic model—it does suggest the central import of the energy sectors in contemporary Houston.

Houston and the World Economy: The 1960s and 1970s

An International City

By the 1960s Houston had evolved into the oil-technology distribution center for the world's oil industries. After the discovery of large Middle Eastern oil fields, advanced oil technologies were required there. By 1980 nearly $7 billion in engineering and related contracts were in effect between Houston and other U.S. oil support companies and public and private enterprises in the Middle Eastern oil fields. Houston companies have been important in the development of many oil fields—in the Middle East, the North Sea, Malaysia, and Indonesia. By the late 1970s about one hundred Houston companies were working in the North Sea fields; and in the early 1980s about one hundred companies were operating in the Malaysia-Indonesia oil fields. During this period the city of Houston developed even more ties outside the U.S. economy.

An international oil city, Houston has been as much affected by decisions made by corporate and political leaders operating outside the United States as by decisions made within the United States. The city's economic and demographic trajectory has frequently been shaped by corporate and governmental policies made in New York, Washington, and international settings. In this regard the large multinational oil companies have been very important; they have played a key role in restructuring the international oil economy in the last third of the twentieth century. Also significant in this regard is the O P E C cartel. In the 1970s O P E C countries gained greater control over their oil, and the big U.S. and British-Dutch oil companies, once dominant controllers of O P E C oil, became partners with O P E C, suppliers of technology, and marketing agents for O P E C oil. U.S. company profits on Middle Eastern oil fell, but the sharp rise in world prices brought substantial increments in profits on oil controlled by U.S. companies elsewhere. Indeed, between 1970 and 1979 the net income of the world's twenty-six largest companies skyrocketed from $6.6 billion to $31.5 billion.[9]

In the early 1980s, just before the collapse in oil prices, Texas led the nation in the number of drilling rigs, oil and gas production, refinery operations, and gas reserves. Between 1973 and the early 1980s the value of the oil and gas in Texas fields grew at the rate of 533 percent, although the amount of oil produced actually *declined* 28 percent. The O P E C-generated price increases changed the economic picture of Houston, bringing expanded profits to the oil industry and enlarging related enterprises, such as Houston's bankholding companies. The rise in prices boosted exploration and drilling, dramatically stimulating the Houston economy in a time of national recession.[10]

More State Aid: The Late 1950s to the 1980s

The profitability of oil companies in the greater Houston area was regularly enhanced by federal and Texas government action and inaction between the 1950s and the 1970s. The U.S. intelligence and military establishments generally protected the engagement in private enterprise in, and the taking of oil from, Middle Eastern and other countries around the globe. One example is the C I A's role in maintaining the power of dictatorial political regimes friendly to the United States and cozy with its oil firms; consider the extensive support for the former Shah of Iran. In addition, the huge navy has protected

U.S. shipping, including the extensive oil trade in the Middle East. There were official protectionist measures as well. In 1959 President Eisenhower set quotas for imported oil, limiting imports to 12 percent of domestic production, a decision justified in terms of national defense; this action helped to hold up domestic oil prices. The government engineered differential probably cost U.S. consumers millions of dollars during the next decade. In addition, numerous tax actions aided the oil industry. In recent decades some members of Congress have attempted to delete the oil depletion allowance. Congress launched a major attack on this tax subsidy for the oil industry in the late 1960s, but only a slight change was made, one supported by major oil company executives for public relations reasons. Other tax subsidies substantially helped the oil industry, including the industry's foreign tax credit and the technical loophole called "expensing of intangibles." [11]

There was also continuing support for the industry by the state of Texas. In a 1978 statement Texas Governor Bill Clements said that if the Texas chief executive was "not already aligned with the oil and gas industry, that's sad commentary on the governor's office." Moreover, the oil companies had helped create the Texas Railroad Commission as a government agency designed to deal with the problem of unrestrained free enterprise in the industry. From the 1950s to the 1970s the commission continued to function as the major U.S. regulatory agency for oil. Conservation of petroleum, the official goal of the agency, took second place to the real goal of promoting the oil industry by stabilizing the price of crude oil. Until O P E C assumed control of oil pricing in the mid-1970s, this Texas governmental agency buttressed the oil and gas industry by maintaining their desired pricing and other regulatory policies, including inaction on environmental questions. In the early 1970s a Texas legislature report criticized the commission for ignoring the environmental damage caused by the oil companies, particularly in offshore areas. The commission had never taken action against an oil company for environmental damage; moreover, it had never denied a drilling permit for environmental reasons. [12]

Even given O P E C's substantial control of oil pricing, the commission still remained important in assisting the U.S. firms, particularly the gas and gas pipeline firms. The fact that this Texas agency was a creature of the oil and gas industry can be documented. For example, in 1970 the industry published an advertisement in a Texas publication openly *thanking* the Railroad Commission for its *service to the oil industry* since 1891. The commission is a major example of how capitalistic enterprises have created state agencies essential to their expansion and profitability. Even Texas politicians have sometimes expressed frustration over the power of the oil and gas industry. Thus, in the late 1940s the chairperson of the Texas Democratic Executive Committee suggested that "It may not be a wholesome thing to say, but the oil industry today is in complete control of State politics and State government." [13]

The Local Business Elite and the Local State

The expansion of the "oil capital of the world" required, in the view of the local business community, substantial governmental assistance. In the last decades of the twentieth century Houston's local government continued both its provision of selected infrastructural facilities and also the tax abatements required by those engaged in commercial, residential, and industrial development projects. As I discussed in the last chapter, governmental bonds have long been used by the business leadership to fund desired infrastructure projects. One major report on Houston politics surveyed several bond elections and noted that local voters "usually approve city requests for bond issues if business groups and the press support the proposals." [14] Since the late 1950s and early 1960s public bonds have been heavily utilized to support business projects, particularly those seen as enhancing the city's ability to compete for business in the world market system. In the late 1950s, for example, Houston's core leadership began working for a new airport, a facility essential for Houston's communication with national and international markets. An attempted bond issue to buy land for a major new airport north of the city was rejected by local voters. However, a group of powerful Houstonians bought 3,000 acres north of the city and held the land under the "Jet Era Ranch Co." They thought they could make an "end run" around the voters by holding the land until voters would support the bonds. And in 1960 the city government did purchase the site. [15]

Another example of state aid is the massive Astrodome project, the first enclosed dome in a U.S. city and a project most of the business community then considered as important as the ship channel to the city's expanding economy. In the late 1950s Harris County voters were persuaded to support a $20-million bond issue to construct the Astrodome. The Houston Sports Association (H S A) was formed by influential business leaders R. E. Smith and Roy Hofheinz, to bring a major league baseball team to the city; the H S A agreed to lease the Astrodome. Soon, however, a larger bond issue was needed. There was some opposition to public funding of a private corporation, but it was largely ignored by sports promoters and most voters. The stadium eventually cost $45.4 million, with $35.4 million from government bonds and other city and state government subsidies. The H S A reportedly paid $6 million toward

Astrodome construction and $750,000 a year (less than 2 percent of their investment) for the lease. Taxpayers again footed most of the bill for a business-generated project.[16]

This pattern of local governmental support for projects designed to make Houston competitive in the world economy has continued to the present day. In 1983 voters were asked to approve millions in taxpayer-supported bonds for a project eagerly desired by the business community: a major convention center facility on the far east side of the downtown. Named after Houston entrepreneur George Brown, this convention center opened in the fall of 1987; it was projected by business proponents to draw 700,000 new visitors and $430 million in expenditures annually to the metropolitan area. But the projections appeared too optimistic. In 1987 actual bookings indicated that the first full year of the center (1988–1989) might bring 129,000 visitors and an expenditure of $57 million. In addition, the bonds had been sold as variable-rate bonds rather than the safer fixed-rate bonds. In the late 1980s some feared that if interest rates ever increased dramatically the government might default on the bonds. In addition, hotel occupancy tax revenues, a source for paying off the bonds, were recalculated to be below initially projected levels.[17]

Restructuring and Recentralization

A major feature of capitalism historically is the constant reorganization and restructuring that occurs in response to the logic of capital accumulation. The changing profitability of investments frequently brings organizational changes. In the decade ending in the early 1970s a number of multinational oil companies shifted subsidiaries to Houston or buttressed existing operations there. Shell relocated its U.S. administrative headquarters from New York to Houston. Exxon, Gulf, and Texaco consolidated some domestic operations in Houston. One reason for this relocation may have been the prominent role Houston had long played in the history of the oil business. As Anthony Sampson put it, "It is in Texas, not New York, that the Exxon men feel more thoroughly at home; and it is the Exxon skyscraper in Houston, the headquarters of Exxon U.S.A., which seems to house the soul of the company." More important was the abundance of oil in the world oil economy, for the relatively stable (and low by late 1970s standards) price of oil in the 1963–1971 period encouraged multinational pruning and consolidation. Yet another reason was the increasing computerization and automation of communications and production being pursued by executives in the oil industry. Automation gave them greater control over their labor forces. Some production facilities, as well as marketing and credit card facilities, were consolidated in Houston.[18]

Oil Dominance on the Houston Scene

Houston remains a major center for oil tools, oil-gas exploration, and oil services, as well as for oil refining and petrochemical production. In the early 1980s about 35 percent of the jobs in the area were directly connected to the oil and gas industry; at least another 20 percent of the city's workers were greatly dependent on the oil and gas industry. Fully 70 percent of the large plants (500 or more employees) in the Houston area were linked to the oil and gas industry. An estimated 60 percent of downtown office space was occupied by energy-related corporations, and much of the rest was occupied by banks, law firms, accounting firms, and other companies which to some extent service oil-gas companies. Eleven of the twenty largest Texas firms were oil and gas companies, eight of which were headquartered in Houston. Thirty-four of the thirty-five largest oil companies had major office and plant facilities in the greater Houston area. And there were an estimated four hundred major oil and gas companies in the metropolitan area, together with hundreds of geological firms, drilling contractors, supply companies, law firms, and other oil-related businesses.[19]

Large oil companies such as Exxon, Shell, Gulf, Texaco, Conoco, and Pennzoil have major manufacturing and other facilities scattered across the southern and eastern sections of the metropolis. In the 1980s Exxon's largest refinery was the Baytown facility. Exxon also built one of the world's largest industrial parks in the Houston metropolitan area. Between the early 1960s and the mid-1980s Exxon's 10,500-acre Bayport Industrial Development received $2 billion in private investment capital. With fifty tenants, mostly major chemical firms, the facility then shipped two billion pounds of chemicals annually. In 1964 Humble Oil, now Exxon, had donated 725 acres to the Harris County Ship Channel Navigation District to allow the Port Authority to build and operate new channel and port facilities at Bayport. Those facilities were built with public bonds, and governmental subsidies were again useful for corporate development. Operated by a subsidiary of Exxon, Bayport is said by its sales managers to have "a favorable tax structure; 90 million gallons-per-day of water capacity; a central waste treatment plant where the user is not required to secure a treated discharge permit; a deep-draft port facility; excellent pipeline and road networks; strict environmental standards; and unmatched raw materials availability."[20] This somewhat contradictory— no permit, but strict standards—statement demonstrates the significance of the good business climate, with its low taxes and government cooperation, for oil and gas firms.

Houston has been a major research and development center for the oil and gas industry. In 1977 the greater Houston area had thirty research and development labs, thus ranking tenth among all U.S. cities—the only old South city in the top twenty. Most major oil companies have had large research labs in Houston, including Exxon and Shell.[21]

Dominance in Petrochemical Production: 1960s–1980s

Over the last few decades debate has recurred among business leaders over diversification in the Texas economy. Historically, diversification along the Gulf Coast has often meant a shift from oil production and refining to other types of oil-related businesses, particularly petrochemical operations. Petrochemicals have their origin in three basic processes, all involving gas or oil: (1) steam cracking of petroleum products to produce ethylene, (2) extracting benzene and other aromatic products from petroleum sources, and (3) production of ammonia by means of oil-based synthesis of gas.

After World War II oil and chemical companies purchased the petrochemical plants they had been operating for the federal government, giving the industry a major boost. In addition, the petrochemical industry was heavily subsidized by the federal government's energy policy; for a long period, particularly in the 1970s and early 1980s, the government kept the price of gas artificially low and thus the feedstocks for petrochemical plants very cheap, a situation European manufacturers complained about. (Ironically, in the late 1980s U.S. petrochemical manufacturers complained about low-cost gas for Canadian petrochemical producers.) Much private capital flowed into these state subsidized chemical facilities after 1945, and by the 1950s and 1960s the petrochemical markets were growing at a rate of 13 to 17 percent annually.[22] The industry grew 800 percent between the 1940s and the 1980s, much faster than U.S. manufacturing as a whole. Dozens of new petrochemical plants were built along the Texas Gulf Coast. By 1982 there were 104 major chemical plants in Texas, with a heavy concentration in the greater Houston area; and the Gulf Coast area produced 40 percent of all petrochemicals in the United States. On the Texas Gulf Coast, as elsewhere, multinational companies controlled most petrochemical facilities.[23]

By the mid-1970s the petrochemical industry was beginning to experience some difficulties rooted in broad changes in the world oil economy. Although petrochemical production had grown rapidly after World War II, the expanding world markets and the cheap oil and gas feedstocks had encouraged the petrochemical executives to build more capacity than needed. When these markets became more competitive and the feedstocks became more expensive after the price hikes in the 1970s, growth in production and markets slowed.

Houston's Position in the Corporate-City Hierarchy

A Center for Corporate Subsidiaries?

Houston has frequently been termed the "oil capital of the United States" and the "oil capital of the world." The data just examined suggest why these sobriquets have been applied to the city. Yet Houston's role in the world oil economy is distinctive, a role primarily in research, exploration, production (extraction), refining, and marketing. Top-level investment, reorganization, and financial decisions supportive of the oil industry are commonly made elsewhere, primarily in New York and a few other northern and California cities. Not one major multinational company has its international headquarters in the city, although most have major subsidiaries located there. The issue of whether Houston and Texas are "colonies" of the Northeast has periodically been raised by scholars, but the issue is not just a matter for scholarly debate. Indeed, the colony question has periodically surfaced in Texas politics; for example, in the late 1930s a politician named Pappy O'Daniel garnered votes for governor and for senator by arguing publicly that Texas should not remain a colony of New York.

In Chapter 3 we noted the role of the east coast financing and control which developed in the early years of the oil industry. Thus at an early point, wealthy eastern banker Andrew Mellon was active in the Texas fields; his Gulf Oil company was formed there. Two authorities on Humble Oil (later Exxon), Larson and Porter, have noted that in the early 1900s the larger Texas-origin companies developed "with the aid of capital from the Northeast" and soon had "headquarters in New York, Philadelphia, or Pittsburgh"; but they argue that Humble Oil itself remained substantially independent of its major stockholder, Standard Oil of New Jersey.[25] Another historian notes that "the national petroleum market provided many goods and services, eastern sources of investment controlled the expansion of the firms, and the sophisticated technological advances that revolutionized the [Houston area] refineries were borrowed from outside the region."[26] In the first decades of the east Texas oil industry much investment capital was supplied by outsiders. The major exceptions to this east coast dominance were the oil and gas drilling firms (the "wildcatters") and the support industry of tools and services, which for the most part remained in the hands of local corporations.[27]

Since the late 1960s both scholarly and mass media analysts have announced that the Texas and Houston oil economies are no longer heavily dependent on the east coast. For example, a 1983 article in *Texas Monthly* asserted that Texas is no longer a "colony of Manhattan" and that "Houston has shoved New York aside to become the center of the international oil business."[28] But this view of Houston neglects the major issue of top management control of much investment, reorganization, and financing. Hymer argued that large corporations have three different functional levels: day-to-day operations, field office management, and top management and planning.[29] The last function is located in a few world-class cities, the field office management in national cities, the day-to-day operations in lesser cities around the world. Top cities have high concentrations of industrial and commercial corporate headquarters, as well as media, law, accounting, art, and brokerage firms.

Corporate cities like Houston differ from the world's leading corporate headquarters cities—for instance, New York and London—because corporate subsidiaries and local companies in middle level cities rely heavily on corporate headquarters and banks in the leading cities, particularly in regard to international *investment* issues. The reverse has usually not been the case. Houston's economy might thus be viewed, in Hymer's terms, as one of "field office management." Unquestionably Houston is not the center of top level investment decision making for the world's largest oil firms, whose international headquarters offices are located on the east and west coasts. Most major oil companies have important domestic subsidiaries in Houston, but these subsidiaries generally depend on the northern or western headquarters of the companies for most of the highest level planning and investment decisions. Thus Shell (U.S.) and Exxon, U.S.A. have their national headquarters in Houston, but the international headquarters of these multinationals are in the Hague and New York. Moreover, oil company executives in the major oil firms tend to be promoted from Houston subsidiaries to New York, sometimes via overseas assignments, rather than vice versa. Although this flow upward brings Texans to top levels of management and keeps east cost control desegregated in reality, it does separate the broadest decision making and investment functions from the operations and research centers in Houston. A partial exception to this continuing dependency on the east coast headquarters for top level decisions seems to be Shell, whose Houston headquarters reportedly operates independently of the international headquarters in Europe.[30]

But to leave the discussion at this point would be to leave an inaccurate picture of the Houston oil economy. Indeed, Hymer's typology of corporate structure is too simple for an analysis of a corporate city like Houston. Houston is a center for much consequential decision making in the oil industry; much of this decision making is centered on research, exploration for oil, production of oil, oil tools and services, refining oil, and producing petrochemicals. Although the city does not house most of the corporate executives who make the broadest worldwide capital investment decisions for the leading multinationals, nonetheless it does concentrate more of the organizational units of oil- and gas-related firms, from the largest multinationals to the smaller "independents," than any other city in the world.

Major decisions are made in three different corporate arenas in the metropolitan Houston area. Leading multinational oil corporations have located their major operating and other subsidiaries in the metropolitan area. These subsidiaries are often functionally rather than geographically structured. They are more than regionalized "field offices," for they often control oil *operations* across the United States, and in some cases across the globe. In addition to the subsidiary firms of the largest multinational oil companies, Houston also houses the headquarters operations and subsidiaries of substantial, if smaller, multinational oil firms. And there are the headquarters and subsidiary operations of the large oil tools and services companies, some of which are the world's leaders in that sector of the industry.[31]

The third arena of international decision-making in the Houston metropolitan area involves the headquarters operations of the very large gas and gas pipeline companies such as Tenneco and Texas Eastern. It is true that much Texas gas production has been controlled by the major oil companies; nine oil giants controlled half the gas production in 1980. However, a few Texas-based corporations, such as Texas Eastern, Transco, Tenneco, Coastal Corporation, and the El Paso Company, have played a major role in the gas and gas pipeline businesses. Firms like Texas Eastern and Tenneco are Houston based and Houston managed, and have become central forces in the national market for natural gas. Tenneco is one of the largest companies headquartered in Houston; in 1984 it was ranked nineteenth among industrial companies in the United States. Given this mixture of decision making at a variety of corporate levels and subsidiaries, it is impossible to position the city in terms of Hymer's limited typology. Clearly, the typology must be expanded to encompass specialized international cities like Houston.[32]

The Issue of Corporate Headquarters: Houston's National Rank

All but one of the chief industrial corporations in the Houston metropolitan area are in the oil and gas business. In 1984 Houston had the headquarters offices of ten Fortune 500 industrial firms: Shell-U.S. (ranked 13th nationally), Tenneco (19th), Coastal Corporation (55th), Pennzoil (147th), Cooper Industries (180th), Anderson Clayton Co. (233rd), Mitchell Energy & Development Co. (315th), Big Three Industries (360th), and Cameron Iron Works (457th). Although Cameron slipped off the Fortune 500 list in 1985, Houston still ranked *sixth* among U.S. cities in the number of industrial firms for that year. Houston was well behind New York (with sixty-six firms), Chicago (twenty-four), and Pittsburgh (fifteen), and just behind Cleveland (ten) and Dallas (ten).[33]

In 1985 Houston also ranked *fourth* among U.S. cities in the number of the nation's largest "service" (e.g., banking, insurance, diversified services, utilities, airlines) firms, with fourteen of the Fortune Service 500 firms. Houston ranked behind New York (fifty-six), Los Angeles (eighteen), and Chicago (eighteen), but ahead of San Francisco (eleven), Philadelphia (eleven), and Dallas (eleven). Among the largest service firms headquartered in Houston were banks such as Texas Commerce Bancshares and First City Bancorporation, insurance companies such as American General and Variable Annuity Life, and an array of other firms such as Texas Air Corporation, Browning-Ferris, U.S. Home, Texas Eastern Corporation, Panhandle Eastern, and Houston Lighting and Power. The Fortune Service 500 ranking for a previous year (1983) had eighteen companies headquartered in Houston, but the slump in the city's economy dropped several off the 1985 Fortune 500 list. The nation's leading industrial and nonindustrial companies have a significant headquarters presence in the city, as the city's sixth- and fourth-place national rankings indicate. Most super-corporations headquartered in the city are tied into the oil and gas industry directly or indirectly.[34]

Banking: A Dependent Relationship?

From the 1910s to the present the city's banks have been involved in oil and gas lending; since the 1950s they have been heavily involved in oil and real estate lending. They have traditionally financed independent operators in production and services, as well as some subsidiaries of major firms. However, we must keep in mind that the major oil companies, such as Exxon and Texaco, have usually drawn on their own resources or have gone to New York or Chicago financial institutions for their most substantial capital needs. For many years the Texas constitution's prohibition on branch banking kept Houston's bankers from developing their own large financial institutions. In the 1970s and 1980s, however, the development of multibank holding companies in Texas circumvented that constitution; these large banks were able to provide more substantial capital for corporate projects. As the leading industry, the oil and gas industry has received what it needs from Houston banks, especially in nonrecessionary times. But other major borrowers, including some large real estate developers, have had to go outside Houston for capital.

Moreover, the dominance of oil lending has held back diversified industrial development, for Houston banks generally lack expertise in other industrial areas, such as the high-tech computer and electronics industries. In one case, an Ohio high-tech company was moving to Houston to exploit the lower labor costs there, but Houston banks, which did not want to loan on the basis of high-tech equipment taken as loan collateral, would not approve financing. This Ohio company had to get an Ohio bank to loan it the capital it needed to move to Houston.[35] From the early 1970s to the 1980s leading Texas corporations secured 80 percent of their credit from out-of-state banks. One author has noted that "more than half of the 42 largest corportions with over $18 billion assets, reported that their company's principal bank was out of state."[36]

By the early 1980s Texas's four largest bankholding companies were among the nation's twenty-five largest banks. Many local business leaders were certain Texas banks were no longer the colonies they once were: "The old colonial process has been reversed: Chase Manhattan, Morgan Guaranty, Manufacturers Hanover, Citibank, and Chemical have come to Texas to compete for loans, along with dozens of foreign banks—32 in Houston alone."[37] One Houston bank prepared a booklet which included the prediction that during the decade of the 1980s Texas cities would "not only expand their roles as the regional financial centers of the South and Southwest, but will also become ever more prominent in the national and international financial structure."[38] However, even before the mid-1980s recession Houston banks were small compared to the nation's "money center" banks. For example, in 1977 Texas Commerce Bancshares was the largest Houston bank with $6.6 billion in assets; but this figure paled in comparison to the assests of Bankamerica Corporation ($82 billion) and Citicorp ($77 billion). In 1981 Houston ranked as the seventh major banking city, with $23.5 billion in bank deposits, but this number was below that of Dallas ($25.1 billion) and far below the banking centers of New York ($155 billion), Chicago ($59 billion), and Los Angeles ($47 billion). It would appear that considerable oil and other Texas capital has flowed to out-of-state financial institutions. There is also the transaction dependency relationship among banks. In 1979 Houston's top two banks owed other U.S. banks $188.9 million and $232.2 million in demand balances—much more than was owed to them by outside banks. Houston's banks have often borrowed more from other U.S. banks than they have loaned.[39]

In the 1970s the outside money center banks began to move some of their banking operations to Texas, in spite of Texas and U.S. banking laws; and they succeeded in getting access to Texas deposits in the mid-1980s, when they began to take over major Texas banks. In the mid-1980s the Texas Commerce Bank, Jesse Jones's creation (see Chapter 5), merged with the Chemical Bank. Banking experts predicted that this and other banking mergers would bring new capital and banking expertise to the city, since the large New York banks are better capitalized. But, in fact, the new banks may move capital out of Houston. The large New York banks are internationally oriented; the regional banks in Houston have traditionally been less involved in overseas loans and financing. As the money center banks develop full-service operations in Texas cities such as Houston, they will doubtless increase the movement of local deposits into international loans, shifting more local capital out of state. In the 1980s big East Coast banks became ever more dominant on the Texas banking scene through mergers with the largest Texas banks.

Trade, Transport, and Houston's Position in the World Economy

The Port of Houston: Prosperity before Decline

In recent decades Houston has been one of the leading seaports in the United States. Because of its ties to 250 ports around the globe and its 180 ship lines it would be difficult to overestimate the importance of the Port of Houston to the development and prosperity of the metropolitan area. Before the downturn in the 1980s an estimated 5,500 ships called each year at the port's extensive and modern wharf facilities. The value of foreign trade through the Port of Houston increased from $2.4 billion in 1970 to $23 billion in 1980. In the early 1980s Houston's top foreign trading partners were Mexico, Saudi Arabia, and Japan. The top countries in terms of receiving exports from the Port of Houston were Mexico, Brazil, and Saudi Arabia. The number one export category, valued at $1.7 billion, encompassed construction, mining, and oilfield machinery. The second most valuable export category was unmilled wheat and corn. Organic chemicals and nonelectrical machinery ranked third and fourth, respectively. But the list of imports contained an irony: In this period oil, once a major export, was the number one commodity *imported* at the Port of Houston; imported crude was valued at $4.5 billion in 1981. The next two categories of imports were steel products and automobiles and transportation equipment. Houston ranked as the second port in the U.S. total cargo tonnage and in foreign trade, a sign of the city's continuing position in the connective tissue of the world trading system. An estimated 32,000 jobs were directly generated by port activity.[40]

The mid-1980s recession hit the Port of Houston hard, in part because the recession was centered in the sectors of oil and agriculture and in part because port facilities were substantially more in private hands than is the case for other ports. Waterborne commerce handled at the Port of Houston declined 7 percent from 1980 to 1981, 25 percent from 1981 to 1982, and 23 percent in the following year. Trade through the Port of Houston facilities rebounded in the first half of 1984, up 45 percent over 1983, dropped off in 1984–1986, then increased a little in the first half of 1987. The sphere of agricultural exports improved by 1986–1987, with the decline in the value of the dollar. Even in the continuing oil crisis, the Port of Houston was shipping large amounts of cotton overseas—an estimated 1.2 million bales in 1986–1987, up from 684,000 bales in 1985. This represented a fifth of all U.S. cotton exports, a continuing sign of the importance of agricultural products to the greater Houston economy. Sugar exports also remained important to the metropolitan economy; and Imperial Sugar's Sugar Land refinery was in the late 1980s one of the largest and most technologically advanced in the United States.[41]

Houston and Important International Trade

Trade through the Port of Houston is another sign of the international linkages of this metropolitan economy. In the 1980s Houston's top trading partners included major countries in Latin America, the Middle East, Asia, and Europe. At least 450 Houston-based companies engaged in international operations and about 600 international companies had operations in Houston before the mid-1980s recession. The number of foreign banks with offices in Houston increased significantly in this period, from fifteen in 1976 to fifty-six in 1981. However, the mid–1980s recession brought cutbacks in more of these foreign-based operations.

The Asian connection remained important for the Houston economy, even during the downturn. Numerous Asian companies have located branch offices in Houston, including Japanese banks and Korean manufacturing firms. For example, a 1980s survey of Park 10, a three-mile-long industrial park in west Houston, found that one office building housed Hyundai, a Korean company that not only manufactures autos and other products but also engineers off-shore drilling platforms around the world. In addition, Houston firms have invested in oil exploration in mainland China. In 1983 Pennzoil, Sun Oil, and two smaller companies agreed to explore for oil along China's coast. In the 1970s Houston's M. W. Kellog Company was the first U.S. engineering and construction company to sign a contract with the Chinese government. By 1984 Kellog was operating a number of ammonia, urea, and fertilizer plants in China, altogether an investment of $1 billion; that same year a top-ranking Chinese official, speaking to the Houston Chamber of Commerce, character-ized Houston as the "world capital of world resources."[42] She also empha-sized the critical importance of Houston companies in developing China's energy resources.[43]

Houston and High-Tech Sectors

Defense-Related High-Tech Industry: The NASA Case

For many decades federal spending has been used to buttress Houston's growth. Since the 1940s some of this federal expenditure has been of a military-industrial nature. To the extent that the U.S. government has a national "in-dustrial policy," it seems enshrined in the routine investment decisions of the Department of Defense. The Pentagon subsidizes many industries that other countries promote by such governmental agencies as the Ministry of Inter-national Trade and Industry (MITI) in Japan and the centralized economic planning units in Europe.[44]

Houston's major space-defense complex is the National Aeronautics and Space Administration (NASA) Johnson Space Center (JSC) facility. This fed-eral intervention into the metropolitan economy was won in competition with other cities by Houston's growth-oriented elite, which included prominent business leaders and local politicians. I will discuss the details of this inter-vention in Chapter 5. By the 1980s the JSC complex employed 10,000 people, two-thirds of them nongovernmental employees; and a half-billion in federal dollars was being spent in the Houston area. In the mid-1980s the facility was assigned the $8 billion space station project, while the University of Houston branch near N A S A beat out Cal Tech and M I T for a joint contract with N A S A to develop a new computer language for the Department of Defense. These contracts insure a military-industrial presence in the greater Houston area for the foreseeable future. Indeed, one diversification goal of the business leadership by the late 1980s was securing a larger portion of the national defense budget for the city.[45]

In 1977 Houston, then the fifth largest city, only ranked tenth among metropolitan areas in federal research and development (R & D) expenditures, much of which went for N A S A programs. Houston's $393 million in R & D money was a modest fraction of that received by private companies in Los Angeles ($3.2 billion), Washington ($1.6 billion), San Francisco ($1.4 billion), New York ($1 billion), and Boston ($1 billion). In the United States federal R & D spending is greatly concentrated in a few research categories; most of it supports defense-related operations such as aerospace, electronics, and military equipment. The Sunbelt cities east of California trail badly in receipt of this federal R & D money and thus in the technology and spinoffs that R & D provides.[46]

Since the late 1970s a number of small high-tech companies have sprung up near N A S A. A few are working with N A S A on such commercial applications of space as electrophoresis and crystal growth. One firm launched the first commercial space vehicle; several companies are applying remote sensing satellite technology to business needs. Some attempts have also been made to wed the needs of N A S A and the Texas Medical Center. And several major developers, including Exxon's Friendswood Development, have tried to make their research parks attractive for new space-related high-tech firms.[47]

Houston's Other High-Tech Companies: Computers and Medical Technology

By the mid-1980s Compaq Computer was Houston's computer company success story. In 1983, the first year after introducing a new computer, it had $111 million in sales. However, only Compaq, Texas Instruments, and Zaisan, Inc. have manufactured a significant number of computers in the Houston area. While computer development has been limited, medical treatment facilities and related medical technology firms have been more significant to the local economy. Houston has become a national medical center. In the early 1980s the Texas Medical Center covered 235 acres with twenty-nine hospitals and research institutions; facilities had specialties in cancer and heart ailments and in biomedical engineering. The economic impact of this medical center has been estimated at $1.5 billion annually, probably more than for the military-space-industrial facilities. However, there are only a few "med-tech" companies in Houston. Indeed, the largest med-tech firm, Intermedics, was created in the 1970s by a Dow Chemical entrepreneur. Although this company regards the Houston medical complex as a customer, it is not a spin-off firm of the medical complex. And much of its developmental work has been done in cooperation with Massachusetts and California firms and universities.[48]

In the mid-1980s the Baylor College of Medicine formed B C M Technologies to help its practitioners and researchers sell technological advances to the private and public sectors. Still, the Texas Medical Center has not been as prominent in creating corporate spinoffs as business leaders would like. The Mayo Clinic and the University of Minnesota hospital complex in the Minneapolis area have generated 150 med-tech companies, but the Houston medical complex has generated a half-dozen major firms. Defenders of the Texas Medical Center emphasize its relative youth. But the fact that Houston's oil-oriented banks and other lenders have little interest in and experience with high-tech investments seems a more important reason for the paucity of spin-off firms.

In addition, venture capital resources for nonoil enterprises are modest. In the U.S. the venture capital industry's estimated worth was about $13 billion in the mid-1970s. But Houston had 1 percent of that business, and Texas just 5 percent, compared to California's 47 percent. In the United States the geographical structure of the finance capital sector, and especially the venture capital subsector, favors east and west coast enterprises in the newer high-tech industries; this geographical concentration will handicap the central areas of the Sunbelt in generating high-tech firms.[49]

Economic Troubles in the Mid-1980s: The Decline in the Oil and Petrochemical Industries

From Boom to Bust: The Oil Industry in Decline

Houston's oil-gas economy buttressed the city against serious economic decline during the Great Depression and all postwar recessions—until the 1980s. Many writers in the 1970s and early 1980s even viewed Houston as "depression-proof." As late as the first quarter of 1982, most assessments of Houston and of Texas were rosy. Indeed, in 1981–1982 the Texas oil industry led the nation in active drilling rigs, wells completed, crude oil production, number of oil refineries, and proven gas reserves. But this rosy picture had clouded by 1982–1983. The sagging price of a barrel of oil brought the U.S. consumer dollar-a-gallon gasoline again; the drop in price to $12 from $18 a barrel in the mid-1980s directly reduced inflation.

What was good for Americans as consumers was bad for Texans as workers and entrepreneurs. The U.S. recession which began in mid-1981 did not hit Houston hard until 1982–1983. Economic activity declined and unemployment rose sharply. Industrial production declined, more rapidly than the national average. The number of active drilling rigs in Texas decreased significantly. The reduction in active drilling rigs brought hard times to Houston's oil production, tools, and supply companies. Problems in the oil industry came to the surface when OPEC began to reduce oil prices. Houston was probably the metropolitan area most directly affected by investment and production shifts in the world oil market.[50]

Declining oil prices and cutbacks in oil production were not the only sources of the economic troubles. There was the negative effect of the overvalued U.S. dollar. Between 1981 and 1985 the price of oil fell 32 percent, but the trade-weighted dollar increased by 56 percent relative to other major currencies. Studies by the Federal Research Bank of Dallas demonstrated that the strong dollar had a more damaging effect on the Houston (and Texas) economy than did the drop in the price of oil. Houston exporters of machinery and agricultural products were significantly affected by the high dollar. As a result of declining oil prices and the high dollar, local companies saw their balance sheets deteriorate significantly. In a survey of Houston's top publicly held companies, the Chamber of Commerce found that fifty-eight of the top one hundred had a decline in earnings per share in 1982, and sixteen of the twenty companies reporting negative earnings per share were energy-related companies. In 1983–1984 a much larger number of companies reported a decline in earnings per share.[51]

Serious Job Losses

The reduction in prices brought a change in the investment activities and strategies of oil-related firms. Disinvestment, the withdrawal of capital in the primary circuit of manufacturing, in the Houston case took the form of major layoffs in the oil and gas industry. The oil tools and supply industry saw major setbacks, with the number of employees dropping 46 percent in 1982–1983 alone. Training programs were cut, facilities were closed, and numerous companies went bankrupt or were acquired by larger companies. The number of oil-field workers in Texas dropped from 313,700 in January 1982 to 260,700 in July 1984. The situation was so bad in 1983 that Governor Mark White told oilfield workers they should train for other work.

Moreover, the downturn in the oil-gas industry had a rippling effect throughout related industries. In the boom times prior to the mid-1980s Houston and other energy-belt cities had attracted a lot of workers from outside the state. Immigration accelerated in the first part of the U.S. recession in the 1980s because of the greater than average economic growth in Texas—and the exaggerated image of that growth in the mass media. Then came the bust, and the state had too many people looking for work, both natives and recent immigrants. By early 1983 there were several camps of the unemployed in the Houston metropolitan area. On the banks of the San Jacinto River, about thirty miles from downtown Houston, 250 people from several states had formed a community of the unemployed poor, a camp called "Tramp City" by its hostile neighbors. Yet these people were not the stereotyped ne'er-do-wells of the popular media; they were displaced families from northern cities with high unemployment. These "Snowbirds" discovered that Houston's workers were facing worse conditions of unemployment than those in some northern cities.[52]

The scale of the job loss for Houston can be estimated from these general employment statistics for 1982, 1983, and May 1986 (Table 4.4).[53] The long recession of 1982–1986 negatively affected employment. In just one year (1982–1983) the number of manufacturing jobs dropped by 77,000, and the total number of jobs dropped by nearly 160,000. By 1986 non-manufacturing recovered but manufacturing positions continued to slump to a 1986 low of only 164,000. Between 1981 and 1986 Houston lost more than 100,000 energy-related industrial jobs and over $4 billion in purchasing power. Correlatively, the unemployment rate grew more rapidly in Houston than in the nation, hitting 9.7 percent in 1983, up sharply from previous years. In 1985 the city's economy briefly resurged, but this was soon followed by a deepening oil crisis. Early in 1986 the jobless rate again jumped to 9.6 percent. Late in 1986 the Chamber of Commerce estimated that the unemployment rate was more than 10 percent; heavy job losses in manufacturing, oil-mining, and construction continued in the twelve months from July 1985 to July 1986. By late 1987 the jobless rate had declined to about 8 percent, a figure still high for Houston. The positive multiplier effects of Houston's energy base on the city's employment for most of the twentieth century turned into negative multiplier effects in the 1980s, as grocers, auto mechanics, and teachers lost jobs because of the downturn in the Houston energy industries. Nonetheless, even in the troubled 1980s optimistic business leaders frequently pointed to the continuing job growth in "services," but these job gains came mostly in the low-wage sectors.[54]

TABLE   4.4.
Employment in Houston: 1982–1986

YEAR	Manufacturing No.	%	Nonmanufacturing No.	%	Total No.	%
1982	254,000	16	1,329,400	84	1,583,400	100
1983	177,000	12	1,246,900	88	1,424,000	100
1986	164,100	11	1,317,400	89	1,481,500	100

Large-Scale Restructuring: The Challenges to the Oil and Petrochemical Industries

An Old Oil Province: Declining Reserves

The Houston area and the rest of Texas not only face the short-run problem of a decrease in oil prices, oil-related operations, and jobs, but they also confront the long-term problem of the reduction in oil reserves. From 1972 to 1983 about 6 billion barrels of oil reserves were discovered in Texas, substantially less than the 10.6 billion barrels pumped out in that period. In the decade of the 1970s oil reserves declined 8 percent annually. During the 1980s recession the rate slowed to 1 to 2 percent a year, but that loss rate will increase with economic recovery. By the mid-1980s Texas oil reserves were only half what they had been in 1952.[55] New reserves will doubtless be discovered, but "enhanced recovery" methods are expensive. As the oil editor of a Dallas paper expressed it: "There have been too many wells drilled in Texas, too many areas explored, too much geophysical work done. . . . Texas is becoming an old oil province. That's the only way I can say it. We're not virgin anymore. We've been had."[56]

Restructuring in Oil Refining

In the 1980s the large oil and gas companies with refineries faced not only the challenges of declining oil reserves but also competition from overseas refineries and a drop in the demand for refined products. Thus, Gulf Coast refineries were importing 33 percent of the oil feedstocks they were processing in the 1980s, a percentage that had been as high as 46 percent in the late

1970s; the comparable figure in 1972 was only 2 percent. Moreover, because the quality of much imported crude oil is not as good as that of domestic oil, new and expensive processing techniques are required; oil companies have invested billions of dollars to convert.[57]

Challenge is also coming from the new state-of-the-art refineries overseas. In 1982 the United States had the world's largest refining capacity, about 18 million barrels per day. Yet this situation is changing. Since the late 1970s construction of numerous large capacity (built for export) refineries has been started in Third World areas, including the Middle East and Asia, while much less new capacity has been built in the United States. If declining oil reserves and overseas refining were not enough trouble, shifts in the demand for oil products have also affected the refining sector. High oil prices in the 1970s stimulated conservation efforts by consumers and corporate executives. U.S. automakers were forced by government fiat to improve the gasoline mileage per gallon on cars. The demand for gasoline dropped from 7.4 million barrels a day in 1978 to 6.5 million barrels in 1982, contributing to a substantial over-capacity in refining. Ending a governmental subsidy program for small re-finers, which allowed them to purchase lower priced foreign crude under import regulations, also accompanied the decreased demand. In addition, many manufacturers and utilities switched from oil to coal and other fuels as a result of the higher prices and the federal Fuel Use Act forcing conversion. In the early 1980s approximately eighty oil refineries were closed in the United States, a process the industry jargon termed "rationalization."[58] Recent forecasts envision more closures of refineries.

Reorganization and Disinvestment in the Oil Industry

Another response to the downturn in the world's oil economy can be seen in the wave of corporate reorganizations and mergers in the oil and gas industry. One result of the recession was the divesting of unrelated companies by firms that had diversified in prior decades. For example, in the earlier expansion Zapata, an offshore drilling company based in Houston, had purchased con-struction, real estate, copper, and fishing companies; now Zapata began to sell subsidiaries because of a high debt burden.

Oil mergers and megacompany buyouts came "thick and fast" in the 1980s; many had an impact on Houston. Standard Oil of California acquired Gulf Oil Company in a $13.2 billion merger, the largest corporate merger to that point. Mobil bought Houston's Superior Oil Company in a $5.7 billion merger. Texaco bought Getty Oil for $10.2 billion, resulting in a major legal struggle with Houston's Pennzoil company which had also sought Getty Oil. Phillips Petroleum tried to acquire Houston's Aminoil USA Inc. for $1.7 billion. Texas Eastern Corporation, another Houston company, bought Petrolane for $1 billion. Houston's M C O Resources, Inc., acquired Houston's Integrated Energy, Inc.; and Houston's Unimar acquired Houston's Enstar Corp. At least a dozen other Houston energy companies were involved in acquisitions or mergers. It had become cheaper for many firms to acquire the proven oil and gas reserves of other companies than to drill for new oil, in part because the risk of finding oil could not be lowered by the application of technology. The conservative Reagan administration did not resist this increased concentration of power in the oil and gas industry.[59]

One effect could be seen in the layoffs of employees in the Houston area. Chevron announced it would transfer or eliminate 2,800 jobs in Houston because of its merger with Gulf. When Superior Oil Company was taken over by Mobil, top executives in Houston were terminated. The mergers made a significant number of oil company employees "redundant," a word that had not been heard in Houston before. One side effect of the mergers was reducing the ability of corporate executives to invest in the exploration for, and thus production from, new oil fields in the United States. Longterm planning was often displaced by shortrun concerns about being raided. The mergers also involved significant debt arrangements requiring high interest payments; such interest payments direct oil company capital to banks rather than to investment in oil-related operations. Again one can discern the contradictory effects of the capitalistic economic system: mergers actually reduce, in many cases, the ability of firms to expand in their traditional fields of productivity.[60]

Recentralization of oil company operations in Houston in the late 1960s and early 1970s preceded the oil crisis. One oil expert has suggested that the recentralization would not have taken place in the Houston metropolitan area if the Texas oil economy in 1970 had been what it became in the 1980s. Such is often the fate of cities tied to one industry, such as auto-dominated Detroit and oil-centered Houston. The historical timing of factors, the conjunction of stable oil prices, automation, and the intent of corporate executives to concentrate their operations are critical to the relocation of operations to the Houston area.[61]

Reorganization
in the Petrochemical Industry

As noted previously, Houston's petrochemical firms have been critical to the economic development and prosperity of the United States since World War

II. The petrochemical industries link downstream to user industries that make a broad array of products, including packaging, pharmaceuticals, fibers, detergents, pesticides, and paints and other construction materials. Problems in these downstream industries mean problems for petrochemical plants, including those in the Houston–Gulf Coast area. For example, smaller houses and fewer building projects meant less demand for many petrochemical products.

In the 1980s declining demand and overcapacity in the world's petrochemical industry created a challenge for Houston area plants. By 1983 overcapacity had increased by 20 to 40 percent in most facilities. Petrochemical executives blamed the overcapacity situation on poor industry data, the recession, the strong dollar, and domestic oil prices falling slower than world oil prices. These were accurate assessments, but there was a deeper reason: classic capitalistic overproduction. For example, executives in the petrochemical firms were reportedly more concerned with what their competitors were doing than with the likely future market for petrochemicals. Competing with each other for market shares, these firms created a situation where overproduction in the world economy finally resulted in recession, major shutdowns, and large-scale cutbacks. Declining oil prices reduced the cost of materials for petrochemical firms, but that feedstock saving did not offset the large-scale overcapacity that developed in the world's petrochemical industry.[62]

Global sourcing of petrochemicals is well underway. Cheaper, foreign-made petrochemical products are having an effect on some Gulf Coast plants. The U.S. petrochemical industry may be facing the same international situation as the auto and steel industries in the North. For example, in 1981 Mexico had sixty-four petrochemical projects planned or under construction, compared to only sixty projects for the United States. Large petrochemical and refining complexes have been constructed in Indonesia, Saudi Arabia, and Kuwait. Two major oil refineries begun in Saudi Arabia in the mid-1980s were joint ventures between S A B I C, a government-owned company, and two U.S. oil companies, Mobil and Shell Oil Co., the latter with its U.S. headquarters in Houston. Exxon and Texaco have joined with Saudi Arabia in joint ventures to construct petrochemical plants. For a short period, the expansion of petrochemical production in Canada cut into the U.S. market, in part because of Canada's relatively cheap natural gas.

The impact of the global expansion on the Houston area petrochemical industry will probably be selective, at least in the near future. Layoffs in some plants will be matched by some hiring in other plants. Because the Houston area has 45 percent of the U.S. base petrochemical capacity in the late 1980s, it is expected to benefit from any national economic recovery and from expansion in demand for certain types of petrochemical products, including specialty chemicals. One estimate from the Houston Economic Development

Council late in 1987 indicated that forty-nine petrochemical construction projects worth $1.5 billion would be completed by 1990. Because of their automated facilities, these plants will not require many new employees, but they will create some demand for construction workers. The future of the Houston area petrochemical industry seems closely linked to research and constant improvements in technology.[63]

The Impact of the Oil Downturn: Numerous Foreclosures and Bankruptcies

Many sectors of the Houston economy felt the impact of the 1980s crisis in the oil industry. In 1984 Armco, Inc. closed its major Houston Works, the second largest steel plant operated by the company and the largest coastal steel plant west of the Mississippi. One of the World War II plants brought to the area under federal subsidization, the steel mill at its peak employed 4,200 people in producing a million tons of steel a year. The huge facility was closed because of the oil downturn and the overvalued dollar. There was a general negative effect on the nearby ship channel as well. Tonnage at the Port of Houston dropped sharply, from 9 million short tons annually in the early 1980s to 6 million tons in 1986.

Building permits dropped from a seasonally adjusted rate of $251 million in 1982 to $64 million in 1986. By 1987 most nonresidential construction still taking place in the city was in the sphere of public works. Moreover, during the oil recession of the 1980s many properties were repossessed given default on mortgage payments. During the first week of June 1986 a major office building and a major hotel were among the 2,500 Houston area properties repossessed by banks and other lenders. For the entire year of 1986 a total of 25,602 properties were foreclosed upon. The next year set some new records. On April 7, 1987, a total of 3,047 residential and commercial properties were posted for foreclosure at the Family Law Center in downtown Houston. Posted foreclosures included major hotels, such as the Westchase Hilton and the French-owned Meridien, and major shopping centers, such as the 100-store Town and Country Village. About 90 percent of the foreclosures involved residential property. This pace had set a new record for the city.[64]

The average number of business bankruptcy filings increased from twenty-five a month in 1980 to ninety-three a month by 1984; a number of these bankruptcies involved firms worth more than $200 million. Oil, real estate, and retailing businesses suffered the greatest pressure. By 1986 the annual number of bankruptcies had increased to 1,618, substantially more than the number for 1984 and 1985: retail firms accounted for 34 percent of the bankruptcies; real estate firms, for 30 percent; and energy firms, for 8 percent. The number of bankrupt energy firms increased to 125 in 1986, up 52 percent from the prior year; however, this was still below the peak of 131 such bankruptcies in 1983. Major Houston firms, including Tenneco and Texas Eastern, were involved in significant corporate restructuring.

Houston and other Texas cities have seen numerous bank failures. Dozens of banks failed in Texas in 1986–1987, including eleven in Houston in the first nine months of 1987, the largest number since the Great Depression. The most dramatic of the bank failures was that of the First City Bankcorporation. In September 1987 the Federal Deposit Insurance Corporation (F D I C) announced a $1 billion bailout of this huge Houston-based bankholding firm—the *second largest bank rescue in F D I C history.* A group of private investors headed by a Chicago banker was set up by the F D I C to take over the First City firm, with the assistance of nearly $1 billion in federal government notes. In addition, retail sales also dropped sharply in Houston. The public sector was seriously affected as well. Sales taxes and oil-gas severance taxes dropped significantly, placing local and state programs in serious financial difficulties. And the city government's ability to issue bonds at low interest rates was endangered by the changes in bond ratings by Standard and Poor and Moody's. Both rating services dropped the bond rating for the city in 1984–1985. In mid-1986 the Houston mayor and other officials even made a pilgrimage to New York to meet with the rating agencies to lobby for improved ratings.[65]

The bright spots in the Houston area economy were limited to two major sectors: the military-space-industrial complex near the N A S A facility in south Houston and the continuing expansion of the Texas Medical Center. Indeed, one 1987 story on the Medical Center noted that construction cranes had disappeared from all areas of the city but the Medical Center, where $1.5 billion in construction was planned for the late 1980s. Business officials publicly noted that this federally supported construction "adds a guaranteed growth dimension for the city."[66] Prominent Houstonians hoped the medical complex would add dynamism to the energy-centered economy.

Conclusion: Recurring Cycles in Energy Economies

This chapter has traced the oscillating trajectory of Houston's development within the world market context. Investment capital flowed into the metropolitan area from the 1960s to the early 1980s. Houston's dramatic growth is signaled by the variety of economic statistics which increased by more than 100 percent in this two-decade period. I have also demonstrated the crucial foundation of energy industries undergirding the Houston economy; this foundation's narrow specialization and dependence on the world oil economy led to serious problems in the mid-1980s. In addition, I have documented the point that Houston is not the leading headquarters city for the world's top oil firms, but rather it houses the major operational subsidiaries for many of the "majors," together with the headquarters offices and subsidiaries of leading oil tools and services firms, secondary oil firms, and leading gas companies.

Perhaps, however, the most important point in this chapter is my documentation of the previous conceptual point that understanding the development, decline, and spatial character of cities like Houston necessitates a serious consideration of the global market context. Houstonians saw the gold-plated prosperity of the 1960s and 1970s rather quickly replaced by the "doom and gloom" of the mid- and late-1980s; local business cycles were directly linked to oil-related and dollar-revalued decisions made in the global economy. When the downturn came, the response of the leaders in the metropolitan business community was rather sluggish, since they had little experience with economic adversity. As I will show in Chapter 6, the leadership did finally create the Houston Economic Development Council, a unique private-public arrangement organized to press for a more diversified economy.

What the future holds in the way of cycles of boom and bust for Houston can only be speculated upon at this juncture. Some recovery in the price of oil had taken place in the first months of 1987, but this was followed by a slump in prices at the end of that year. Although there was some local economic recovery until the price drop late in 1987, the initial effect was primarily to reverse the sharp decline in the job situation; other aspects of the local economy, such as mortgage foreclosures and bank failures, were still at crisis levels. The effect of the 1987 drop in prices to the job situation in Houston in the near future is at this point unclear. Oscillation in the price of oil and the city's economy seems probable in the near future, but a medium-term increase in the price of oil is likely; that would bring the type of economic recovery to reinvigorate the city. However, that recovery is also likely to be followed at some later point by yet another fall in price, followed by other boom-bust oscillations—a typical story of urban economies tied to primary resource extraction industries.

5

| Who Runs Houston?

| The Succession

| of Business Elites

In the last two chapters I examined the economic and state structure of the capitalistic development which characterized the Houston metropolitan area from the 1830s to the late 1980s. This political-economic structure is the broad framework within which, and through which, the actors in the Houston drama in fact carried out their critical objectives and responsibilities. In Chapter 2 I noted that some critical urban scholars emphasize that the actors within the economic and political structures should become a major focus for researchers concerned with understanding the realities of urban growth and decline.

The Importance of Powerful Actors on the Urban Scene

Particular urban actors make the concrete everyday decisions that in effect create or shape economic and political institutions. Gottdiener's emphasis on the point that urban spatial forms are contingent on the dialectical articulation between action and structures can be extended to include the restructuring of economic and political forms as well. Institutional changes are processed through human actions taken under specific historical conditions.

In Chapter 2 I examined the work of Harvey Molotch and Bill Domhoff, both of whom have stressed agency and action in their research on cities. Molotch has brought urban growth coalitions, organizations of local land-oriented capitalists working for growth, to the center of urban analysis. And Domhoff has noted the close linkage between these capitalists at the local level and those at the helm of national corporations who provide the outside investment critical to local business prosperity. Agency analysts such as Molotch and Domhoff have been criticized for deemphasizing structure in their concern with powerful actors, for failing to show how the elites themselves are constituent elements of a wider structural and institutional order.

106

My purpose in this chapter is to examine Houston's succession of business leaders and elites with a focus on who they are and how they have operated to promote the growth of the city by both private and public means. In undertaking this task, I will attempt to show how the elites are linked to the wider social order. Actions of elite actors create economic and governmental structures, which later shape the actions of these same and subsequent powerful actors.

The Houston Leadership: An Overview

Houston has been ruled by a strong business elite from its first decade. The character of that establishment has changed over time, but in most decades since the 1830s the local power structure has been dominated by business leaders such as merchants, cotton "factors," bankers, oil entrepreneurs, developers, lawyers, and corporate executives in multinational firms. In some cities politicians have emerged out of urban machines or union backgrounds to compete with business leaders, but not generally in Houston. The top city politicians, with rare exceptions, have been members of or heavily dependent on the business elites. There is a correspondence between the character of the actors dominant in the power structure in a particular period and the economic organizations characteristic of, or emerging in, that same period (see Table 5.1). The first group to dominate the city was composed of the founding entrepreneurs, the Allen brothers, and a few other merchants. General and cotton merchants were very influential over the next few decades, making the initial economic and political decisions that created the city of Houston. But they made those decisions within the context of, and limited by the logic of, the precapitalist plantation economy and the commercial capitalistic economy.

In the 1880s and 1890s the merchant aggregation was supplemented with a group of bankers, lawyers, and railroad entrepreneurs. They, too, made decisions that shaped the economic structure and spatial layout of the city, but within a more national political-economic framework than their predecessors. This framework allowed a broader range of decisions because of greater available resources. But it also, depending on the issue, provided more institutional restrictions, as we will discover in examining the ties of the municipal bond structure to the troubled national banking system. By the late 1920s a few oil entrepreneurs had become part of the city's power structure.

In the late 1930s the most cohesive clique emerged, one with a distinctive name (later called the "Suite 8F crowd"). This elite appears to have been the most powerful in the city's history, largely because of its cohesion and its distinctive personalities as well as its corporate networks and national and inter-

TABLE   5.1.
Economic Sectors and Business Elites

Emerging Economic Sector	Approximate Date of Emergence	Selected Members of Core Elite
Agricultural production, marketing	1840s–1880s	Allen brothers, W. M. Rice, T. W. House
Railroad industries	1880s–1910s	J. A. Baker, W. Baker, H. Rice, J. H. Kirby, J. Jones, O. Holcombe
Primary commodity production; oil tools; banking	1920s–1960s	J. Jones, W. S. Farish, Suite 8F crowd
Medical services; space-related industry	1970s–1980s	Chamber of Commerce, other business groups

national resources. Operating in an expanding world economy, this group presided over several decades of Houston's formative city growth and development. When Suite 8F power waned in the 1970s, a larger and less cohesive power structure emerged; the Houston Chamber of Commerce more or less moved to the center of the business leadership. This organization is headed by an assortment of principal corporate executives, but its influence has been limited by the larger contextual factors associated with a major disinvestment and declining-rate-of-profit cycle in the sectors of the capitalistic economy vital to the city of Houston.

Characteristics of the Houston Business Elites

A number of important characteristics link these successive business elites. First, and perhaps most important, has been a vigorous commitment to a laissez-faire, "free enterprise" philosophy—one characterized by an intense belief in economic growth, private property, private investment control, private profit, and government action tailored to business needs. Houston is a city whose leaders have propagated the strongest possible ideology of the free market and laissez-faire government. The 1980 advertisement for the metropolis cited in Chapter 2 was published by the local business leadership in *Fortune* magazine. It accented the good business climate, the free enterprise gospel, and the probusiness state: "Houston, by virtue of being in Texas, reaps the benefits of a state that has one of the best business climates in the nation. . . . Free enterprise is still the gospel." [1] This view has been amplified and proclaimed in various publications of the business elites, including the Chamber of Commerce. The social science literature on growth coalitions suggests the importance of this free enterprise growth ideology to the legitimation of localized capital accumulation. Urban development is more than a matter of money, bulldozers, and buildings; it also requires an ideology legitimating the activities of the powerful actors engaged in investment in the various circuits of capital. The ideology more or less consistently espoused by the succession of business elites in Houston has been an extreme version of the laissez-faire free enterprise philosophy.

Second, these business elites have been willing to use all levels of government to promote and support capitalistic endeavors. As I have documented in previous chapters, Houston's business community has never been committed to "laissez-faire" government in the real world of metropolitan life. In Chapter 2 I assessed the research of Swanstrom and Mollenkopf, who focus on the role of politicians in local growth politics. Swanstrom distinguishes between liberal and conservative growth politics. *Liberal* growth politics is a balancing act, with local politicians providing incentives for wealthy investors interested in growth and also providing some redistributive support for their nonwealthy constituents. In *conservative* growth politics planning and implementation of economic growth are left primarily to the private sector; this type rejects redistributive policies benefiting ordinary urbanites below the upper-income level. This useful distinction assumes a somewhat independent political apparatus.

However, in some U.S. cities there have been few independent politicians. This has been the case for Houston, which provides a clear example of local government that is, to use the conceptual language associated with Miliband and Domhoff's research, the *instrument* of the local business community. Since the 1830s Houston's business leaders have consciously sought governmental action and capitalization in regard to a broad range of business-facilitating infrastructure projects, as well as governmental intervention to deal with the urban irrationalities created by an unrestrained pursuit of private profit. There have been few breaks in this overwhelming business dominance of the local economy and polity. Conservative growth politics, the emphasis on private planning for growth and the rejection of redistributive programs, characterizes the city because business elites have so designed the operation of local politics. The business leaders have not only sought and received capital, tax, and regulatory assistance from all levels of government, but they have also controlled to a substantial degree the character and composition of the local (and, on occasion, the Texas) governments.

Cooperative government is emphasized in business-oriented publications, such as a 1980 guidebook on Houston published by Macmillan: "Much of the city's growth can be attributed to the local government's attitude of cooperation with the business community. . . . Perhaps the key element in Houston's continually growing and historically sound economy has been a consistently positive attitude towards the free enterprise system." [2] The business leadership has to some extent been limited by democratic political institutions, but rarely by major opposition movements stemming from the city's workforce. Houston and Texas data on these state-related issues are so substantial as to require, it would seem, some rethinking of certain major perspectives on the state, especially the "independent state" theories.

Third, Houston's power structure is an organized network of powerful individuals seeking generalized business goals. It is accurate to emphasize the social organization and cohesiveness of the ruling elite, for these have been neither isolated individuals nor for the most part independent operators. The elites are enmeshed in a variety of informal organizations, corporations, and state positions. They exercise their power from organizational heights of industrial firms, banks, law firms, business organizations, and state agencies. Yet it is also accurate to speak of these influential business cliques as composed of distinctive actors with differentiated interests and distinctive personalities. Virtually all leaders have been capitalists with a strong commitment to private profit making, and they have routinely operated to foster the individual and collective interests of capital against that of the general citizenry. But there have also been serious conflicts *within* the business elite, because individual members have acted in their own specific business interests and in the context of their own family and personal histories. I will now examine these business leaders, perhaps the most consequential actors in Houston's urban drama over the course of the city's first century and a half of development.

The Agricultural Marketing Period: Founding a City

Successful Town Entrepreneurs

Town entrepreneurs have been important in the history of the location and early development of U.S. cities. Houston began in 1836 as a land development scheme of two entrepreneurs: J. K. and A. C. Allen bought 6,000 acres of land in southeast Texas for a little more than a dollar an acre and laid out their projected city in a gridiron pattern considered profitable for speculative land sales. The Allen brothers talked military hero General Sam Houston into giving his name to their development scheme, for which favor they offered him land. The Allens marketed their land as desirable and healthful to outsiders, including land investors and settlers from the East, many of whom were unaware that the area was marshy, mosquito-infested, and extraordinarily hot and humid.

An 1836 newspaper advertisement placed by the Allens proclaimed: "The town of Houston is located at the point on the river which must ever command the trade of the largest and richest portion of Texas. . . . [It] will warrant the employment of at least *One Million Dollars* of capital, and when the rich lands of this country shall be settled, a trade will flow to it, making it, beyond all doubt, the great interior commercial emporium of Texas."[3] These entrepreneurs solicited much outside capital and offered land to investors, merchants, and settlers, with the expressed view that Houston would become the regional center of commercial capitalism and the government of the new Texas Republic. Even at this early point here is a primary example of the urban boosterism so characteristic of those local promotional groups which scholars would later term "growth coalitions." These growth coalitions, typically including land-interested capitalists at their core, have engaged in aggressive advertising of their particular towns and cities. Note, too, the importance of the growth ideology. The mix of agency and structure can be seen in the founding of Houston. While these town entrepreneurs made the decisions about where to locate the city, how to promote it, and how to attract the physical location of the state, their actions were constrained by the need for outside capital and the workings of the larger capital markets.

By the spring of 1837 the city with 500 residents was the capital of the new Republic of Texas. A boomtown, Houston by the late 1830s had tripled its population to 1,500. The Allen brothers had succeeded in attracting the new Republic's government to Houston, but, because of the inclement weather, yellow fever, and competititon from land speculators in other towns, within a few years the Texas capital was moved to Austin. Still, the Houston area grew with the expansion of trade and agricultural marketing. The Allen brothers dominated the power structure in the first years, although John K. Allen died in an early yellow fever epidemic. In the first decade they were joined in the ruling circle by general and cotton merchants. Among those who became prominent were the Bordens, who published Houston's first newspaper, the *Texas Telegraph and Register*. Gail Borden would later become famous as the inventor of condensed milk.[4]

Among the powerful leaders in the 1840–1880 period were Thomas W. House and William M. Rice, merchants who engaged in multiple business activities. Arriving in Houston in the 1830s, House soon became a major dry goods merchant and cotton trader. By the 1850s he owned the largest wholesale firm in Texas and invested in shipping and railroad firms. The Civil War made him one of the wealthiest merchants in the Southwest. Merchants such as House supplied the Confederacy and brought out cotton through an extensive smuggling system; by the end of the war he had $300,000 in gold. After the war House became involved in the international cotton trade to English cities, Liverpool and Manchester. Likewise prominent in business, William M. Rice came to Houston in 1839 from New England. For two decades Rice built up one of the major fortunes in Houston as a dry goods merchant, cotton broker, real estate investor, and railroad entrepreneur. By the 1850s he owned a shipping company operating on Buffalo Bayou, the city's commercial watercourse. Opposed to secession during the Civil War, Rice moved to Mexico, where he sold Texas cotton to British ship captains and thereby became a millionaire.[5]

Merchants with a Global Vision

Even at this early stage of Houston's development, business leaders were consciously acting to bind the city to the global market system. While there certainly were structural, logic-of-capital-accumulation reasons for the merchant capitalists to take such action, its timing and effectiveness are shaped by particular historical conditions. These conditions included the farsighted local entrepreneurs. Indeed, the business leadership in competing Gulf Coast towns and cities did not, in the next few decades, act as effectively as this Houston business elite.

Rice and House were central guiding figures in the local business elite, which was greatly concerned in these early decades with matters of transportation. They organized the Houston Navigation Company to run steamships out Buffalo Bayou to the Gulf of Mexico. The local merchants successfully lobbied the Texas legislature in the 1850s for support of a privately-owned development plan which would tie Texas railroads into the expanding national railroad system. Some in this merchant elite set up their own railroad corporations, drawing in part on public taxes. The cotton moving to Houston's wharves increased sharply by the 1860s; this expanding cotton trade generated a significant increase in local profits and a real estate boom.[6]

Utilizing the State

After the Civil War, Rice made his permanent home on the East Coast and no longer played a role in the city's power structure. House, in contrast, became active in extending credit to farmers and planters and in the burgeoning cotton trade. Like many business leaders after him, House served at the helm of the local government—a member of the board of aldermen and mayor. He also formed the first gas light company, a venture successful largely because of local government subsidies. The Texas legislature granted a right-of-way for this private company's distribution system and made any attacks upon its property a criminal offense; and the city council gave House's firm a monopoly on gas lighting for twenty-five years.[7]

At this early stage, Houston's entrepreneurs had developed and used a public sector which could facilitate their business requirements. Here are two different ways of using the local state: One is to serve in the state itself; the other is to lobby the state's legislative organs for business support. These two activities were to remain closely interrelated in subsequent decades of Houston's development.

The Railroad and Banking Era: Building Infrastructure

By the 1880s Houston had become a railroad hub in the Southwest. However, the national railroad entrepreneurs, who generally lived elsewhere, played little part in running the city. The railroads brought many blue- and white-collar workers to the city. These new industrial facilities also stimulated a number of associated enterprises, such as the lumber, law, and banking firms that provided local business leaders over the next few decades.

Some Local Lawyers and Bankers

Leading entrepreneur William Baker made his fortune in railroads, utilities, and banking. He was a major stockholder in the Houston Electric Light and Power Co., a utility he helped organize in 1882. Baker also controlled the city's major newspaper, the *Daily Post*. In 1880 Baker, then president of the City Bank, was elected mayor, an important political event to which I will return later.

Unrelated to William Baker, James A. Baker was one of the chief members of the business community in the 1890–1930 period. By 1887 he was a partner in Baker & Botts (the later name of the firm), his father's law firm. Founded in 1866, this firm has been for more than a century one of the city's most consequential. The growth of railroads was a force behind the expansion

of the firm. Many major railroad firms operating in Texas, including Jay
Gould's Missouri Pacific system and the Southern Pacific, were represented
by Baker & Botts. Baker presided over the rapid growth of the firm; he
worked closely with local utility companies and local governments. In 1894
Baker was the corporation attorney for and a director in a local water company
investigated by a city government committee, and in 1901–1902 the new
owners of the private Houston Electric Railway company hired his firm to negotiate for them with the city council. By 1916 Baker was president of the
South Texas Commercial National Bank, whose directors included cotton and
grain company executives, other bankers, and railroad executives. A key
member of the Business League, the forerunner of the Houston Chamber of
Commerce, Baker was an officer and director in many businesses, including
Bankers Trust, Guardian Trust, and the Houston Gas Company. Buenger and
Pratt describe him as "probably more than any other man of his day . . . posi-
tioned to influence and observe all facets of Houston's business community." [8]

The Baker & Botts firm was not only influential in the region, but it also
maintained probably the first direct and substantial local ties to the national
business aristocracy and the federal government. For example, Edwin Parker,
a major figure in Baker & Botts, served on the War Industries Board in World
War I and on the International Court of Claims. He also became the general
counsel for Texaco. Robert S. Lovett, onetime railroad specialist at Baker &
Botts, became a protégé of E. H. Harriman and eventually chairperson of the
board of the Southern Pacific and Union Pacific railroads. And several partners of the law firm were active in Electric Bond and Share, a New York holding company which owned several utility firms including Houston Light and
Power. [9]

Leading Lumber Entrepreneurs

The railroads and accompanying real estate developments greatly stimulated
the lumber industry in Texas. Several lumber entrepreneurs, including John H.
Kirby and Jesse H. Jones, were powerful members of the business elite. In the
1880s the young Kirby convinced prominent Boston capitalists to invest
$400,000 in the timbered lands of east Texas and build a railroad to the out-
side world. Kirby eventually became a timber baron and controlled 1.1 million acres of east Texas. He built important bridges between east coast banks
and Texas enterprises, bringing east coast capital to Gulf Coast enterprises
and thereby establishing a tradition of investment in a then risky frontier area.
Having made $300,000 in three years in east Texas, in 1890 Kirby moved to
Houston; from this city he directed his lumber, railroad, and real estate invest-

ments. By the early 1900s Kirby, senior partner of the Houston law firm of Kirby, Martin, and Eagle, was also president of the important Planters and Mechanics National Bank.[10]

Kirby became active in the Houston power structure in the 1890s; he was sent by the older business leaders to Washington, D.C., to secure government help in dealing with a navigation problem on Buffalo Bayou. In the next decade Kirby's rise to economic prominence was accompanied by rising power in the local business elite. Like some of his predecessors he was very active in local and national politics as well, serving two terms in the Texas legislature; in 1914 he was urged to become governor of Texas. During World War I, at the request of Woodrow Wilson's adviser Bernard Baruch, Kirby served on the Raw Materials Committee of the Council of National Defense in Washington, D.C. Kirby provided yet another personal link between Washington and the Houston business elite.[11]

One of the sons of the aforementioned William M. Rice was a business associate of Kirby. Joe Rice became head of the Kirby Lumber Co., the Great Southern Life Insurance Co., and the Union Bank. He was part of the group of merchants, often called "our crowd," that selected gubernatorial candidates and generally controlled Texas politics between 1895 and 1905. This wealthy lumber and finance capitalist was well integrated into the important social networks, clubs, and corporate boards in the city. Also linked to Kirby was H. Baldwin Rice, a nephew of William M. Rice and another member of the inner circle; Rice was a vice-president of a bank and also of Kirby-owned timber and oil ventures.[12]

At this point it is important to note particular business actors linking different fractions of capital. Specific business leaders provide the concrete, everyday links. For example, Baker was a principal lawyer and directly involved in utility and banking businesses. Baker, Lovett, and Kirby illustrate the importance of the conscious actions of indigenous capitalists in establishing the character of local political-economic structures and the significance of the assertion that often individuals provide the concrete nodal connections between the abstract institutional structures of local and national economies and local and national states. This type of agent linkage has remained central to the coordination and function of Houston's business sector for more than a century. Economic and political structures are very important to an analysis of urban development, but it is also clear that the evolution of a specific city in a particular historical period involves a distinctive web of relationships. Often powerful individuals tie together formally and informally the macrostructural realities termed the "state" and the "economy." These entrepreneurs and investors are acting individuals who built a city, but they are also part of the wider social order emphasized by analysts like Dear and Clark. They not only acted as individuals limited by that larger political-economic order, but they also changed and shaped that wider social order for subsequent generations.

Organizing the Business Elite

By the 1890s the business community had grown to such a size that integrative organizations of a formal nature became essential. The Business League, created in 1895, was renamed Chamber of Commerce in 1910. Earlier business organizations, including one called a "Chamber of Commerce," had come and gone, but the Business League was the first with staying power. In the 1890s the league pressed for a professional fire department, gave out a million pieces of booster advertising on the city at the Atlanta Exposition, prepared research reports on sewage and water problems, and organized local protests against a railroad tariff. The league became a primary vehicle of local business action; by the early 1900s the league was coordinating major business groups— the Cotton Exchange, the Banker's Clearing House, and the Manufacturer's Association—and local political campaigns. By 1905 it included most of the city's business and professional elite. At the heart of the League were men like H. Baldwin Rice, John Kirby, T. W. House, Jr., and James Baker. In 1911 the organization had 1,200 members and an income of $17,000.[13] Among other actions, Kirby and several Business League members became active in economic support actions such as organizing pipeline companies to bring newly discovered oil to Houston as a cheap source of fuel and directing the infrastructure decisions of city government.

These organized business leaders publicly delineated their growth-oriented vision of a "Greater Houston." They discussed the requirements necessary for Houston to become a major metropolis; commercial and industrial development became a top priority. One business booster's view was typical: "[more] cooperation among the businessmen and property owners, more thought, more getting together. . . . Industrial development is the important factor in citybuilding. . . . The world is now a neighborhood, made so by rapid transit and competition in the carrying trade by rail and water." [14] The *world* context was explicitly recognized.

Business Control of City Government

Since its founding, leading business figures have, with few exceptions, directly or indirectly dominated mayoral and city council positions in Houston. The inner circle of the business elite has, on occasion, provided mayors. This was the case in the 1860s, when T. W. House, Sr., served as mayor; and it was true again in the 1880s when William R. Baker served three terms as mayor. In the 1880s Baker joined with other notables serving in the city administration, including merchant T. W. House, Jr., and Cotton Exchange head William D. Cleveland, to resolve the credit problems noted in Chapter 3.

In the 1880s this business dominance was, for a brief period, challenged by the growing working-class population. In 1886 Houston politics became ward-based and thus more democratic. Several candidates ran for most government positions; there was extensive organizing and campaigning at the neighborhood level. The old business elite was forced to share power with skilled workers. In 1886 Mayor William Baker was challenged by Dan C. Smith, a railroad mechanic and union member who represented the blue-collar population. Working in coalition with a group of lawyers and executives opposed to the old leadership, Smith won by only four votes. Under the previous mayor eight of the ten council members had been business leaders, but under Mayor Smith the members included a painter, two railroad superintendents, a yardmaster, a saloon keeper, and a grocer. Smith and his council succeeded in resolving the controversy over the municipal debt which had raged for more than a decade, and public works projects for all areas of the city were expanded.[15]

In this period much utility growth in American cities was often in private hands. In the late 1880s a Chicago capitalist bought Houston's street railway monopoly. However, the newly democratized city council granted another firm a franchise to put up a competing system. The Chicago entrepreneur was so angry that he cancelled a half-million dollar modernization plan. Yet the council-fostered competition did stimulate an expansion of transit services into neighborhoods formerly excluded. The representative city council managed to exact tax and regulatory concessions from the private utility entrepreneurs. For a time council actions scared some northern investors out of a city which had gained the reputation of being unfriendly to private utility monopolies, but the business elite soon regained control. In 1890 they succeeded in getting their preferred choice, Henry Scherffius, elected mayor.[16]

In the mid-1890s growing numbers of Houstonians were pressing for improved services to neighborhoods. Banker H. Baldwin Rice, elected as a business-backed mayor in 1896, faced a challenge in 1898 from Samuel H. Brashear. While both candidates were members of the business elite, Brashear opposed Mayor Rice's view of government as primarily the promoter of business and instead argued for neighborhood services. With labor support Brashear won the Democratic primary over Rice, and as mayor he shifted the balance of power toward the neighborhoods and pressed for an expanded public sector. Brashear built a modern sanitation system, pressed for a new city charter, increased regulation of privately owned utilities, and collected back taxes from wealthy property holders. He worked hard for the public ownership of utilities: the utilities owned by outsiders had not been responsive to community needs, and his municipal ownership would put services under local public control. There was a stormy battle in 1900 over a proposal to erect a municipal light plant. A divided city council and the mayor blocked each other's proposals. Heavy pressure was applied to council members by private utility firms, and no municipal utility was built.[17]

In 1902 the Business League successfully organized opposition to neighborhood-oriented reform and put Oran T. Holt into office, a man who pressed for "scientific management" and business-like efficiency in government agencies. Holt started in the Democratic ward politics of the Dan Smith era, but by the early 1900s he had thrown in his lot with the antidemocratic Business League. Fearful that the neighborhood-oriented philosophy would scare off outside capital and retard the city's growth, Kirby and his entrepreneurial associates more or less ran the successful political campaign of Holt from the league. Once elected, Holt reformed the city's budgetary practices by bringing in outside "experts." Holt's administration also denied municipal services to black Houstonians. Indeed, the early 1900s were hard years for the black voters. Black voters had been effectively disenfranchised in 1898 when they were excluded from the Democratic primary in Texas. In 1900 the ward system of elections was replaced by the at-large system, and in 1903 a state poll tax further discriminated against poorer voters.

In 1904–1905 the Business League and the business-dominated council persuaded the state legislature to accept a mayor-commission form of local government; this action mainly guaranteed rule by the business leaders. Platt notes that the "suppression of urban democracy and its ward-centered system of politics was a high price to pay for the modernization of the Texas city's society and environment."[18] By 1905 the business elite had regained complete control, having elected former mayor H. Baldwin Rice to office, a reign of another eight years. The at-large election format gave the elite the power to select acceptable business candidates for top office in local government; the few at the top of the elected structure were supported by a handful of "experts" managing the city under the commission form of government. Indeed, Houston was the first city in the United States to set up a commission form of government under normal political circumstances. From this period to the present the business community has retained substantial and instrumental control of the political institutions.[19]

Seeking Federal Government Aid

In Chapters 3 and 4 I chronicled the close relationship between governmental action and the needs of the business elite. This can be seen in the role that banker and mayor H. B. Rice played in working for improved port facilities. Since the 1830s a critical issue for the city's elite had been the dredging of Buffalo Bayou so that Houston could become a deepwater port. Prior to the 1890s the local government, as well as private sources, had spent significant funds to improve the Bayou channel. In the 1890s members of Houston's elite such as John Kirby and William Chew of the Commercial National Bank went to Washington, D.C., to plead for federal funds to dredge the ship channel to a more adequate depth.

Moreover, in January 1909 several Houston capitalists, including local bankers, cotton merchants, and lumber company executives, met at Mayor H. B. Rice's office to work out a plan for the federal government to match local funds for making Houston a deepwater port. Although I reviewed the details of this project in Chapter 3, it is important to note here that the plan was developed by the business leadership, working through their entrepreneurial mayor. As part of the plan, the local government was to match the federal grant. Since the city had no authority to issue bonds for projects outside its city limits, attorneys were sent to the Texas legislature to secure a law permitting a Houston navigation district to issue local bonds for improving the channel. Many of the bonds to dredge the ship channel were bought by local bankers. After the initial decisions about the channel were reached, the Chamber of Commerce played a part in drawing citizen approval. The chamber helped with various bond issues in the 1910s and made a study of the Manchester (England) ship channel, which had been dug to the sea by that inland city's leaders in the late nineteenth century. The Houston leadership actually modeled the development of the Houston ship channel on that of Manchester.

The early decades of the twentieth century constituted a heady period of rapid growth, elite involvement in government, and an increasingly aggressive promotion of the city. The boosterism of the Houston growth coalitions continued into the twentieth century. For example, in 1909 the *New York Times* published an article on "Cities that Advertise." In that article the writer noted that Houston was offering inducements to "investors and homeseekers" in national ads that ran as follows: "Her city hall is a business house. She has no wards, no ward politicians, no graft." Even in this early period the city hall was advertised as a business house with *no interference* from the now disenfranchised working-class citizenry. The city hall was advertised as a part of the good business climate. [20]

The 1920s: A Bridging Era in Elite History

The 1920s was an era of rapid growth in the city of Houston, a point underscored in Chapter 3. Not much data is readily available on the leadership in this bridging era. However, in 1930 a leading Houston advertising executive, writing in the new chamber magazine *Houston,* made a brief list of Houston's most influential leaders in the growth period of the 1920s. At the top of his list was Jesse H. Jones, a "master of men and money" who as a developer has "decorated the city's towering skyline." High on his list were two bankers, John T. Scott and J. W. Neal, and two Humble Oil executives, W. S. Farish and Ross Sterling, the latter also chair of the Texas Highway Commission. Also included were Captain James A. Baker, "a power in politics and business and general affairs extending from Houston to Washington," and Will Clayton of Anderson, Clayton. These men led the city in the prosperous 1920s, and, as I will document, several would continue as principal figures for the next decade and beyond.[21]

Another important figure in this period was real estate developer and business leader Oscar Holcombe, who served, off and on, as mayor for more than twenty years. An entrepreneur with political ambition, Holcombe was elected mayor for eleven terms between 1921 and 1958. The Ku Klux Klan was a major force in midwestern and southern politics in the 1920s, and Houston was the first Texas city to see the organization of a chapter of the resurgent Ku Klux Klan in the 1920s. Holcombe himself had joined the Klan, but he quit after one meeting. In the 1922 election he was strongly opposed by the Klan, which at the time controlled the Harris County government. The Klan pressured him to fire Catholics serving in city positions, but Holcombe refused. Although the Houston business elite at first flirted with the Klan, key members of the local elite—men like Kirby, Jones, and Holcombe—soon discovered that the violent Klan was bad for business and a stable political and economic situation.[22]

From the 1930s to the 1960s:
The Background and Emergence
of the Suite 8F Crowd

The Background of the Suite 8F Crowd

Houston's business community from the late 1930s to the 1960s was primarily centered in the Suite 8F crowd, a loose coalition of business leaders who called themselves the "builders" of modern Houston. The Suite 8F group was frequently referred to as the "unofficial capital of Texas" or the "Establishment." These top leaders had a threefold power base: substantial wealth founded on corporate development, general support of the local business community, and intimate ties to major officials in local and national politics. From the 1930s to the 1960s the entrepreneurs who met regularly in such places as George Brown's Suite 8F in the Lamar Hotel dominated the important business and political decisions in both Houston and, in many cases, the rest of Texas. Although this Suite 8F crowd did not coalesce until the 1930s, several members were powerful figures in Houston by the 1910s and 1920s, and, as I just noted, they provided the bridging links between the business elite of the early 1900s and that of the later period. While the actual membership fluctuated, the core of the Suite 8F crowd included Jesse H. Jones, Herman and George Brown, James A. Elkins, Sr., Gus Wortham, and James Abercrombie.

Jesse H. Jones: "Mr. Houston"

Of all the influential business leaders who have dominated the city—and to some degree the state of Texas and the nation—since the 1920s, the single most powerful was Jesse H. Jones. In 1939 *Fortune* magazine called Jones the man "who runs Houston" and the most powerful capitalist on the Gulf Coast. Making his home in Houston from 1898 to 1956, Jones was termed "Mr. Houston" for more than forty years. Well over six feet, Jones was aggressive and took himself seriously, so much so that President Franklin Roosevelt, among others, reportedly referred to him on occasion as "Jesus H. Jones." [23]

Jones was one of Houston's most vigorous boosters. In 1923 Jones compared growth in Houston to that of Chicago:

> Chicago, the miracle in growth of modern cities, has not become what it is because of any unusual natural advantages, but because it was in the lines of travel and progress by land and water. . . . There is now a decided movement of business and population southward. . . . Capital has begun to flow in and population has begun to flow in, both seeking new opportunities. Our ship channel and the great transcontinental railway systems, meeting deep water here, make Houston the inevitable gateway through which the products of this growing southern and western empire can best reach the market of the world.
>
> We pride ourselves that, by the expenditure of a few million dollars of public funds, we have provided navigable waters up to our city for ocean-going vessels. [24]

As did other Houston leaders, the perspicacious Jones saw Chicago as a model for Houston. The capital flowing into Houston from the North, he notes with accuracy, was stimulated by *public* investments in Houston's transport infrastructure. Business-centered growth is a central emphasis in Jones's perspective.

Jesse H. Jones was a capitalist with many talents; during his long life he was a lumber entrepreneur, a developer, a banker, an oil investor, a newspaper owner, and a leading federal government official. Jones came to Houston from Dallas to become general manager of his uncle's lumber company, where he worked under the auspices of T. W. House, a banker who was president of that lumber company and a member of one of Houston's oldest families. Jones invested in a large section of timber, borrowing the money from a Dallas bank; that investment was the foundation of his fortune. Perhaps as a consequence of his lumber operations, Jones became a builder and developer.

Charles G. Dawes, who served as Reconstruction Finance Corporation (R F C) chair before Jones, once portrayed Jones as an empire builder like the famous Briton Cecil Rhodes who helped to colonize Africa. However, Jones preferred his "empire" in the form of major buildings in U.S. cities. Between 1908 and 1956, operating as a developer, he averaged one major building a year in cities such as Houston, Fort Worth, and New York. By 1912 Jones had built three large office buildings and a hotel in downtown Houston. In 1912 he tore down the old Rice Hotel and constructed a large edifice in its place; the top floor of that new hotel became the site for the first Petroleum Club, a place where early oil and other business deals were made. A few years later Jones built a ten-story building for the new Texas Company, which had moved its oil headquarters from Beaumont to Houston. A decade later, in 1928, he completed construction of a skyscraper for Gulf Oil Company; indeed, Jones had played an important role in convincing the new Gulf Oil Company to leave Beaumont. By the mid-1920s this developer had constructed thirty important commercial buildings in the city. Jones was the first of Houston's major property developers, first in a long line of large-scale developer-investors moving money into Houston's secondary circuit of capital.[25]

Jones had a number of "leg men" working under him. From the mid-1920s to the late 1950s Alfred C. Finn was Houston's principal architect, working on numerous development projects for Jones. When Jones became the chair of President Roosevelt's R F C, Finn became the first architectural supervisor for the Federal Housing Administration: Finn's firm received many federal projects. Finn designed many of Houston's monumental landmarks, including the federally subsidized San Jacinto monument and Jones's Gulf building. Finn was the prototype of a business architect, one who "could provide the client with usable working structures in which spaces function the way the client needs and wants. In this regard, he was more of a businessman in temperament than many architects of the period."[26]

Jones's real estate activities led to his newspaper ownership. In 1908 he constructed a building for the publisher of the Houston *Chronicle* and received half-interest in the paper as a downpayment on the building. After buying the other half-interest in 1926, Jones became sole owner of the *Chronicle*. At one time he owned Houston's other major paper as well; in 1931 he purchased the *Houston Post-Dispatch* from the then bankrupt oil entrepreneur Ross Sterling. He quickly sold that paper to ex-governor W. P. Hobby, whose family controlled that paper into the 1980s. Jones was briefly in the oil business. An original stockholder in the Humble Oil and Refining company, with Ross Sterling and W. S. Farish, Jones soon sold his stock; as he said, he had bought the stock to insure Humble's headquarters in Houston. It is significant that Jesse Jones not only sought to expand his own capitalistic enterprises but also worked to center the emerging petroleum industry in the city of Houston. His role in influencing Gulf Oil to move its early headquarters to the city and in helping capitalize Humble Oil is evident. The agents of capital are as important as the institutions of capital in urban development.[27]

A Leader of Finance Capitalism: Jones in Houston and Washington

Perhaps the most significant business activities conducted by Jones were in the area of finance capitalism; he was active in the private banking sphere locally and in running the federal government's banking system for more than a decade. To finance his real estate projects Jones borrowed from Houston, Dallas, New York, and Chicago banks, which gave him a vested interest in developing more accessible banking facilities. By 1905 Jesse Jones was moving into banking; in that year he became a major stockholder in the Union Bank and Trust Company. In 1908 Jones played a key role in bailing out troubled local banks; by 1915 Jones was a major owner of the National Bank of Commerce, where he became president in 1922. In 1929 the National Bank of Commerce, forerunner of the Texas Bank of Commerce, moved into Jones's Gulf Building; from that year to 1956 Jones served as that bank's chair of the board.

Two Houston banks were in major trouble in the early 1930s, but Jones and his associates rescued them. In 1931 Jones called a group of Houston's banking and other business leaders into his office. In two days a strategy was worked out for healthy banks to bail out those in trouble. The bailout meeting included executives such as W. L. Clayton of Anderson, Clayton and W. S. Farish and H. C. Weiss of Humble Oil. The arrangement was complicated: Humble Oil agreed to purchase an oil terminal company from Ross Sterling, which enabled Sterling to reduce his problem loans to Houston National, one of the troubled banks; Jones's National Bank of Commerce acquired the other troubled bank. Not surprisingly, in 1932 President Herbert Hoover appointed

Jones to his new Reconstruction Finance Corporation (R F C), an agency which for the next decade spent billions of federal dollars to bail out many banks, farms, and other businesses in bankruptcy. In 1933 Jones became R F C chair; he has been credited with restoring the health of the U.S. banking system.[28] Jones, later Secretary of Commerce, was a key figure in the extraordinarily powerful Business Council in the 1930s and 1940s. Jones provides a clear example of the importance of powerful capitalistic actors at both the economic and state levels.

Some Other Members of the Suite 8F Crowd: James A. Elkins, Sr.

A trio of other business leaders—Herman and George Brown and Judge James A. Elkins, Sr.—was second only to Jones in dominating Houston and Texas affairs in this period. Coming to Houston in 1917, Elkins was one of the founders of the law firm Vinson and Elkins; in the 1980s it was one of the nation's largest. In 1924 Elkins founded what became Houston's largest bank, the First City Bancorporation, in the 1980s; this bank was the first leading Houston bank with serious financial difficulty in the late 1980s, to the extent of being bailed out by the federal government. Elkins was instrumental in the creation of American General Insurance Co., the South's largest insurance firm. Elkins's law firm and bank grew in tandem; the clients of the one were often referred to the other. Reportedly, Elkins's firm, specializing in petroleum law, serviced local oil entrepreneurs who did not like eastern law firms. By the early 1950s Judge Elkins served on the boards of four affiliate banks, thus unofficially creating a Texas banking empire. Over his lifetime Elkins served as a director of many banks, railroads, oil companies, and insurance firms. Like his associates in the Suite 8F crowd Elkins participated in the system of interlocking directorates by which individual capitalists bind together the corporate institutions of modern capitalism.

Elkins was reputed to be very powerful in local and Texas politics. Take the case of Mayor Holcombe, who in the 1930s came to be linked to the Suite 8F crowd. Working with the core elite, Holcombe was aggressive in sponsoring major infrastructure improvements such as roads and sewage systems. However, in 1952 the Suite 8F crowd interviewed county judge Roy Hofheinz and decided that he should be the next mayor of the city. Even though he had already printed up campaign literature, Holcombe was asked to retire, which he did. Reportedly James Elkins was a key figure in removing Holcombe. However, when Hofheinz became too progressive, Elkins and others supported Holcombe again in his successful 1955 campaign to defeat Hofheinz.[29]

The Brown Brothers: Partners
in Large-Scale Construction

Herman and George Brown were among the most powerful Houstonians during their adult lifetimes, which spanned the decades from the 1920s to the 1980s. In the 1920s Herman created the small construction firm which became Brown and Root, later one of the world's largest construction and development firms. This company headquarters was moved from Austin to Houston in the mid-1920s, and the company grew steadily from the late 1930s to the 1960s, depending heavily on federally subsidized large-scale construction projects. During this period George made his Suite 8F in the Lamar Hotel famous as a gathering place for men like Jesse Jones and Judge Elkins as well as prominent politicians like Lyndon B. Johnson and Sam Rayburn. George and Herman Brown were particularly effective in building bridges to politicians at the national level. Indeed, New Deal contracts helped establish Brown and Root as a principal construction firm and saved the company from bankruptcy in the 1930s.

During the 1960s George Brown's corporation, Texas Eastern, became the major developer of a thirty-two-block project in downtown Houston called Houston Center. Brown got city government permission to build the innovative megastructure over city streets, gaining millions of square feet at a small cost. The projected megastructure, initially projected to be twice the size of the World Trade Center in New York, was called by some the largest urban development project in world history. I will assess this project in more detail in Chapter 7. Moreover, unlike other members of Houston's postwar elite, the omnipresent Brown was the target of overt protests against his activities. For example, Rice University students would occasionally protest his presence on their campus, because Brown and Root had done much construction during the Viet Nam War.[30]

An Insurance Entrepreneur: Gus Wortham

Another important figure in the Suite 8F crowd was Gus Wortham. Founder of the American General Insurance Co., one of the twenty largest in the United States, Wortham was an outside activist for the Suite 8F clique. The young Wortham had served on the Texas Fire Rating Board; he subsequently used the knowledge gained to set up his own insurance company. By the mid-1920s Wortham had the legal authority to create a major insurance company in Houston, which he accomplished with the financial backing of James Elkins,

Sr., and Jesse Jones. During the 1930s Wortham also began investing in Houston real estate, investments which buttressed his substantial wealth.[31] Wortham played a central role in linking the Suite 8F crowd to the larger business and civic communities in Houston. He was a public figure; he chaired fund drives for charities, served on the board of trustees for Rice University, and worked on behalf of art institutions, including the Houston Grand Opera, the Houston Symphony, and the Society for the Performing Arts. Explicitly recognizing the importance of local cultural institutions in attracting outside investors to the city, the Suite 8F elite fostered local colleges and art facilities.

An Oil Entrepreneur: James Abercrombie

Between the 1930s and the 1960s independent oil capitalists were not as prominent in running Houston as one might expect. But one oil entrepreneur who was a member of the 8F crowd was James Abercrombie. Abercrombie had gone into the oil drilling business in the late 1910s; in 1920 he created the Cameron Iron Works, which eventually became one of the world's leading oil tools manufacturing firms—with 7,000 employees and sixteen plants scattered from the United States to Europe and Asia before the mid-1980s recession. Abercrombie was a major figure, together with the reclusive Howard Hughes, in putting Houston at the center of the world's oil tools and services industry. And he also played an important role in local philanthropic activities, including building up the Texas Medical Center.[32]

Lesser Figures

From time to time a number of business and civic leaders have been mentioned by various writers as members of the Suite 8F crowd, including Leon Jaworski of Watergate fame, R. E. "Bob" Smith, a prominent oil entrepreneur, Walter Mischer, a real estate developer and banker, and former governor William P. Hobby and his wife Oveta Culp Hobby. The Hobbys were influential because they controlled certain communications media in the city, including a principal newspaper and a major TV station. Oveta Culp Hobby was one of few women ever to exert much power in Houston. One of the most influential of Houston's oil entrepreneurs was Bob Smith, who played a central role in real estate and politics for three decades; he invested in thousands of acres of land on the suburban edge of the city. A later addition to the group, Walter Mischer built a banking empire called Allied Bancshares and was important as a local developer.[33]

Most members of the 8F crowd had become known to ordinary Houstonians by the 1950s. Indeed, by the 1950s the city sometimes seemed to be bragging about its successful elite. A visitor to the Houston International Airport in 1955 would have found fifteen portraits of Houston's prominent leaders proudly displayed on a restaurant wall. These included members of the Suite 8F crowd (Elkins, George Brown, Abercrombie, Smith, and Hobby), the maverick Hugh R. Cullen, the leading partners in two major law firms, as well as less influential civic and religious leaders. City officials installing the portraits included the most powerful members of the local elite but may have added less powerful people to play down the power of the core elite.

Outside the Suite 8F Crowd: Other Business Leaders

The Internationalist: Will Clayton

Several important capitalists remained largely outside the local Suite 8F establishment in this period. Two of these had roots in the Anderson, Clayton firm, a major Houston trading corporation. Monroe D. Anderson, one of the founders, became wealthy in the 1920s, and he translated some of his wealth into philanthropic contributions to university and medical center developments in Houston. Will Clayton played an especially important part in tying the Houston business community to the world market system and to the federal government. Clayton was often the "public man" for Anderson, Clayton; the firm became nationally visible when it was accused of monopolizing the cotton marketing industry during a series of congressional investigations between 1928 and 1936. Clayton vigorously defended the company at the hearings.

During the Great Depression the firm expanded its multinational operations. The early years of the depression resulted in a drop in cotton exports to Europe and a significant increase in foreign cotton production. As a result, U.S. cotton trading never resumed its earlier importance, and over the next few decades Anderson, Clayton withdrew from cotton marketing and developed as a conglomerate. With expanding international interests, Clayton emerged as one of the outspoken defenders of worldwide enterprise and opponents of protectionism. Clayton also moved into federal government positions. He served on the cotton committee of the War Industries Board during World War I. In the 1930s, when Jesse Jones became Federal Loan Administrator, he brought Clayton into the government as his deputy.

After Jones, Clayton may well have been the most important link between the Houston and Texas business elites and the federal government in this period. After serving as Jones's deputy, Clayton was appointed Assistant Secretary of State, in which position he reportedly played a principal role as one architect of the famous Marshall Plan. Clayton was also very active in the Business Council, which took an internationalist position on issues. Clayton served as a chief trade negotiator for the United States after World War II and negotiated the first international (G A T T) trade agreement. Clayton helped integrate the Houston business community into international markets and politics. These extensive outside activities may account for his lesser role in the local power structure.[34]

In addition to Suite 8F figures and to Clayton, the larger power structure of the city, according to one 1960 study, included two Humble Oil (later Exxon) executives, Morgan J. Davis and Rex Baker. However, these men seem to have devoted most of their time to Humble Oil and the oil business. Hines H. Baker and W. B. Bates were mentioned in the same study as partners in leading law firms, but they do not surface elsewhere as influential leaders, except on a few specialized issues. Another prominent local lawyer, Dillon Anderson, was very active in national politics as special assistant to President Eisenhower but seldom in local matters. This study of the local elite reported that a few other executives were mentioned locally as influential: Palmer Bradley, a Sun Oil executive; Al Parish, head of Houston Light and Power; Lamar Fleming, head of Anderson, Clayton; and L. F. McCollum, an executive at a firm then called Continental Oil. It would appear, however, that these latter influentials played a less significant role than 8F members on most major local issues.[35]

Flamboyant Oil Entrepreneurs

Houston's business elite has often been misperceived by the outside mass media. For several decades media analysts have commonly emphasized certain local oil entrepreneurs in assessing the dominant families in the city. Two of the most famous media stars were Glen H. McCarthy and Hugh R. Cullen. Glen H. McCarthy began oil wildcatting in the 1930s and 1940s. Flush with wealth from his successful oil and gas ventures, he built the famous Shamrock Hotel in an undeveloped area several miles south of the center of Houston. At the time, the $21-million hotel was one of the most opulent in the United States, with mahogany paneling, televisions in rooms, its own tailor, and a unique swimming pool. Painted in many shades of green in honor of McCarthy's Irish heritage, the hotel was opened in 1949 with a champagne party attended by 50,000 people, including Hollywood stars. The hotel was widely viewed in the national media as the symbol of "nouveau riche" Houston.

Hugh R. Cullen started out in real estate ventures; he purchased land along the ship channel, a venture which brought him into conflict with Jesse Jones. He did not prosper in these early ventures, but his fortunes changed rapidly as he got into wildcatting where a series of oil wells brought him great wealth. However, Cullen reportedly was not much of a team player, and this seems to have reduced his local power. After World War II Cullen became an active supporter of Senator Joe McCarthy and other anticommunism crusades, including the Liberty Lobby. He supported anticommunist groups in Houston and helped to secure the firing of the chancellor of the University of Houston, whom Cullen and others mistakenly thought a communist. In addition, Cullen gave most of his personal oil fortune away to the University of Houston and to local hospitals. For this reason, he is perhaps the best known of Houston's oil philanthropists.[36]

A comprehensive analysis of Houston's flamboyant oil men would also have to include the mysterious and reclusive Howard Hughes, who inherited a major Houston oil tools firm, Hughes Tool, from his father. Of course, the eccentric Hughes played little role in Houston's local power elite.

Integrating the Business Community: Law Firms, Banks, and Other Corporations

Essential Corporate Ties

The Suite 8F elite, as well as its predecessors and successor elites, was not composed of loners. A corporate base undergirded the power of these leaders. Each person founded at least one major corporation. Jesse Jones founded the bank that became Texas Commerce Bancshares, one of the nation's largest, and he was instrumental in the founding of Tenneco, a Fortune 500 conglomerate. Judge James Elkins, Sr., founded the First City Bancorporation and the Vinson and Elkins law firm. Gus Wortham founded American General, the insurance conglomerate. And Herman and George Brown were the entrepreneurs behind Brown and Root, the world-class construction firm, and Texas Eastern, a Fortune 500 energy company. Speaking of his friends in the power structure, George Brown once said that "we just formed one corporation after another after that. Business was more fun in those days."[37]

In addition to these corporate ties, most members of this business aristocracy built a web of interlocking relationships to numerous corporations. Each served as directors on the boards of other companies, some locally headquartered firms created by other members of the 8F elite and some northern-based multinationals. The ties between the firms headed by Jesse Jones and other Texas and national firms reached legendary proportions. In the late 1940s, for example, Jones's National Bank of Commerce was linked through interlocking directorates with the Houston Deep Water Land Co., Gulf Oil, Dillon, Reed and Co., the Missouri Pacific railroad, Anderson, Clayton, and Wessen Oil, to mention only a few. Burch's research on 1960 linkages found that George Brown served on the board of I T T and his brother Herman served on the board of A R M C O steel, while Gus Wortham served on the board of Missouri-Pacific and James A. Elkins, Jr., son of Judge Elkins, held a position on the board of Eastern Airlines. These linkages indicate the Suite 8F crowd's tie to national and international corporate networks. Moreover, several of the Suite 8F group had ties to the mass media. Both of Houston's major newspapers (*Post* and *Chronicle*), one major TV station, and several local radio stations were at times controlled by members of the group.[38]

Law Firms and Banks

The core members of the Suite 8F group were founders of, or major figures in, leading banks and law firms. It is sometimes difficult to determine where the corporate structure of the major law firms ends and the corporate structure of leading banks begins; substantial overlapping has been characteristic of these interrelationships. Houston's law firms have not only played an integrating and service role for a succession of local business cliques, but they have also linked Houston firms to large corporations outside the city. The large law firms have been central players in local and national politics. Three of the nation's largest law firms, all based in Houston, were linked to the Suite 8F crowd: Vinson and Elkins, Fulbright and Jaworski, and Baker & Botts. Since the 1930s these firms have been part of the glue binding together Houston's establishment.

Each law firm has had ties to bankholding companies. One of the largest, First City Bancorporation, has been closely associated with Vinson and Elkins. The City National Bank and Elkins's First National Bank merged in 1956 to become the First City National Bank, the immediate progenitor of First City Bancorporation. In the early 1980s James A. Elkins, Jr. headed that bankholding firm. The board of directors for the bank included a rancher, the president of Cameron Iron Works, a former ambassador to Great Britain, and executives from Exxon, Superior Oil, Gulf States Utilities, and L T V. The close ties between these banks and leading oil and gas companies are visible at the level of the board of directors.[39]

The law firm of Fulbright and Jaworski has been linked with Anderson,

Clayton as well as with the bank called Southwest Bancshares. The late Leon Jaworski, of the law firm Fulbright and Jaworski, was chair of the board of Southwest Bancshares. Moreover, in the early 1980s Houston's most powerful bank was Texas Commerce Bancshares, a bank initially shaped by Jesse Jones. In the decade after World War II the predecessor bank to Texas Commerce Bancshares, Jones's National Bank of Commerce, did very well. By July 1949 the National Bank of Commerce was Houston's largest; in 1964 it merged with the Texas National Bank, creating the Texas National Bank of Commerce, with a quarter of all local bank deposits. The board of directors then included many top oil and gas executives and executives from a major supermarket chain, a newspaper chain, a food company, and a world-class construction company. In addition, Texas Commerce Bancshares has had close ties to local law firms, including Baker & Botts, whose managing partner served as a director of the bank.[40]

Integrating the Business Elite: Clubs, Ranches, and Private Schools

In his work on the national ruling class in the United States, G. William Domhoff has shown that this class is not simply a category of powerful individuals, but rather a *socially integrated* group, one tied together by clubs, schools, social life, and intermarriages. This pattern holds true for business elites in Houston and other Texas cities. By the 1910s and 1920s Houston's business community had created a number of private clubs. For example, in 1921 the membership of the Eagle Lake Rod and Gun Club, a social club with facilities on Eagle Lake, included key members of Houston's establishment— W. S. Farish (Humble Oil), James A. Baker and James A. Baker, Jr. (Baker & Botts), Howard Hughes (Hughes Tool), and H. C. Weiss (Humble Oil). This particular club integrated the oil and law sectors of the business community.[41]

A number of business clubs and country clubs facilitated the integration of the 8F elite. In addition to the informal social club at the Browns' Lamar Hotel suite, associations such as the Houston Country Club, the Bayou Club, the Ramada Club, and the Houston Club were meeting places. The gatherings there linked core leaders with "leg men" who implemented their decisions. An examination of the 1963 *Houston Social Register* (see Table 5.2) reveals ties several members of the Suite 8F crowd had to five major clubs.[42] The Suite 8F crowd was well-integrated socially. Members belonged to these five major country and social clubs, with each person belonging to at least two. It is in-

TABLE   5.2.
Club Memberships (1963)

Members of the Suite 8F Crowd	Houston Country Club	River Oaks Country Club	Bayou Club	Ramada Club	Houston Club
J. S. Abercrombie	x	x	x	x	x
George R. Brown		x	x		
Herman Brown	x			x	x
Leon Jaworski	x				x
Gus Wortham	x			x	
R. E. "Bob" Smith		x			x
William P. Hobby (Oveta Culp)	x		x	x	x

SOURCE: *Houston Social Register* (Houston, 1963).

teresting that the controversial oil entrepreneurs Hugh Roy Cullen and Gene McCarthy are not in the 1963 *Social Register,* even though they were the two most famous Houstonians in the national mass media. Moreover, a review of the *Social Register* suggests that a distinction between locally oriented leaders and nationally focused leaders might be hazarded. Certain business leaders, such as Morgan Davis, top executive and director at Humble Oil, held several memberships in these clubs, yet their names rarely surface as important in local decision making. Apparently they limited their local activities to their particular corporations and left most broader business decisions to members of the Suite 8F crowd.

The Ranch

Another aspect of the social integration of the Houston elite is "the ranch" and the parties associated with this venerable institution. Regular pilgrimages to ranches and hunting leases have been important in building social bonds in Texas. Lyndon B. Johnson's ranch in central Texas played this role. And one of Gus Wortham's ranches—the Nine Bar in Cypress, Texas—was on occasion a gathering place for the wealthy and the powerful, including the Suite 8F crowd and its associated politicians, Lyndon Baines Johnson and John Connally, as well as members of the national ruling class such as Winthrop Rockefeller.[43]

Ties to the National Ruling Class

I have already shown that Houston's business establishments, such as the Suite 8F crowd, were not composed of isolated or independent "cowboy" capitalists but rather were well-integrated—locally, regionally, and nationally—through interlocking directorates and social gatherings at clubs and ranches. But there were other important national connections. During the 1960s and 1970s prominent members of the business community belonged to the premier private clubs binding together the national business elite. Houstonians belonged to the Links Club in New York, the Duquesne in Pittsburgh, and the Bohemian in San Francisco. Among the Houston members of the Boston Club (located in New Orleans) were Morgan Davis, Sr. (Humble Oil) and John W. Mecom, a wealthy local oil entrepreneur. George Brown and James A. Elkins, Jr., were members of the Links Club, as were Houstonians Gardiner Symonds and Francis G. Coates.[44]

Moreover, in the mid-1960s the Houston Committee of the Council of Foreign Relations—a principal organization of the dreaded Eastern Establishment—had no less than sixty-five members, including foremost members of the local business community. Among its members were Leon Jaworski, W. L. Clayton, John T. Jones (nephew of Jesse Jones), and W. P. Hobby, Jr. Also included on the Houston Committee were a number of other business leaders, including Dillon Anderson, a director at Westinghouse and Monsanto; J. C. Hutcheson III, a director at Schlumberger; and Gardiner Symonds, director at a Chicago bank and on numerous oil company boards. Four Houstonians, including George Brown, were members of the extraordinarily powerful Business Council in the late 1960s, a national group whose early development was fostered by Jesse Jones in Washington, D.C., during the 1930s.

The children of Houston's business elite have also been integrated into the social networks of the national ruling class. Tabulations by Domhoff indicate that many of Houston's leaders have gone to northern prep schools and colleges or have sent their children to such schools. The numbers of Houstonians who went to non-Texas prep schools in the years running from 1910 to 1970 were:

> Kent—12
> St. Mark's—3
> University School—8
> Portsmouth Abbey—5
> Episcopal High School—54
> Hill—60

Cranbrook—8
Woodbury Forest—37
St. Paul's—27
Deerfield—31
Hotchkiss—21
Lawrenceville—87
Milton Academy—3
St. George's—4
St. Louis—7[45]

Included among the graduates of these northern prep schools have been James A. Baker, Jr., James A. Baker III (Chief of Staff and Secretary of the Treasury under Ronald Reagan), and James A. Elkins, Jr. Surprisingly, Domhoff's data on the children of Houston's business elite indicate that a large proportion of them have gone to East Coast colleges and universities, including Ivy League schools; the attendance figures rival those for the University of Texas.

The Houston Chamber of Commerce: Action Arm of the Business Leadership

A Voluntary Association of Citizens

The Business League of the late nineteenth and early twentieth century was renamed the Houston Chamber of Commerce in 1910. Over the next several decades it was destined to become an important action arm for a succession of business elites. The chamber's top officials saw their organization as "a voluntary association of interested citizens that does those things for the community which most people think just happen," simply as one part of the "volunteer sector" in Houston.[46] However, this undue modesty obscures the real significance of the chamber, which has been in effect the action arm of the business leadership for decades. The chamber has been used as a forum for the airing of ideas, a channel of study and investigation, and, as I will demonstrate in the next chapter, often the de facto "planning department" for the city.

Although the most powerful business leaders have been members of the chamber, they frequently have not played a visible, public leadership role, preferring instead to operate behind the scenes. For example, the Suite 8F elite operated in various ways. On some issues they worked behind the scenes;

for other issues the 8F leaders would create a general committee of twelve to twenty people, some from the elite and some from outside, to deal publicly with a particular problem. In many cases the chamber officials would be encouraged by Suite 8F leaders to get involved in research and planning. However, with the demise of the Suite 8F group came greater independence for the chamber and a broadening of the city's business leadership.

The Top Officers of the Chamber:
An Overview

An examination of the chamber's executive committee and board of directors demonstrates that the city's dominant economic sectors have usually been represented. In 1924 the chamber included among its top six officers three local bank vice-presidents, an insurance executive, and a railroad president. On the larger executive board were W. L. Clayton of Anderson, Clayton and W. R. Scott, president of Southern Pacific. Not one of the top sixteen chamber officials was primarily in the oil business. Most were bankers, cotton merchants, railroad presidents, or retail and wholesale merchants. Then came the oil company expansion of the 1920s. By 1930 among those on the executive committee and board of directors were the vice-president of Hughes Tool, a vice-president of a major bank, president of a steamship company, president of a grain company, a vice-president of Humble Oil, president of Houston Oil, six banking executives, a vice-president of Southern Pacific, and a number of major local merchants. In 1930 the extensive participation of oil industry officials on the board signaled the growing dominance of oil in Houston's economy.

In the 1930s and 1940s the Chamber of Commerce became one action arm of the Suite 8F crowd. All Suite 8F members belonged to the chamber; some served as officers. Gus Wortham was perhaps the most active. In the mid-1930s he was a two-term president of the chamber, and he served on the nominating committee of the chamber for the rest of the 1930s. In the late 1940s he was a director of the U.S. Chamber of Commerce. In this fashion he tied the Suite 8F crowd into the organizations of the national business community.[47]

By 1949, the year General Dwight Eisenhower spoke to the annual chamber banquet, the executive board and board of directors of the chamber included a construction company president, a vice-president of Humble Oil, several other oil company executives, as well as George Brown and James A. Elkins, two well-known Suite 8F names. The 1959 executive committee of the chamber included another member of the Suite 8F group, Leon Jaworski, as well as vice-presidents of Shell Oil and Houston Lighting and Power, the president of a steel company, the general manager of Southwestern Bell, and several attorneys. The 1969 executive committee included the president of Brown and Root, a partner with Vinson and Elkins, the president of American General Life Insurance Company, and several major oil-gas company executives. Among the other directors were James A. Elkins, Jr., and W. P. Hobby, Jr. Also on the board were the president of Jesse Jones's Texas National Bank of Commerce and the president of Tenneco. Two major developers appear among the directors for the first time, Gerald D. Hines and Walter Mischer, the latter sometimes mentioned as a later addition to the Suite 8F crowd.

On occasion, some members of the business establishment tried to set up alternative action organizations, but none replaced the chamber as the visible arm of the elite. For example, in 1955, R. E. Smith tried to bring the leading men of Houston into an official organization called the "Committee of 1,000," a group modeled on the successful Dallas business organization called the Dallas Citizen's Council, but his efforts were unsuccessful. Smith was more successful in building up the Petroleum Club, an exclusive club now at the top of the Exxon skyscraper in the downtown area, a place where Houston's oil industry decision makers have held court since the late 1950s.[48]

The Chamber in Action: Lobbying for Houston Industry

The chamber has functioned as Houston's unofficial booster organization and economic development council for many decades. By the late 1920s chamber officials were working vigorously to expand foreign trade. The chamber set up a Foreign Trade Committee and tours to Latin America; it aggressively promoted Houston as an international center. As one chamber official put it, "present day competition between cities makes necessary the use of the most intelligent salesmanship in the race for supremacy."[49] In the summer of 1930, a chamber-sponsored group of industrial and commercial leaders made a 5,700-mile tour of the East, North, and Middle West to sell the city to investors outside the region. The train tour went to dozens of cities—from Houston to Chicago, Detroit, New York, Philadelphia, and St. Louis. Houston specialists had conferences with corporate officials at each stop. The emphasis was on attracting new rubber, iron and steel, furniture, and chemical firms to the Houston area. During the 1930s and 1940s articles in the chamber magazine *Houston* explicitly proclaimed the goal of "selling" growth and development in Houston.[50]

A Note on Wealth, Arts, and Charitable Contributions

Historically, the chamber has also been active in the development of the local arts and medical institutions. Houston capitalists have developed foundations to support the fine arts, but the chamber seems to have provided much of the ideological framework, particularly by arguing publicly for the civic and economic significance of developing the fine arts, which were seen as a way of putting the city on the national map.

Houston's civic-minded capitalists, including its real estate and oil entrepreneurs, have given many millions of dollars to a variety of arts and medical causes over the course of the city's history. With the help of contributions from the public-spirited Hogg family and other local entrepreneurs the city had developed a nationally recognized orchestra by the 1960s. By 1966 the orchestra was playing in an impressive Jones Hall, one built with a major donation from Houston Endowment, the foundation created by Jesse Jones. The Jones's foundation also provided the land for the nationally prominent Alley Theatre. The Houston Art Museum prospered with substantial contributions from Ima Hogg and other members of the Hogg family, as well as from the Brown Foundation. John and Dominique de Menil, prominent figures at Schlumberger, a French oil tools company operating in Texas, donated an ecumenical chapel designed by architect Philip Johnson to house abstract paintings by Mark Rothko. Rice University and the University of Houston have benefited greatly from the philanthropy of prominent Houstonians, including William M. Rice, Hugh R. Cullen, George R. Brown, Jesse H. Jones, W. W. Fondren, J. S. Abercrombie, and M. D. Anderson.

During the 1940s the Texas Medical Center was conceived by Houston's business leaders, and substantial contributions from the M. D. Anderson Foundation helped establish the Baylor College of Medicine and the M. D. Anderson cancer hospital as anchors of the medical complex a few miles south of downtown. Many of the city's civic-minded oil entrepreneurs have contributed substantial sums to the construction of nearly a dozen hospitals and clinics for the treatment of diseases. I have already noted the substantial contributions of Cullen and Abercrombie to creating the medical complex. While the philanthropy of these entrepreneurs did lay the foundation for a more diversified economy in the Houston metropolis, they did not seem to have that goal in mind. Their concerns seem to have been with the health of particular groups of people, such as disabled children, or perhaps in some cases with their own mortality. Yet their charitable contributions had the very important consequences of creating a biotech and med-tech complex which in the long run has played an important role in diversifying the city's economy.[51]

The Business Elites and Several Levels of Government

Elite Involvement at the Federal Level

Houston's history is a history of the business establishment creating, shaping, and running local governmental bodies, as well as securing aid from and participating in the running of State of Texas agencies and of certain federal agencies. Houston's business leaders have been involved with national politics and the federal government since before World War I. I have previously noted the activities of Edwin Parker and John Kirby, but Jesse Jones was perhaps the most active at the federal level. Jones was a major force behind the proposal to the U.S. Congress to pay half the cost of improving the Houston ship channel. In the early 1900s Jones led a group of business leaders to Washington, D.C., to convince Congress to fund half the cost of dredging Buffalo Bayou; he headed the Houston Harbor Board that supervised the dredging project, completed in 1914 and celebrated with a cannon firing triggered by President Wilson from the White House. Wilson later invited Jones to be Assistant Secretary of the Treasury and Secretary of Commerce.

Jones had become a major powerbroker in the Democratic party by the 1920s. He was a Texas delegate to the Democratic convention in 1924 and became director of finance for that ill-fated presidential campaign. In the late 1920s Jones used his position in the Democratic party to put Houston on the political map. When the time came for various city elites to bid for the location of the 1928 Democratic party convention, San Francisco's business leadership offered $250,000. Jones himself countered with a successful recommendation that Houston be chosen as the site, wrote out a personal check for $200,000 and promised a 25,000-seat hall for the convention; it was barely completed in time for the delegates to see the Catholic New Yorker Al Smith nominated by Franklin Roosevelt in Houston, a Protestant town of the Old South. Moreover, during the 1930s and 1940s Jones served President Roosevelt as head of the RFC, as Federal Loan Administrator, and Secretary of Commerce. Yet during these years Jones kept in constant contact with his National Bank of Commerce back home; he set bank policy and attended some board meetings while a Washington official.[52]

Beginning in the 1930s, Houston and other Texas cities had a lot of power-ful friends in Washington, D.C. John Nance Garner, as House member and vice-president, had represented Texas for decades. A Texas senator chaired the Senate military affairs committee, while Texas House members chaired the judiciary, agriculture, and rivers and harbors committees. Between the 1930s and the 1960s there were many direct links between Houston's business leadership and the federal government. An important politician associated with the Suite 8F crowd was House Majority Leader and Speaker of the House Sam Rayburn. In his 1944 campaign Rayburn faced a tough opponent, and, although regarded as "not conservative enough" by many Texans, Rayburn received behind-the-scenes backing from the Suite 8F crowd, particularly Judge Elkins.[53] But perhaps the most important politician associated with the Suite 8F crowd was Lyndon B. Johnson.

The Brown brothers were effective in cultivating national politicians. Dur-ing the Great Depression New Deal contracts helped save Brown and Root from bankruptcy. In the mid-1930s the Browns had received a federal contract to build a dam project near Austin, but Brown and Root's contract needed further congressional approval. The brothers helped get a young New Deal representative named Lyndon B. Johnson elected. Within two weeks of his arrival in Washington, Johnson got the necessary approval for the dam. Johnson became a full-fledged member of the Suite 8F crowd. The Brown brothers were sometimes called "New Deal capitalists" because of the federal contracts they received, which in the 1930s and 1940s included dams, naval air stations, and warships. After World War II the Brown brothers bid on two war surplus pipelines, and the Texas Eastern Co., now a Fortune 500 firm, was created to operate the pipelines.[54]

During World War II there was much contact between the local business leadership and the federal government, in addition to the individual work of Jones, the Browns, Lyndon Johnson, and Will Clayton. For example, during the war the chamber was involved in bringing war projects to the Houston area. Correspondence between chamber officials and federal officials was fre-quent. More than a year before Pearl Harbor, W. N. Blanton, general man-ager, wrote to Albert Thomas, Houston's prominent House member; Blanton sent two copies of a chamber "brief" presenting Houston's case for being the location of a major airplane plant. Thomas sent the brief to the war depart-ment and received a speedy reply from the Assistant Secretary of War. Simi-larly, in 1945, the secretary of the chamber's military affairs committee lobbied Thomas, the Secretary of War, the commanding general of the Army Air Forces, and the entire Texas delegation to Congress in an attempt to keep a military installation called Ellington Field in South Houston and to maintain the Army Air Field in Galveston.[55]

After World War II the ties to the federal government remained strong. From the 1950s to the 1970s a number of Texans connected to the Suite 8F crowd played significant parts in the federal government. In addition to Lyndon Johnson's role, Oveta Culp Hobby served as the first Secretary of Health, Education and Welfare in Washington, D.C. Former Texas governor and partner at Houston's Vinson and Elkins law firm, John Connally, served as the Secretary of Navy; in 1987 Connally faced business and personal bankruptcy, in part because of real estate investments that relied upon continuing population growth in Texas. Leon Jaworski served as special Watergate prosecutor in the early 1970s. Other members of the local business community also served in Washington, including Dillon Anderson as national security adviser in the 1950s.

These ties to the federal government were sometimes used by local business leaders to spur the growth and development of Houston. For example, study the relationship between Leon Jaworski, a member of the Suite 8F crowd and sometime president of the chamber, and Houston Representative Albert Thomas. On December 16, 1959, Thomas wrote Jaworski a letter of congratulations on his election as president of the chamber and said that "whenever I can cooperate with you, the other officers and directors, it will be my pleasure to do so. Don't hesitate to call on me whenever I can be of any service whatsoever." On April 1, 1960, Thomas again wrote Jaworski asking for the chamber's active participation in supporting "the project of widening and deepening the San Jacinto River as an adjunct to the Port of Houston." In a follow-up letter, Thomas wrote to Jaworski: "You are a honey. You came through with flying colors. I know that the resolution of the Houston Chamber of Commerce will have great influence with the Port Commission. As I mentioned to you before, this project should be consummated now for the future growth and welfare of Harris County." Later, Thomas wrote Jaworski saying that he had "enjoyed visiting" with Jaworski in his office in Washington. He further noted that Houston had been put on the F A A's airport program for a new airport, a major goal of the chamber. And in closing, Thomas reiterated his role as a foot soldier for the chamber: "Don't hesitate to call on me whenever there is any foot-work I can do for you. You have only to say the word."[56] This correspondence illustrates the importance of individuals in integrating the organizations and institutions of the society—in this case the federal government and a major business organization.

The N A S A Manned Spacecraft Center provides another example. In 1961 N A S A was seeking a site for its new Manned Spacecraft Center. Vice-President Lyndon Johnson was head of the National Aeronautics and Space Council. Working together with the Suite 8F crowd and Houston Representative Albert Thomas, who headed the key House committee, Johnson pressed vigorously for the Houston location. A major oil company entered the picture at this point. In 1938 Humble Oil Company (now Exxon) had bought 30,000 acres southeast of Houston for oil exploration. In the early 1960s the president of Humble Oil gave 1,000 acres of this land to Rice University, which Rice in turn gave to N A S A for the Space Center. As chair of the Rice board of trustees, George Brown had helped in arranging the land transfer. Brown and Root, later part of Halliburton Co., got a contract for architectural and other work on N A S A's $125-million project. Humble Oil announced major commercial and residential developments on the remaining land near the new N A S A center. Houston's climate and terrain were not the only factors in the N A S A decision; the aggressive boosterism of the local business elite and its connections with the federal state were critical.[57]

Elite Involvement in State of Texas Politics

In the Suite 8F crowd the Browns, Judge Elkins, and the Hobbys were particularly influential at the Texas government level. Herman Brown reportedly exercised a lot of influence over Texas legislators, so much so that he was described in 1951 as the "most powerful man in Texas." Moreover, William P. Hobby had served as governor of Texas from 1917 to 1921. After that service, Hobby and his wife, Oveta Culp Hobby, remained influential in Texas politics for many years.[58]

The law firms associated with the core members of the Houston business elite have been prominent in local and national politics. For several decades the law firms associated with the Suite 8F crowd played an important role in screening potential candidates for elective offices. A former state legislator has noted how "unless you get their [the top partners in the law firms] blessing, you couldn't get money from the client."[59] Most Texas governors between the late 1930s and the 1970s were the candidates of the big Texas law firms or were at least acceptable to them. These firms reportedly have had the power to kill bills in the committes of the Texas legislature.[60]

On occasion, the corrupt nature of some connections of Houston entrepreneurs to Texas politicians has been made public. Houston was the center of a major banking scandal in the 1970s. Frank Sharp, a prominent Houston developer, controlled the Sharpstown Bank. Federal investigations revealed that Speaker of the Texas House Gus Mutscher had pushed bills insuring bank deposits through the Texas legislature for Frank Sharp, a local banker and developer who sought this legislation. Sharp offered state officials stock in his company, including Mutscher, the governor of Texas, and several others.

Mutscher was convicted of accepting a bribe; other powerful politicians were tarnished by suspect trading in Sharp's stock and by no-collateral loans from Sharp's bank.[61]

Beyond the Texas and federal levels of government is, of course, the local state. The business elites and their chamber arm have been intimately involved in local government. I will reserve a detailed discussion of the local state for the next chapter.

The Changing Guard: An Expanded Business Leadership

The Rise of Corporate Leadership

By the 1970s the Suite 8F group was seriously weakened by the deaths of core members and the arrival of numerous corporate executives from across the nation. Between the late 1960s and the late 1970s more than 150 companies moved subsidiaries, divisions, or headquarters to Houston. The magazine *Texas Business* commented that the older movers and shakers in Texas were being eclipsed, in part, by urban-based capitalists from outside and that the "influx of corporations into the state has both enhanced and diminished the power of the business establishment."[62] Chandler Davidson has argued that since the 1970s the Suite 8F oligarchy has been replaced by "a more expanded oligarchy in which the key institution is the Chamber of Commerce, whose job is made more difficult by the politicized electorate."[63]

Since the 1970s there seems to have been an effort to include most executives of major Houston corporations on the Board of the Houston Chamber of Commerce (renamed the Greater Houston Chamber of Commerce in 1987). Table 5.3 presents a listing of the 1985–1986 Board of Directors of the chamber. On that board were the top executives of a majority of Houston's major industrial corporations, banks, newspapers, and law firms, as well as a token number of educational officials. Notably, the board includes representatives from most of the Suite 8F-origin firms: Vinson and Elkins; Fulbright and Jaworski; First City Bancorporation; Texas Commerce Bancshares; Texas Eastern; Tenneco; Brown and Root; and the Houston *Chronicle*. The oil, banking, insurance, law, and industrial firms created by the Suite 8F crowd still have major representatives at the chamber. However, the leading executives in these firms do not wield the great personal power the members of the Suite 8F crowd once did.

Corporate executives on the board signal the centrality of the large multinational corporation in contemporary Houston—firms that are major employers and taxpayers. And the executives in these firms often serve on the boards of other firms, the interlocking directorates used effectively by earlier generations of Houston's business leaders. Moreover, real estate developers constitute a distinctive interest group. Kenneth Schnitzer, head of the Century Development Corporation, symbolizes the growing importance of the major developers in Houston's business leadership in the 1970s and 1980s. As shown in Table 5.3, some developers—Schnitzer, Gerald D. Hines, Walter Mischer, George P. Mitchell—had become members of the chamber's board of directors. The developers have had an influence on the shift of the chamber to concerns with the decaying infrastructure of the city, as well as with the diversification of the economy.

Reportedly, in the late 1980s a few men on the chamber board had the power to significantly improve the chances of a favorable decision or block a major decision in a situation where the local business community faced either a crisis or a major development project. Although there is no longer a small oligarchy of a half dozen or so men running the city, there is still, depending on the particular issue, a group of men who constitute what one informant called a "yes or no" elite. These men—and they are still virtually all men— have substantial power to shape the economic and political agendas for the city of Houston.

With the decline in importance of the Suite 8F elite, the Ramada and Coronado clubs, River Oaks Country Club, and a few other socializing centers replaced George Brown's suite. Referring to the Ramada Club, a *Texas Monthly* article noted that "there is no place in Texas where so many people nominated as the most powerful in Texas meet so often and for such an extended period." [64] In addition to the Ramada Club, numerous social networks (for example, those maintained at ranch parties) continue to integrate the present incarnation of Houston's business elite, although the increased size of that elite has meant a less personalized exercise of power in the city.

Action by the New Elite

Since the 1970s the chamber's governing board of top corporate executives, although much larger than the old Suite 8F crowd, has pursued similar goals: to protect, enhance, and expand business investments in the city. But they have faced both a deteriorating infrastructure of roads, sewers, and water systems and the major economic recession of the 1980s. In Chapter 6 I will examine a broad array of chamber planning reports, prepared at the behest of

TABLE 5.3.
1985–1986 Board of Directors, Houston Chamber of Commerce

EUGENE V. AMOROSO, President & C.E.O., Coca-Cola Foods, A Division of the Coca-Cola Company

DANIEL C. ARNOLD, President, First City Bancorporation, Inc. of Texas

J. EVANS ATTWELL, Managing Partner, Vinson & Elkins

JOE E. BAILEY, Chairman & C.E.O., InterFirst Bank Houston, N.A.

T. J. BARLOW, Chairman of the Board, Anderson, Clayton & Company

JACK S. BLANTON, Chairman of the Board & C.E.O., Scurlock Oil Company

JOHN F. BOOKOUT, President & C.E.O., Shell Oil Company

W. J. BOWEN, Chairman of the Board & C.E.O., Transco Energy Company

ROBERT S. BRADEN, President, Turner Collie & Braden, Inc.

I. DAVID BUFKIN, Chairman of the Board & C.E.O., Texas Eastern Corporation

DR. WILLIAM T. BUTLER, President, Baylor College of Medicine

EARL C. CALKINS, Founder/Chairman, Mustang Tractor & Equipment Company

C. STERLING CORNELIUS, Chairman of the Board, President & C.E.O., Cornelius Nurseries, Inc.

ROBERT J. CRUIKSHANK, Partner-in-Charge, Deloitte, Haskins & Sells

CHARLES W. DUNCAN, JR., Duncan Interests

T. J. FEEHAN, Chairman of the Board, Brown & Root, Inc.

CHARLES E. FOSTER, Vice President, Southwestern Bell Telephone Company

GIBSON GAYLE, JR., Chairman of the Executive Committee, Fulbright & Jaworski

REX R. GIVAN, General Manager, South Texas Area, Sears Roebuck & Company

HARRY A. GOLEMON, President & Chairman, Golemon & Rolfe Associates, Inc.

ARTIE LEE HINDS, Investment/Management

GERALD D. HINES, Owner, Gerald D. Hines Interests

NED S. HOLMES, Chairman, Parkway Investments/Texas, Inc.

HOWARD W. HORNE, Chairman of the Board, The Horne Company, Realtors

RICHARD J. V. JOHNSON, President, The Houston *Chronicle*

DON D. JORDAN, Chairman of the Board & C.E.O., Houston Lighting & Power Company

JAMES L. KETELSEN, Chairman & C.E.O., Tenneco, Inc.

R. C. LASSITER, President & C.E.O., Zapata Corporation

KENNETH L. LAY, Chairman & C.E.O., Houston Natural Gas Corporation

DR. C. A. LeMAISTRE, President, University of Texas System Cancer Center at Houston

HENRY F. LeMIEUX, Chairman & C.E.O., Raymond International, Inc.

JAMES R. LESCH, Chairman of the Board & C.E.O., Hughes Tool Company

LEO E. LINBECK, JR., Chairman & C.E.O., Linbeck Construction Corporation

FRANK LORENZO, President & C.E.O., Texas Air Corporation and Chairman of the Board & C.E.O., Continental Airlines, Inc.

BEN F. LOVE, Chairman of the Board & C.E.O., Texas Commerce Bancshares, Inc.

LASKER M. MEYER, Chairman & C.E.O., Foley's

RANDAL MEYER, President, Exxon Company, U.S.A.

CHARLES MILLER, President & C.E.O., Criterion Group

WALTER MISCHER, SR., Chairman of the Board, Allied Bancshares, Inc.

GEORGE P. MITCHELL, Chairman and President, Mitchell Energy & Development Corp.

S. I. MORRIS, Partner, Morris/Aubry Architects

DENNIS E. MURPHREE, Chairman of the Board, Murphree Company

ROBERT R. ONSTEAD, Chairman, President & C.E.O., Randall's Food Markets, Inc.

ROBERT W. PAGE, SR., Chairman & C.E.O., Kellogg Rust, Inc.

MARCELLA D. PERRY, Senior Chairman of the Board, First Pasadena State Bank

JACK M. RAINS, Chairman of the Board, 3D/International

DR. BILLY R. REAGAN, General Superintendent, Houston Independent School District

J. HUGH ROFF, JR., Chairman of the Board, President & C.E.O., United Energy Resources, Inc.

JOE E. RUSSO, President, The Russo Companies

ROBERT T. SAKOWITZ, Chairman, President & C.E.O., Sakowitz, Inc.

KENNETH L. SCHNITZER, Chairman of the Board, Century Development Corporation

DR. LEONARD H. O. SPEARMAN, President, Texas Southern University

GEORGE F. ENDRES, JR., Financial Counselor, CIGNA Individual Financial Services

---

SOURCE: Houston Chamber of Commerce

these corporate executives, on such infrastructure issues as flooding and pollution; occasionally they have been implemented by city government.

Other Business Organizations in the 1970s and 1980s

In addition to the chamber, other powerful local business associations have shaped the city's development. Some organizations, such as the Houston Board of Realtors and the Associated General Contractors, tend to focus on real estate development issues, including opposition to ordinances designed to introduce substantial development and zoning controls for Houston. Semi-secret organizations such as the C Club, a powerful political action committee (P A C) created in the 1960s to promote "conservative government," also exist. The C Club became active in mayoral and other local political races in the 1970s and 1980s. Limited to 100 male members, the organization has pumped money into the campaigns of candidates whose philosophies pass conservative tests and has taken a more active role in recruiting candidates for public office. In 1985 the president of the C Club was quoted in the *Houston Business Journal*: "I don't think of it ('good old boys') as a derogatory term. It's what gets things done." [65] And he was right. The C Club is generally considered one of the more powerful P A Cs active in Texas politics. Another important organization was the Greater Houston Association; this group has important real estate interests. This organization worked in the 1980s to support local business candidates for governmental positions. Still, the C Club and Greater Houston Association are just two of several business organizations which have influenced Houston politics since the 1970s.

Conclusion: Several Generations of Business Influence

The data in this chapter illustrate the importance of conscious human actions in creating and maintaining social structures and social frameworks. In cities such as Houston economic and political structures do not develop according to inevitable general laws or inexorable necessity; instead, they develop in coordination with the conscious actions of human agents. But the decisions of the agents are not random. The array of possible decisions is limited or shaped by the economic and political frameworks inherited from the past. Business decisions, particularly investments made in consonance with the logic of capital accumulation, created or did not create jobs for workers in selected industries and created corporations. And then there are the business elite decisions to create the type of local government that can meet both business requirements and the pressures for services from the general citizenry. In the struggle for control over government, however, the contest has been one-sided. The business elite, in the form of Kirby or Jones, of the Suite 8F crowd or the chamber, has done much goal setting and planning for Houston; that elite has also provided government officials. Although all cities seem to have elite power structures, Houston's extraordinarily powerful capitalists, generally unrestrained by labor unions or local government officials, would seem distinctive even among U.S. cities. The instrumentalist view of the state seems well supported in the Houston case.

Powerful actors such as Baker, Kirby, and Jones show in their everyday decision making the importance of conscious actions in establishing the character of local institutional structures, both economic and political. Jesse Jones provides a conspicuous example of the importance of agency and actors in an adequate theory of urban development. If Jones had been a typical Texas oil entrepreneur, he probably could not have become the central link in the Houston and Texas political economies in the first five decades of the twentieth century. The fact that his own economic base was in the area of real estate development and banking seems to have given him both the vision and the resources to see beyond the parochial limits of the oil entrepreneurial philosophy to the broader social context. Jones was concerned with his own personal profit and that of his friends, but he could also see the need for linking institutions, those effectively binding capitalistic fractions together at both the local and the national levels. Thus, he worked to bring Gulf and Humble Oil to the city. And he recognized, more clearly than most, the extraordinary importance of the state in bailing out capitalism, especially in times of great crisis.

Moreover, Jones personally provided a critical node joining factions of local Houston capital and national capital, as well as two levels of the state and various levels of the business community. But these important points about the life and times of Jesse Jones do not exhaust the significance of Jones for a theoretical consideration of the dialectical articulation of institutional structures with agency. Jones's personality was very strong, and in government as in business he worked to maximize control over his own particular turf and territory as well as to foster capitalism in a broader sense. Thus, in his federal government activities he sometimes acted to preserve his own bureaucratic control, such as that over federal government loan programs, even at the expense of the interests of the U.S. business community more generally.[66] These influential urban actors and their consequential decisions illustrate the point that individuals provide the concrete connections between the abstract institutional structures of local and national economies and local and national states.

6

"The Business of Government
Is Business": Local Government
and Privatized Planning

In earlier chapters I have assessed the relationship between Houston's free enterprise system and the state. It is evident that the commitment to a free enterprise philosophy by elites has never meant a rejection of extensive governmental intervention; from the beginning there has been a willingness to use all levels of government to promote business goals.

Thus, in Chapter 3 I explored the early days of the city and the emergence of a close relationship between the free enterprise elites and the state, with at least three dimensions to that relationship: (1) control over and participation in the government itself; (2) subsidization in the form of social capital expenditures; and (3) the structuring of governmental regulation so that it facilitates capital accumulation. And in Chapter 5 I reviewed the succession of business elites and the elites' use of and participation in Texas and federal government agencies. My purpose in this chapter is to examine in more depth the structure of the city government and the way in which that local government has been connected to the business elites, with a particular emphasis on the last half of the twentieth century.

In contrast to cities like New York and Chicago, Houston has rarely had major grass-roots input into local political decisions, and there have been no immigrant political machines. For virtually all of its history, and without any major interruptions since the early 1900s, the local business elites have been able to dominate governmental decisions and nondecisions about most major issues, including determinations on planning and zoning mechanisms. One major consequence of this business dominance of the city government is the "planless city," a phrase meaning an absence of public planning. Houston's planning agencies have been relatively weak, often responding to the needs and demands of the city's business leaders and real estate developers. Much infrastructural and other planning has been done by outside state agencies and by private organizations such as the Chamber of Commerce. Houston developed *privatization* in planning and the deliverance of services long before that word had become part of the national debate on urban public policy. In the years between the early 1970s and the mid-1980s the city of Houston was often held up, in U.S. and foreign news media and in governmental policy circles, as a major example of how unrestrained free enterprise works better than state planning in creating a healthy and prosperous city. Attempting to evaluate these assumptions, in this chapter and Chapters 7, 8, and 9 I will explore various aspects of the character and consequences of unrestrained private development in the planless city.

The Structure and Character of Local Government

Dimensions of the Business Approach: Subsidies and Limited Regulation

Between the 1830s and the 1880s the business elites' basic approach to government was established; this approach would persist to the present. It included the aforementioned dimensions of control over political officials, public expenditures for business goals, and limited regulation.

The subsidization of infrastructure was an initial characteristic of the business approach to government in this free enterprise city. I have shown how the Allen brothers used local and Texas governments to subsidize their town creation project. Local government funds and bonds were used to build the infrastructure desired by business elites from the 1830s to the present. The tremendous expansion of infrastructure in the nineteenth century included a range of projects from grading principal streets and giving franchises to private utility companies to dredging Buffalo Bayou. Business leaders pressed for their priority projects, even if that meant neglecting the needs of neighborhoods for basic public services; they focused their concern on the business areas. The business solutions to various infrastructure crises included the issuance of millions of dollars in municipal government bonds for city projects. Subsequent business elites pursued this general approach to infrastructural development, but none of them would secure substantial citizen input into the decision making. Thus in Chapter 4 I examined the extensive use of public bonds to fund a broad array of business-generated support projects in recent decades. Public bonds have been used to create a massive international airport, the huge Astrodome, and a major convention center.

I have also documented the solicitation of federal funds by the business elite for a range of infrastructure projects in the twentieth century, including a variety of New Deal construction projects—for example, the refurbishment of the city's roads and schools—and the recurrent dredging of the Houston ship channel. Federal subsidization can also be seen in the local elite's seeking the N A S A Space Center and other military-industrial facilities for the Houston metropolitan area.

The third dimension of the business approach to local government mentioned above involves regulation. In earlier chapters I discussed the opposition of the Houston business community to most types of regulation. In particular, the federal regulations tied to social programs, as well as most real estate regulations, have been anathema to the business elites. In the postwar years opposition to federal funding for most social welfare programs and a variety of community programs remained strong among business leaders. The city government rejected federal aid for community programs and public housing; and the school board at times even rejected school lunch money.

In addition, the business community has been touchy about the regulation of development. In contrast to most other major cities, Houston had *no* federal urban renewal program. Many real estate developers and other business leaders considered such programs to be socialist because of government regulations covering such funds. Of course, the business leadership has not opposed all forms of regulation, for they have begged for regulation when it suited their business purposes, as in the case of the overproduction of oil in the East Texas oil fields in the 1930s. This rejection of governmental regulation can also be seen as limiting taxation to a low level. To maintain the city's image of fiscal conservatism (in the 1970s Houston was the only major city with a A A A bond rating by Wall Street), for decades the local elite has kept government operating expenditures and property taxes relatively low.

Participation in Government: Business and the Mayors

Another aspect of the business elites' approach to government has involved actual participation in government or choosing government officials to serve there. Businessmen (few have been women) have dominated mayoral and city council positions in Houston. The inner circle of the business elite has, on occasion, provided mayors. For example, one of the city's foremost merchants, T. W. House, Sr. served at the helm of the local government, as a member of the board of aldermen, and as mayor; in the 1880s William R. Baker served three terms as mayor.

In Chapter 3 I discussed one revolt of the working-class population against business dominance. For a time in the 1880s the business elite was forced to share some political power with skilled workers, but the business leaders soon regained control of city politics. In the 1890s, moreover, the conservative business elite faced a challenge from one of its own, Samuel H. Brashear, a progressive business leader supported by labor and black voters for his program of improving neighborhood services. Nonetheless, the people-oriented administrations were short-lived, and by the early 1900s the business community was firmly in control. The structure of local government, as in other cities, was "reformed" at the turn of the century in a way that improved business control of city affairs. The conservative majority in the business clique worked to replace the ward system with the at-large system. And in 1904–1905 the Business League and the business-dominated council forced the state legislature to agree to a mayor-commission form of local government, reinforcing business control of local government. The new political arrangements stipulated at-large elections; politicians sympathetic to business goals were elected. In 1913 Houston voters approved city charter amendments designating the four city "aldermen" as the heads of the four major city departments called tax and land, fire, water, and streets and bridges. The mayor was relatively weak·and did not at that time appoint the department heads.

From Oscar Holcombe to Louie Welch

The structure of the local government changed slowly over the next few decades in the direction of increased power for the mayor. Within a few years the mayor had control over the department heads. One of the most influential of Houston's mayors was Oscar Holcombe, a real estate developer who served, off and on, as mayor for more than twenty years. An entrepreneur and early real estate developer with political ambition, Holcombe was elected mayor for eleven terms between 1921 and 1958, illustrating the importance of real estate developers in the city's leadership. He built thousands of homes and the Palm Center, one of the first shopping centers in the metropolitan area. Working with the core elite, including the Suite 8F crowd, Holcombe was aggressive in sponsoring major infrastructure improvements such as roads, sewage systems, traffic signals, and motorized fire departments. As was the case for most mayors before and after him, Holcombe had a vision of wide open growth for the metropolitan area. As former Houston mayor Neal Pickett put it at the time of Holcombe's death, "his vision of a great city never dimmed and he encouraged many young men and women, years ago, to dream of the great metropolis we have today."[1]

Holcombe had his opponents. In an attempt to reduce the power of the mayor and cut down on the power of his political "machine," anti-Holcombe and other governmental reformers advocated a city manager system. One newspaper reporter noted that opponents of the city manager plan were asserting that its adoption "would permit Negroes a vote in the Democratic primary." Race baiting was used to try to stop the reformers. Nonetheless, in 1942 Houston voters approved a council-manager form of local government; the new city manager had direct authority over city departments. But Holcombe had suffered only a temporary defeat; he was able to convince the voters to abolish the city manager system just five years later. When the city manager format was abandoned, Mayor Holcombe emerged as much more powerful, for under the new mayor-council system the mayor apppointed all city department heads.[2] Subsequent mayors would benefit from this "strong mayor" form of government.

For decades City Hall has been organized around a strong mayor; all city department heads, except the city controller, report directly to, and are appointed by, the mayor. The Public Works Department is generally considered the most important, since it is responsible for much public construction in the city. This dominant mayor structure of government has generally facilitated the dominance of the local business leadership. The mayor often sets the agenda for the city council. When ready for political input in designing major projects, business leaders have often met with the mayor first; then the mayor consults with department heads and the city council. Major business projects generally receive priority treatment.[3]

From 1947 to the early 1970s Houston had only four mayors, Oscar Holcombe, Lewis Cutrer, Roy Hofheinz, and Louie Welch, all of whom more or less depended on the Suite 8F crowd. Generally speaking the core of the business elite controlled the composition and major activities of the mayor's office.[4]

All of Houston's mayors in this century have been business-oriented. However, some Houston mayors, particularly Roy Hofheinz (1953–1955), Fred Hofheinz (1974–1978), and Kathy Whitmire (1982–present), have been rooted in the moderate wing of the city's business community. On occasion, these three mayors have fought with the more conservative majority of the business community on particular social issues, such as the rights of minorities and homosexuals. But even these moderate business leaders have been limited in their ability to confront the conservative majority, in part because they have personally supported most business goals, including economic growth. And if they proceeded too far in a progressive direction or disagreed with the business elite on a major issue, as both Roy and Fred Hofheinz found out, the more conservative business leaders would organize to defeat them in the next election. Thus, in 1953 Roy Hofheinz became mayor when Holcombe was eased out by the local business elite. Hofheinz was reputed to be more progressive than Holcombe and was tied not only to the local business but also to minority community leaders. Holcombe preferred to work behind the scenes, but Hofheinz had a more confrontational style. During his second term Hofheinz's support of a property reassessment drive, which would have meant large increases in the assessments of downtown property, reportedly got him in trouble with James Elkins and other members of the Suite 8F crowd. As a result of this, and of clashes with city council members, there were several attempts by the council to limit his powers, even to impeach him. In 1955 prominent business leaders, including some of the Suite 8F crowd, asked Holcombe to run against Hofheinz. Holcombe beat Hofheinz with 57 percent of the vote. In Houston mayors have been expected to toe the business line.[5]

Louie Welch, who served as mayor from 1964 to 1974, was a local business leader who promoted the city usually in alliance with the Suite 8F crowd and the Chamber of Commerce. He was fond of speaking of Houston's prosperity as deriving from its status as a "free market city," one with a "partnership between the local government and the private sector." This close working relationship was, he noted, "perhaps unique in the world."[6] The close relationship between the business elite and the mayor's office can be seen in the fact that Welch moved out of the mayor's office to head the Chamber of Commerce, a step local observers considered a promotion.

A local lawyer and son of Mayor Roy Hofheinz, Fred Hofheinz, served as mayor from 1974 to 1978. He was a moderately progressive mayor and benefited from the newly enfranchised minority voters of the city. By the 1970s the administration of Mayor Fred Hofheinz had abandoned the long-standing policy of rejecting federal aid for most social and community programs. With the enfranchisement of minority voters, and after much local civil rights organizing, came the election of some mayors more sensitive to the needs of the city's minority residents. Prior to the mid-1970s the business elite and the city government it dominated were generally able to ignore the needs of inner-city minority communities, but the growing power of minority voters led to a more representative mayor and city council—and thus to successful pressures from central city residents to expand public services. The effective enfranchisement of minority voters also put upward pressure on the city government's budget and contributed to the fiscal crisis I will discuss in detail in a later chapter.[7]

Jim McConn and Kathy Whitmire

The importance of the real estate interests in Houston could again be seen in the mayor who followed Hofheinz. From 1978 to 1982 the mayor, Jim McConn, was a long-time member of the city council and a real estate developer. In addition, in 1981 one-third of the city council was in real estate or related fields.[8]

With the election of Kathy Whitmire in 1981, the relationship between local city government and the business leadership, including the Chamber of Commerce, changed somewhat. Although the business elite was split over Whitmire's candidacy because of her liberalism on social issues (for example, feminism and gay rights), most recognized that she was conservative on other business and government issues. Strongly probusiness, she had been an accountant before she became mayor. Some younger business leaders and newcomers to the city felt that as mayor she might improve the city's "good old boy" image. After Whitmire's election the relationship between the mayor's office and the chamber became more formal than it had been in recent decades. But as long as Whitmire kept taxes low and accepted the pro-growth business philosophy, she was grudgingly accepted by much of the business leadership.

Whitmire made some changes at City Hall. Houston's City Hall had traditionally been run as a relaxed "good old boy" institution with the friendliness of a local grocery store. Many contracts were let without competitive bidding to friends of politicians and departmental heads, and some departmental promotions were reportedly made on the basis of friendships. But Whitmire began to alter those practices. She replaced mediocre department heads with knowledgeable administrators. She named a black police chief to head a predominantly white police department famous for its brutality and racism. She reduced waste in city government by reforming civil service rules and requiring competitive bidding for contracts. And her 1982–1983 city budget was the first city budget in twenty-five years that was presented and adopted on time.[9]

This new "efficiency" approach to local government angered some city political brokers. The mayor's decisions on a number of issues, such as not to support the Houston Economic Development Council with city funds (see below), angered some in the business community. As a result, in 1985 some members of the chamber played a key role in supporting the chamber's head, former mayor Louie Welch, to run against Whitmire. Welch lost in a close race, primarily because Houston's large gay and minority communities, particularly the black community, supported Whitmire. Nonetheless, Mayor Whitmire remained a strong advocate of a probusiness approach to local government and of bringing new companies to the city. She did not alter, in any fundamental way, the dependence of local government on private enterprise; and she did not respond to her voters by calling for expanded women's rights, minority rights, or for more neighborhood participation at City Hall. The more savvy business leaders recognized that the government was run more efficiently, "like a business."

Houston city council budgets have increased substantially over the decades of the twentieth century. In 1908 the total budget for the city of Houston was about $900,000, including $245,000 for interest on bonds. By fiscal 1985 the general fund expenditures were $684.3 million, with debt service at $70.7 million. About half the general fund expenditures in the budget have been spent for police and fire services, with debt service being second on the list. The crash of the 1980s brought Houston's new mayor face to face with the first major fiscal crisis the city had faced in many decades. Like northern "fiscal crisis" governments, criticized for fiscal irresponsibility by some Sunbelt leaders, the Houston city government found itself with expenditures rising much more rapidly than tax revenues. There was the usual "fancy footwork" to create the image of a balanced budget. For example, creative accounting was used to show a $16-million surplus in June 1983, a surplus promised to bond rating agencies; the city officials juggled funds from the revenue sharing account to the general account, a strategy similar to those tried in other cities in crisis such as New York and Cleveland. In 1987 Mayor Kathy Whitmire unveiled her budget for the operation of the city for fiscal 1987–1988. Faced with a projected deficit of sizable proportions, she took the usual approach of "no new property taxes." This traditional approach left her the conservative options of laying off city employees—303 employees, to be exact—and raising numerous fees for city services. An interesting aspect of the budget generation process is the in-depth review given by the Chamber of Commerce. In a summer 1987 newsletter, for example, the chamber noted that "city officials requested input" and a "Chamber group met periodically with the Mayor, Controller, six council members, and several department heads." Chamber officials recommended a $22 million cut in expenditures, a $27 million increase in revenue enhancements, and protection of the "business climate." [10]

Battles over Zoning:
The Prodevelopment City

The History of the Zoning Struggle:
The First Stage

Houston is unique among major cities in the United States: it has no traditional zoning laws to control the pattern of land use. This situation did not occur without a struggle. Even the business leaders have been divided over zoning. Real estate interests, speculators, and small property owners have generally opposed zoning. Yet other business and professional leaders, such as architects, have supported prozoning efforts since the 1920s.

The lengthy struggle over zoning highlights a number of features of Houston's political-economic history. First, it reveals the depth of the conservative laissez-faire philosophy among the city's leaders, even when that philosophy interferes with other interests of the leadership, such as protecting elite residential neighborhoods from commercial encroachment. Even those business leaders who supported a moderate degree of zoning found themselves backing off when other leaders organized an open attack on zoning proposals. Second, the failure to implement zoning accents the power of the real estate and development capitalists in the city, for these interests have traditionally been the most consistently opposed to zoning. Third, Houston represents the nearly unique failure to implement professional planning in a principal Sunbelt metropolis. After examining the zoning history and some of its consequences, I will analyze the broader question of planning in Houston.

Local citizens' groups have tried several times to convince the city council or the voters-at-large to accept zoning ordinances. In 1927, a year after the *Euclid* v. *Ambler* Supreme Court decision which upheld the constitutionality of zoning ordinances, the Houston city government created a City Planning Department and reestablished a City Planning Commission chaired by Will C. Hogg, an influential business leader and developer of the elite River Oaks residential area in the inner city just west of downtown. Hogg and certain other wealthy individuals living in the inner city "gilded ghettos" were concerned about mixed-use encroachments on elite residential areas; Hogg worked diligently to bring professional planning and zoning to Houston. In 1927 he helped secure passage of a law by the Texas legislature which permitted cities to adopt zoning laws and control subdivision planning. A major zoning ordinance and a street and park plan were presented to the city council in the late 1920s. However, real estate interests, including the powerful lumber and real estate entrepreneur John H. Kirby, organized the Property Owners League, which in 1930 brought out 350 people to protest zoning at city council hearings. Zoning was heatedly decried as interfering with the rights of those engaged in private real estate transactions. As a result of this well-organized pressure, the support receded, and the council adopted a resolution against zoning.[11]

Later Attempts at City Zoning

In 1938 the city council attempted to resurrect the zoning ordinance; again hundreds of real estate and other business opponents packed the city council chambers. Zoning was attacked as corrupting and undemocratic, and the city council again retreated from its plan to establish a zoning commission. In addition, both the City Planning Commission and the City Planning Department were eliminated. Yet another try was made to resurrect zoning in 1945 by outgoing mayor Otis Massey. Over the next two years there was considerable citywide debate on the Massey proposal for zoning; a referendum was held on the issue in 1947. As before, a strong antizoning coalition, including real estate groups such as the Houston Property Owners Association, worked vigorously to convince the general public that city planning and zoning were "un-American and German" and a threat to personal freedom and personal property. One full-page advertisement argued that we must "kill this legalistic monster, spawned in Europe and disguised in the slum-ridden eastern cities as a device to protect your homes." [12] In the referendum local property holders overwhelmingly defeated the zoning proposal.

In 1959 another zoning study group was established by Mayor Lewis Cutrer. After twenty public hearings, the study group voted to recommend zoning. And in 1962, after several years of additional study, another referendum was held. Opposition again came from organized real estate interests, whose leaders charged now that zoning, "against our free enterprise way of life," was "socialized real estate." By calling zoning "socialism" and "communism" the antizoning groups used scare tactics in this era of Cold War tensions. Right-wing groups, including the John Birch Society, supported the antizoning campaign. In the 1962 referendum a majority of the voters agreed with opponents and again defeated what was to be the city's last zoning vote. [13]

The Importance of the Antizoning Ideology

Over the years the ideological attack on zoning has involved the equation of governmental zoning with the violation of personal property rights. I have emphasized several times the general strength of the free enterprise, antigovernment regulation ideology of the city's business community. Houston's real estate segment has held perhaps the most vigorous commitment to weak governmental regulation of the local built environment. Major real estate interests gained the support of smaller landowners by drawing heavily on the ideology of free enterprise and laissez-faire government. The usual defense of zoning as a protection of private residential property from encroachment of "bad" land uses lost out to the defense of property by those capitalists engaged in land deals in this freewheeling boomtown. Also involved in the zoning debate was the notion that zoning was somehow a foreign and radical philosophy. There is even a touch of anti-Semitism in some of the opposition.

The real estate interests in Houston's growth coalition have developed a number of myths to buttress local opposition to zoning. Author Neal Peirce asked a local editor why the city had no zoning. The editor's reply was the common one: "Houston is populated with people from small towns and farms of the old, rural South. Their salient characteristic is fierce, don't-fence-me-in individualism—the psychology that 'If I want to have a pigpen in my backyard, by God I can!'"[14] Yet this view is misleading. More than a third of Houston's citizenry are renters without property to protect, and many moderate-income and some high-income homeowners have supported the development of zoning laws historically. Far more important than the views of the "little people" have been the views of the city's powerful real estate interests and right-wing political groups—those who actively and successfully used the free enterprise ideology and their control of the mass media to persuade the voters to reject "zoning socialism." Interestingly, many social problems of the city, particularly traffic jams, which became so serious as to impress even the freewheeling real estate sector, had by the 1980s led a few large developers to favor some regulation of real estate development.

The struggle against zoning has been of more than local interest. Houston has become a much-cited example in national and international political struggles over the regulation of land use. Houston's lack of zoning and generally weak planning laws have been used by some advocates as a defense of the viability of "private planning" without public intervention. Thus, Houston was used as the major example of Bernard Siegan's argument that city zoning is a bad idea; in his *Land Use without Zoning* Siegan argues that the market-regulated city is better planned than the publicly planned city.[15]

Deed Restrictions: A Local Substitute for Zoning?

Siegan and others point to the effectiveness of private controls such as deed restrictions in land use protection. Deed restrictions and the rationing of land use by price have been principal reasons why Houston's physical appearance and land use patterns are not greatly different, at least in broad contours, from those in other spread cities. Restrictive covenants and civic associations to enforce covenants have been the mechanisms protecting residential areas since the 1920s. The developers of the elite inner suburb, River Oaks, pioneered in the development of stiff deed restrictions in the 1920s and 1930s. From the 1940s to the 1980s, deed restrictions, as well as private master plans, were generated for the hundreds of shopping centers, garden apartment complexes, and industrial and office parks in the Houston metropolitan area. In the mid-1970s it was estimated that 10,000 deed instruments covered about two-thirds of the city. These private "zoning" regulations have been imposed by real estate developers and homeowners. Moreover, in 1965 the Texas legislature permitted city governments, as well as local civic associations, to enforce these private deed restrictions.[16]

One problem with the private deed restrictions is their variance from area to area in content and enforcement. Many of these instruments have been enforced and also renewed at the time of expiration; others have been allowed to lapse. According to planning officials, in some areas, particularly minority communities, landowners and developers have simply ignored these private deed covenants, for once the new development projects are started it is usually too late to force major changes. In addition, in major projects developers can sometimes buy out local homeowners, acquire title, and "vote" to change deed restrictions from residential to commercial, a point to which I will return in Chapter 7.

Neighborhood Organizations and Deed Restrictions: The Racial Dimension

The enforcement of deed restrictions has generally been relegated to local residential associations. Although Houston's citizenry has in most respects been less well organized than that in other cities, Houstonians residing in residential communities have organized hundreds of local civic clubs. Prior to the 1890s residential areas in the city were settled without deed restrictions. After 1890, however, several subdivisions were developed on the edges of the inner city; these residential areas had deed restrictions designed to protect property values by specifying permissible housing construction, banning commercial development and, to quote one covenant, prohibiting "colored neighbors."[17] Civic clubs were created both to enforce these deed restrictions and to lobby City Hall for better public services. Moreover, when subdivision development accelerated on Houston's periphery in the 1920s, many new civic clubs were created.[18]

The Absence of Zoning: Assessing the Urban Impact

Analysts such as Siegan frequently argue that the absence of zoning makes no difference to metropolitan development. However, the lack of zoning in Houston has had several major effects on overall land use patterns. There is more commercial strip development along major arterial streets than in zoned cities. And the lack of zoning has meant a larger than average number of oddly mixed land uses: massage parlors are built across the street from churches, and office towers are erected in the backyards of wealthy suburbanites. Yet at the broadest level the city's land use map is similar to the spread city pattern common to many Sunbelt cities. Three factors contribute to these unofficial zoning results: (1) Houston land prices; (2) deed restrictions; and (3) decisions favoring developers in cities with zoning commissions.

The lack of zoning and the weakness of most other planning restrictions have meant that Houston developers generally face less red tape and shorter project development times. In a city with stricter zoning and planning, such as Dallas, it might take a year or two to get a plan for a megastructure project approved and underway, but in Houston it sometimes takes only six months. The lack of zoning has also facilitated the growth of the eighteen business activity centers which I will discuss in the next chapter.[19]

Public and Private Planning in Houston

The Early History of Local Planning

The history of planning in Houston has been intertwined with the history of zoning. The development of public planning for the city has been slow and halting. Just after the turn of the century some efforts were made by the business-oriented city councils and boards to study the needs of the city, albeit primarily the needs of the business community, and to undertake limited planning for the city's development. In 1913, at the request of a newly created park board, a master plan for parks and thoroughfares was submitted by Arthur C. Comey, a prominent Boston planner. Comey's plan for landscaped parkways in the central city area was partially implemented by the city government because these thoroughfares appealed to the business elite.

In 1924 Mayor Oscar Holcombe appointed a permanent City Planning Commission, the first one established by the City Council. The firm of Hare and Hare, planning consultants from Kansas City, was hired by the commission to come up with a zoning plan, a street plan, and a plan to beautify the bayous of the city. Hare and Hare presented its plans in 1926, but the commission expired when its appropriation ceased. This master plan was ignored by the city council. Nonetheless, a few prominent citizens, particularly the family of Will Hogg, pressed for planned city development, including zoning. Hogg almost singlehandedly brought the concept of city planning to Houston in the 1920s; he worked hard to get legislative support for planning at the state capitol and City Hall. He spent his own money to buy land for a parkway. In

1927 the mayor of Houston appointed Hogg to chair a resurrected City Planning Commission, but Hogg soon resigned in despair over the opposition of many in the local elite to planning and zoning. After a checkered career, including another abolition in the late 1930s, in 1940 the City Planning Commission and a City Planning Department were permanently reestablished.[20]

A Modest City Planning Structure

In 1940 a permanent City Planning Department was established with a tiny staff of professional planners who were given the task of general planning for roads and parks. In 1940 the City Planning Department had a budget of only $10,000 and a staff of three employees for a city with a population of 384,000. Nearly two decades later in 1959 the budget was $176,785, and there were twenty full-time employees; the city population was just under one million. This inadequate staffing reflects the weak commitment of the city's elite to planning, a commitment that persists into the late twentieth century. By 1980 the budget was $920,301 with a staff of sixty. This would appear to be a significant increase, but only twenty-nine of the employees were actually professional planners, in a city that then exceeded 1.6 million. Remarkably few dollars from the hundreds of millions in the annual city budget were being spent on metropolitan planning activities. On a per capita basis, the Houston city planning budget was *one-fifth* of the Dallas city planning budget and one-ninth of the Austin budget. Yet this minuscule planning department had responsibility for more than 500 square miles of development in the city limits and for a 1,500-square-mile extraterritorial jurisdiction.[21]

The Character of Planning in Houston

During my interview with the chief of Houston's comprehensive planning division in the City Planning Department in the spring of 1981 he commented, "We plan for Houston's future like weathermen for the next weekend; we do short-range planning." Long-range planning is missing. According to this planning official the large private projects are planned by developers with little or no input from city departments and agencies. As he put it, "In Houston the project just happens."[22] There is often an aspect of mystery to the large developments, as far as the general public and planners are concerned. As a result, effective government planning is virtually impossible.

From 1964 to 1983 head of the City Planning Department Roscoe H. Jones restricted the department to the modest role of research, record keeping, and plat checking during these decades of extraordinarily vigorous growth.

Roscoe's department spent most of its time documenting and describing the city's rapid growth. Beyond this record keeping, the City Planning Department reviewed and approved subdivision plats and provided modest supervision of the extraterritorial jurisdiction.

Because of the weak City Planning Department, in the mid-1970s Mayor Fred Hofheinz created divisions of Economic Development and Community Development within the mayor's office. In many cities these are traditional functions of a city planning department. When Hofheinz was replaced with more conservative mayors, the planning functions of City Hall were reduced, and the planning department was again encouraged to stick to its limited functions. When in 1980 the planning department tentatively moved away from its traditional activities by considering the problem of traffic snarls in the Galleria/Post Oak area, a large commercial and office tower complex about five miles west of downtown, then Mayor Jim McConn cut money for that purpose out of the city budget.[23]

As a result of this lack of city planning other state agencies sometimes must take up the slack. Outside public agencies, including the Texas Highway Department and the Harris County Flood Control District, have been forced on occasion to undertake critical long-range planning and infrastructural construction efforts for the city. In addition, although the Public Works Department is the largest city agency in terms of personnel, local accounting and contracting firms have provided much of the day-to-day project planning for the city. One prominent private engineering firm, sometimes called the "other public works department," not only has developed the primary water and sewer engineering plans for the city but also has been important, together with a few other firms, in restructuring the city's tax structure and airport planning. Such firms not only get planning contracts from City Hall but often the later implementation contracts as well. Moreover, in the early 1980s Browning-Ferris Industries, a private disposal firm, was doing solid waste planning for the city. Public decisions have often been delegated to private firms which, journalist Burka notes, "are really extensions of city hall." In general, city departments, such as Public Works, have been known for their close cooperation with developers and other real estate interests.[24]

Outside the city limits the developers have created their own utility "plans" for areas the municipal government is unable to supply with utility services. The Texas Annexation Act of 1963 permits major Texas cities to create "an extraterritorial jurisdiction" (E T J) five miles beyond the city limits for the purpose of regulating subdivisions and other development. In theory, if not always in practice, a developer's subdivision plans for the E T J must be reviewed by city planners to determine utility requirements and specifications. If the city cannot provide utility services, the developer can create, with governmental permission, a municipal utility district (M U D) with the authority to sell bonds for utility construction. In effect, the developers decide where the water, sewer, and other utility systems will be extended next—a type of privatized planning. As I will show in the next chapter, the social cost of this privatized infrastructure planning and provision can be enormous, for inadequate sewer systems in outlying subdivisions have polluted water sources.

By 1986 the metropolitan area had 411 Municipal Utility Districts (M U DS), about three-quarters of all such districts in the state of Texas. Even during the first years of the economic downturn in the mid-1980s a few developers continued to create new M U DS to raise money for water and sewage infrastructure facilities, although by 1987 the creation of new M U DS near Houston had ground to a halt. The city government is supposed to review the financing proposal and the quality of utility services with an eye to future annexation and assumption of operation of the M U D utility systems. As a rule, the city eventually annexes the subdivisions and takes over the utility system, often incurring substantial debt. Although the Houston annexation policy has kept many suburbanites within the official city boundaries, this inclusion has introduced the problems of inadequately planned utility systems.[25]

Houston: A Pioneer in the Privatization of Planning

The Business Elites and the Chamber

In the 1980s the offices of the Chamber of Commerce were high in a modern glass and steel skyscraper in the heart of downtown Houston. These luxurious accommodations soared above the old city hall building and permitted the chief executive of the chamber literally to look down on local government. This fortuitous spatial relationship is indicative of the actual power relationship. Mayors, city councils, and planning commissions have generally depended on the business interests represented by the chamber. The business elite has controlled the pace and character of local public planning. Indeed, important debates over the character of government planning have often been conducted within chamber committees. For example, one study done by the Future Studies Committee of the Chamber of Commerce went so far as to recommend long-range governmental planning for water needs, but this caused controversy on the chamber's board given the concept of public water planning involved.

The weakness of public planning has meant that Houston's citizenry beheld the *privatization* of long-range planning at an early stage. When long-range planning is viewed as necessary, it has often been carried out under the auspices of the business elites, such as the Suite 8F crowd, or by important committees of the Chamber of Commerce. Much chamber activity has reflected the interest of Houston's business leadership in privatized planning for the metropolitan area. By the early 1980s the chamber was a large organization with a staff larger than that of the City Planning Department. The expansion of the chamber's board during the 1970s and early 1980s likewise expanded the size of the support staff. In the early 1980s the staff of the Chamber of Commerce reached its peak size of about eighty employees, up significantly from its twenty staff members of the 1930s; however, the economic downturn reduced the chamber staff to about fifty-five employees by 1987.

The chamber has been the planning agency trying to develop reasonable and business-oriented solutions for many of Houston's problems. One report noted that the broad influence of the chamber on city hall cannot be exaggerated: "In fact, one had only to study the goals listed by the Chamber of Commerce each year to get a good indication of what City Hall would be working on in years and decades to come." [26]

The Chamber's Major Planning Committees

Since the 1930s the chamber has created occasional research and planning committees to deal with Houston's water, waste, and other growth dilemmas—as they were envisioned by the local business community. In 1935, for example, the chamber prepared a comprehensive study of flood problems, an examination which helped spur some construction of prevention projects. The chamber's Flood Control Committee worked with the city Public Works Department to improve the drainage system. Flooding has remained a persistent concern; thus, in the 1980s the chamber's Regional Service Systems Task Force issued major recommendations for another flood control program. Furthermore, in 1955 the chamber created a Long-Range Planning Committee to begin, tentatively, long-term planning and a Committee on the Sciences to monitor technological trends.

Chamber officials established a Waste Disposal Committee in 1945, and in the late 1950s the chamber sponsored an air pollution survey which found that "Houston had no air-pollution problems that either affected the entire community or that persisted in specific areas over prolonged periods of time." [27] The chamber had thereby whitewashed the serious air pollution problem. In the mid-1970s the chamber sponsored a $1.4 million Houston Area Oxidant Study. From the 1960s to the 1980s chamber task forces also studied water supply problems and made construction recommendations. For example, in the 1960s this business association sponsored the Lake Livingston Water project, a program to use social capital expenditures to provide large amounts of water needed for industrial development. Local government officials filed an unprecedented application with the State of Texas to build a reservoir outside Houston's own watershed on the Trinity River. When the Trinity River Authority protested Houston's encroachment on its water resources, a former president of the Houston chamber negotiated with the authority for a jointly-operated reservoir project.[28]

As one might expect, given the role of developers in Houston's business elites, roads and highways have been a long-range planning target. By the 1920s the chamber was firmly committed to auto-centered transport; since the 1930s the chamber's Highway Committee, one of the chamber's strongest, has pressed successfully for major road improvements. The absence of business support for mass transit contributed to the abandonment of the city's streetcars in 1941. In the 1960s both W. P. Hobby and John T. Jones were on that highway committee; both of them had ties to the Suite 8F crowd. This committee had a major influence on the planning of the 244-mile freeway grid then being developed around the city. In the 1980s a chamber-developed Regional Mobility Plan, which spelled out serious local traffic problems, was being partially implemented by local governments.

Adequate airports to support business expansion have been another transportation concern. In the 1950s the chamber's Aviation Committee prepared a report on local airport needs and worked with airlines to increase service.[29] Moreover, in 1958–1959 the chamber's Metropolitan Area Committee drafted a proposal giving Texas cities home rule powers and submitted it to the state legislature, which passed the necessary laws. This law greatly strengthened the power of cities like Houston and gave them power to annex much adjacent land. This annexation was of great concern to real estate interests; it committed city governments to the provision of infrastructure for new residential developments.[30]

Economic Development Planning

By the 1980s the economic downturn in Houston had generated a growing concern about the relative lack of economic diversity in the metropolitan area, particularly the heavy dependence on the oil-related enterprises. The Chamber of Commerce created a number of committees concerned with economic development questions, including an Aerospace and Technology Task Force. Perhaps most interesting was the creation of a new form of private-public partnership by the business leadership. In a capitalistic society moments of crisis often precipitate innovations in state intervention.

Many scholars have written about the widespread, federally funded, urban redevelopment and urban renewal programs in many U.S. cities since the 1950s. Over several decades billions of dollars were spent by local and federal governments to destroy older buildings in central city areas and to construct new buildings on the government-cleared land. In the 1970s these massive, federally funded renewal programs were replaced by new arrangements called "public-private partnerships." In the face of the accelerated movement of corporations and capital investment on a global scale, alliances were forged at the municipal level between public officials and business interests to promote new corporate investments in the cities. Yet in Sunbelt cities like Houston the emphasis on the private sector in these cooperative endeavors has been so substantial that these alliances would best be termed "private-public" partnerships.[31]

Houston's Private-Public Collaboration

The movement of the Houston business elite in this direction was belated. In 1984 the business leaders of the Chamber of Commerce set up the Houston Economic Development Council (H E D C) under Kenneth Schnitzer, chair of the board of Century Development Corporation, a large real estate development firm. Appointed as vice-chairs on the H E D C were top executives of the two local papers, top executives at the four largest banks, an independent oil entrepreneur and real estate developer, a local entrepreneur heading a city booster organization called Pro-Houston, and the treasurer of the Harris county A F L-C I O. Chamber officials also appointed the city mayor and the county executive to serve with the council's fifty business members. The H E D C's chair and vice-chairs came mostly from Houston's growth coalition.[32]

The H E D C was created and funds were raised before a clear vision of H E D C action and goals was articulated. H E D C's first two years were spent organizing a plan of action and raising money for its efforts. The H E D C raised $6.3 million for its first two years of operation, mostly from the local business community, and was set up in a way that permitted business contributions to be deducted as "investment expenses." Most of the budget for the first two years was spent on consultants, salaries, and rent and renovations of its office.

New Governmental Subsidies for Corporate Action

The H E D C was created by the business community, but local governments have played a considerable role in financing. The city government contributed a $150,000 grant for the first two-year budget. And in March 1986 the Houston City Council unanimously voted to match private contributions to the H E D C, up to a figure of $1.25 million annually. Mayor Whitmire tried to defeat this subsidy. Whitmire encouraged a black council member to sponsor a rider calling for minority business participation in the program. But proponents of the H E D C accepted the rider and the city controller found $1.9 million in unused city budget money to support the H E D C. The mayor was defeated. The Greater Houston Political Action Committee, a business group, had worked hard to get this maximum government assistance for the H E D C.[34]

In June 1986 several council members were upset that the H E D C had not yet signed a contract with the city government. A few blamed the mayor for foot dragging on the project, but at least as much foot dragging came from the H E D C; several leaders feared that such a strong financial tie to local government would mean closer public scrutiny of both H E D C operations, some of which had been kept secret, and H E D C expenditures. H E D C officials, including its president, worried openly that, if the new organization accepted $1.25 million in governmental grants, it would have to operate in a less secretive fashion. Indeed, the H E D C president noted that companies considering locating in Houston often like to keep the decision-making process secret, and he expressed the hope that elected officials would respect "the sacred character of our business transactions."[35]

Officials' Setting and Changing Goals

In 1984 the H E D C publicly pinpointed nine categories of business firms as the most important in broadening the Houston economy: (1) biomedical research and development; (2) research and development laboratories; (3) instruments, particularly medical and computer equipment; (4) communications equipment; (5) chemicals, including plastics and drugs; (6) materials processing research; (7) computers and office machines; (8) engineering and architectural services; and (9) distribution services. The notable omissions from the categories proclaimed in the initial statements were oil, petrochemicals, construction, and most types of manufacturing—Houston's core enterprises. Ostensibly the omissions reflected concern for broadening the local economy and the huge losses in employment in these traditional areas during the 1980s recession.[36]

The Center for Enterprising at Southern Methodist University prepared a research study on Houston suggesting that the city's leaders look to certain forgotten areas of Houston's manufacturing for diversification ideas, that is, to agricultural and food processing, printing, paper, and pharmaceuticals, rather than to the faddish areas of biotechnology and computers. Another ingredient in the mix of pressures leading to the reorientation of H E D C goals was a recognition of the importance of education and university research. In a May 1986 issue of *Houston* the chamber published an article, "What Can Houston Learn from Massachusetts?" The article and the new attitude suggested in its title were surprising, for Houston's leaders have traditionally detested "Yankees" and their ideas. The article praised a symposium which featured Massachusetts public officials and educators lecturing to Houston leaders. The symposium's basic theme was that the presence of leading research universities in northern metropolitan areas had created the large reserve of innovative researchers and potential entrepreneurs. Houston had no research universities and no federal research and development laboratories; moreover, the University of Houston and Rice University did not receive sufficient research funding. Sponsored research at these two institutions was $34 million in 1985, compared to M I T's $250 million. The Massachusetts officials asserted that Houston's leaders should not go after high-tech electronics firms but rather should build on traditional industrial firms, on N A S A, on chemical and mechanical engineering firms, and on medical institutions.[37]

By mid-1986 H E D C leaders recognized that cities with substantial high-tech industries had first-rate educational institutions and national research labs. H E D C now made several recommendations: (1) a communitywide task force should be created by the chamber to strengthen research and graduate training in local universities; (2) the chamber should work to establish technology transfer organizations and federal R & D laboratories; and (3) the chamber should seek increased federal funds to the medical center and N A S A facilities. The H E D C's 1986 Strategic Priorities Agenda emphasized the need to target energy, biotechnology, space enterprises, international business, and conventions/tourism as areas of reinvigorated economic development. The exotic objectives of biotechnology and space were now embedded in a revised list of goals.[38]

New Spending for Public Relations

The lion's share of the H E D C budgets in the first years was spent for communications, public relations, and marketing efforts. H E D C was preoccupied with the city's image. The national media have been repeatedly attacked by local business leaders for portraying the Houston metropolis in negative terms. Desiring to find out more about the image of the city in national business circles, the H E D C sponsored a survey of U.S. business leaders; it revealed that executives whose companies had no contact with the Houston area harbored a negative view of the region as a low-tech, single-industry "cowtown." H E D C leaders were upset at these survey results and set as a priority the creation of positive attitudes about Houston among decision makers— locally, nationally, and overseas.[39]

Northern public relations firms were hired to advertise the city. A Chicago firm sent letters to 120 media outlets, primarily on the East Coast, protesting the negative image of the city and praising the city's virtues. The H E D C set up the "Houston Marketing Network," encouraging local executives to extol the city's virtues to their business associates across the nation, and a program called "Houston Beautiful," a beautification campaign. Another public relations strategy, "Houston Proud," was an effort to make Houstonians think positively about the city. As part of its effort to market the city more positively, the H E D C developed numerous advertisements and brochures.

Business Leaders Taking Action: Corporate and State Projects

Early efforts of H E D C officials included sponsoring a European trade mission and attempting to secure the proposed General Motors automated Saturn automobile facility and a Navy homeport for the Houston-Galveston area. The private organization of the H E D C has not precluded its pursuit of state-funded projects, such as those in the military-industrial complex. Working with Galveston officials, the H E D C put together an $18 million incentive package to secure a proposed naval base for a U.S. battleship group. The H E D C interest in the project was underscored in a Houston magazine article, which noted that "the homeport is also expected to lessen the housing surplus and encourage the development of defense and high-tech industries in Houston and Galveston."[40]

The October 13, 1986, issue of the *Houston Business Journal* reported that Houston business elite had succeeded in recruiting a major military-industrial firm, Grumman, to the Clear Lake City area near the N A S A spacecraft facility. The incentive package which attracted Grumman included $24 million in state-of-Texas-subsidized job training programs for Grumman employees, a $20-million tax abatement from city government, special education programs at the Clear Lake branch of the University of Houston, a special Houston Relocation Taskforce of realtors and lenders to help employees find reasonably priced housing, special airfares for Grumman employees provided by Continental Airlines, and coordination of informational flow by the H E D C. Although the major attraction for Grumman was the N A S A center, Grumman's prime customer, the incentive package was viewed by local business leaders as quite important. Social capital expenditures by local governments were again at the heart of the proposal. The Grumman effort was one of the first formally organized and coordinated private-public efforts to recruit new industrial corporations to Houston. Business leaders commented to the press that Houston was finally learning to play the "economic development game."

Why was the business leadership so slow in working out development and diversification efforts to deal with the oil-related depression of the 1980s? Mainly until the 1980s economic development seemed to take care of itself. The headline of the October 6, 1986, issue of the *Houston Business Journal* read "The Many Roads to Economic Recovery: Other U.S. Cities Have Solved the Riddle of Economic Development." The first paragraph of this unique story began: "For decades, Houston business leaders weren't really interested in economic development. They simply didn't see the need. . . . With the drop in oil prices, all that began to change."[41] As a group, Houston's leaders had never faced the problem of diversification before.

The Goal of the Good Business Climate

A major expressed goal of the H E D C has been to maintain Houston's "good business climate"—explicitly including anti-union laws, government officials sympathetic to business, low taxes, balanced government budgets, weak regulation of real estate, and governmental reluctance to expand social programs. The same Strategic Priorities Agenda which explicitly and vigorously advocated this "good business climate" agenda on one page also discussed serious problems with the local "quality of life" on the next. The report noted that Houston's many social problems include serious traffic problems, major flooding, water pollution, crime, air pollution, lack of parks, and sewage crises— problems I will assess in detail in Chapter 8. Yet the H E D C Agenda proposed only weak "quality of life" initiatives to deal with these pressing problems: one focusing on beautification and the other on welcome-orientation services for visitors.[42] Neither the chamber nor H E D C leaders have recognized that the low taxes associated with the good business climate are a major reason why cities like Houston lack responses to many social costs of growth.

The Concept of State "Para-apparatus": The HEDC

Generated by the private sector, the H E D C, in contrast to public-private partnerships in other cities, involves the state primarily as a financial partner. The H E D C board of directors has been drawn for the most part from business corporations; its staff constitutes a private bureaucracy. Clark and Dear have developed a suggestive analysis of state bureaucracy and function. They make several distinctions: the "state apparatus" is the total of those mechanisms and agencies through which the state operates; the "sub-apparatus" is the set of agencies implementing a specific state goal; and the "para-apparatus" is the group of auxiliary agencies separate from the state but performing state functions.[43] The H E D C fits loosely into the para-apparatus category; it is a privately-created independent organization carrying out typical local state functions and substantially funded by local tax revenues.

Recent Ordinances:
Backdoor Planning and Zoning?

By the 1980s the Houston City Council was belatedly taking modest steps to deal with the city's massive development problems. In 1985 the *Houston Business Journal* ran a scare headline: "Look out Houston, here comes zoning." The specter of zoning was allegedly haunting the city's business community. However, the headline referred to a number of proposed ordinances to restrict land use in Houston in very limited ways. In the mid-1980s the City Planning Commission recommended limited growth control ordinances to the city council: restrictions on the location of pornography shops, off-street parking requirements for stores, mobile home restrictions, and a limited building setback ordinance. These moderate recommendations for development restrictions were described, not surprisingly, as "backdoor zoning" by some real estate interests.

Led by member Eleanor Tinsley, the city council passed several ordinances. The most important requires commercial structures outside the downtown area to be built at least twenty-five feet from major thoroughfares, prohibits dead-end streets in subdivisions, and restricts blocks to certain lengths. These limited restrictions require more active intervention by the planning department into the activities of real estate developers. The modest restrictions were such startling news in this free enterprise city that they received prominent coverage in the front sections of both local papers and national newspapers, such as the *New York Times* and the *International Herald Tribune*.

In addition, in 1986–1987 the city council debated and approved the drafting of a comprehensive study of and plan for development in and around the city. This plan was expected to take four years to complete. In the 1986 discussion the plan generated fierce opposition from the local real estate community, which quickly labeled it "zoning." By late 1987, however, the Chamber of Commerce, as a local newspaper noted quaintly, had give the plan its "blessing." In effect, the comprehensive city plan would emphasize *public* construction projects, and the private sector recommendations would be *non-binding*. In addition, the council members made it clear that developers and business groups would play a *central* role in the planning recommendations. The city council efforts did not signal the arrival of large-scale zoning efforts but rather belated and piecemeal attempts, coordinated with the Chamber of Commerce and other business groups, to grapple with the metropolitan sprawl and the social costs of freewheeling development in the city and county.[44]

Conclusion: The Privatization of Planning

The refusal of Houston's leadership to extend the public planning function to the usual array of public infrastructural and economic development purposes is unique among U.S. cities. Phillip Lopate has suggested that Houston, and presumably its elite, refuse to recognize its urbanity: "Its resistance to city planning is partly a way of putting off acceptance of its urban nature, and partly a dread of the often messy negotiations between conflicting political interests which an open planning process necessitates."[45] This is an interesting observation about the fear of open political conflict, but Lopate fails to specify the most fearful group: the city's powerful business aristocracy. The business elites have intentionally rejected broad public planning for more than a century.

Houston is indeed the planless city, if by planning we mean significant governmental planning and zoning in the public interest for a broad range of infrastructural and socioeconomic problems of development. Much "public" planning has often been privatized and haphazard, and the dictates of the investment market have been primary. This situation has created serious social and environmental problems. Among these are the absence of zoning laws protecting residential areas from encroachment, the excessive freedom for developers whose actions can bring major infrastructural crises for neighborhoods, and a city hall often unresponsive to the particular needs of neighborhoods. In Chapters 8 and 9 I will examine in some detail the specific consequences of unrestrained development on communities in Houston. By the mid-1980s there were pressures for change in the direction of increased public planning and zoning; the city's planners, though handicapped by budget austerity, were having a greater impact.

7

The Spatial Dimensions of

Houston's Development:

Investments in

the Built Environment

Early ecologists analyzed the spatial layout of cities. These urban scholars viewed the competition in urban markets as resulting in unplanned regularities of land use patterns; and thus it generated a map of concentric zones moving out in waves from a central business district. They were particularly interested in the types of human populations that inhabited these zones. Little attention was given to the character of the built environment, the actual physical construction on the landed zones, or the structure or agents of real estate capitalism critical to that constructed environment.

Theoretical Issues

The Chicago School

At one point, in a classic 1926 article, R. D. McKenzie, of the University of Chicago, gave brief attention to "the more fixed aspects of human habitation, the buildings, roads, and centers of association."[1] Since McKenzie's trenchant analysis, most urban ecologists and many other urban social scientists have been more interested in urban and metropolitan demographic trends than in the geographical mapping of human populations. They have sometimes preferred explanations of urban development in terms of technological determinism—the inevitability of the auto-centered system. Moreover, mainstream analysis tends to view the urban spatial inequities which show up in their demographic analyses as both an inevitable consequence of market-oriented competition for the highest and best use of space and an inevitable functional differentiation.

174

Industrial and Development Capital

In this chapter I will explore the flow of private and public capital into the physical environment of the city. I will analyze the capitalistic forces and actors which have shaped what McKenzie termed the "fixed aspects of human habitation." Scholars developing the new critical paradigm have taught that capitalism has survived by the constant production and shaping of space. Central in shaping the sociospatial patterns of cities is the development sector of capital examined in Chapter 2. Since the 1930s the development process in Houston has involved several major categories of development-related decisions—corporate location, land ownership, land development and speculation, public infrastructure construction, building construction, and land and construction financing. The initial actors in many cases are the top corporate executives in the industrial and commercial corporations seeking a place to locate plant, warehouse, or office facilities. These have included cotton firms, oil and petrochemical companies, and a great variety of commercial, retail sales, and service corporations.

Development firms help create the built environment for the commercial and industrial companies. In the boom period from the early 1970s to the early 1980s Houston probably led the nation in the number of land-oriented speculators, developers, and financiers operating within its metropolitan boundaries. Some land-oriented entrepreneurs and companies specialize in one area, such as construction or land ownership, but most large development companies are multifaceted. Even industrial corporations have added real estate development subsidiaries in recent decades. For example, Exxon's Friendswood Development subsidary has played a major role in real estate development in metropolitan Houston. Moreover, many land use actors operate in dozens of cities across regional and international boundaries. For example, as of the early 1980s Canada's Cadillac-Fairview Corporation, one of the ten largest firms operating in the United States, had eight divisions, including financing, shopping center, and construction divisions. Part of its land empire was the massive Houston Center project in downtown Houston. Similarly some Houston development firms (e.g., Gerald Hines Interests) started after World War II as local firms tied into a local growth coalition, but they later became complex bureaucracies developing projects in numerous cities and engaging in a variety of financial, landowning, construction, and marketing operations.

Multinodal Cities and the State

The result of the creation and recreation of the land and built environments of cities by these development interests is the modern decentralized city. Over the course of United States urban history a general decentralization trend can be seen in the periodic surges of suburbanization. Particularly in the last several decades, Sunbelt cities have developed a distinctive "spread city" version of the decentralized metropolis. Houston represents the current spread city form. The development of multinodal spread cities is relatively recent, and this change is more than the result of technological developments.

The growth of the spread city has heavily depended on infusions of capital into the "secondary circuit" of residential and commercial construction. But the spread city does not heavily depend on localized processes of central agglomeration and center-generated dispersal, the commonplace theory of spread development. In fact, as Gottdiener has reminded us, the sprawl city is more dependent on broader societal forces such as the state actions subsidizing suburban development and on the global investment processes such as capital flight, disinvestment, and reinvestment. Gottdiener argues that modern cities are likely to be multinodal realms, metropolises with a less central focus than most prior cities. Houston is a premier example of this multinodal realm.[2]

The Role of State in Development

The Fainsteins, Gottdiener, Smith, and other critical urban analysts have emphasized the importance of examining the role of the state in urban real estate.[3] In many cities the local state supports the needs of industrial, development, and financial capital. The state plays a crucial, albeit sometimes dysfunctional, role in fostering capital accumulation by industrial, commerical, financial, and development capital within the urban political-economic system. The role of the federal and local state in shaping the flow of public capital into urban infrastructure essential for private investment can be seen clearly in Houston. In addition, absent zoning and weak public planning, which I explained in Chapter 6, have given developers and industrial companies a relatively free hand in making and remaking the face of the city.

The Houston Metropolis: An Overview

A recent visitor to Houston reportedly commented that Houston's creation was "neither an act of God nor of nature, but an act of real estate." In the 1920s Houston's secondary circuit of real estate became a major avenue for investment. Even in the Great Depression of the 1930s Houston ranked second only to Washington, D.C., in growth and real estate construction. Since World War II Houston's developers and builders have built more large-scale projects than their counterparts in most other cities. For example, in the three years immediately following World War II, Harris County ranked first in the United States in the value of construction. From that period to the mid-1980s Houston or Harris County would regularly rank at or near the top of the construction value list of all American cities.

The impact of this construction can be seen in the spatial map of the city of Houston. The metropolitan land use pattern is similar to that of other spread cities. The central business district has a major concentration of commercial and office buildings, while the eastern and southeastern sections have concentrations of heavy industries. These heavy industries are supported by a large-scale infrastructure of railroad lines and Port of Houston facilities. Most commercial and light industrial activities, as well as numerous office complexes, are located near major highways, particularly Loop 610 and other interstate freeways. Major highway interchanges are favorite locations for the larger commercial and office complexes.

Residential areas are distributed across the entire city, but they are most common on the northern, western, and southern sides. High density, multifamily residential areas tend to be located along major travel corridors. Single-family housing can be found inside and outside Loop 610. Typically this housing is in subdivisions. Many older residential areas with detached houses ring the central business district, particularly on the north and west. Houston has many distinctive geographical areas, including numerous identifiable communities and neighborhoods. In the late nineteenth century some definable communities within Loop 610 came to be called by their local political jurisdictions, such as the Third and Fourth wards, names which persist to the present day. As the city expanded during its first century, most residential development took place to the north and south of the downtown area, with less development moving out in eastern and western directions. Most suburban development in recent decades has taken place on the western and northern sides of the city, with the greatest development running in a band along the outside of Loop 610 from the Houston Intercontinental Airport on the north to the "southwest corridor."

One of the most distinctive features of the Houston spatial layout is the great amount of undeveloped land scattered throughout the central city and outlying areas. Houston is a spacious city with many vacant lots and much undeveloped acreage within the central city. As Phillip Lopate wrote, "This is a city three-fourths of which sometimes gives the impression of being at the edge of town."[4]

The Spatial Distribution of Industrial Workplaces

Important Location Decisions

The character and existence of Sunbelt and Frostbelt cities reflect the choices of powerful decision makers. Among these decision makers have been corporate owners and top executives seeking sites for their enterprises. Where corporate executives decide to locate their production and distribution facilities directly or indirectly affects the lives of most urbanites, whether the choices involve locating a new facility in a suburb, deciding on a downtown location for an office tower, or moving investments from northern cities to the Sunbelt. Typically, a few key industries are at the heart of each successive epoch of economic growth in a metropolitan area. Usually the location decision of any one company does not give a city its characteristic industrial structure; rather, the set of decisions made by several, dozens, or hundreds of related companies are involved. In each distinctive period of a city's economic growth older industries, such as the cotton brokerage firms in Houston, do not necessarily die out, but they may become less dominant. And each new wave, such as the petrochemical industrialization in the 1940s in Houston, is reflected in distinctive forms of urban spatial development.

The Spatial Aspects of Manufacturing

After several decades of railroad growth in the nineteenth century, Houston had become by the mid-1880s a leading railroad city with major foundries and railroad shops. The first industrial areas were those concentrating the railroad and related machine shops along the tracks in the northeastern and eastern sectors of the city. There were also agricultural processing facilities in the central city area. With the expansion and development of the ship channel in the first decades of the twentieth century there was new industrial development running east from the downtown area along the ship channel to the out-

TABLE   7.1.
Larger Manufacturing Plants in the Houston
Metropolitan Area, 1982

Location in Houston	Total Plants		Chemical/ Oil/Gas		Metals		Machinery		Other	
	N	%	N	%	N	%	N	%	N	%
Northwest area[a]	182	(17)	7	(5)	62	(21)	38	(19)	75	(17)
Southwest area[b]	219	(20)	18	(13)	48	(16)	53	(26)	100	(23)
Northeast area[c]	119	(11)	12	(9)	41	(14)	26	(13)	40	(9)
Inner South- east area[d]	260	(24)	38	(28)	69	(23)	47	(23)	106	(25)
Outer South- east area[e]	293	(27)	62	(45)	80	(27)	40	(20)	111	(26)
TOTAL (all areas)	1,073	(99)	137	(100)	300	(101)	204	(101)	432	(100)

SOURCE: Calculated by author from data on Bank of the Southwest, "Industrial Map of Metropolitan Houston," 10th ed.; and from Houston City Planning Commission, "Houston Year 2000
Map," Houston, October 1980.
NOTES: Plants have twenty-five or more employees. "Other" category includes a few plants with
unclear marking on maps.
[a] North of IH 10 and west of IH 45.
[b] South of IH 10 and west of IH 45/South Freeway.
[c] East of IH 45 and north of IH 10.
[d] South of IH 10 between IH 45/South Freeway and East Belt (existing and proposed), includes
Galena Park, South Houston.
[e] South of IH 10 and east of East Belt, includes Baytown, Deer Park, NASA.

lying cities of Deer Park and Baytown. From the 1920s through the 1940s the
eastern side of the city was the site for locating most oil refining, petrochemical, and metal-related plants. Numerous refineries and other oil-related
facilities were built in Houston because of the wealth of necessary raw materials—and in the eastern sector of the city because of the state-subsidized port
facilities. By the early 1930s the metropolitan area had more than 420 manufacturing plants of all sizes, most on the eastern side.
    In the mid-1980s much of Houston's industrial manufacturing plant was
still concentrated on the east side of the city, along and south of the ship channel. Table 7.1 demonstrates this industrial geography of metropolitan Houston. The large southeastern quadrant contains 51 percent of all the major

manufacturing plants with twenty-five or more employees in the metropolitan area, as well as 73 percent of the chemical plants, oil refineries, and other oil-related facilities. Steel and other metals facilities are also disproportionately located in this southeastern quadrant. The easternmost section of this quadrant, particularly that near Galveston Bay, has much of Houston's heavy industry. The 1982 list of major plants in this area reads like a Who's Who of U.S. industry; Exxon Chemical Co., U.S.A.; Shell Oil Co.; Stauffer Chemical Co.; and Goodyear Tire and Rubber Co. This area includes a number of contiguous industrial satellite cities such as Baytown. And in the southernmost part of the quadrant are Exxon's huge industrial park, Bayport, and a cluster of newer aerospace and electronics plants near the N A S A spacecraft center. Houston now has a number of very large industrial parks, most on the eastern side of the city. The manufacturing facilities outside the southeast quadrant are mostly clustered near major roads and highways, such as IH 10 and the Southwest Freeway, and near the Houston Intercontinental Airport in the far north area of the city.

An Excess of Fixed Capital

The economic downturn of the mid-1980s hit the industrial developers and landlords very hard. The decline in oil-related and agriculture-related activities had a major impact on industrial real estate. In June 1986, Houston had 38.3 million square feet of vacant industrial space in single-tenant service centers, multitenant and single-tenant warehouses, and fabrication facilities. Most of this vacant space was in the northwest, southeast, and western industrial areas. Symbolic of Houston's problem was the vacant 4.1 million square feet of fabrication space in the Armco Steel Plant which was closed in 1984. With the vacancy rate in the 25 to 30 percent range industrial developers and brokers were laying off employees, and the construction of new facilities ceased.[5]

The Ownership of Corporate Property in Houston

Much of the land and built environment in the city of Houston is owned by large corporations. In 1980 the ten largest taxpayers in the Houston Independent School District (H I S D), which encompasses most of the City of Houston, were as follows:

	Assessed Value of Property (in millions)
Southwestern Bell Telephone	905.1
Houston Lighting and Power	464.1
Gerald Hines Interests	438.7
Hughes Tool	213.5
First City National Bank	208.8
Texas Commerce Bank	180.6
Exxon	163.2
Tenneco	145.6
IBM	138.8
Texas Eastern	127.8

Together these ten private companies accounted for one-sixth of all the taxable property, such as office buildings, shopping malls, and land, in the H I S D. The list includes four of the city's largest oil and gas firms, two big private utilities, the two largest banks, the city's leading development company, and I B M. I B M and Exxon are the only nonlocal multinational firms represented on the list. In Houston the corporation gets a break: the assessed valuation, at $2,986 billion, was well below the actual market value of the property. Indeed, the underassessed property in the downtown area, for a brief moment in the early 1980s, became a political issue for citizen's groups.[6]

Highways: The State and Houston's Spread Development

The Traditional Ecological View

Mainstream ecologists frequently view the development and spread of cities as determined largely by transportation and communication technologies, technologies which are too quickly abstracted from their economic and political contexts. For example, Kasarda views the rapid growth of Sunbelt cities substantially in terms of both new technological developments, such as highway systems, and the better business climate of Sunbelt cities.[7] The political-economic history of these transport technologies is not carefully examined.

New Federal Highway Investments

Federal government subsidies have been critical to the process by which auto-mobile transportation has substantially replaced rail transportation in the United States. This can be seen in the development of massive intracity and intercity road and highway complexes, particularly the Interstate Highway System so visible in the spatial layout of cities such as Houston. Military de-fense needs constituted the rationale President Eisenhower used in defending his mid-1950s proposal for a $50 billion intercontinental highway network. Testifying before Congress on the highway bills in the mid-1950s, Robert Moses, the most prominent highway builder in United States history, said, "I still have not found anybody who can tell me how you are going to keep on turning out all these cars without decent, first-class modern highways for them to run on, in particular on the routes that connect the big cities and their sub-urbs, and run through the cities, because that is what we have today."[8] Not only does Moses explicitly link automobile production to expanded highway systems, but he also emphasizes the role of these road systems in organizing the shaping land development in cities and suburbs. Private-sector capitalists, many associated directly with the auto and road construction industries, and government officials developed a major public relations campaign to generate public support for a tax-funded national highway system. In the mid-1950s a law was passed setting up a Highway Trust Fund collected from gasoline taxes to build an interstate highway system.

The highway construction and auto-oil lobbies have dominated the Federal Highway Administration as well as local agencies such as the powerful Texas Highway Department. Thus, in 1963 the *Asphalt Institute Quarterly* strongly supported a statement by then Secretary of Commerce Hodges, who said that traffic problems would be solved by providing better roads for cars, not by restricting the number or caliber of cars: "We shout a 'Hear, hear!' and let's construct those better roads out of asphalt so they will cost less to build and thus be easy on taxes—at the same time providing more roads for more cars to travel more miles and use more petroleum products."[9] Such a view has been especially popular in oil-centered Houston.

Houston: The Early Decades

One of the ironies of Houston's history is that this auto-centered metropolis first rose to economic greatness on the foundation of rail transport. In the early 1900s so many railroads converged on Houston that it was called the "Iron-ribbed city" and the commercial junction "where seventeen railroads meet the sea." Within the local area mass rail transport linked many residential and industrial sectors. Houston had an extensive intraurban rail transit system. Yet the local shift to industries closely tied to the automobile and the federal shift toward subsidizing the automobile and highways were well underway by the 1920s and 1930s, and the days of Houston's trolley system were numbered.

In this period the business elite and the Chamber of Commerce played a significant role in street and highway development in the Houston metropolitan area. As I noted in Chapter 6, since the 1930s the chamber's Highway Committee has lobbied successfully for federal and local government funding for streets, freeways, and bridges. Street expansion within the city was extensive in the 1920s and the 1930s. Significant improvements were made in the Houston street and bridge system under the New Deal programs in the 1930s.[10]

The World War II Period

During World War II Houston-based firms benefited greatly from the investment of federal capital in war-related industries. The Houston area also benefited from the use of federal capital for the construction of many military installations. In 1941 a member of the Texas Highway Commission noted that Texas had the nation's major military complex, "with 41 Army, Navy and Air Corps posts, forts, training bases, fields, [and] camps."[11] He argued that the gasoline taxes should be used to expand the Texas highway system linking these military installations.

In addition, the Secretary of War supported substantial federal appropriations for improving highways for military purposes. Texas was a major beneficiary of this program. Many highways were permanently paved during this period, including major roads to Houston. Moreover, at this time the new director of the Houston City Planning Department, landscape architect Ralph Ellifrit, began to develop a plan for a freeway network. Later the Texas Highway Department elaborated this plan as the basis for the Houston freeway system. After World War II, streets and freeways were at the center of private and public planning efforts for the city. The Major Street and Thoroughfare Plan of 1943 became, in effect, the "comprehensive plan" for the city.[12]

The Changes in the Postwar Era

Major divided highways became part of Houston's structure in the late 1940s, when the Texas Highway Commission undertook a massive construction program. Much of the total Texas expenditure for highways was actually spent in the Houston area. In 1946 an $18-million program was started to provide a major north-south highway (75) and a major east-west highway (90).[13] Five miles of the Gulf Freeway (now Interstate 45) to Galveston were opened in the late 1940s. Congressional appropriations under the new interstate highway law had facilitated extensive freeway development by the 1980s. In fact, by the 1980s more than three-quarters of a billion dollars had been spent to create a wheel-and-spoke system with 210 miles of freeways. Several major multi-lane highways converge on the downtown business district, including U.S. Hwy. 59, Interstate 45 (Gulf Freeway), and Interstate 10, the major east-west freeway. A circumferential belt freeway (Loop 610), circles the central area of the city and links the radial freeways. An outer loop (Beltway 8) is currently under construction, and a Grand Parkway has been proposed as a far outer loop.

The central role of the local business elite in these highway projects can be seen in the many discussions held on roads by the Houston Chamber of Commerce and its Highway Committee from the 1930s to the present. This committee had a major influence on the planning of the freeway grid being developed around the city. In the 1980s a chamber-developed Regional Mobility Plan was being implemented by local government. Much road planning has occurred in this private business organization, an all-white association in the critical 1930–1960 period. Because of this racial skew in Houston's leadership composition, Houston's nonwhite communities paid a substantial price for some highway development. Sections of the Fourth Ward, an important black community west of downtown created by freed slaves after the Civil War, were destroyed as Houston's freeway system developed. The Fifth Ward black community, north of the downtown area, was severely disrupted by the construction of two major highway systems now called Interstate 10 and Interstate 59. In addition, the Hispanic communities of Houston have periodically suffered from the bulldozers and earthmovers associated with freeway development.[14]

Road Development: Parkway Privatization

Houston's business leadership never seems content with the local highway system. The extensive freeway system and the inner belt currently under construction are viewed as inadequate to the development needs and profits of Houston's real estate elite. Public development of the road system seems too slow for this elite. One novel developer scheme for further expansion of Houston's freeway system is the Grand Parkway, an outer 155-mile loop already under development by private interests.

Pushed by west Houston landowners and developers who wish to open new land for development, this scheme has involved the creation of a Grand Parkway Association. In 1984 this private organization helped secure the Texas legislature's approval for private organizations to accumulate land for state road projects. In the late 1980s this Grand Parkway association was securing donations of right-of-way land from landowners and cash donations for private, not governmental, design and engineering work on the highway loop. After this initial developmental work is done privately, for an anticipated cost of $56 million, then the Texas Highway Department is expected to take over the project and build the Grand Parkway with taxpayers' money. Houston developers and land speculators are betting that the city's future lies in decentralized villages many miles from the downtown center. Moreover, one developer was quoted as saying that "in 20 years almost every major freeway built within a metropolitan area will be done this way." Houston is pioneering in a "build-your-own-road" approach to urban development that could conceivably signal a wave of such privatized development in metropolitan areas.[15]

Suburban Development in a Spread City

The First Decades of Houston's Expansion

Until the early 1900s Houston's city limits enclosed less than nine square miles; there was little commercial or residential development outside those boundaries. The earliest expansion of the metropolitan area was along the rail lines and the ship channel. By the 1890s developers had created residential areas beyond the original city boundaries, including Deer Park, South Houston, and the Heights. A few close-in suburban subdivisions were created in the 1902–1919 period. Woodland Heights, created in 1907, was advertised in a fashion that would become widespread across the United States: a "charming suburban park dotted with comfortable and artistic homes."[16]

By the 1920s the suburbanization paralleled the expansion and development of the road and highway system. Between the 1920s and the 1940s, for example, the self-contained suburban community of West University was substantially developed; it was created on reclaimed swamp land along major east-west thoroughfares a few miles southwest of the downtown area. West University grew slowly in the 1920s and 1930s, but by the late 1940s it was one of the fastest growing residential areas. It is a separate city with its own government and strong zoning and building ordinances, laws which have protected property values and kept the inner city suburb residential to the present day. Both inside and outside the central city area, most of Houston's residential space is occupied by single-family homes. In the older areas of the city these are mostly smaller homes with relatively little open space around them. There is considerable mixing of commercial strip development, mostly along thoroughfares, within the central city subdivisions. Some industrial areas are adjacent to these older residential areas, particularly on the east side of the city. The flow of capital into Houston's secondary circuit of real estate put the city on the national investment map. Carleton and Kreneck quote one business observer who, at an early point, was impressed by the dramatic residential development: "The wonderful growth of Houston is the topic of the hour among capitalists throughout the entire country." [17]

Development in Recent Decades

The major round of suburbanization took place from the late 1940s to the early 1980s. A construction boom was a part of the 1950s dynamism. In the 1950s no fewer than 99,000 new homes were built, thus expanding suburbia in the metropolitan area. By the 1960s apartment construction became a high proportion of all dwelling units constructed. Three-quarters of the residential development in Houston has been built since World War II, much of it in large-scale tract developments farther out from the central city. By the 1970s the area outside the central city, defined by Loop 610, had become a complex of suburban subdivisions, ranging from garden apartment complexes to mega-tract developments such as Kingwood (Exxon) and the Woodlands (see next section). In one twelve-year period culminating in the late 1970s Houston developers built several hundred suburban subdivisions with conventional names like Kings Forest, Pecan Grove Plantation, Golf Villas, and Whispering Pines, many on the western side of the city.

Federally subsidized highways and federal home mortgage programs made expansive suburbanization possible. The absence of zoning ordinances facilitated the proliferation of a series of suburbs fanning out along the interstate highway spokes radiating from Houston's downtown hub. Scattered among these outlying residential areas are numerous large shopping centers and regional shopping malls. In 1980 Houston had 200 shopping centers outside the downtown area; seventeen of these were in the "super-mall" category of over 750,000 square feet. [18]

The Woodlands: A Planned Satellite City

Moving farther out from the center of Houston than most outlying residential suburbs, one comes to a number of satellite city projects. One of the largest in the nation is The Woodlands, a project with twenty-five thousand acres of construction twenty-seven miles from downtown. The project is the brainchild of a Texas oil capitalist, George P. Mitchell, who in the 1960s began to invest some surplus capital and personal efforts into the building of a $5-billion satellite city of his design. Built by Woodlands Development Corporation, a subsidiary of Mitchell's oil company, the "planned unit development" is intended to be a city of 160,000 people by the time its thirty-six-year master plan is completed in the twenty-first century. Schools, shopping malls, condominiums, apartments, single-family homes, churches, recreational facilities, and transportation lines will be provided.[19]

The mid-1980s downturn in the Houston economy slowed development significantly. By 1987 20,000 people lived in 8,700 dwelling units, together with two shopping centers, seven schools, twenty-two churches, and 300 businesses with 6,000 employees. The developer had attracted a small university research center and a few high-tech firms to the area. Although Mitchell had expected to have 35,000 people by this point in time, he was undaunted by the downturn; he was quoted as saying that "this is something Houston needs, and that's why I continue with the project."[20] Mitchell's view of what he is doing is distinctive. Public relations brochures for the Woodlands speak of it as follows: "The hometown idea is refreshingly simple. You'll sense it during your first visit here." But his view of this hometown is more idealistic than that of most major urban developers.

Mitchell speaks of lower- and moderate-income housing as part of The Woodlands. He has insisted that The Woodlands eventually be annexed by the city of Houston so it will not become just another white upper-middle-income enclave feeding off an increasingly nonwhite central city. The Woodlands represents Mitchell's vision of solving current urban and suburban problems. He sees his philosophy providing a better quality of life by offering a well-planned city guided by wise executives in a private development corporation. For his part, Mitchell has moved investment capital from oil to satellite suburban-city development. Mitchell explains:

> Energy is a very fast moving business on pay-out. I have to drill a well every seven years because the well's gone by then, produced out. But if I build a building, it has a 40-year life. The longterm economics are what make it look interesting.
>
> If we do this well and build human resources and make a profit, then other people will have to do the same to compete with us.[21]

The Woodlands, Mitchell further notes, is "not Utopia, but it's a step better than anything done in the past."[22]

Mitchell's vision of a satellite city where the poor and the rich mingle in one planned suburban development will not be fulfilled. The profit logic of modern capitalism is such that new low- and moderate-income housing, in other than modest amounts, is practically beyond the pale, for it generates little or no profit. Thus, Mitchell's surplus capital will likely create another upper-middle-income residential suburb of Houston, but one with its own careful private planning, industrial parks, shopping centers, and recreational facilities. Interestingly Mitchell recognizes that such huge satellite suburbs require big companies, both development corporations and financial institutions, to provide the capital and governments for essential subsidies.

A significant feature of these large-scale planned unit developments, in many cities across the nation, is the role of the state. Federal government loan guarantees have been provided for $50 million in loans for The Woodlands project. The state provides essential social capital expenditure support for developments which generate privately appropriated profits. In addition, federal funds of $16.1 million were given to the developer as matching grants for community improvements, and another $9.7 million in federal money went to local governments and other organizations for projects in The Woodlands area. Here those involved in capital accumulation in suburban real estate received significant government assistance.[23]

A Note on Housing Investment

All was not rosy for Houston's residential developers and home-owning suburbanites in the 1980s. Shifts in the city's oil-based economy had a major impact on the bedroom communities. When the mid-1980s economic recession hit the city, several developers of suburban homesites went bankrupt. Many thousands of homeowners lost their jobs and, as a result, their homes. By 1986 the eighteen-mile arc of new subdivisions on the west side of the city had so many mortgage foreclosures that it was called the "foreclosure rainbow." In numerous subdivisions there were foreclosed houses on many blocks; some subdivisions had many vacant lots and vandalized, abandoned "new" homes. These tragic events point to the consequences of overinvestment in residential subdivisions. The Houston oil boom attracted a lot of capital and developers to the city in the 1960s and 1970s. Many subdivisions were built under the boom-generated promise of easy profits, and many residents were encouraged to overextend themselves for the enticing suburban dream. These dreams became a nightmare for both investors and ordinary suburbanites.

The impact of the downturn on housing was not confined to homeowners and suburbanites. One newspaper story in November 1987 discussed the bulldozing of 4,100 apartments in forty apartment complexes. The largest projects demolished had been built since 1956. Another 10,567 units had been taken off the market, most of which were not being renovated. Many owners had taken possession of the projects because of foreclosure; the news story noted that the investors could no longer profitably rent their complexes. They reduced their taxes and maintenance costs by destroying the apartment complexes. Such actions suggest the negative evaluation of prospects for profit among apartment investors and the short-lived character of much housing construction in this free enterprise city. These actions also reduced the housing available to renters, both in the present and the future.[24]

The Impact of Capital Investment: Houston's Office Buildings

The Importance of Office Buildings

Manhattan-scapes of high-rise towers, hotels, and apartment buildings are a relatively new development, for until the 1940s and 1950s most cities had modest-sized buildings either downtown or in outlying areas. Most high-rise office buildings in metropolitan areas have been built since World War II, a phenomenon associated with the growth in importance of large corporations. There is a close relationship between the character of capitalism in a particular historical period and its urban form. Office buildings are at the heart of the physical structure of modern capitalism, providing the places where the administrative, accounting, and other white-collar activities of dominant corporations and allied business service firms are located and interrelated. Larger corporations tend to build, or have built, tall skyscrapers.

Why are such skyscrapers constructed? Tall buildings are considerably more expensive to construct than are shorter and wider buildings with the same amount of floor space. It is estimated that the taller office towers cost at least 20 percent more per square foot than an equivalent building with fewer floors. The high price of land often justifies the creation of the super-skyscraper in downtown areas; however, the savings in land costs do not offset the premium building cost for a high-rise building.

Wittenberg has reported on a major office project in downtown Houston. The land cost $12.5 million, about 10 percent of the total cost, $127.5 million, of the building itself.[25] The land cost was no more than the cost of the expensive elevator system for this high-rise structure. If a larger lot had been purchased, the added cost of the land would have been much less than the added cost of high-rise elevator and air conditioning/heating systems. The reason for the high-rise buildings does not seem to be the high cost of the land in downtown Houston or other metropolitan areas; instead, the high-rise towers have been constructed both to facilitate the integration of large corporations, internally and externally with their support service firms, and to symbolize corporate presence and dominance. To quote the urban theorist Lamarche, "They are first and foremost the physical expression of the concentration of capital and of the close ties linking the headquarters of industry and the financial world." [26] Office buildings are not simply the products of an architect's imagination but rather a geographical solution to the integration of modern capitalism.

Office Development in the First Decades

Downtown Houston was the center of office development for the first few decades. Between 1908 and 1913 the expansion of the cotton firms and the oil corporations endowed downtown Houston with a skyline of buildings ranging from seven to seventeen stories. Following decreased construction after 1913, this real estate investment resurged in the roaring 1920s. Oil-fueled growth brought a spurt of residential, industrial, and office building construction. And there was a general increase in the height of the new structures. As Fox has expressed it, Houston's business leadership held the omnipresent romantic mythology that portrayed the high-rise office buildings as symbols of a modern era of urban civilization. [27] The erection of tall office and hotel buildings continued in the downtown area. Jesse Jones's thirty-seven-story Gulf Building (1929), the tallest west of the Mississippi at the time, and the twenty-one-story Sterling Building (1931) were constructed in the Art Deco style.

Moreover, high-rise construction spread to outlying areas. Two high-rise hotels constructed several miles south of downtown caused Houstonians in neighborhoods of single-family homes to decry the malignant spread of high-rise construction. A City Planning Commission report in 1929 pointed to an apartment hotel encroaching on the Montrose residential area to emphasize the negative consequences of absent zoning ordinances. With the onset of the Great Depression this type of construction slowed, and high-rise expansion outside the downtown area was curtailed.

High-Rise Construction in Boomtown

In an important report the Urban Land Institute, the U.S. think tank for large developers, documented the fact that since 1945 "new office buildings and

TABLE   7.2.
Number of Office Buildings
and Towers: 1899–1987

YEARS	Size (100,000 ft^2 or more)
1899–1910	3
1911–1920	6
1921–1930	10
1931–1940	1
1941–1950	2
1951–1960	15
1961–1970	38
1971–1980	159
1981–1987	251
TOTAL	485

SOURCE: Calculated by author from directory in the Houston Chamber of Commerce Economic Development Council, "1985 Guide to Office Space," *Houston* 56 (February 1985), pp. 35–62; and "By Area, Construction is Down as Market Works Off an Oversupply," *Houston* 57 (February 1986), pp. 35–54.
NOTE: Extant buildings by date of completion or projected completion.

office parks have accounted for an ever-increasing share of the capital devoted to real estate." [28] This was the case for the Houston metropolitan area from the late 1940s to the early 1980s. During this period numerous large office and commercial buildings were completed, creating many business activity centers outside the downtown area. One of the first decentralization moves involved a hotel. In 1949 the Shamrock, a major hotel, was built several miles south of the old downtown area. It was soon joined by the Prudential Insurance Company building. These major projects became the anchors for large-scale development on undeveloped land several miles south of downtown.

Beginning in the 1960s, Houston's population and industrial growth were matched with increments in the built environment of office buildings. Table 7.2 presents a historical overview of major office buildings in Houston. Altogether 485 sizable office buildings of at least 100,000 square feet had been built or were under construction; another 400 were in the 50,000 to 100,000 square foot size category. Among extant buildings only nine were built before 1920.

The most spectacular real estate investment boom took place in the 1971–1987 period, when more than 80 percent of *all* major office buildings were constructed in the metropolitan area. These buildings represent billions of dollars in real estate investment. This spectacular construction boom had a profound effect on the downtown area. Although the new buildings had an extremely dramatic effect on the skyline, they generally were inward-looking, often plaza-centered; they were all the same in their unrelieved massive architecture, and they drove out the mixed uses of retail commerce and entertainment that had once characterized the downtown area. Where there were no buildings, the land was often cleared and "banked" in blacktopped parking lots.[29]

Table 7.3 plots this office development on an annual basis between 1971 and 1987. The pattern is one of an oscillating number completed. There is a general increase from 1971 to 1983, then a precipitous decline from 1983 to 1987 in buildings constructed or under construction. In 1971 just nineteen large buildings were completed. The number of major buildings completed drops to a low of 7 to 8 in 1974–1975, then begins to climb more or less regularly to a peak of seventy-nine major buildings in 1982. Between 1982 and 1987 a remarkable decrease in construction took place; in 1985 only fifteen buildings were completed, and only two buildings were scheduled for completion in 1987. The pattern of square footage added generally follows this same pattern, although the completion of a very large building significantly inflates the space for certain years.

Since World War II the total square footage of office space in Houston has increased dramatically:

1949   6.9 million
1959   12.3 million
1969   18.6 million
1979   85.2 million
1985   159.2 million
1986   163.5 million

Office buildings are usually built in one of two ways: either for one particular tenant or on a multitenant basis. In 1985 Houston had about 159.2 million square feet of office space, with 133 million square feet in multitenant buildings. Houston's square footage in office space was reportedly the third largest amount for any city in the United States. When compared to cities of similar size like Philadelphia, with 41.8 million square feet, or Boston, with 58.4 million square feet, the enormity of the investments in Houston's office construction boom becomes clear.[30]

TABLE   7.3.
Major Office Buildings by Date of Completion,
Paralleled with Crude Oil Prices (Houston
Metropolitan Area)

DATE	Number of Large Office Bldgs	Sq. Ft. Added[c]	Crude Oil Price (Bbl) (in $)
1971	19	5,002,000	3.39
1972	11	3,347,000	3.39
1973	13	5,392,000	3.89
1974	7	2,935,000	6.87
1975	8	3,053,000	7.67
1976	11	2,829,000	8.19
1977	21	4,112,000	8.57
1978	16	6,841,000	9.00
1979	21	6,222,000	12.64
1980	32	10,297,000	21.59
1981	46	13,892,000	31.77
1982	79	21,760,000	28.52
1983	75	20,123,000	26.19
1984	27	8,181,000	25.91
1985	15	3,780,000	24.00
1986	7	3,800,000	12.51
1987	2[a]	—[b]	15.41

SOURCES: Department of Energy, Energy Information Administration, *Monthly Energy Review,*
January 1985; Economic Development Council, "1985 Guide to Office Space," *Houston* 56 (February 1985), pp. 35–62; Research Division, Houston Chamber of Commerce, "A Year-by-Year
Survey of Houston Office Building Development: 1949–1985," *Houston Business Journal,* July
30, 1984, p. 26c; "By Area, Construction is Down as Market Works Off an Oversupply," *Houston*
57 (February 1986), pp. 34–54.
[a]Expected date of completion for buildings under construction in 1986.
[b]Data unavailable at this time.
[c]Multiple-tenant buildings only.

Decentralization of Development: Houston's Western Tilt

Interestingly, much of Houston's development has had a western orientation.
Many of the residential subdivisions, apartment complexes, and retail shopping centers have been built in the western half of the metropolitan area. In

recent decades development has not spread evenly from the center of the city, a center that once dominated the city's built environment. Extensive highway subsidization by the state, coupled with relatively weak regulation of development, facilitated the move to the west. Decentralization of office construction has also tilted in the westward direction.

Within the Houston metropolitan area four geographical areas have substantial office development: downtown, the southwest corridor spreading out from downtown, the international airport area, and the northwest corridor spreading out from downtown. The largest buildings, including ten of the twelve buildings over fifty stories in height and thirty-four of those from twenty to forty-nine stories in height, are downtown. Outside the downtown blocks only the southwest area has a significant number of very tall buildings; this area was the first to be developed beyond the center in the 1950s. In this "energy corridor" area well over half of all Houston's office buildings have been constructed. Both the northwest corridor and airport areas were expanded later, during the capital infusion of the 1970s and 1980s. Few of Houston's major office buildings can be found in the eastern half of the metropolitan area.

Downtown and Other
Business Activity Centers

Within the broad areas just delineated there are eighteen definable business centers, each with its own concentration of major buildings. Map 7.1 plots the eighteen major activity centers. In addition to the downtown complex there are several major concentrations in the central city. Twelve important office activity centers lie outside the central city (Loop 610) and include concentrations at Clear Lake (N A S A) and Post Oak (Galleria). Some of these dispersed concentrations have less than one million square feet of total office space, but others are in the ten to thirty-five million square feet range, the equivalent of the total office space in many downtown urban areas. This highly decentralized pattern of office development is distinctive. While other major cities have few large buildings outside the downtown area, Houston has many.

Among the major office centers, the downtown area is the largest. In the postwar period downtown space went through an extended period of commercial and office development; some construction involved major private redevelopment. Between 1945 and 1970 several dozen downtown office buildings were constructed. From 1970 to 1987 many more office buildings were built. In this 1,000-acre complex are Houston's tallest buildings; the tallest is the seventy-

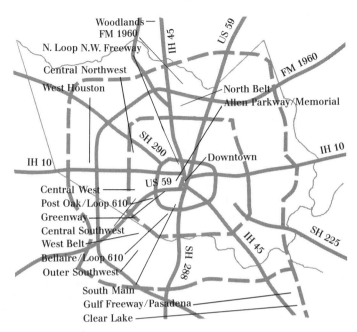

MAP 7.1. Eighteen Major and Developing Office Activity Centers in Houston

SOURCE: Rice Center, "Questionnaire Results on Office Location Issues in Houston," *Research Brief 4* (Houston: Rice Center, 1980), p. 3. By permission of Rice Center

five-story Texas Commerce Bank building (1.7 million square feet), whose developer/owners in the early 1980s were Gerald P. Hines Interests, one of the nation's two top developers, and the Texas Commerce Bank, one of the nation's twenty-five largest banks.

Most of these downtown office building projects required some privately funded clearance of earlier structures, including warehouses, stores, and older office buildings. The largest of these downtown clearance projects, the Houston Center multiple-use development, was inaugurated by the leader of the Suite 8F crowd, George Brown. Houston developers have been pioneers in multiple-use developments (M X DS), one of the newest types of urban development. Some developers see M X DS as part of a development wave reshaping metropolitan life. According to the Urban Land Institute an M X D is a large-scale real estate venture with three or more types of profit-generating activities integrated into one land-intensive development project.[31] These activities can include office buildings, shopping malls, apartment buildings, convention centers, and hotels—all as part of one integrated megastructure complex. Houston's multiple-use projects have been built on a huge scale, one that rivals the biggest building projects in all of human history. Three M X DS—the downtown Houston Center and the decentralized Greenway Plaza and Galleria complexes—are among the largest in the United States, each built by a major national developer.

The Houston Center project was begun in the late 1960s by George Brown's Texas Eastern Corporation, which bought thirty-three square blocks on the east side of downtown Houston. At the time of purchase this was a diverse area of older commercial buildings, small hotels, apartment houses, and homes. The project has been proclaimed by its developer as remolding urban life: Houston Center means "the creation of an entirely new city offering fresh approaches to work, recreation and residence. It may well be the prototype of the city of the future." [32]

In a speech an executive of the Houston Center project emphasized that the development group seeks to revitalize the downtown area so it is more than a place to work, "to restore a mix of activities by including hotel, retail, residential and leisure-time [activities] within the project." [33] The developer received permission from the city government to close some streets entirely to remake this section of the downtown area. By the mid-1980s the Houston Center included a forty-four-story office tower and a forty-six-story office tower linked together by an eight-story street-spanning wing with a landscaped plaza. Two additional blocks had been sold to a major bank, which built another office tower and a garage. A thirty-story hotel had been constructed as part of the project along with an exclusive athletic and dining club. In the works were other major office buildings.

By 1983 the Houston Center complex contained twenty thousand workers and residents. Houston Center was originally expected to provide more than twenty million square feet of megastructures—hotels, office towers, stores, people-mover vehicles, and parking for forty thousand cars—integrated into one complex. [34] In the mid-1970s Texas Eastern lagged in its development schedule; the firm sold half interest in major sections of the project to Canadian-based Cadillac Fairview, at the time one of the world's largest development corporations. The developer also gave several blocks farthest from the center of downtown to the local government so that city authorities could build the convention center complex discussed in Chapter 4.

Energy Complexes

Much of the office tower development has been generated to house energy-related corporations. Major oil and gas companies require large amounts of space for their managerial, financial, exploration, research, marketing, and accounting operations. In the mid-1980s, about 61 percent of the office space in the downtown area was occupied by energy-related firms, with banks, law firms, and accounting firms occupying another 30 percent. Thirty-three corporations with offices in downtown Houston employed more than 1,000 people, including Exxon, Gulf, and Shell.[35] Note the symbiotic relationship between the administrative centers of the energy and business service firms. The significance of this symbiosis can be seen in a survey of tenants in downtown office buildings. Hyland asked the tenants what items were most important in locating their offices. The items most often cited were (1) nearness to banks and other financial institutions, (2) cost, and (3) location near highways. This finding underscores the importance of finance capital institutions and state-provided highways in the location decisions of industrial and business service firms.[36]

Decentralized Business Activity Centers

Developers have played a key role in decentralizing office space, as they have sought out lower-priced land outside the downtown area. And the decentralized office projects have accelerated the construction of adjacent residential and shopping mall projects. Thus urban theories which accent abstracted technological forces neglect the important role of particular capitalistic actors, those whose investment-oriented actions shape not only the large-scale projects they develop but also areas around those projects. Outside the downtown area the most important business activity centers lie in the southwest corridor, the area running from downtown west to Memorial Park and southwest roughly along the Southwest Freeway (Interstate 59). This most intensively developed business corridor in the city encompasses unique concentrations such as the Texas Medical Center four miles south of downtown. The medical complex includes more than thirty different educational, research, treatment, and support facilities and institutions. Nearby are the South Main commercial area, Rice University, and the Astrodome entertainment complex.

Particularly significant in the southwest corridor are the Greenway Plaza and Post Oak office and commercial complexes about five miles southwest of downtown. These office-centered, multiple-use developments are closely linked to Houston's regional freeway network. A critical transportation feature of this sector of Houston is the western section of Interstate Highway Loop 610. The first section of this freeway opened in 1962–1963, facilitating the rise of the Post Oak area as a major retail and office center. The largest office complex outside downtown Houston can be found in the Post Oak area. In the mid-1980s the area had more than twenty million square feet of office space.

Although this area is not a centrally planned development, it does center on the Galleria, a famous regional shopping mall on two hundred acres (developed by Gerald Hines Interests), a twenty-two-story Post Oak Tower, a four-hundred-room hotel, other large office buildings, hotels, and apartment buildings.[37] Numerous corporate, divisional, and regional headquarters for oil, gas, computer, and real estate companies are located here. About half are energy or engineering firms.

In 1982 one-fifth of Houston's new housing units were within a thirty-minute drive of the Post Oak area at peak driving periods. Neighborhood access can be very important to firms locating in office buildings. Much development capital flows into accessible residential projects, including single-family homes and apartment buildings. An Urban Land Institute analysis of Houston suggests that this decentralization of office construction has followed, not led, the decentralization of residential subdivisions populated by white-collar workers. Office towers are said to have been built close to white-collar workers to reduce communting times. Yet this view overlooks the determinative importance of investor and developer actions and related state highway decisions which at an early point channeled and facilitated the office decentralization to sections like the Post Oak area.[38]

The major investment builder in the Galleria/Post Oak complex is Gerald D. Hines. At least $2 billion worth of office buildings, shopping malls, and other large projects have been erected by Hines's company in cities from New York to San Francisco. Between the 1950s and the 1980s Hines's company built 273 projects, altogether about 55 million square feet of space. Headquartered in Houston, Hines's company is internationally famous for architecturally distinctive buildings and showy openings.[39]

The Greenway Plaza: A Planned MXD Complex

In the mid-1980s the Greenway Plaza area was the third largest office complex in Houston. Four miles from downtown, this island of office towers, also in the southwest energy corridor, centers around Century Development Corporation's development called the Greenway Plaza. The construction of this M X D complex of office and commercial buildings involved the buying up of three hundred single-family homes in four residential subdivisions. Century Development Corporation bought up houses from middle-income residents at above-market prices. Once the houses had been bought, the developer changed subdivision deed restrictions from residential to commercial. Greenway Plaza is of such a scale that it required financing from major U.S. financial capital firms, the Equitable Life and Northwestern Mutual Life companies. Construction of Greenway Plaza is projected to be finished in the late 1980s, at a total cost of more than $1 billion. This megastructure project encompasses 127 acres of central city land, an area about the size of sixty downtown blocks. In its first two phases, nearly four million square feet of office space were constructed. By the 1980s Greenway Plaza included a thirty-two-story oil tower, an eleven-story Union Carbide building, a nine-story Dow Center complex, a twenty-two-story building, the Richmond and Buffalo towers, a chemical company building, a luxury hotel, high-rise apartment buildings, a huge parking garage, a heliport, and a major sports arena. By the mid-1980s the general Greenway Plaza area had more than ten million square feet of office space, housing 41,000 employees. About 70 percent of the space was occupied by energy and engineering companies.[40]

The Source of Capital for the Construction Boom

Investing in Houston Real Estate

The rapid flow of capital into Houston during the boom of the 1967–1982 period was central to this surge of industrial, commercial, and residential construction. David Harvey has extensively explored the concept of the secondary circuit of capital, a concept drawn from Henri Lefebvre and one with substantial potential for analysis of the shifting capital flows into the built environments essential to production and consumption. In Harvey's view a surplus of capital in the primary circuit of commodity production can result in the flow of capital to the built environment. Overproduction and overaccumulation are chronic problems in a capitalistic system. Surplus money capital is typically recirculated through a variety of financial institutions. The movement of capital into the secondary circuit of real estate construction thus contributes to the generation of a finance capital system. A major aspect of Harvey's argument about the secondary circuit is that investment in the built environment is undertaken not only for the obvious use-value reasons—more office space for large corporations—but also for financial reasons, that is, as part of the quest for the highest rate of return on investment of excess capital. State and financial institutions play a strong mediating role in shifting capital into and out of the primary and secondary circuits.

In *The Urbanization of Capital*, Harvey's empirical analysis illustrates the

importance of the secondary circuit of real estate investment in broad historical periods.[41] The two global economic crises of the 1930s and the 1970s were
preceded in countries like the United States and Great Britain by major movements of capital into long-term real estate development, a capital mobility
which Harvey views as a last-ditch attempt to find productive uses for an excessive surplus of capital in the primary circuit of investment in such items as
manufacturing operations. Gottdiener has criticized Harvey for failing to
specify adequately the relationship between the state and space and for failing
to understand that investment in land has its own dynamic, to a substantial
extent independent of overaccumulation problems in the primary circuit of investment. Spatial production is the material manifestation of complex political and economic processes associated with phases of capitalist development.
Moreover, sociospatial patterns are the product of contradictory processes of
capitalistic development, rather than being necessarily functional for capital
accumulation.[42]

Where did the surplus capital which flowed into the secondary circuit in
Houston come from? What was its principal source? Harvey argues that a
boom in investment in the secondary circuit is fueled by surplus capital which
cannot find an acceptable rate of return in the primary circuit of production.
This is a plausible argument, for which there is some evidence in the Houston
data. However, as Gottdiener has emphasized, investment in space has a logic
of its own. The real estate investment sector is a highly leveraged sector, with
its own distinctive tax advantages and, in boom situations, a high rate of return on capital. Moreover, capital invested in urban real estate may not stem
from the primary circuit, at a particular time.

What was the source of the massive amounts of capital that flowed into the
secondary circuit of Houston real estate? We can exclude one reasonable explanation in this regard. Analysts have suggested that the building boom in
certain Sunbelt cities was funded by the direct recycling of oil company profits from the nearly tenfold rise in the price of oil during the 1971–1981 decade. These huge profits stemmed ultimately from the extraction of oil from
the ground and from oil refining as well. Petrodollars flowed into major U.S.
banks, including to some extent Houston banks. Thus, it would seem reasonable that some of this surplus capital, unable to find profitable oil investments
and mediated by the banks, flowed into Houston real estate. Indeed, the data
in the last column of Table 7.3 suggest an apparent connection between the
rising price of a barrel of crude oil and, with a two- to three-year time lag, an
increase in office building construction in Houston. Oil prices increased from
$3.39 a barrel in 1971 to $31.77 a barrel in 1981, then decreased significantly.
It would seem logical then that the city often called the "oil capital of the
world" would prosper physically, as well as in economic terms, as the profu-

sion of petrodollars sought out new investments. Moreover, according to this line of argument, when the price of a barrel of oil declines, building construction plummets sharply.

Yet the evidence weighs against this explanation of the source of most surplus capital which poured into office and other large-scale construction. My interviews with lending officials in Houston uncovered the fact that only a modest proportion of the surging oil company ("windfall") profits actually flowed into U.S. real estate, including Houston area development projects. This finding is buttressed by other studies of these new petrodollars that show the flow of such dollars into top executive salaries, shareholder dividends, acquisitions of nonoil firms, expensive oil company mergers, and multibillion dollar loans (often via multinational banks) to Third World countries. These newly generated petrodollars did not constitute the primary source of the surplus capital flowing into Houston development projects.[43]

Finance Capital and the World Market

The key to the mystery lies in finance capital institutions inside and outside Texas: the commercial banks, investment trusts, and insurance and mortgage companies. These financial institutions channeled much surplus capital from various sources into Houston real estate during the growth period. In Houston, as elsewhere, development corporations rely heavily on national and international finance capital in building projects such as office towers, shopping malls, and suburban subdivisions. Financing large-scale urban projects such as major office towers is usually complicated. A commercial bank may provide the short-term construction financing, while a real estate investment trust, foreign investor, or insurance company may provide the long-term mortgage financing. Insurance companies have become very important in financing large-scale projects. For example, by 1980 Prudential Insurance and its real estate subsidiary held $2 billion in real estate assets in Houston alone.[44]

Houston's major local banks became heavily involved in real estate loans by the late 1960s and early 1970s. As a rule the banks' loan portfolios were in the areas of oil-gas and real estate loans. The capital for these loans came from many sources, including syndications with "upstream" banks, the deposits of ordinary Houstonians, and corporate deposits. To some extent corporate deposits included oil-gas company profits. As a result of these heavy banking commitments to the oil and real estate sectors, when the severe recession of the mid-1980s hit, the big Houston banks faced financial difficulties.

A major source of the surplus capital circulating into Houston land and construction has come from overseas. Foreign investments in Houston have frequently poured into the office buildings and multiple-use developments. By the early 1970s Houston was part of a world market in investments. And in the late 1970s Houston was second only to New York as a place for foreign capital to invest in office buildings. European, Middle Eastern, and South American firms and individuals invested substantially in central city and suburban real estate. In the late 1980s a Coldwell Banker survey found that 39 percent of downtown office buildings were owned wholly or in part by foreign investors, mostly by West Germans, Saudi Arabians, and other Middle Eastern investors. The Deutschebank of West Germany, for example, owned 80 percent of the Pennzoil twin towers and also 50 percent of the fifty-story Shell building. A British pension fund was involved with office buildings downtown, and other British invested in suburban subdivisions.[45]

During the boom period, outside investors said to their banks and other brokers, according to one local expert, "if it's in Houston, I want it." An array of experienced and inexperienced developers surfaced to exploit this demand for a high return on investment capital. Lenders often accepted what the developers told them about the viability of a projected office building project; meanwhile some developers aggressively pushed questionable development projects.[46] Many institutions wanted to lend to developers; during the building boom at least sixty major outside lenders were active in Houston, including major foreign banks. Speaking about the behavior of finance capital during the boom, one prominent Houston broker argued that "when there is money to build buildings, developers will arise to relieve the banks of those monies. . . . The source of [much of] this funding did not come from [Texas banks]. . . . It came from outside lenders . . . basically responding not to any market place, but to a need to lend funds, and to the fact that certain parties had a need to buy a product."[47] Clearly the facts indicate Harvey's point: much of the capital flowing into the secondary circuit in Houston was surplus capital which had to be placed by institutional investors. Moreover, a former Citibank executive pointed out that Houston's overbuilt environment shows that finance capital has a "herd mentality"; lenders move to "hot" cities. He noted that in the boom period Houston became a world money center with "plenty of money available at the best possible world rates."[48]

Finance capital consists of differentiated fractions, including not only banks and mortgage companies but also a variety of syndication firms. By the late 1970s real estate syndication deals had become important for the Houston real estate boom, particularly limited partnerships which allowed wealthy investors to join with a developer to buy office buildings and other projects. During the boom period syndicators from all parts of the country bought commercial property to sell to investors, small and large, including northern and foreign concerns. In this period about 80 percent of syndications in Houston involved office buildings, shopping centers, and apartment projects, with the remaining 20 percent in land deals.

While outside banks and outside investors working through syndications became important sources of capital during the boom years in Houston, large Texas banks played a significant role as conduits of local and outside capital, linking the large U.S. multinational banks into the process by means of "correspondent" arrangements. Indeed, the complexity of the banking arrangements is such that one can raise serious questions about a too elementary picture of surplus capital flowing from the primary circuit into the secondary circuit. Although it is impossible to secure data from the world banking system on specific sources of capital, partial data for Houston indicate that surplus capital lurks in many nooks in the world capitalist system, not just in situations of overproduction in the primary circuit. Surplus capital may exist in the coffers of manufacturing corporations or financial institutions in one region or country, and that capital may flow into another country when it is profitable to do so. This appears to have been the case in the Houston real estate expansion, when surplus capital from the Middle East, South America, and Europe flowed into Houston real estate through various finance capital intermediaries. Probably much of that capital was already well removed from the primary circuit and resided in banks or even in real estate outside the Sunbelt. Land investment is often attractive to investors, whatever happens in the primary investment circuit.

The Central Role of the State in the Construction Boom

Local and Federal State Intervention

Harvey, Gottdiener, and other critical urban theorists have emphasized the important role of government in facilitating and creating urban real estate development. Both local state aid and federal state intervention have played significant roles in spurring office tower and other real estate investment in all areas of Houston. Earlier in this chapter I explored the important role of the federal state in providing massive infusions of public investment capital into auto-centered transport networks. The weak regulatory environment provided by the local government, including the lack of zoning, encouraged decentralized development and accelerated the actual production of commercial structures across the metropolitan area. In addition, major state action at the federal level helps spur office and other commercial construction.

For years the U.S. federal tax code had a generous tax loophole ("tax expenditure") for real estate investors. Owning property such as apartment buildings and office towers could involve large tax deductions for building depreciation where a certain percentage of a building's cost could be deducted each year. This deduction reflects a fictitious notion because many buildings do not in fact depreciate in worth at that annual rate.[49] Between 1969 and 1981 the depreciation deduction was gradually liberalized at the federal level—a result of successful lobbying by the real estate industry. Because of the liberal depreciation allowances in the U.S. tax code, much office construction in Houston has been "tax-driven"; that is, investments have been made in office tower projects not only to make profits from leasing building space itself but also to save substantial amounts in federal taxes. This clearly demonstrates a capitalistic market being channeled by state-provided advantages. Changes in the tax code in the mid-1980s may alter this loophole substantially.

The Houston Case

The role of the state is very important in the real estate arena, not only in regard to taxation but also in regard to the many types of subsidies provided for attracting industrial capital to urban locations. Both the federal and the local states have substantially contributed to creating an extraordinarily favorable growth and business climate in Houston. Local political officials have advanced private real estate development by refraining from imposing significant planning, building, and zoning restrictions on Houston developers; and they have worked closely with the business elite to disburse federal funds for infrastructure development. Yet this development aid is not the only example of federal state intervention. This federal largess—for example, extensive federal aid for freeway expansion and federal assistance for Houston's growing dependence on nuclear powered electric utilities—facilitated the construction of large-scale development projects.

The Consequences of Overbuilt Housing Markets: The Office Building Case

Overproduction of Space

The rapid increase in construction of large-scale real estate projects led to a number of problems, including inferior construction. The office boom created millions of square footage in poorly constructed buildings. One development executive stated: "Amateur developers who had never built an office building before got into the market and threw something up. . . . There are buildings that don't have things like adequate air conditioners, or adequate elevators. Location was always the biggest mistake." [50]

The Impact of High Vacancy Rates

When the mid-1980s oil-gas recession came to Houston, both corporate work-forces and leased office and commercial space were reduced. High vacancy rates for industrial plants resulted. Similarly, by 1984 the vacancy rate in Houston office buildings was running four times the rate normally considered profitable. Between 1978 and 1987 the vacancy rate for all buildings in the Houston downtown area ran as follows, compared to the rate for all U.S. cities:

	Houston	U.S. Cities
1978	2.5%	6.9%
1982	2.3	7.1
1985	24.0	20.1
1987(mid)	30.6	not available

Between 1978 and 1982 the vacancy rate in Houston was lower than the national average, but by 1983 it was rising dramatically. Late in 1984 prime ("Class A") office space in Houston was running at a 19 percent vacancy rate in the downtown area and a 29 percent rate in the decentralized business centers. The total vacancy figure was more than 21 percent for all office buildings in the entire city. These 1984 rates were much higher than in Frostbelt cities such as New York (6 percent, downtown; 9 percent, suburban) and Chicago (11 percent, downtown; 8 percent, suburban). By 1986 the vacancy rate had climbed to one-quarter of all the office space; in mid-1987 the figure was approaching one-third. [51]

In addition, a game of "musical buildings" was created in which some office buildings completed before 1980 had a vacancy rate of 40 percent or more, while some newer buildings had lower rates secured by stealing tenants from older buildings. This resulted in a chessboard of occupied and unoccupied space. Compared to other cities, in 1985 Houston had the most unleased office space and also the greatest increase in newly leased and occupied space. The corporate movement out of older buildings into new buildings explained this apparent contradiction.

The Need for Leasing Concessions

In 1979–1981 the high cost of leasing office space in downtown Houston had driven tenants to outlying office complexes. But by 1984 the rising vacancy rate brought many back to the downtown area, where they were then seeking leasing concessions. A 1985 survey of corporate tenants in six downtown buildings found that 86 percent had received some type of rent concession. Half had received free rent for six to twelve months, and some received lower rent payments, old-lease buyouts, or moving expenses. "Banking" cheaper square footage, numerous companies were found to be leasing more office space than they currently needed; thus, the official vacancy rate was not as high as the actual vacancy rate.[52]

A related response to the overbuilding was an increase in aggressive courting of tenants by developer-owners. Unusual epideictic displays could be seen, for example, in the actions of a developer of an eleven-story building a great distance from downtown Houston. Although the building was in a depressed office market area, it was 85 percent leased. The developer had, as one real estate broker put it, "a reputation for enjoyable parties and a cooperative attitude toward brokers." This development firm threw a lavish opening party for its new building, complete with a safari theme, a wild game dinner, and champagne. No fewer than 1,200 people drove, many a long distance, to the party.[53]

The Trickle of Real Estate Capital

In the mid-1980s recession the movement of capital into the secondary circuit of real estate development in Houston slowed significantly. This situation underscores Harvey's point about the oscillation of investment flows from one circuit to another over time. Overproduction can be as real in the secondary circuit of speculative real estate as in the primary circuit. When the mid-1980s oil-gas recession came, outside syndicators and other lenders left Houston in large numbers. Northern investors, one expert noted, were "ready to write off all of Texas" and Houston as places to participate in real estate deals. When the downturn began to deepen and spread to all types of megastructure projects, the growing vacancy rates brought developers and other office building owners into financial crisis. As a result, the developers' banks faced substantial amounts of what they termed, euphemistically, "nonperforming loans" and "charge-offs." Nonperforming loans are those either not paid back on a timely basis or renegotiated to prevent foreclosure. Charge-off loans are noncollectible loans written off as bank losses.

For example, in the first six months of 1985 the eleven largest bank holding companies in Texas, many of them involved in Houston real estate loans, saw an increase of $368 million in nonperforming real estate loans. Charge-offs increased by $200 million in the same period. For the entire year of 1985 major Houston-based bankholding companies such as Texas Commerce Banc-shares, Inc., and First City Bancorporation experienced sharp increases in non-performing loans over 1984, to $654 million and $563 million respectively. Charge-offs for these two banks were also up significantly, to $186 million and $260 million respectively. Although these figures include not only real estate loans but also energy and miscellaneous loans, they do signal a major crisis in the banking mediators which channel surplus capital into real estate. First City failed in 1987 and required a federal bailout. Moreover, many Houston and other Texas banks failed during the 1980s oil and real estate crisis. Other Houston banks became involved in the rash of corporate mergers in the 1980s. In 1986 Jesse Jones's Texas Commerce Bank merged with New York's Chemical Bank to create the fourth largest bankholding firm in the United States.[54]

Channeling the Flow of Investment Capital: The Role of Image

Understanding pouring surplus capital into the secondary circuit of real estate requires understanding why key actors in banking and development firms be-have the way they do. It might be expected that decisions to invest in major office building projects in specific cities would involve careful cost-accounting research on the market setting, as well as careful analysis of what other devel-opment capitalists are doing. Yet interviews with real estate actors and experts in the Gulf Coast area revealed that the built environments of cities like Hous-ton gain a reputation among investors and investment brokers for being "hot" or "cold" for investments. Cities like Houston become "hot" areas for in-vestors who, as one local housing researcher put it, are like "hogs running to the trough."[55]

Why a particular city gets this reputation would be an important subject for research. Gerald Suttles has explored the reasons that cities get journalistic characterizations such as "space" or "oil city" in Houston's case.[56] But city images are a bit different for investors. Apparently cities gain "hot" images based on how they are assessed by major corporate location firms such as the Fantus company and by major business media such as the *Wall Street Journal* or *Business Week*. Also important in generating the "hot" image is a real eco-nomic boom. In the case of Houston the oil-gas boom during the 1970s gave Houston a low unemployment rate, a soaring economy, and much exaggerated media coverage. The business media hyped the hot image of the city as a place to invest well beyond the point where economic bust was the underlying reality.

Harvey views investment in the secondary circuit as consistently functional for a capitalist system whose primary circuit is overloaded. But the Houston data indicate how dysfunctional real estate investments can be, not only for the ordinary citizens whose housing needs are not met but also for capitalists themselves. Development and finance capitalists frequently make decisions about urban development projects which are irrational from a tough cost-accounting approach. As investors themselves note in business newspapers, many development decisions are made on the basis of "feel" and "image." There is a social psychological dimension to capital investments flowing into the real estate environment. One real estate expert in Houston noted in the *Houston Business Journal* that "for what would seem to be sophisticated business, real estate is awfully unsophisticated. It's done by feel or by stomach. Buildings go up and are financed and designed without a lot of research." [57]

Real estate investment is to a substantial degree based on faith, on speculative guesses about what inflation and leasing rates will be over a period of three to thirty years. This same expert spoke further of "an inordinate amount of self-gratification" by office building developers, who feel that the distinctiveness and location of their particular building will overcome the competition and any economic crisis. Research studies by social psychologists on individual and group decision making have found that individuals vary greatly in their willingness to make risky choices. But researchers also found that in group decision making the group tends to make more risky choices than most of the group's members would make alone. This may be one factor in the social psychology of capital investors who flocked to Houston for a time and then quickly moved en masse when the city gained a "cold" image. [58]

Conclusion: The Real Estate Circuit of Capital

Understanding capital flow is important to understanding how cities are built. Like other major cities in the Sunbelt, Houston has provided in its fixed-capital real estate sector a major outlet for surplus capital of all types. Houston real estate developments have absorbed large amounts of surplus capital, not just from U.S. financial institutions but also from foreign investors. Over-accumulation of capital in the primary circuit and elsewhere is a recurring problem for capitalism, fueling a broad array of investment ventures from office tower development to frequent mergers of large companies to speculation in the stock markets.

But the flow of capital into manufacturing plants, office buildings, shopping malls, and residential subdivisions has its own logic as well; it does not simply depend on excess capital in the primary investment circuit. The built environment of cities functions as the general precondition for both production and consumption forces. Space must be rearranged and produced for that production and consumption to occur. But that space is also a major place for the investment of capital, an investment process linked to increasing the value of footloose capital, whether or not there is great utility for production or consumption purposes. With finance capitalists aggressively seeking the highest rate of return for investors, depositors, or shareholders, investment speed can accelerate or decelerate depending on either world conditions of real estate profitability or the amount of surplus capital.

The role of the state is very important, in regard to taxation and the many subsidies provided for attracting industrial capital to urban locations. Tax and grant subsidies are provided for attracting industrial capital to urban locations. Local governments usually have close ties to the local growth coalitions composed of the land-interested local business ventures emphasized. State actions in the form of freeway expenditures or weak governmental building regulations, usually at the behest of business lobbying, can greatly affect the profitability of real estate investments—and thus shape the built environment in those areas of investment.

Harvey has suggested that cycles of speculative investment in the city environment generate a chaotic ferment out of which new spatial configurations can grow. A built environment of office buildings on Houston's 160-million-square-feet scale can be a major *barrier* to new spatial configurations. Just as one Houston developer in the mid-1980s tore down a twenty-story office building to make way for a (now postponed) eighty-two-story supertower, many of today's large office buildings would have to be torn down, before their time, to make way for new spatial configurations; thus, much capital embedded in the built environment of Houston and similar cities would be permanently destroyed. In addition, it is frequently advantageous for manufacturing and commercial firms if the capital embedded in land and buildings is owned by someone else because that situation increases their own ability to move. There is the potential conflict among different factions of capital in this situation: "If the capital locked into the built environment is owned by a separate faction of capital, then the stage is also set for inter-factional conflict."[59] Industrial firms and developers may, eventually if not currently, have different interests. In the case of Houston, the circulation of capital through the built environment of cities has created a highly specialized system with diverse capitalistic agents involved in the process.

8

Problems in a Free Enterprise
Paradise: The Social Costs of
the Good Business Climate

Many urban problems are the social costs of the private enterprise system predominant in U.S. and western European cities. Much discussion of urban problems has targeted declining cities with long-term negative prospects such as Detroit and Newark. But the social costs of growth in boomtowns have received much less attention. Because the preeminent U.S. boomtown from the 1940s to the early 1980s was Houston, it is instructive to examine the social consequences of urban growth in this "capital of the Sunbelt." The Houston case is even more interesting given the unexpected and severe economic downturn that struck the city in the mid-1980s. In effect, Houston has been both a premier boomtown and a leading "busttown" in the late twentieth century.

Calculating the Price of Growth

All cities have urban problems associated with growth and decline. Serious infrastructural and environmental problems can be found in many U.S. cities, but the character, scope, and recurrence of these problems are different in cities where the business elites have carefully maintained a good business climate with low taxes and weak local governmental regulation. It is not my purpose in this chapter to argue that free enterprise Houston is a unique city in its social and infrastructural problems—most Houston problems can be found elsewhere. However, it is instructive to examine the remarkable array and seriousness of the basic problems that now plague this largely unregulated and unplanned city. Houston does appear to be at the extreme end of an urban problems continuum. In this examination I have suggested that, whatever the quality of the business climate, Houston is not the untarnished mecca of the good life that national and international image makers frequently proclaimed in the prosperous days from the late 1960s to the early 1980s. Under the city's prosperity lurks a problematical quality of life for the citizenry.

210

Firm-level Profit and the Idea of Growth

The capitalistic system of investment, production, and marketing is a powerful machine for the social and physical transformation of cities. Growth in capitalist cities typically hinges on the decisions made by controllers of capital calculating profit at the firm level. Social costs have been defined by some economists as the negative consequences of for-profit capitalistic production; business expansion and production create these costs, which are not paid for by an individual firm but are shifted onto third parties such as individuals and communities living in the vicinity.[1] Costs are calculated at the microeconomic level of the individual company in terms of its profits, its future net revenues, or its share of the market. Corporate decision making by this criterion will seek to reduce business costs and, if possible, to ignore costs of economic growth that can be displaced onto third persons. Many urban problems are created because corporate decision making about the quality of life in surrounding cities involves no democratic input from or regulation by the citizenry.

Profit is linked to expansion and growth, measured in terms of jobs, production, and population. Billboards across the nation proclaim that "profits mean jobs." The idea that profit seeking can be antisocial is explicitly rejected. President C. E. Wilson of General Electric once emphasized this view: "Certainly there is nothing antisocial in profit. I think the truth of the matter is that—given access to all as buyers and sellers—the profit earned by the wise businessman is a measure of the service he has rendered to his market, in terms of a value placed on those services by the buyers, individually and collectively."[2] One review of the U.S. business school literature found that new managers are taught to make decisions based on such factors as short-run profitability, market share, and annual sales growth.[3]

Markets are sacred in U.S. society. Conservatives and liberals alike accept decisions aimed at the market as the primary adjudicator of what is or is not produced. But market prices do not necessarily reflect the larger community and social costs generated by corporate decisions, either individually or collectively. When numerous companies make decisions which create, for example, high urban unemployment from corporate relocation, subsidence from unregulated development, or cancer-causing pollution, it becomes clear that the market process can be very negative for the larger urban context. Large corporations are able to create environmental and other social costs because they have great economic and political power.

The context of narrow, firm-level cost accounting can multiply the negative effects. The physical environment has its own regularities and laws—for example, ground and surface water flows, air patterns, rainfall, and soil characteristics. If these environmental facts are ignored in profit-centered investment and production decisions, then their consequences may be negative. Within a given natural environment, the rate of economic growth is linked to the velocity of capital investment, as Bluestone and Harrison have discussed:

> How much expansion can be absorbed, and how quickly, depends on the dynamics of the people and the environment of the community involved. . . . With suitable planning and reasonable forecasts, new schools can be built, teachers hired, roadways, water, and sewage systems constructed, and job training. . . . But when the capital influx is totally unrestrained, the absorptive capacity of the social system can be quickly overwhelmed.[4]

In a context with little planning, the high velocity of investment into, and later out of, Houston accentuated or created major infrastructural problems, including sewage crises, water pollution, traffic congestion, subsidence, and toxic waste contamination and disposal. In addition, it is difficult for a city with weak planning and weak regulatory agencies to measure and assess the range of social costs; indeed, many costs of unrestrained corporate growth (for example, high cancer rates from extensive pollution) may take a long time to appear in either individuals or communities.[5]

Coping with Costs: Governmental Responses

In most cities the business elite pressures the local government to subsidize the location, development, and infrastructural costs of companies making capital investments within its boundaries. But local government also faces pressures from its citizenry to deal with the community services requirements and the many problems created by the velocity of investment flows into and out of the city. Local government is often in partnership with private entrepreneurs, furnishing subsidies essential to profit making. When local governments operate to facilitate the location or expansion of firms or when they retreat from the planning and intervention necessary to deal with the broad public services problems created by private profit making, they cooperate in inflicting the social costs of private enterprise on the citizenry. Some defensive expenditures for certain infrastructural needs, such as roads and sewers, will be made, although who directs the selection of infrastructural projects is a central question.

In cities like Houston the business leadership usually determines, directly or indirectly, the broad contours of infrastructural development. And often infrastructural expenditures are kept at the level consistent with business needs and with keeping the citizenry from political protests. The reason for this is that too much governmental action on schools, social programs, neighborhood sewers, water systems, and toxic waste problems can be costly in terms of individual and business fees and taxes. Since the local growth coalition demands a good business climate with relatively low taxes, it follows that public services and defensive infrastructural expenditures must be kept at the minimal level consistent with low taxes. However, although reducing support for infrastructure can sometimes be done in the short run, in the long run someone will have to pay for much of that infrastructure. Often present and future ordinary taxpayers pay for much of the community cost of unrestrained and underregulated corporate growth. Moreover, the social costs of investment-spurred growth in a particular urban area are not borne equally by all citizens. The poor and minorities and those living in certain areas—such as central cities, growth corridors, or near toxic waste dumps—frequently bear more of the social costs than others.[6]

Given its limited government approach, Houston has been unable to absorb its high velocity of investment and population growth without much pain and many infrastructural crises. Billions of dollars of investments have been channeled into oil refineries, petrochemical complexes, office towers, residential subdivisions, and shopping malls. This capital flow has generated a broad array of skilled and unskilled jobs and stimulated Houston's growth from a city of 385,000 in 1940 to a city of 1.7 million in the late 1980s. But the rapid industrial and population increase has accentuated the city's infrastructure needs and problems, particularly given the past underdevelopment and undermaintenance of the infrastructure and the laissez-faire government.

Toxic Waste Disposal: The Industrial Growth Problem

Tons of Annual Waste in Houston

One major social cost of rapid industrial growth in a city with a laissez-faire government ideology can be seen in Houston's toxic waste problems. Since cheap and generally unrestricted toxic waste dumping is linked to industrial profitability, it is not surprising that some of Houston's residential communities face the looming specter of a Love Canal disaster. The societal cost of the toxic waste dumps has not for the most part been tallied on chemical firm ledgers; instead, it will be and is being paid for by the local citizenry.

Expanding industrial investment since the 1920s has brought a rapid growth in toxic waste, particularly during the postwar period. Houston–Gulf Coast area industries produced three million tons of toxic waste each year in the early 1980s. In addition, billions of gallons of contaminated water were being dumped into local wells. Much hazardous waste flows to or through Houston by barge, truck, airplane, railroad car, and pipeline; in 1982 alone a total of 1.9 billion gallons of hazardous waste was handled. Periodically there is a major transport disaster: for example, in 1976 an ammonia truck plunged off a highway ramp, killing six people and injuring two hundred with its poisonous vapor discharge.[7]

In the mid-1980s the head of the Environmental Protection Agency (E P A), William Ruckelshaus, described the greater Houston area as one of the worst hazardous waste disposal areas in the nation because of its nine major toxic waste dumps then on the Superfund list, as well as its one hundred toxic waste sites not on that list. Ruckelshaus said that "the Houston area has bigger problems because it has more of the industries [that produce waste]."[8] He was referring to the large number of chemical and petrochemical plants in the area. As a principal center of growth in this type of industrial production between 1920 and the early 1980s, Houston has many serious toxic waste problems not yet cleaned up. The Texas Water Commission regularly issues lists of the worst operating records at hazardous waste disposal facilities in Texas; Houston area facilities usually place high on the lists. Such great quantities of industrial waste would be a problem in any metropolitan area, but the magnitude of the problem in Houston has been exacerbated through nonexistent or weak regulation of disposal by the local and federal governments and the lack of attention to this problem by the private sector. In the early 1980s there were only fourteen waste disposal firms for the entire nine-county area around Houston.

Local Residential Communities
Struggling with Waste

Each year Houston papers are filled with articles indicating the array of toxic waste and pollution problems. In 1985 a helicopter search of 150 square miles between Houston and Galveston discovered two "hot spots" where low-level radioactive waste had been dumped.[9] Regularly stories in the press indicate the impact of toxic waste on local residential communities, as well as the occasional citizen protests over this pollution. For example, a waste disposal firm, Nuclear Resources and Services, applied for a permit to expand waste facilities in southeast Houston. At the site construction equipment was burned, perhaps by local residents, and an executive of the firm had to be protected from an angry crowd by the Houston police. In another case the residents of a subdivision in northeast Houston organized protests against a proposed poly-chlorinated biphenyl (P C B) waste storage site. A disposal company was pro-posing to store more than 50,000 gallons of dangerous P C Bs. In this case a blue-collar community decided to fight. As one woman put it, "We're very blue-collar out here. We don't have a lot of money. But we plan to hire a law-yer and fight this all the way." [10]

Southern and southeastern areas of the city seem to have the greatest num-ber of toxic waste problems. In 1983–1984 local officials in the South Hous-ton community were pressing the federal E P A to clean up a thirteen-acre dump thought to be contaminating ground water with cancer-causing P C B-waste and twelve other toxic waste chemicals. A trained geologist, the mayor of this city of 14,000, publicly argued that the toxic waste was contaminating drinking water in the area. Most city residents live within a mile of the dump. The Texas Department of Water Resources had recommended the dangerous dump to the E P A for federal Superfund cleanup, but the E P A was very slow in providing aid. Local residents were fearful that P C Bs and other toxic wastes were spreading throughout the underground water system because of the many abandoned oil and gas wells in the area. Moveover, in the spring of 1986 more than 360 homeowners in the Southbend subdivision of Friendswood sued the project's developer and home builders for withholding information about a dangerous waste site near the homes. The pits reportedly contained chemical wastes such as vinyl chloride and styrene tar from local refinery and chemical plants, some of which had seeped into surface water. Local residents, fearing long-range cancer problems, filed suit against the real estate firms, whose lawyers in turn argued it was the obligation of the government not the builders to inform the residents. Local newspapers compared these court suits to those brought by the homeowners at Love Canal. [11]

Houston's central commercial artery, the ship channel, is characterized by large-scale industrial development, but it is also surrounded by residential communities. From the 1960s to the 1980s the ship channel was lined with more than 130 chemical and oil refining plants. During some periods in these decades the water was so polluted that local residents were cautioned not to let it touch their skins. One analyst writing in the 1970s noted that the channel was devoid of plant and fish life; "the surface is frequently covered with float-ing grease, oil, debris, and colored chemicals." [12] In addition, several dozen major landfill areas have been built in this southeast area of Houston since the chemical revolution of the 1940s. Deer Park, a ship channel community of

25,000 residents in the southeastern sector, has numerous waste dump sites. Commenting on one highrise landfill there, a local resident noted that "This is a mountain of Class I [most poisonous] waste. I'm scared to death that a hurricane or tornado will knock the thing over. Mother Earth can't hold it. This is not a democracy. It is a dictatorship by industry when we have to live like this." [13] Rapid industrial growth in a laissez-faire government situation where citizens have little or no democratic input has produced significant neglect of the massive problem of toxic industrial waste.

But toxic waste is not the only toxic materials problem created by rapid and uncontrolled industrial growth in the Houston metropolitan area. For example, in 1986 the citizens of Mont Belvieu, a small community on the far eastern edge of the metropolitan area, faced an explosive problem created by firms in the sophisticated petrochemical complex there. These companies had over the years stored millions of barrels of liquid petroleum gas and other volatile materials in a huge salt dome under the community. But leaking gases from the salt dome caused numerous explosions, blowouts, and fires. By the early 1980s the quality of life and the values of homes in the area were rapidly deteriorating. Indeed, the situation had become so dangerous by mid-1986 that a group of thirteen petrochemical firms even offered to move 350 families to new homes at a cost of $16 to $20 million. Many local citizens were dissatisfied with the proposal because it did not include enough of the area's endangered families. [14]

Sewage and Garbage Disposal in Houston

Past and Present Sewage Problems

Rapid population growth has paralleled rapid industrial growth; and industrial and population growth in a weak-services, low-taxes governmental framework has meant major problems in routine sewage and garbage disposal. By the early 1900s the growth of the city was making the use of the bayous a major health problem for the city. In 1916 Houston's mayor reported that 70 to 80 percent of the sewage was dumped into the Buffalo Bayou, a central watercourse that had become an open sewer. Into the 1980s Buffalo Bayou remained a major artery for disposing of sewage, including millions of gallons of raw sewage from the elite residential area of River Oaks. [15]

By the mid-1980s millions of gallons of wastewater were flowing down that polluted bayou from city and private-development sewage plants. The Bayou had become anaerobic in some places, with little in the way of aquatic life. Since it flows through the city's finest park and through a planned downtown river walk, the Buffalo Bayou sewer was not a hidden problem. Enormous quantities of sewage have been dumped in other city bayous. As one resident at a hearing on a sewer plant permit application put it, "The issue is whether Houston is just going to be a good place to make money and then get out, or a good place to live." [16]

Routine Garbage Disposal

Disposal of the city's garbage is another significant waste problem. Rapid metropolitan growth has meant increasing garbage and thus an accelerating demand for landfill areas in which to bury trash. No residential community wants such garbage disposal areas developed near them. Traditionally, as I will substantiate in the next chapter, a disproportionate number of these trash dumps have been located in or near minority communities. By the 1980s the city was seeing a growing number of battles over where to locate new landfill areas in which to bury the city's constant flow of garbage.

Water Problems:
Subsidence, Flooding, and Pollution

The Unique Issue of Subsidence

Sustained metropolitan growth has created several interrelated water problems, which have been aggravated by the velocity of growth and the low-taxes, low-budget approach of local government. Many areas of Houston are actually sinking as a result of vigorous development. Houston citizens and industries have in recent decades drawn about 60 percent of their water supply from wells and the rest from lake reservoirs. By the 1980s this dependence on pumping water from wells was changing because of the soil subsidence. The compacting of clay soils as water and oil are pumped out of the soil creates this subsidence, and the construction of megastructure projects contributes to its existence. Some areas of southeast Houston have sunk six to eight feet since 1943, and central city areas have subsided three to five feet in the same period. One large northwest area sank two to three inches in 1983; its total drop in the 1975–1983 period was fourteen inches. In the southwest quadrant land is sinking even more rapidly, with a three to four inch drop in 1983 alone. Much of the west side subsided seven to twelve inches in the 1978–1983 period, largely because much ground water still being pumped in the greater Houston area is coming from under the rapid development areas on the west side. Such subsidence continues to exact substantial costs from ordinary homeowners. In 1985 just one foundation company reported that it was repairing 200 home foundations annually because of subsidence, at an average cost of $5,000 per foundation.[17]

Houston's Regular Flooding

Flooding problems have increased as a result of subsidence. Again, rapid uncontrolled growth is responsible. In the mid-1980s, Joseph Goldman, chairperson of disaster services for the Red Cross in Houston, noted that with the number and intensity of floods in the Houston area increasing "faster than you'd expect" the number of flood victims was rising. The area has a high level of rainfall. In the mid-nineteenth century the first capital of the Republic of Texas was moved from Houston in part because of the rains, mud, and mosquitoes. Periodic flooding has become a major problem. Because of subsidence, high annual rainfall, and flat topography, Houston had major flooding in two dozen of the years between 1907 and 1987. A 1935 flood caused $2.6 million in damages; a 1949 flood, $5 million; a July 1979 flood, $83 million; a September 1979 flood, $25 million. Average annual losses in the 1970s and 1980s were running more than $30 million. The costs are often more than monetary. For example, in June 1987 several days of substantial rain flooded large areas of the city, particularly along creeks, bayous, and rivers; one person drowned, and 250 homes were seriously damaged.[18]

When subsidence in a residential area is coupled with increased water runoff from hard surfacing in development projects upstream, downstream areas along creeks and bayous can suffer serious routine flooding. Moreover, about one-fifth of Harris County's flood plain area has extant real estate development, along bayous, streams, and other watercourses. There has been massive residential and commercial development in the watershed areas on the west side of Houston. Since natural drainage in the Houston metropolitan area is generally from west to east, a high level of westside development has substantially increased water runoff after rains, flooding some westside areas as well as areas to the east.[19] Some of these areas have fought the flooding consequences of unregulated development with interesting strategies. For example, sections of the affluent southwest Meyerland area suffered *six* major floods between 1973 and 1983; in 1984 the disgruntled homeowners in Section 4 of Meyerland decided to sell all their homes to a development firm that wished to expand a nearby shopping mall.[20]

Adequate Water Supplies?

Houston is located over large reservoirs of ground water. During several decades of economic development much of this ground water has been consumed by local industries, at relatively low prices. The rapid industrial growth from the 1940s to the 1980s seriously depleted the water supply. Business leaders began to develop surface water sources. Water supplies for the city, drawn increasingly from surface water sources, are projected to be adequate for the growth expected in the Houston area until 1992, but there are periodic problems with water pressure. A summer 1980 heat wave dropped the water level in Lake Houston, and inadequate water lines and pumping stations forced the city to reduce water pressure to residents very substantially.[21]

Persisting Water Pollution

The quality of surface water in the Houston metropolitan area has deteriorated because of growth. One example is Lake Houston, the source of drinking water for four in ten Houstonians in the mid-1980s. The Houston health department reported that water samples taken from Lake Houston had fecal coliform bacteria counts ranging up to 5,500 to 17,000 organisms, well above the "safe" standard of 400 per 100 milliliters of water. An environmental specialist advised Houstonians not to swim in Lake Houston because of these high coliform counts.[22]

Given rapid suburban development in the lake area, sewage flows through small treatment plants, especially in the outlying Municipal Utility Districts, into the lake. Some plants are overloaded and discharge inadequately treated effluent. Private developers have created the sewage problems, but they themselves do not pay the major costs. According to a mid-1980s city council study more than 200 small sewage treatment plants in the Lake Houston watershed released fifty million gallons of effluent *daily* into the lake. Many plants met minimal treatment standards and lacked on-site operators.[23]

Real estate investment in the 300-square-mile watershed of Lake Houston is the critical generating factor behind the lake's severe pollution problems. In the mid-1980s about 140 to 160 million gallons of water from this lake were being treated daily for drinking water by the East Water Treatment Plant, a plant with a rated capacity of only 100 million gallons. In 1983 the Texas attorney general filed a lawsuit against a developer and a private utility company for operating a polluting sewage plant. The suit alleged that homeowners served by the plant had been deceived into believing that the plant was approved. A second lawsuit against another utility responsible for an inoperative sewage plant was filed at the same time. Both plants were discharging raw or partially treated effluent into Lake Houston. Five other sewage plants were being considered for similar suits.[24]

Large corporations, including local utilities, have played significant roles in Houston's water pollution problems, as I observed in the discussion of toxic waste impact on ground water. For example, in the mid-1980s the federal E P A ordered Houston Lighting and Power, a private firm, to cease discharging millions of gallons of untreated wastewater into lakes and streams near its coal-fired plants. Rapid growth in electricity demand in the Houston area has meant major construction projects by this large private utility firm, some of which have generated far more coal ash and untreated wastewater than their designers had projected.[25]

The Cost of Office Buildings

One reason for the pressure to expand electricity generation is the merciless heat and humidity of the Houston climate during six months of each year. In 1978 it was estimated that Houston's residents paid $250 million annually just to cool the air in homes, offices, and stores. This figure probably increased sharply over the next several years of electric rate increases and construction expansion. Expanded electricity generating power is necessary to maintain high-rise construction in the eighteen business activity centers of the city.

Office towers consume large quantities of energy. Gordon Wittenberg has thoroughly examined this issue for the city of Houston. He notes that office buildings consume about 75,000 B T Us of end-use energy and that the taller buildings consume even more, an estimated 90,000 B T Us of end-use energy. At these high rates of energy consumption the energy costs for an office building are so expensive that they *exceed* the construction costs in about eleven years.[26] Several features of large office buildings, including size and mass, account for the high energy consumption. Wittenberg notes that one major cost is in the elevators and pumps used to service the upper floors. In addition, lighting systems require huge energy consumption. Not only is there the direct cost of the lighting, but there is also the cost of the air conditioning necessary to offset heating the building by the extensive lighting system. Wittenberg estimates that approximately 40 percent of the air-conditioning tonnage in high-rise buildings is used for this purpose alone.

Since Houston has one of the largest concentrations of office buildings in the world, this use of space creates a heavy drag on the city's utility systems and increases local utility rates. This is obvious in the case of electricity, wastewater, and water usage. Office building utility requirements have contributed to the city's recurring fiscal crises.

The Impact of Air Pollution

The Human Costs of Industrialization

Houston's air pollution problem is serious. Ordinarily Houstonians are exposed to unhealthy ozone levels many times a year. The greater Houston area has hundreds of industrial plants spewing pollutants into the air; two million motor vehicles contribute to the smog. The eastside heavily industrialized sector is made up of a number of industrial and residential areas along the ship channel and Galveston Bay; some of these are within the city limits. Politically separate but well integrated into the Houston economy are outside cities such as Texas City and Deer Park.

The complexity of chemical-related accident, waste, and pollution problems can be seen in an area like Texas City in the southeastern metropolitan area. Texas City is composed of about ten square miles of chemical plants, oil refineries, and industrial waste incinerators. In 1947 a vessel loaded with ammonium nitrate exploded; the chemical explosion and accompanying fire killed 576 people and injured 4,000. Since then a few workers have been killed every year or two in various explosions, fires, and toxic exposure incidents at industrial plants in the area. Some of the nation's most toxic waste dumps are there as well. Local citizens have complained of accidents at the work place and of cancers resulting from working and living in Texas City. One study at a major chemical plant producing 375 million pounds of chemicals and plastics annually found a high rate of brain cancer among the workers there. Moreover, air pollution in the area is a serious problem.[27]

Air pollution associated with industrialization has long been a major social cost of Houston's national leadership in manufacturing growth. In 1981 a

Houston newspaper article began with the following comments on an area in the industrialized southeast: "Lifeless bodies of small blackbirds dot the roadside leading to the Battleship Texas [a local monument]. And wild rabbits romp along the Battleground Road in the buff, for they have lost their fur. Oak trees behind the San Jacinto Monument are stripped too—of their tinsel-like Spanish moss." [28] Both researchers and local residents have attributed these problems to air pollution. But air problems are neither confined to this southeastern area, nor is the human population exempt. One study of cancer death rates by the M. D. Anderson Hospital and Tumor Institute revealed that the metropolitan area had one of the highest lung cancer death rates in the United States, at 47 deaths annually per 100,000 population, twice the national rate of 22 per 100,000. Air pollution is one likely cause of this lung cancer crisis.

Burning PCBs

Industrial pollution contributes to Houston's air problems. Into the 1980s in the southeast community of Deer Park, polychlorinated biphenyls (PCBs) were burned legally. Millions of pounds of PCBs have been burned at one Deer Park facility, as well as a million pounds of other highly toxic deadly chemicals. PCBs have been banned from production in the United States, but there are plenty of chemicals in dump sites in industrial cities such as Deer Park. Deer Park residents have complained that their trees and grass are dying and that people there suffer excessively from skin rashes and respiratory problems. Homeowners in residential areas near industrial plants in the southeastern quadrant have reported a disproportionate incidence of vasculitis and other skin diseases thought to derive from toxic air and water pollution. There has been some limited protest against these serious social costs of industrial development. Local residents have held meetings with hundreds in attendance and have picketed the landfills that have permits to burn PCBs. Moreover, accidental chemical fires have generated air pollution; in mid-1986 the *Houston Post* ran a front page story about the evacuation of 3,000 people along the ship channel because of toxic fumes from a major fire at a chemical company's sulfur storage facility. [29]

In the 1980s the Texas Air Control Board began a research effort to examine systematically air pollution in four countries in Houston and adjacent Gulf Coast areas. Ten substances, including PCBs and vinyl chloride, were examined. Preliminary surveys revealed that 235 industrial plants in the four counties were emitting hazardous substances into the air. The head of the Texas Air Control Board noted that, in contrast to other Sunbelt cities, the air pollution in Houston was related more to industrial plants than to cars. [30]

Persisting Traffic Problems in a Spread City

Commonplace Auto Congestion

Automobiles are at the heart of the most heralded of Houston's growth problems. In the late 1980s headlines sometimes read: "Frantic Freeways Forecast for City." Surveys of Houstonians that ask for the "single biggest problem" in Houston often get traffic and mobility as the leading responses. There is a mistaken impression that the structures of cities such as Houston and Los Angeles are the deterministic result of automobile technology. Yet both cities were originally laid out, to a substantial degree, as streetcar and street railway cities. Into the early twentieth century Houston was a railroad and streetcar city. As late as September 1909 Houston, then a city of only 78,000, had 51.4 miles of street car lines. By the 1940s Houston had lost its railway system and the city was becoming auto-centered.[31]

Dramatic growth has significantly decreased geographical mobility. With nearly 2.5 million registered vehicles in the city, the city's 4,600 miles of roads cannot accommodate a substantial percentage of the vehicles without significant congestion. And the spread city means that the average motorist drives an estimated twenty-four miles a day. A local publisher has printed a book-length guide with the explicit purpose of helping frustrated Houstonians find short-cuts through their congested streets. The transportation system is overloaded.[32] One survey of six major freeways found that in peak traffic periods the average distance one could drive from the downtown area in a thirty-minute period had been reduced by one-third between 1969 and 1979. On several major roads the distance one could travel from downtown at peak hours had dropped by 50 percent. The major reasons for this sharp drop in distance traveled are that autos increased at a rate twice that of population increase and that freeway use increased at a rate more than four times the rate of increased freeway capacity. In 1985 the Texas Department of Highways and Public Transportation commissioned a twenty-one-month study of severe traffic problems on IH 10, Houston's major east-west highway. Reasonable traffic per lane is 11,000 vehicles a day, but each day this freeway carries at least 28,000 vehicles per lane on its most congested sections. Moreover, a mid-1980s Federal Highway Administration study of thirty-seven metropolitan areas found Houston to have the worst traffic problems in the nation.[33]

The omnipresent traffic congestion has contributed to a high death rate. For some years in the 1980s Houston was the most dangerous of the larger U.S. cities to drive in; its traffic fatality rate of 23 per 100,000 per year was nearly twice that of Detroit (12.7) and more than twice that of cities like New York (9) and Philadelphia (7.5). In addition, there is some violent conflict between drivers on Houston's streets and freeways. During one ten-month period in the mid-1980s the Houston Police Department received 161 formal complaints of violent conflict on the congested major roads, including some that resulted in serious injuries. And hundreds of incidents go unreported. In this case Southern male culture may contribute to the negative impact of growth because many male drivers carry a rifle or handgun in their vehicles. When traffic grinds to a halt during Houston's long rush hours in the morning and evening, tempers can flare, and knives or guns may be used.

One other traffic-related problem has contributed to the city's budget crisis. The rapidly increasing truck and auto traffic coupled with rainfall and shifting clay soils have caused a rapid deteriorioration of many city streets. In the 1980s Houston's one to two million potholes were said to be the nation's worst example of street deterioration.[34]

Traffic and Central City Gentrification

Houston's massive traffic problems have resulted in a search by some affluent families for shorter commuting times. As a result, some central city areas traditionally occupied by moderate- and middle-income families have undergone substantial gentrification. One of these central city residential areas is West University, among the few self-contained and incorporated areas within the city limits of Houston. This area of residential dwellings with strict restrictions on commercial and industrial development is within easy commuting distance of the downtown and other central city business complexes. In the late 1960s and 1970s the area attracted many professional and managerial families, thereby driving house prices to extraordinarily high levels. Houses built in the 1930s and 1940s for less than $5,000 to $10,000 were now selling in the $100,000 to $300,000 range. Some older houses were demolished and replaced by developers with very expensive ($265,000 to $900,000) homes. There was a gradual transition from an older generation of low-middle-income and middle-income families in West University to a generation of upper-middle-income families. Moreover, in several other central city communities some minority Houstonians have been displaced in classic gentrification fashion.[35]

Citizens View Houston's Problems

Awareness of the costs of growth increased in the decade of the 1980s. A major survey of Houstonians by Stephen Klineberg at Rice University found that when asked about rapid growth and development, 71 percent of the sample said growth was *not* good or had mixed feelings about it; only 28 percent felt growth was unequivocally good. Moreover, surveys of Houston residents in the four years between 1982 and 1985 found a growing percentage who felt that private/public control of air and water pollution was poor or fair, rising from 67 percent in 1982 to 70 percent in 1985. In three surveys between 1983 and 1985 the overwhelming majority thought living conditions in the city had not improved, or had stayed the same, over the last three or four years. Surveys conducted by the Center for Public Policy at the University of Houston in 1983–1986 found that one-quarter of Houstonians felt that industrial pollution of the water and air was a serious problem, and another 60 percent felt that air and water pollution might become a serious health hazard. In 1986 two-thirds of those interviewed saw the air quality as "only fair" or "poor."[36]

By the 1980s Houston's residents were supporters of environmental action by government, even if such action meant higher taxes. In Klineberg's 1985 survey 46 percent felt government was spending "too little" on protecting the environment, while only 7 percent said "too much"; 62 percent opposed any relaxation of efforts to control pollution in Houston, even if that would stimulate the local economy. And 61 percent felt that protecting the environment was so important that improvements should be made, whatever the cost. Klineberg's surveys revealed that Houstonians saw some improvements in transportation and policing by the mid-1980s. Ironically, at first the recession and the end of rapid growth enabled the local government to improve some services. However, with the inevitable fiscal crises came a decline in services; the Houstonians surveyed in 1987 perceived the deterioration in police services and in efforts to improve transportation.[37]

Public Services and Social Costs: The Consequences of Laissez-Faire Government

Early Public Services and the Business Elite

I have discussed the Houston business elite's pressures on local government to subsidize the development costs of Houston investors, as well as the community pressures to provide services and deal with problems of industrial growth. From the earliest period Houston's public infrastructure developed under control of the business elite. Neighborhood needs and concerns were frequently slighted in preference for providing infrastructural facilities for business areas. There were no surfaced streets in any neighborhoods of the city until 1882; and early in the city's history raw sewage was dumped into Buffalo Bayou, a source of drinking water. Fifth Ward residents became so angry about the lack of a bridge across Buffalo Bayou and related amenities that they twice threatened to *secede* from the city. A 1912 city council report catalogued severe service deficiencies: few sidewalks, few sewers, one-eighth the needed paved roads, and half the needed water service.

In the early 1920s public pressure forced the city fathers to improve utility services. Sewer construction was increased. Although nearly forty miles of sewers were constructed by city government in 1921–1924, an additional forty-five miles of sewers were constructed by private owners during this same period. Privatization of sewer provision was important at an early stage in Houston.[38]

Service crises have continued to plague the metropolitan area. A 1959–1960 survey reported serious shortages in police and fire personnel and library personnel and major deficiencies in sewer, water, and street light facilities. Yet one top official noted that "This city doesn't want to pay more taxes, period!"[39] What this probably meant, appropriately translated, was that the local business leadership did not want to pay more taxes for services. To maintain the city's image of fiscal conservatism—in the 1970s Houston was the only major city with a A A A bond rating by Wall Street—for many years that business elite has kept the government operating expenditures relatively low, thus permitting a modest tax rate. One result of these historically low operating expenditures for certain categories of service projects has been a limited array of city services and an infrastructure of aging streets, inadequate and aging water and sewer systems, and substandard police and fire facilities, particularly in the central city area.

The Distinctiveness of Houston's Sewage Crisis

By the early 1980s the city of Houston had 4,000 miles of sewers and forty-four treatment plants. The plants have regularly violated state wastewater effluent standards; in January 1980 twenty-two plants were in noncompliance. In the mid-1970s the Texas Water Quality Board ordered the city to improve its underdeveloped sewage system. The reaction was a sewer connection moratorium on new construction in three-quarters of the city to reduce significantly the raw sewage processed at many treatment plants. Many developers and homeowners were forced to revise building plans as a result. Large tracts of land could not be sold or developed because of a lack of sewer capacity. Moreover, developers who had already secured sewer permits on parcels of land sometimes traded them to other developers without permits; this informal trading was called locally "poop futures." This sewer connection moratorium cramped the activities of developers in many areas, but not in the downtown district.

Wittenberg notes that "In what has often been described as a 'brilliant' stratagem, the city managed to trade plant capacity so that construction was limited to existing capacity in all areas but the central business district."[40] Few restrictions on sewer hookups were placed on the city's powerful downtown developers. Moreover, in 1986 the Texas Water Commission placed Houston's Southwest Plant on its list of Texas's worst water polluters because that plant released millions of gallons of raw sewage into Brays Bayou. In March 1987 the water commission fined the city government $500,000 for what they regarded as the worst municipal sewage disposal problem in Texas, and local officials agreed to a compliance order which required sewage improvements at a high cost. The sewer crises make it clear that even capitalists pay in the long run for the laissez-faire city.[41]

The crises have resulted from more than a lack of capacity. They are also a matter of inadequate public capital investment in sewer lines. For example, late in 1983 a 200-million-gallons-per-day sewer processing facility was completed in north Houston, technically releasing portions of the northern area from the moratorium. Yet there was no rush to use the new facility; the mid-1980s recession had arrived in Houston, and there were inadequate pumping stations and sewer lines for many areas serviceable by the new treatment plant. Even with the new plant, most development areas in the central city remained under a sewer moratorium in the late 1980s.[42]

One result of the moratorium has been a significant increase in the number of small ("package") sewer plants constructed by private developers. In many cases the city government is eventually required to repay a developer for the plant and replace the temporary facility with regular city service. The developer, in the meantime, is supposed to maintain the plant. But privatized plants are sometimes not well regulated; state and local governments in Texas generally do not have the staff and/or the authority to make sure such facilities as sewage plants meet quality standards. As a result, some private plants are a source of surface water pollution.[43]

One should note that the sewage crisis is linked to the weakness of local planning efforts discussed in Chapter 6. The head of the city's wastewater division has explained his dependence on the whims of local developers: "And in many cases a developer would first build a warehouse structure that had low-volume sewage needs and then, after the city had built lines to serve it, would change the use of the land to high-rise condominiums or other buildings that need much larger sewer lines."[44] These comments reveal the absence of government zoning and the weak character of local government planning. The sewage problem has been costly in terms of the city government budget. In 1983 the city's wastewater department implemented a new user's fee for larger development projects in order to collect money for new sewer line and pumping station construction, as well as to give the wastewater department some notice of anticipated usage in new development projects. And in the same year council member Eleanor Tinsley proposed a new sewer ordinance that would require developers of large projects to put up money in advance to help the city finance sewer treatment plants. About the same time the city's sewer bonds were downgraded in rating by national bond-rating agencies, thus raising the cost of securing money for infrastructure.

Reaction to the Garbage Crisis

A major story in the mass media in the late 1980s was the looming garbage crisis in many American cities. In Houston the garbage crisis has been aggravated by the low-tax government. Routine disposal of city garbage has been a recurring predicament. The city government has not developed many resource recovery facilities; in the early 1980s about three-quarters of the city's refuse went directly to landfill areas well out from the center of Houston. The largest landfill was exhausted in the mid-1980s because of population growth. The garbage crisis became so severe that the Chamber of Commerce conducted a major study of the matter. Its 1983 report highlighted the severity of Houston's waste problems and recommended that the city contract privately for all garbage pickup (58 percent was contracted in 1983), build new landfill sites in all quadrants of the city, and put a half billion dollars into waste-to-energy facilities.[45]

Water-related Problems: Coping with Flooding and Subsidence

Government attempts to deal with the city's water problems, including flooding and subsidence, have ranged from inadequate to nonexistent. Dealing with subsidence has mainly involved a shift from using underground water systems to using surface water. Thus, there have been plans to deal with subsidence in the west Houston area by building two major water treatment plants for increased use of surface water. But the cost of this obvious solution is prohibitively high, requiring huge increases in water rates and major capital improvement bonds. Past neglect of this water-related problem portends expensive solutions in the future.[46]

Local officials have dealt with flood problems by relying on a disaster relief approach involving insurance. A government plan seriously restricting development in flood prone areas has long been considered too interventionist for the local business elite.[47] A local flood control district office controls flooding along watercourses in the Houston area. Until 1970 the U.S. Army Corps of Engineers was a major partner with the district, spending as much money as the district to reduce flooding. Since then the corps has assisted only with planning and a few modest flood control projects. The corps did propose a substantial solution to serious flooding along the central Buffalo Bayou, but county officials rejected it as too expensive. Corps officials have criticized local politicians for moving slowly in developing a master flood control and drainage plan.[48]

By the mid-1980s the size of the problem was beginning to be discussed by city and county officials. Some modest action was taken. The Harris County Flood Control District required that detention ponds be built by developers putting large-scale real estate projects in areas where the drainage systems have been overloaded. Yet because existing developments were not covered, this requirement did not reduce much flooding. The magnitude of the flooding crisis can be seen in the chamber's responses. In 1984 a chamber task force group on planning recommended a $922-million improvement program over twenty-five years, to correct the pressing drainage problems. Although it emphasized drainage construction projects, there was some recognition among the corporate elite that *long-range* planning was required to pay the costs of past unrestrained development. However, the long-range strategy for and construction of flood projects has not as yet been implemented because of the massive cost and, doubtless, the extent of the intervention required in the private real estate market.[49]

Water-Related Problems: Distribution and Treatment

Although the amount of water available for the Houston metropolitan area is considered adequate until the late 1990s, the pumping stations and treatment facilities necessary to maintaining adequate pressure during periods of drought have not been constructed. Indeed, in 1984 the Texas health department withdrew its special "state approved" designation for Houston's water systems because the city did not have adequate water storage facilities, particularly for a time of crisis such as drought or hurricane. A city planning commission report, moreover, noted that Houston's water system of pipes and facilities will not be able to handle Houston's expected growth after 1992.[50] A city council report noted "some concern for the treatment process" and further that the "Public Works Department has stated that the water is safe to drink despite the fact that its odor and color may not always be appealing."[51] That same report called for an aggressive attempt to improve water quality in Lake Houston, even if that meant a "moratorium on the construction of wastewater treatment facilities" by developers of residential subdivisions around the lake.

Coping with Air Pollution

The city government has vacillated on the enforcement of air pollution standards for local industries. For example, in the mid-1980s the city council voted unanimously to sue a local chemical company because of air pollution resulting from handling toxic chemicals. The city's legal department argued that haphazard handling of toxic chemicals such as methyl bromide and malathion had resulted in air pollution. In another case the city's health department decided not to process local citizen complaints about air pollution at a U S S Chemicals facility but rather to pass the complaints along to the state air control board. Local residents had complained a number of times about air pollution from that particular chemical plant. State officials filed a lawsuit against the company for repeated pollution violations, but city government officials refused to participate because, they said, the company had made a "good faith" effort to correct the problem.[52]

In the early 1980s the federal E P A put Houston authorities on notice that certain types of construction might be banned and that federal funds might be terminated if air pollution were not reduced. Citing Harris County for high levels of ozone and suspended particulates, the E P A proposed a ban on the construction of new oil refineries and petrochemical plants. Under federal law there would be a ban on industrial construction that might add to ozone levels if the city and county did not meet the federal government standard by the end of 1987. Not surprisingly, by late 1987 the city's political and economic leaders were debating new legislation proposed in the U.S. Congress to give the city ten more years to clean up its air. Yet the legislation would also require testing for several pollutants besides ozone and would impose more severe sanctions for failure to comply. The Chamber of Commerce's Ozone Task Force, another "planning" effort which included some governmental representatives, publicly worried about the consequences of such rigorous new legislation. This task force behaved like a government department; members traveled to Washington to brief E P A officials on the pollution situation. Moreover, in the debate city leaders admitted that there had been virtually no change in Houston's ozone levels during the last eight years.[53]

The Inadequate Governmental Response to Traffic

In the United States the extensive highway-centered transportation system has become costly to maintain, and few cities will ever be able to raise the money to maintain and rebuild their concrete and asphalt conduits for motor vehicles. Billions of dollars will be needed for basic repairs. Texas has benefited more than any other state from federal intervention; 40 percent of the cost of the state highway program has been federally subsidized. Yet even with this mammoth subsidy, highway-dependent Texas cities like Houston will be unable to afford to maintain their highway systems in the long run. We have noted the disrepair of the streets and highways in Houston, the "pothole capital." Because of its weak tax base, the city government's approach to street maintenance has been to patch rather than resurface. In 1978, for example, city crews filled 800,000 potholes, compared to 109,000 in the similar spread city of Los Angeles. Government maintenance costs sharply increased, from $14.2 million in 1975 to $46 million in 1980. Even with these large increases in expenditures, Houston has spent less money on repairing streets than comparable cities. One 1978 study of Houston's per capita expenditures for street maintenance compared Houston with eleven other Sunbelt cities, and Houston spent less per capita than nine of the other cities. To maintain low taxes and fiscal conservatism, preventive road maintenance has often been neglected in Houston; in the long run this has cost city residents millions of dollars in damaged vehicles and belated catch-up repairs.[54]

The traffic and road crises have received considerable attention from the business leadership. For example, indicating its private planning priorities, the chamber undertook a study of road problems; its report proposed spending no less than $16.2 billion (thirteen times the 1987 annual budget of the city government) for 300 miles of new freeways and 30 miles of high-capacity transitways. State of Texas outlays on repairing Houston's state-maintained roads had become very expensive by the late 1980s—one billion dollars a year. Furthermore, traffic problems were so serious by 1978 that many business leaders actively favored government-subsidized rail mass transit. In a local election Houstonians approved the creation of a Metropolitan Transit Authority (M T A), to be funded by a 1 percent sales tax, with a mandate to improve the bus system and move toward a rail transit system.

In the early 1980s Houston's mass transit (bus) system carried only 54 million passengers annually; in the city of Pittsburgh, roughly comparable to Houston, the mass transit system carried 103 million riders. A study by the American Public Transit Association reported that Houston had one of the worst public transit systems in the United States, provided by low taxes and laissez-faire government. As the head of the M T A board put it, "Nobody paid attention to transit here for 20 years or more. Our bus service was probably the worst in the country. We got so much growth, people did not prepare; people were complacent."[55] By the late 1980s, however, this administrator had sharply reduced accidents and bus failures in the system, and therefore costs. The number of passengers carried had increased to 74 million in 1987. Still, only 3 percent of all Houston trips took place on a city bus.

Moreover, in 1982 Houston's M T A approved the construction of a $2.1 billion heavy rail system to run from downtown out the southwest corridor, in order to help solve severe traffic problems in that booming area of the city. Given the traffic nightmare, many business leaders have been willing to accept federal funding for the transit plan. As usual, the plan was designed to meet business needs. The proposed M T A system would guarantee that much of the city's future development would be centered on the downtown area. And the system would connect that downtown center to the key outlying business activity centers, such as the Post Oak and Greenway Plaza needs. Not surprisingly, this heavy rail proposal was soundly vetoed by the voters in 1983, and the city transit authority switched to support of a light rail concept in the late 1980s. The debate late in 1987 was over a M T A construction program to increase transitway development, to build overpasses and streets, and to build a light rail system. Officials at the Chamber of Commerce viewed this plan as implementation of the recommendations of its Regional Mobility Plan published in the early 1980s. Other Houstonians, however, were arguing that the M T A tax should be reduced or abolished.

Houston's traffic dilemma has been aggravated by the absence of zoning and planning. This has permitted huge buildings to be located very close to major traffic arteries and has allowed critical cross-streets to be closed for developers to create large megablocks of development. Finally, in the 1980s the formerly laissez-faire council adopted an ordinance imposing some modest restrictions on development, the main purpose of which was to improve traffic flow. New buildings were required to have greater setbacks from the street; blocks must be of manageable length; and all commercial development must be submitted to the planning commission for review. Yet the ordinance specifically excluded downtown development projects.[56]

The Government Response to Other Service Deficiencies

Rapid growth has brought other problems for the local government to cope with. For example, there are overcrowded jail facilities. In 1983 two police officers sued the city over unsafe conditions at the city jail, including crowded corridors and cells. The city jail was built in 1952 for a city of 700,000; it had become seriously overcrowded and a firetrap. The number of prisoners going through the facility had increased from 98,466 in 1976 to 114,205 in 1982, with no change in the number of officers on duty. By the early 1980s the city government had activated no program to alleviate the crowded conditions.[57]

One does not have to drive many miles in the central area of Houston to notice one telling sign of a starved public infrastructure for local residential neighborhoods. Although the city has long had many imposing office buildings, Houston has little public space such as parks, squares, fountains, and monuments. Recreational facilities have not kept up with growth. In 1910 Houston had only 115 acres of park land for a population of 78,000, the lowest per capita acreage of any major city in the United States. The situation did not improve much in succeeding decades. In 1977 a U.S. Interior Department study ranked Houston 140th among cities in park land per capita. Then the fifth largest city in terms of population, Houston had more than 500 square miles of territory but only 6,200 acres of park land. By the mid-1980s city government efforts had increased the park land, but the city still ranked very low. Houston had far less park land (4.9 acres per 1,000 people) than compa-rable Sunbelt cities such as Phoenix (34 acres per 1,000) and Dallas (27 acres per 1,000).

Houston has been so slow to develop recreational park facilities that in the 1980s the Texas Parks and Wildlife Commission rejected Houston's request for an additional $2 million in state money to build new parks because of slow progress in spending earlier grants.[58] Various explanations have been given for this lack of public space, ranging from the hot climate to the free enterprise mentality of developers. But other cities with hot climates have far more pub-lic space. Even some developers in other cities have, to a greater extent than in Houston, recognized the advantages of public space for making private devel-opment more profitable. The private fortunes in Houston have built a number of important public spaces, such as art museums and sculpture exhibits; yet most entrepreneurs behind those fortunes have been unwilling to see tax mon-ies spent on public space.[59]

This low-tax city has periodically experienced serious shortages of govern-ment personnel. Between the early 1970s and the early 1980s Houston was the construction capital of the United States. Yet between 1978 and 1983 the city of Houston actually decreased its staff of building inspectors from the already low figure of 128 to 116, most of whom were thereby forced to make dozens of inspections a day at a speed not conducive to thoroughness. Moreover, in 1980 the city government had only three traffic light repair crews, two of which were assigned to the downtown area. Some traffic lights remained unre-paired for months. The city's garbage trucks were another problem. Because there was no preventive maintenance program, on an average day in the early 1980s half the trucks were out of service.[60]

From 1975 to 1980 Houston's firefighting personnel grew 18 percent, less than the population growth of that period. The fire department's operating bud-get nearly doubled during those years, from $43.9 million to $82.2 million, but these budget increases did not bring the city up to national firefighting stan-dards. In 1980 the city had only 1.5 firefighters per 1,000 population, below the national standard of 2 firefighters per 1,000. Houston's ratio declined be-tween 1971 and 1980. A similar problem existed in regard to police protec-tion. Houston's 1.7 police officers per 1,000 population was also below the accepted national standard. This police figure was gradually improved by the mid-1980s, with the arrival of a new police chief under Mayor Kathy Whit-mire. Still, some residential subdivisions hired their own private police offi-cers because the response time of Houston police to calls for help was slow. Overall Houston has fewer municipal employees; in the early 1980s Houston's 8.7 employees per 1,000 was much lower than the 17 to 19 per 1,000 in cities such as Atlanta and Denver.[61]

The Free Enterprise City in Fiscal Crisis

Budget Crises in Context

A spring 1983 issue of the *Houston Business Journal* heralded: CITY IN THE RED: HOUSTON FEELS THE HEAT OF FISCAL CRISIS. The lead sentence in the front page article asked, "Is Boomtown going bust? Is Bayou City sailing into the straits of New York City?" Since Houston's leaders and citizens have traditionally envisioned their circumstances as radically different from those of their northern counterparts, these questions would have been unthinkable just a few months before. But now metropolitan newspapers were dramatizing the unprecedented fiscal crisis in the "shining buckle of the Sunbelt."

City of Houston and Harris County government debt was at record levels in the 1980s; by 1987 the combined city-county debt was reported to be the *highest* in the nation. Moreover, in 1981 Houston's general fund balance was $70 million; in 1982 this dropped to only $16 million, and by fiscal 1983 it slumped to a projected deficit of $43 million. Over the next several years the city faced a chronic budget deficit. In 1986 the city projected a $93 million revenue shortfall. And in summer 1987 a $48 million shortfall in revenues for fiscal 1987–1988 was predicted. I noted in Chapter 6 that city officials at first engaged in creative accounting to show a small surplus in June 1983, a surplus promised to outside bond rating agencies, but creative accounting did not suffice. Substantial cutbacks in city services and increases in local fees were dictated by the continuing economic crisis. Not surprisingly, in 1986 water and sewer rates were increased by 20 percent.

The crisis was so serious that budget cuts were made in most city government departments, and the local property tax was increased by 7 percent. In June 1987 Mayor Whitmire unveiled her $1.29-billion budget for the operation of the city for fiscal 1987–1988. Faced with a deficit of $44 million, she adopted the fiscal conservatism approach of "no new property taxes." This approach left her the fiscally conservative options of laying off many city employees and raising numerous fees for city services; she proposed a garbage collection fee, a zoo admission fee, higher court fees, an electricity sales tax, a 20 percent increase in water rates, the latter coming on top of a recent one-third increase in sewer charges. The last two increases were recognized as necessary to upgrade the city's troubled sewer and water systems. Indeed, the sewer increase had been forced on the city by the Texas Water Commission's mandated improvements. In July the city council voted not to increase most of the fees proposed by the mayor; instead, they voted to balance the new budget with a 3 percent cut. Various city departments were faced with another round of cutbacks in employees and services. Particularly serious were the likely reductions in both police personnel and patrols for the city.[62]

A New York City?

One intriguing aspect of Houston's financial crises is that they were *not* caused by factors alleged to have created a fiscal trauma in northern cities. Houston's business-oriented government managed to engineer fiscal crises without high taxes, "troublesome" unions, or "high-paid" government workers. Why then is Houston suffering the same fiscal crisis as New York and Cleveland? Some have attributed the crisis to the oil-gas recession which hit the Gulf Coast hard in the mid-1980s. Certainly this is part of the story, but only part. The more fundamental reasons are closely tied to the postponed costs of industrial and population growth examined previously. In the mid-1980s Houston's city controller noted in a speech that a gloomy fiscal picture faced Houston, a retrenchment period with the possibility of service cutbacks. He attributed the problem to required increases in spending for local services and to the persisting lack of *planning* by government officials, noting optimistically that the "ill-planned days of the past are over in Houston."[63]

In the 1970–1982 period Houston saw government revenues soar from $300 million to $1 billion. But in the 1977–1982 period revenue increases from local property and sales taxes slowed considerably. In the same period, local government expenditures increased much more rapidly, with requisite sewer expenditures alone going up 88 percent. Sharply rising costs for the services required by business interests, demanded by neighborhoods, and mandated by Texas regulatory agencies forced budget increases. Costs were rising largely because of past growth and neglected infrastructure—the underbuilt and inadequately maintained facilities across the city. The modest government approach of Houston's first 140 years was becoming less viable; its long-term costs were being recognized in official city reports.

Inadequately maintained infrastructure facilities in the central city, built between 1910 and 1970, are aging rapidly. The inner city infrastructure is not only aging, but also much of it is missing. In addition, many rank-and-file Houstonians, particularly recent migrants from northern cities with better services, have pressed for improved city services. Ironically, the 1980s budget cuts of the Reagan administration had serious implications for Houston's city government; most federal funds received by the local state have traditionally been used for capital construction projects. Reagan's cuts reduced the local government's ability to fund development of infrastructural projects desired by the business coalition and citizens in general, such as sewer facilities, airline terminals, and mass transit systems, and at the same time to fund programs for its now politically active minorities. In the 1970s tax stabilization had been a major benefit of federal aid to the city of Houston; otherwise, a sharp increase in local taxes would have been required if federal aid had not been increased.[64]

Taxation in Houston

Another aspect of Houston's fiscal crisis is the city's tax structure. The fiscally conservative philosophy guiding Houston has resulted in a modest tax base for Houston's government. Property taxes, set at a relatively low level, have been a major source of revenue. The mid-1980s recession affected oil and real estate companies and thus reduced local tax revenues. In addition, the 400-plus M U Ds in the Houston area have created major service liabilities for the city. When the M U D areas are annexed, the city sometimes has faced substantial expenditures to provide adequate utilities to replace the developers' poorly-built or poorly-maintained facilities. M U Ds enabled the city government, for a time, to avoid expenditures for facilities; by the 1980s the postponed costs were coming home to roost. Furthermore, in the past Houston has relied heavily on aggressive annexation of nearby areas to expand its tax base to cover city government and public services. Yet the cost of providing adequate services in annexed areas has reduced the utility of this strategy for raising revenue.

Taxes seem of less concern to the citizens than to the business elites which worry about the "good business climate." In several public opinion surveys of Houstonians on the issue of taxes, more than half of Houstonains interviewed said they would, if given a choice between raising taxes or reducing major city services, prefer an increase in taxes. It is a good thing, too, that Houstonians are willing to pay higher taxes. Since the city's ruling elite has postponed paying for many social costs for so long, and since a massive property tax increase, especially on business property, is unlikely, the likely politicians' response will be higher taxes (short of a massive increase) and cutbacks which mean deteriorating service delivery. Houston's problems demonstrate that, in the long run at least, unrestrained capitalistic development and a first-rate quality of life may be incompatible in a modern city.[65]

Conclusion: The Sobering Cost
of a Free Enterprise City

Growth in Houston brought many social problems in its wake, and the era of decline in the 1980s made it even more difficult for government and the citizenry to cope with these social costs of free enterprise. Just how this Sunbelt capital is doing depends on one's perspective. From a corporate view of profit making, Houston's market-oriented economy was, until the downturn of the mid-1980s, very good. Centered on agriculture, exports, and the oil and gas industry, and assisted by major retail successes, Houston's economy had until the mid-1980s been very prosperous, especially for those with the wealth to invest in industrial, commercial, and real estate projects. Periodic recessions may force some belt tightening, but there is still a good business climate; there are still no state or local income taxes and few unions. And there is business-oriented city government. Yet, since the late 1970s, the seriousness of Houston's problems has become so obvious that complaints from the citizenry have become a source of concern for the city's elite. One leadership tack has been to blame the *general public* either for creating the problems themselves or for an unwillingness to pay for the needed services. Another tack can be seen in a mid-1980s boosterism campaign designed to reduce citizen complaints about social problems. A new business organization, "Pro-Houston," was created—with prominent Houston executives from major oil companies and banks on its board—to diminish local social problems, emphasize what "the city is doing right," and motivate the citizens to volunteer to solve the problems. Another business initiative, "Houston Proud," even developed an Adopt-a-Park program, in which volunteers donate their time and services to improve the city's deteriorated parks. This same strategy, ironically, was adopted in Detroit in the midst of the fiscal crisis there. When the total cost of the good business climate was becoming conspicuous to many citizens, one prominent response of the business community was yet another call for the privatization of city services.[66]

By the early 1980s, if not before, the rank-and-file Houstonian was becoming increasingly concerned about the low-service city and its array of problems. Periodic flooding, subsidence, peeling paint and lung diseases, polluted water, late buses, water pressure problems, chronic air pollution, shortage of park land, slow police and fire department response times, defective traffic signals, variable garbage service, and absent zoning protection for neighborhoods made the ideological blandishments of the power elite about the benefits of the free market, laissez-faire city seem increasingly hollow. Moreover, it was clear long ago to some Houstonians, particularly in the less affluent white and minority neighborhohods, that the free enterprise city means a starved public infrastructure and therefore difficult problems in coping with the everyday life in this spreading metropolis.

Why has the public infrastructure been starved? Clearly the answer does not lie in the hot climate or the terrain of this Sunbelt metropolis. The central reason for this failure to provide adequate public services lies in the extremely individualistic character of the capitalism practiced by the city's guiding entrepreneurs. Their outspoken opposition to taxes for neighborhood services, their emphasis on governmental support for business concerns, and their preoccupation with the idea that public planning is "socialistic" have led them to reject public expenditures for many community services necessary to provide a good urban quality of life for most citizens—and to reject taxes at the level necessary to provide those services. The lack of a noblesse-oblige civicmindedness on the part of most of the city's leading entrepreneurs seems distinctive. But the failure must also be placed at the feet of rank-and-file Houstonians. The relatively weaker political organization of the residents of most of Houston's communities places the city in contrast to other cities (for example, Minneapolis) where political action by citizens' organizations has historically accounted in part for the public amenities. Apathy does not seem to be the primary problem; lack of organization and intense individualism are likely reasons for inaction (see Chapter 10).

The business community has not been apathetic; in fact, it has taken the lead in developing an array of private planning committees, most of which have been generated by the Chamber of Commerce. As I have shown in earlier chapters, much planning for Houston on many local social cost problems has been done by an array of chamber committees, task forces, and councils, from the Ozone Task Force and the Aerospace and Technology Task Force to the Houston Economic Development Council.

9

The Delivery of Services

to Houston's Minority and

Low-Income Communities

From the 1830s to the early 1980s the generally booming economy of Houston was accompanied by a substantial growth in population. The city imported large numbers of rural and urban workers from various areas in Texas, adjacent states, and the midwestern states. In the first eight decades these workers were for the most part blacks and whites. Hispanic immigration began in the 1910s, but it did not expand rapidly until the post-1960 decades. Asian immigration accelerated in the 1970s. The migration of large groups of whites, blacks, Hispanics, and Asians has created the complex mosaic of vital racial and ethnic communities that is modern Houston. And the families in these communities provided the labor that brought prosperity to the city. Particularly important to the city's growth and development has been the labor of those residing in the city's minority neighborhoods. Yet the minorities' hard work and other contributions to the city's prosperity have not been equitably rewarded. Indeed, many social costs of growth, and of the 1980s recession as well, have been disproportionately borne by the city's minority and low-income white residents. In this chapter I will describe the history and problems of the minority and low-income residents, as well as the character and quality of the governmental services and programs they have received.

The Formation of Black Communities

The Early Period

Among the first workers in the city and surrounding areas were large numbers of African and Afro-American slaves, involuntary migrants to the region. In the first decades of its existence Houston grew as a commercial and marketing center which substantially supported the plantation agriculture in the area. These white-owned plantations used slave labor to produce much wealth. Thus, the foundation of the prosperity for the white business community dis-

240

cussed in Chapters 3 and 5 was the extreme exploitation of the area's major nonwhite minority—the Afro-American Texans and Houstonians. This dimension of the city's history is important for understanding the problems, including growth cost and service delivery dilemmas, faced by minority communities.

Slavery

Black Houstonians initially occupied the city as the slaves of white masters who moved to the city. By 1860 there were hundreds of slaves in Houston. Surrounding plantations had large numbers of slaves, so many in fact that the present Houston metropolitan area was then about half black. After the Civil War the black population faced severe economic difficulties; most went to work in semislavery conditions in agriculture or in the hardest urban jobs. Many exslaves came to Houston seeking work, food, and housing. During the postwar period blacks did gain some voting rights and voting power in Texas and Houston, but in a few decades these voting rights were terminated by the white primary and other racist devices supported by white leaders and workers at the turn of the century. Politically disenfranchised by the early 1900s, black Houstonians were to face many racial barriers in the decades to come.

By 1870 these black Houstonians were doing much of the city's dirtiest work in construction and services; in that year they constituted approximately 40 percent of the city population. For all of the city's history black Houstonians have provided a substantial portion of the labor that built and maintained the city. Much of the wealth of white Houstonians and other south Texans, not just in the past but also in the present, is ultimately rooted in uncompensated slave labor or poorly compensated free black labor. Houston is a southern city, historically part of the plantation South, and this is an important part of the racial culture or "mind of the city," to borrow from Cash's phrase about the South.[1] The presence of many black slaves and, later, many black workers in a segregated rural and urban caste system created racial division that would handicap not only black Texans but white workers as well; race was used by the elites to divide black and white workers who might otherwise have organized to bring change.

Racism and Segregation Patterns

In 1880 blacks made up nearly 40 percent of the population. But white immigrants poured into the city in the next few decades, and by 1930 the percentage of black residents had dropped to 22 percent. The initial pattern of residential development for black Houstonians was scattered, with blacks living in large numbers in several of the city's political wards. In 1890 there were black residents in all six of the municipal wards, but the largest number lived in the Third Ward to the south and east of downtown and in neighborhoods on the fringe of the Fourth Ward to the west of downtown. This housing pattern is typical of southern cities. More rigid residential segregation was apparent in the next few decades.[2]

As was true for many cities of the South, segregation in most Houston facilities increased between the late 1870s and the 1920s. Thus, in 1876 school segregation was imposed by the new Texas constitution. State of Texas and city laws gradually expanded legal segregation to hotels, restaurants, theaters, and other public facilities by 1907. In 1913 the train station segregated its waiting rooms, and the city hall segregated drinking fountains. In 1928 the Democratic National Convention even went so far as to segregate black spectators behind chicken wire.

Residential segregation also increased during this period. A 1920s plan presented by William C. Hogg called on the city to expand its park system and to adopt zoning. Segregation of the races in Houston was recognized by the Hogg planning report, which noted three areas of black concentration. The earlier pattern of residential scattering was officially recognized as being a problem for whites; the Hogg report recommended that the scattering be replaced by thoroughgoing housing segregation. The Hogg report suggested that certain sectors should be set aside for blacks: "Because of long established racial prejudices, it is best for both races that living areas be segregated."[3]

Moreover, Houston was the first Texas city to have an organized chapter of the Ku Klux Klan in the 1920s. The Sam Houston Klan Number One selected a former Harris County deputy sheriff as its leader, and then Mayor Oscar Holcombe joined the Klan for a brief time. The Klan even controlled the Harris County government. At first the Houston business elite flirted with the Klan, but it soon found a somewhat less flamboyant type of racial discrimination more useful and acceptable.

The blatant and extremely stereotyped images many white Houstonians held in regard to the large black community are captured in these opening lines from a *Houston Press* reporter's story titled "Houston's Little Harlem Thrives on Laughter":

> Strike a note of life that vibrates somewhere in the misty region between the throb of a jungle tom-tom and the sharp, clear tones of an Anglo-Saxon civilization and the answer comes throbbing back from the thousands of negroes who are living their day in the heart of Houston. Down Prairie and Preston Avenue from Travis and Louisiana streets, and on Milam street life moves along to the

indolent rhythm of the black man's heart—now childish and carefree—now depressed—and now dangerous as the leap of a jungle cat.[4]

Segregation in a Southern City

From the 1920s to the 1970s majorities of the business community and the white working class were hostile to attempts to desegregate the city's basic institutions. For example, against the backdrop of harsh racial discrimination in this Old South city, in February 1955 the Houston *Chronicle* announced on its front page the dramatic news that in 1956 the city's symphony director would be none other than the legendary Leopold Stokowski. The city's leaders viewed this event as important in overcoming the cowtown and unsophisticated image of the city. But Stokowski's relationship to the orchestral board, part of the local elite, gradually broke down over the next several years. The final break came over a racial issue. In 1960, well into the desegregation era in U.S. race relations, Stokowski decided to have the all-black chorus at the principal local black university, Texas Southern University, sing in a performance of a Schoenberg work, but the white management refused. The reason was obvious in this southern metropolis. The local symphony concerts were segregated, and blacks would not normally be allowed on the stage.[5] This decision was not reached by prejudiced white workers in a blue-collar suburb. Well into the civil rights revolution which began in the 1950s, the educated, white leadership of this southern city was unprepared to extend basic human rights to its local black residents.

Residential segregation was rigidly enforced in the 1950s and 1960s. As I discussed in Chapter 6, private deed restrictions have been used to keep areas segregated. Houston's civic clubs in these residential communities were not initially used to exclude black residents, but the overturning of segregation laws and the wave of suburbanization in the 1950s were accompanied by increasing white concern with racial integration. The aggressive black civil rights movement scared white Houstonians, especially those in residential areas near black subdivisions. The Greater Riverside Property Owners Association was organized on the east side to protect an older white area from black in-migration. In 1953 the first black family to move into the area was bombed. Moreover, in the 1950s an umbrella organization, the Allied Civic Club, was created to link civic clubs in southwestern neighborhoods. This organization coordinated white opposition to racial integration.[6]

The white clubs received the backing of many in the business community. In the 1950s and early 1960s the Suite 8F group poured money into the political campaigns of racial segregationists running for the city council and the school board. In these years the city had extensive racial segregation in public accommodations, housing, jobs, and education. Moreover, the rigid wall of economic and housing segregation, *legally* enforced in Houston until the 1960s, fostered the development of self-contained black communities with their own institutions—churches, schools, newspapers, parks, restaurants, movie theaters, and businesses. Strong black institutions resulted. But the cost of this segregation has been high: poor housing, low-wage jobs, poorly supported schools, and inferior public services.[7]

Migration and the Location of Black Communities

Black southerners in the rural areas of the South moved to the cities during the two world war periods, but in Texas the migration was most substantial during and after World War II. Between 1940 and the early 1980s black migration to Houston dramatically increased the size and number of the city's black residential areas. The city's black population increased from 86,300 to 440,250 in this period. Older black communities in the Third, Fourth, and Fifth wards grew substantially, sometimes spilling over into adjacent white communities. In addition, many new subdivisions were built to the north, south, and east of the central city.[8]

The geographic center of the black population has shifted over time. In 1900 the largest number lived in the Third and Fourth wards. Black schools and churches had been established in these communities well before 1900. Until the 1940s the economic and recreational center of black Houston was located in these two wards. In the next two decades the heart of the black community moved just northeast of the downtown district to the Fifth Ward— a vibrant black community with important jazz clubs and many black businesses. Indeed, some called the Lyons Street area one of the major black cultural centers in the United States. With the partial destruction of that community by the highway developments examined in Chapter 6 and the new inmigration after the 1950s, the economic center of black Houston shifted back to the Third Ward. A mid-1970s study of the Third Ward found it to be a high density area with 51,300 residents, 91 percent black and 3 percent Mexican American. Texas Southern University and the main campus of the University of Houston are located in the area.[9] The area also housed a major black-owned bank, a black-owned savings and loan, and the black Chamber of Commerce.

There was some residential desegregation in formerly all-white residential areas in the 1970s, and some black middle- and upper-income Houstonians moved out of the traditional inner city areas during the next decade. Still, in the mid-1980s three-quarters of black Houstonians resided in predominantly black areas. Houston's black communities are generally segregated and distinctive. Most of Houston's black population remains concentrated in the Fourth Ward and in a broad belt on the eastern side of the city. The school system is also de facto segregated; 44 percent of the children are black and 32 percent Hispanic.[10]

In addition, the economic and health conditions of the black community were deteriorating in the mid- to late-1980s. In the summer of 1985 black unemployment had climbed to 12.3 percent in the metropolitan area, compared to 9.7 percent for Hispanics and to 5.6 percent for the nonminority population. The black infant mortality rate was 17.2 deaths of children under one year of age for every 1,000 live births, while the white rate was only 12.3.[11]

The Provision of Services to Black Communities

The Historical Background

Discussing the disenfranchisement of black Texans at the turn of the century, Platt notes that the new plan of the business leadership for Houston intentionally resulted in "two segregated communities—one modern and one unimproved."[12] The experience of black communities was one of uneven development within a city of growing wealth and resources. Urban social scientists frequently assess the uneven development that occurs across regions, but equally important is the uneven development that takes place *within* cities themselves. In the slave system and the subsequent semislave segregation system low-wage jobs, subemployment, constantly threatening unemployment, and poor public services have long been recurrent problems facing Houston's black citizens.

For many decades most minority residential areas have had poor public services, including one or more of the following: inadequate sewage treatment plants and lines, inadequate water lines, inferior water and sewer systems, poor storm drainage, problematical public transportation, and segregated schools. Most black Houstonians, residing near the central business district, greatly depend on the insufficient and routinely troubled mass transit (bus) system. Basic infrastructure facilities in the central city, especially for residential neighborhoods and mostly built between 1910 and 1970, have been inadequately maintained and thus are aging rapidly. In a 1978 application for a federal development grant even city officials admitted that they had starved central city neighborhoods:

The city, in its efforts to keep up with the tremendous growth of population and land areas away from the inner city, has been unable to maintain and upgrade the infrastructure of the inner city. These inner-city neighborhoods (lying in the intermediate zone between the Central Business District and the outlying fringe) are plagued by inadequate infrastructures (including unpaved streets, inadequate water and sewer capacity, nonexistent street lighting, decaying telephone and electrical lines) which are not adequately maintained and which negate locational advantages these areas may have to attract private investment.[13]

The inner-city infrastructure is not only aging but also missing; those guiding the city government have intentionally provided inferior facilities for minority communities. This quote, moreover, indicates that possible private investment, not citizen rights, is motivating infrastructural change.

Public services have traditionally been distributed in a discriminatory fashion in the city of Houston. As late as 1940, nearly 25 percent of black households had no running water, compared to 5 percent of white-occupied housing units. In addition, black "neighborhoods often did not have paved streets, street lights, and sidewalks, and typically they suffered from poor drainage that regularly made them inaccessible after heavy rains."[14] This neglect forced black communities to create civic and community associations with the dual tasks of improving their neighborhoods with volunteer efforts and of pressuring, albeit gently, the white business elite to make neighborhood improvements. On the whole, except for occasional infrastructural projects and repairs, the business elite was unresponsive in the early decades of the twentieth century. During the New Deal period the city government officials, flush with federal money, did provide some modest improvements for black communities. In the late 1930s and 1940s the new Houston Housing Authority built 3,800 federally-funded public housing units in black residential areas. At the same time, however, a large housing project for low-income whites was located in one of the oldest black neighborhoods, displacing hundreds of black residents. On the whole, from the early 1900s to the political resurgence of minority voters in the 1970s, black communities were the last areas to receive attention from city government.[15]

Services in Recent Decades

We have already noted the discrimination black Houstonians faced from police. Historically, black communities have also faced a low level of routine police services. Indeed, for decades the city of Houston was famous in minority circles for its high level of police brutality, evidenced in the number of blacks and Hispanics killed or seriously injured by the police, and for very slow response times to black requests for police assistance. In the 1980s, however, the increased political influence of the black population could be seen in the improvements in police services. In a dramatic move reflecting her own social liberalism Mayor Whitmire appointed a black police chief in 1982; by 1986 he had reformed the police department in regard to police brutality and provision of services to minority communities, and he had more than doubled the number of black police officers. However, in budget crises in the late 1980s the number of officers was reduced, and progress was threatened.[16]

In most other areas black Houstonians have had to tolerate either persisting discrimination in public services or no redress for the present results of past service discrimination. In Chapter 8 I examined the garbage crisis of the metropolitan area. Historically, much of Houston waste has been dumped in or near the minority neighborhoods; Houston's oldest garbage dump is in the black Fourth Ward area. Between the 1950s and the 1970s a total of twenty-one solid waste sites were authorized by the Texas Department of Health for the Houston area. Of these, eleven (52 percent) were located in or near black areas, even though blacks occupy less than 20 percent of residential space in the city. Six landfill areas with state permits received municipal garbage between 1970 and 1978; *five* of these were in black neighborhoods at the time they opened, and the sixth was becoming a predominantly black area in the early 1980s.[17] Moreover, Houston's five garbage incinerators operating from the 1920s to the 1970s were located in black or Hispanic neighborhoods. Here is a clear example of unequal payment of the social costs of development in a free enterprise modus operandi. Minority Houstonians have suffered most of the site selection effects of Houston's garbage crisis.[18]

Problems in Specific Black Communities

In the 1970s and 1980s most black and Hispanic communities have faced serious water, sewage, and flooding problems, often but not always worse than those faced by white residential areas. For example, in the mid-1970s an evaluation by the City Planning Department of the utility services to the Montrose and Fourth Ward areas, both with substantial minority populations, revealed serious deficiencies. One of the sewerage districts serving the area was operating far above capacity, and many of the sewer lines were old and inadequate. These two areas also had fifty-three miles of water pipe below the minimum standard, and both reportedly had serious storm drainage and flooding problems. In addition, small areas of the Third Ward did not yet have sewer connections. Sewage facilities were generally adequate, but most water lines were below standard. In the Southpark/MacGregor area there were also service deficiencies. One sewer district was operating treatment plants above capacity, and several residential areas had inadequate water lines and difficult access to the municipal water supply. Just under half the blocks in the area had no storm sewers.[19]

Some black communities have suffered even greater discrimination in the provision of public services. For example, Riceville, an all-black neighborhood in the southwest, is a century-old area annexed in the mid-1960s. As late as the 1980s the area had not been provided with such services as water facilities, sanitary sewers, storm drainage, or paved roads. Surrounded by white subdivisions with better facilities, the Riceville and similar black communities symbolize the racial aspect of the uneven development within the metropolitan area.[20]

The Destruction of Black Communities

Uneven Development within the City: The Fifth Ward

White-dominated development has destroyed the vitality of one black community in the central city area, and it is about to destroy another. The Fifth Ward in northeast Houston has suffered from the growth plans of the white business elite. Its Lyons Avenue area was once a major center for Houston's black citizens, with provisions for entertainment, black businesses, and churches. Today the area has long stretches of abandoned houses and boarded-up stores; indeed, the avenue is now called "Pearl Harbor" because of its bombed-out look.

Once a partially integrated area, by the early 1980s the Lyons area was predominately composed of low- and moderate-income black families. Decisions by Houston's developers to build two major highways through the area, starting in the 1940s, have destroyed this black community. The 40,000-person neighborhood was severely disrupted by the construction of two major highway systems now called Interstate 10 and U.S. Hwy. 59. These two freeway systems literally crucified the area by creating large freeways in a cross pattern through its heart. This massive cross disrupted community life during and after construction and permanently destroyed many black homes and businesses; the roads also separated many residents from convenient access to other business and church facilities. The initial decisions leading to destruction of this residential community were made by white leaders in the interest of business-oriented growth.[21]

Redeveloping the Fourth Ward?

Although some of the nation's richest and most powerful white men live on Houston's inner west side, their elite residential areas (for example, River Oaks) are only part of the Houston story. As Garreau has noted in *The Nine Nations of North America:* "Almost literally in the shadow of the tall buildings at Houston's core are black slums straight out of the heart of Mississippi."[22] Just west of new downtown towers lies the two-mile-square Fourth Ward; by the late 1970s it was 72 percent black and 9 percent Hispanic. The area has long been a cohesive black community, with friendly neighborhoods, numerous churches, and black-owned businesses.[23]

Since World War II the community has suffered from construction projects. The construction of Interstate 45 and adjacent developments, favorite projects of the city's white elite, destroyed several important black landmarks in the Fourth Ward. In the late 1970s, moreover, because of its nearness to the booming downtown district, development capitalists seeking to build office buildings and luxury apartment complexes eyed the area for private redevelopment. To legitimate bulldozing the area newspaper editors and other leaders described the area as a "blighted neighborhood" or as a "bleak collection of shacks." Although this verbal labeling of an area is essential to legitimate its destruction, one Houston resident who knows the area disagrees with the verbal attack: "The Fourth Ward I know is a beautiful place, where neighbors actually know each other, kids play outside in the streets, older folks sit on their porches and chat with neighbors. . . . and there's a warm feeling of community that's found almost nowhere else in Houston."[24] The 7,000 mostly black residents had been anticipating redevelopment for more than a decade; the wooden shotgun houses had been allowed to decay by absentee landlords. Portions of the Fourth Ward had already been transformed into parking lots and glassy office towers.

Consultant reports to the city government suggested that the area be redeveloped, but they offered no real solutions to the housing plight of black tenants. Development plans for the area included tearing down a major public housing project called Allen Parkway Village. In July 1984, the Houston city council approved a plan of the Houston Housing Authority to demolish Allen Parkway Village. However, the American Civil Liberties Union (A C L U) submitted a brief on behalf of public housing applicants charging the housing authority with deliberately being "overly bleak" in assessing the Village's physical condition in order to bypass federal standards prohibiting destruction of public housing. The city's housing authority estimated rehabilitation costs for the project at a rather extreme figure of $36,000 per unit. Business-oriented city officials were planning to destroy the project and lease the property to private developers—an action made easier under the Reagan administration.

In September 1984 the housing authority applied to the federal Department of Housing and Urban Development to bulldoze the project, build 975 new public housing units, and erect 525 private apartments available to low-income people elsewhere in the city. Thus, the Village site itself would be made available to developers. The A C L U brief charged that the Village was still structurally sound and that city housing officials had withheld $10 million in federal dollars received in 1979 to rehabilitate public housing units. The brief also charged the housing authority with excluding blacks from the Village in favor of Indochinese tenants who would be easier to evict once the project was cleared for destruction by the federal government.[25]

By late 1986 the Houston housing authority had boarded up 800 of the 1,000 apartments in Allen Parkway Village. The housing authority was waiting for the U.S. Department of Housing and Urban Development to fund the demolition of 1,000 units and approve sale of the thirty-seven acres of prime land to real estate developers. Nearby private houses were also demolished in 1985–1987, and the predominantly white absentee property holders in the area were expecting to profit significantly from their land once Houston's recovery begins. The destruction of minority communities with the help of city of Houston officials is rooted ultimately in the city's racist past.[26]

Black Protest and Politics: Attempts to Improve Public Services

Protesting Racial Discrimination

In comparison with the communities of other cities, Houston's black communities have produced relatively less in the way of civil rights protest. The major riot in the city's history was carried out by northern black soldiers during World War I. A northern unit of black soldiers was sent to Camp Logan in west Houston to provide security for army property. These soldiers had to endure the intense racial discrimination rigidly enforced by white Houstonians. In August 1917 two white police officers raided a dice game and beat up a black soldier, taking him and a woman to jail. A black military police officer had heated words with the arresting officers; the white officers hit the black military official and took him to jail. Seeking to punish the Houston police and fearful of a white attack on their camp, seventy-five to one hundred black soldiers armed themselves and marched into central Houston. They killed several whites, including a number of police officers. A thousand soldiers were brought in to suppress the rebellion. Thirteen of the soldiers were hung, in what appeared to be a legal lynching. Many others were imprisoned. This rebellion only contributed to the established racial fears of white leaders and workers over the next decade.[27]

Beginning in the 1950s, major changes took place in Houston's segregated public accommodations and schooling patterns. A series of N A A C P-supported and other court suits brought against white authorities, combined with a few black protests, forced the abolition of racial barriers at the municipal golf courses (1950), the public library (1953), city buses (1954), public schools (1960, 1966), restaurants (1960), and most other public facilities (1960–1963). The most visible protest demonstrations were carried out by students at Texas Southern University. In 1960 the students engaged in a number of sit-ins at local lunch counters. As a result, several members of the white business leadership, led by the chief executive at the principal downtown department store, moved to desegregate the restaurants without fanfare.

The university students also engaged in two other struggles with the city's white authorities; in 1965 and in 1967 black students protested against local police actions, generally regarded among the most brutal in the country. In 1967 there was a police riot in response to student protest. Although there is no evidence that the protesting students were armed, the 500 police officers called out fired no less than 4,000 rounds of ammunition, many of them at student dormitories. One officer was killed, probably by a police bullet, and 489 students were jailed in what has locally been termed a "student riot."[28]

Perhaps the longest civil rights struggle, a court struggle persisting into the 1980s, took place over school desegregation. In 1877 the Houston city government set up free public schools in the form of a racially segregated system. In 1923 the Houston Independent School District (H I S D) was created as a separate political entity to run the public schools. For decades conservative interests controlled the bare-bones school system and worked to keep H I S D spending and taxes low, particularly for the minority schools. The conservative, all-white school board even refused to accept federal lunch programs for disadvantaged students.

After a brief period of moderate-liberal control in the early 1950s, right-wing segregationists regained control in 1956. In 1959–1960 the H I S D had 168,000 students in 177 schools in one of the country's largest racially segregated school systems. Because of the 1954–1955 *Brown* decisions and local black opposition, there was substantial pressure on the H I S D to desegregate the schools, but the school board moved slowly in that direction. This issue, one observer noted in an assessment of Houston politics in 1960, was the "top political issue in Houston."[29] The N A A C P and other black organizations conducted an extended struggle to integrate the Houston public schools. Between 1959 and 1966 there were a number of court cases and hearings on the segregation of Houston public schools, but not until 1962 did a federal appeals court decision in New Orleans force the H I S D to cease its overt resistance to desegregation. In 1966–1967 the H I S D finally completed a meaningful desegregation program. But the controversy over de facto racial segregation of the public schools and white flight to private and suburban schools persisted into the late 1980s.[30]

Blacks in Local Politics

After the Civil War black slaves were given their freedom in Texas, and growing numbers exercised their right to vote from the 1870s to the 1890s. The votes of black Houstonians gave the city some of its most progressive governments in this period. Because of this voting power, in the 1898 municipal election the conservative white Democratic leaders decided to prohibit black voters from any further participation in party elections. The primaries became private, white-only gatherings.[31] In the 1898–1904 period the white primary rule and the Texas poll tax sharply reduced Houston's voter registration rolls, thus allowing the white business elite to consolidate its control over the city. The politics of "progressivism" in Texas was also the white politics of minority exclusion. Black Texans, as well as the poor white Texans, were excluded from fundamental political institutions. This in turn reinforced the increasing wall of segregation, where cracks developed after World War II; but no major changes took place until the 1970s.

The major crack in the wall of political discrimination came in the early 1970s with increased voter input from the black and Hispanic communities. This increased voter power resulted in part from structural changes forced on the white establishment through a suit undertaken by members of the city's minority communities. This legal battle was required to force replacement of an eight-member at-large council with one made up of nine members elected from specific districts and five elected at-large. This was perhaps the most significant internal change in Houston's politics since the so-called "progressivism" brought to City Hall by the business elite in the early 1900s.

With the enfranchisement of minority voters in the 1970s came the election of white mayors and partially desegregated city councils somewhat more sensitive to the needs of minority residents. Prior to that decade the business elite and the city government it dominated were generally able to ignore the needs of inner-city communities. By the mid-1970s the city administration of Mayor Fred Hofheinz had rejected the longstanding policy of not accepting federal aid for most social and community programs, especially those beneficial to minority communities. He was also the first Houston mayor in the twentieth century to pay even modest attention to serious problems of minority Houstonians. Moreover, this reenfranchisement of minority voters brought minority representatives to the city council, including several black city council members. As I have noted in earlier chapters, these minority representatives have been able to bring some services to their constituencies. Indeed, by 1987 two of the black politicians were considering running in the 1989 mayor's race.

Hispanic Houstonians: Communities and Crisis

Historical and Recent Hispanic Immigration

Houston is more than a city with Deep South roots in slavery and racism; it is also a southwestern city. Houston has a history as a frontier city, later a global city, looking toward the Southwest and Latin America. At the turn of the century railroad construction and machine shops brought the first Hispanic workers and their families into the greater Houston area. In the next few decades the expansion of the oil and real estate industries generated further migration to the city.

Over the course of the twentieth century the economic development of metropolitan Houston has involved an infusion of thousands of Mexican and Central American workers. Again, as in the case of black Houstonians, the urban growth machine does not run solely on the fuel of money capital; it also requires the labor and vigor of the city's workers. Houston is a part of a worldwide labor system, not just of a global investment system. Hispanic migration flows have paralleled investment flows, and both have been shaped by the requirements of the global economic system. From the early 1900s to the 1980s,

Houston has drawn heavily on migrating workers from Third World regions, particularly Mexico and Central America.

Diversity in the Hispanic Population

In 1900 there was a small Mexican American community of about 1,000 in the "barrios" (neighborhoods) of Houston. The population grew over the next two decades with the addition of large numbers of immigrant laborers from Mexico, and by 1940 the Mexican American population had grown to about 20,000. During World War II Mexican laborers were imported to work in agricultural areas because of the labor shortage in the United States.[32] The migration streams from south of the border grew gradually over the next few decades, then expanded rapidly during the 1970s and 1980s. In these latter decades thousands of Hispanic workers from Mexico and Central America arrived in Houston; many did not have legal documents. Although many were Mexican immigrants, others were political and economic refugees from Central America. In the 1960s and 1970s, most immigrants were undocumented Mexican workers, many of whom were temporary migrants who worked in the United States. Hard times in several Central American countries sent undocumented immigrants to the Houston area. In the 1980s the number of undocumented Central American immigrants grew rapidly, almost to the level of Mexican migrants. Undocumented immigrants from El Salvador became a significant portion of the resident population. By the late 1980s estimates of the number of Salvadorans ranged from 80,000 to 140,000, thus establishing the Houston area as the home of one of the largest Salvadoran communities in the world.

The director of a local immigration agency estimated that in the mid-1980s there were 100,000 Salvadorans, 30,000 Guatemalans, and 10,000 Hondurans, Nicaraguans, and Costa Ricans in Houston. At that time there were at least 250,000 Hispanics in the city of Houston, with another 150,000 outside the city limits. However, these are conservative figures, and most experts estimated the Hispanic population to be larger than these figures suggest. Indeed, a marketing survey of the twenty-county "Houston market" estimated the Hispanic population of that area to be 706,000, which ranked the city just behind San Francisco and Chicago as the seventh largest Hispanic market in the United States. The same survey also estimated that most Hispanic Houstonians were under thirty-five years of age; therefore, many were citizens by birth. The future growth of the Hispanic population will probably come from natural increase and from migration within the United States. The 1986 immigration law will doubtless slow the number of Mexican and Central American residents coming to the city from outside the country and thus reduce the growth of the Hispanic communities from immigration.[33]

Problems of Employment and Migration

This Hispanic immigration flow is another signal of the important global capitalistic system in Houston's development. Immigrants from a variety of Third World countries have played a paramount role in building the city; they have done substantial construction, maintenance, and service work. Why has Houston become a center of Hispanic immigration? A former director of the U.S. Immigration and Naturalization Servcie explained that at first the Houston job market was attractive. But by the 1980s the presence of large and vibrant Hispanic communities, the critical enclaves that ease settlement in the United States, was a critical issue. Immigrants from the most remote villages of Guatemala know exactly to which neighborhood in Houston they must go in order to settle among hometown people. Although jobs are still the major pull, the large Hispanic enclaves provide the critical support networks necessary for survival in a strange country with a different language and culture.[34]

A recent development in the history of immigration is the 1986 Immigration Act. By late 1987 this act was having a significant impact on Houston's Hispanic populations. Interviews with undocumented workers by local journalists found that fearful employers had begun to fire workers they knew or suspected to be undocumented. Because the immigration law assesses fines for employers of "illegal" aliens, these employers have fired many workers unnecessarily and have slammed the door on others looking for jobs. Confused employers were not fully informed on the law. For example, contrary to the belief of many, under the law they will not be fined for undocumented workers they hired before the law was passed. The result of these firings will be long-term unemployment for many undocumented and some Mexican American workers. "We can't live here without work," said a twenty-three-year-old Salvadoran in Houston interviewed in mid-1987.[35] It seems likely that these workers, many of whom worked long hours building the city of Houston, will return to their home countries.

Discrimination and the Location of Hispanic Communities

In the early decades of the twentieth century most of the Mexican American barrios were in industrial areas: in the Second Ward, which extended directly east of the downtown business district into industrial and port areas, and in the Magnolia area southeast of the Second Ward and near the ship channel. White real estate and governmental officials played an important role in channeling Mexican American families to segregated residential areas. From the 1910s to the 1950s the growing Mexican American population faced racial and language discrimination. Dark-skinned Mexican Americans were treated just like black Houstonians. Many suffered discrimination in housing and employment; they were largely excluded from political participation. Mexican American children were punished for speaking Spanish in school. Most attempts to combat the blatant discrimination were unsuccessful until the 1950s and 1960s.

Between the early decades and the 1980s communities sprang up in many parts of the city. In the late 1980s Hispanic communities—Mexican American, Mexican (undocumented), Honduran, Salvadoran, Guatamalan, Central American Indian—were for the most part on the eastern side of the city, with large numbers in an eastern corridor moving out from downtown. Although there were Hispanic areas in many parts of the city, the greatest concentrations were in the old Second Ward, Magnolia, and Denver Harbor areas, older areas to the east with well-established Mexican and Mexican American communities—Mexican folk culture, businesses, Catholic churches, theaters, and entertainment.[36] By the late 1980s there were many different types of Hispanic communities. Perhaps the largest of the non-Mexican communities was the Salvadoran community, a dispersed population; many resided outside the traditional Hispanic communities. One knowledgeable Houston lawyer noted, "You'll find them in Bellaire and southwest Houston, all over the city, and that's one of the reasons it has become so difficult for us who work with voter registration projects."[37]

Problems with City Services: The Impact of Growth on the Hispanic Community

A Range of Service Delivery Issues

We have observed the service delivery problems that have been the scourge of black communities for generations in Houston. Some of the communities already discussed also have Hispanic neighborhoods, including the Montrose and Fourth Ward districts. Moreover, concentrated Hispanic areas such as Magnolia and Denver Harbor have experienced serious difficulties with water, sewage, and other utility services. In the traditional Hispanic area of Magnolia a city planning department study found that one sewer district had treatment plants operating above capacity and that most water lines were below standard. Storm drainage and flooding were major problems for that residential community. Recall also that certain Hispanic communities have been confronted with Houston's garbage disposal facilities in their backyards. In addition, numerous Hispanic communities have periodically suffered from the bulldozers and earthmovers associated with road and freeway development.[38]

In recent years some of the city's Hispanic leaders have criticized the quality of police services provided to Hispanic communities. Given the Houston police department's reputation for brutality not only against black residents but also against Mexican American residents of the city, several Mexican and Mexican American young people have been killed by the police under questionable circumstances. When Whitmire became mayor in the early 1980s, one of her first reforms was replacing the police chief. Although the new black chief reformed the police department and changed its image in the black communities, city council member Ben Reyes complained that he had not placed enough emphasis on hiring Hispanics. In 1987 black officers constituted one-eighth of the police force, compared to one-tenth for Hispanics, arguably the larger of the two minority populations. The shortage of Hispanic officers meant that not enough Houston police officers could speak Spanish; thus, police service to Hispanic communities was inadequate. It is noteworthy that this Hispanic political leader was also critical of certain private companies in Houston for not providing adequate services to the growing Hispanic communities. For example, Reyes was contemptuous of the *Houston Post* for "just a steady, steady, steady, steady" stream of negative coverage of such Hispanic community issues as the federal foreclosure on the El Mercado shopping mall, a center set up by local business leaders in the 1980s to serve the flourishing Hispanic community.[39]

Attempts to Organize for Change: Hispanic Houston

Issues of Voting and Protest

Political disenfranchisement in effect characterized the minority communities of Houston until the 1970s. We have already noted that civil rights litigation was required to enfranchise the city's minority communities. No Hispanic Houstonian served on the Houston city council until 1979. Since then council member Ben Reyes has been outspoken in asserting the needs and concerns of the Hispanic community. By the late 1980s a principal topic of debate in the Houston political circles was the voting potential of this Hispanic community. From 1970 to 1980 the Hispanic population in Houston increased by more than 60 percent; yet this growth was not matched by a major improvement in the political condition of Hispanics.

Ethnic and national diversity of the Hispanic population and its dispersal across several geographical areas of the city, as well as the large number of undocumented residents, will make it difficult for the Hispanic community to secure political power in the near future. "While we may be 55 percent of the first-grade class at H I S D . . . we're only 8 percent of the voters," Leonel Castillo explained to a journalist in 1987.[40] In the late 1980s a majority of the Hispanic community could not vote because of age or illegal status. Some Mexican workers were expected to be able to become citizens under the amnesty provision of the 1986 immigration act. Since most Salvadorans will not qualify under the amnesty provision, they are unlikely to play a role in the future political power of Houston's Hispanic community. Leonel Castillo has estimated that perhaps 100,000 of the undocumented aliens in Houston will try to become citizens under the immigration law, but other analysts of the Houston scene are skeptical about that high figure.[41]

Militant Protest

Outside the ballot box there has been some militant protest against discrimination in the history of the Mexican American community in Houston. For example, there was the 1978 protest against police brutality. In 1977 Houston police officers arrested a Mexican American, Joe Torres, for drunkenness; he was later beaten by the police and thrown into Buffalo Bayou. His drowning triggered the creation of a militant organization, People United to Fight Police Brutality, and subsequent marches and leafleting. A state court convicted the offending officers of a misdemeanor and fined them one dollar each; the decision provoked more demonstrations in the Mexican American neighborhoods. When the officers were tried in federal court for violating the civil rights of Torres, they received what were, in effect, nine-month sentences. A month after the decision, a crowd of 3,000 Mexican Americans was celebrating the Mexican Cinco de Mayo holiday in Houston's Moody Park. Although the exact cause of the ensuing riot remains unclear—some accused the police of intentionally provoking it—there was a major riot against the police in the park area. Four hundred people were arrested, and the city's business leadership, following the almost obligatory behavior of southern white officials, accused outside agitators and radical organizations of stirring up trouble in the Mexican American community. The hypocrisy of the white leadership, heavily implicated in the economic crisis and discrimination facing Hispanic Houston, was obvious to the city's minority residents.

Linguistic Conflict

One problem facing the Hispanic community that does not face the black community is language. Some among the city's Anglo leadership have long been critical of the bilingual emphasis in the Hispanic community and have supported the jingoistic movement to make English the official language of Texas and the United States. This view seems to reflect both the past anti-Mexican attitudes of many white Texans and the present fear of political and economic power among the growing Mexican and Mexican American populations. The large-scale immigration of the 1970s and 1980s represents in one sense an Hispanicization of the Houston area. "We're more Mexican than San Antonio," commented Leonel Castillo, former commissioner of the U.S. Immigration and Naturalization Service. "San Antonio has more *ambience,* or atmosphere, but fewer Mexicans. San Antonio also has fewer people who speak Spanish only."[42] While Hispanic leaders such as Castillo view this change positively, many Anglo Houston leaders and citizens are afraid of the future political power of the Hispanic community, as well as the cost, as they see it, of a large unemployed population of undocumented workers. A local Hispanic bishop was quoted in 1987: "They feel threatened. I hope I am completely wrong, but I fear that unless things are handled properly, we might see very ugly situations in the not-so-distant future."[43]

Persisting Poverty
in the Free Enterprise City

Business Views Houston's Poor

The city's business leaders have had little understanding of the lives of the city's poor white and minority populations. Indeed, free enterprise dynamism in the city has been viewed as minimizing social problems such as poverty, a point emphasized by former mayor and Chamber of Commerce head Louie Welch: "The free market place has functioned in Houston like no other place in America. It has a method of purging itself of slums. No city is without poor people, but the opportunity not to be poor is greater than in most cities. The work ethic, and opportunities, are strong here."[44] The sad irony in this statement is that Houston has actually fostered some large poverty areas.

This free market city has more than not purged itself of slums. According to the U.S. census nearly 200,000 Houstonians, about 13 percent of the population in the city limits, fell below the federal poverty line in 1979, at the peak of the city's prosperity. The percentage was relatively low compared to other major cities, but the absolute number was the sixth largest in the United States. During the city's years of prosperity the relatively low unemployment rate reduced the number of persons falling below the poverty line, but this prosperity by no means purged the city of its 200,000 residents in poverty-stricken areas. In addition, the prosperous years brought many residents low-wage employment, which kept them just above the poverty line. Unlike residents in northern cities Houstonians of modest means have had little in the way of governmental programs to extend their incomes and provide a safety net for hard times.

During the major economic downturn in the mid-1980s the city's white and minority workers were faced with high unemployment in a relatively low-service setting. The city, county, and state of Texas programs for the unemployed and the poor vary from minimal to nonexistent. In Texas, as in most southern states, able-bodied unemployed men with families do not qualify for federally funded welfare programs. And, in the late 1980s, families with husbandless unemployed mothers and several children qualified for less than $200 a month in basic welfare stipends. Indeed, many Texas business and political leaders seemed proud of the fact that the state ranked forty-sixth among the fifty states in spending for public services. In addition, federal cutbacks in public service programs under the Reagan administration in the 1980s made the situation even more grim.

Hunger and Homelessness in Houston

Hunger has been a chronic problem for poorer Houstonians, but in the 1980s hunger also received some local media attention, in large part because of the economic recession. In 1982 the nonprofit Houston Food Bank distributed 268,000 pounds of food; by 1984 this distribution had grown to *three million* pounds. By 1985 dozens of church and other nonprofit food pantries were distributing food to the hungry. A survey of the directors of the food distribution centers found that most saw the economic recession as responsible for the increasing hunger problem, and the majority of the directors said that most requests for food were coming from families. High unemployment and the Reagan administration cutbacks in food programs were primary causes of increased hunger. A 1987 newspaper story covered the distribution of food at three Salvation Army centers on one day. The Department of Agriculture had provided surplus food for distribution, and more than 3,000 people came to secure the treasured commodities, many waiting for hours in the rain and cold. The centers distributed 84,000 pounds of cheese, rice, butter, and powdered milk. "We're getting more people because the unemployment is so bad," reported the city commander of the Salvation Army. Because the federal government threatened to cancel the program the Salvation Army distributed two months' worth at one time. "I need whatever they can give," said one former construction worker on disability relief. "If I have to wait in line, I will—I got my two kids, my wife and my baby granddaughter at home."[45] Houston has not purged itself of either poverty or hunger.

Homelessness is yet another uncelebrated dimension of the Houston scene in the panegyrics on the city during the boom period from the 1970s to the 1980s. However, the economic downturn of the mid- and late-1980s sparked local media interest in Houston's large homeless population, estimated to be at least 15,000. In 1986 the city's shelters for the homeless were overflowing, with significant numbers of families seeking refuge there. The Star of Hope Mission's family shelter had 180 beds, but was housing 240 people, including 90 to 95 children, each night, in addition to the 500-plus single men housed in the Mission's main shelter—reportedly the *largest* mission shelter for the homeless in the United States. In addition, many others stayed in the Salvation Army facilities, also the largest such shelter in the country. Other Houstonians lived under bridges or in the Tent City, a makeshift community of the unemployed adults and families living out on the edge of the metropolitan area. Some of the city's homeless were workers who had come to the city but had been unable to find jobs; however, others were longterm residents of the city, many of whom had longstanding housing difficulties.[46]

Houston's Housing Crisis: A Social Cost of Private Enterprise?

A Free Enterprise Model?

With the conservative ideological wave in the late 1970s and early 1980s came a number of scholarly publications that featured Houston as a free enterprise model for other cities and their private and public leaders to follow. One of these important books was *Resolving the Housing Crisis,* a book edited by M. Bruce Johnson and highly praised by the prominent housing policy analysts George Sternlieb and Anthony Downs. Central to the book is the idea that governmental laws, such as zoning and rent control ordinances, have interfered enough with the urban housing market in most cities to create a housing crisis. The solution posed by most analysts in the book is deregulation of the housing markets in cities, including the rollback of land use, zoning, and rent control legislation. Again, as in the British books I have discussed elsewhere (see Chapters 1 and 10), Houston is cited as a model of affordable housing generation in a less restrained free market context. Contrary to what this conservative perspective suggests, however, the free enterprise city has not solved the urban housing crisis.[47]

In earlier chapters I have described Houston's recent crisis in housing for homeowners. With the employment collapse of the 1980s came a housing crisis for numerous moderate-income and middle-income homeowners, as well as for some high-income owners, many of whom not only lost their jobs but also their houses. In 1986 there were 25,602 (mostly residential) foreclosures in Houston, a 65 percent increase over 1985 and a 178 percent increase over 1980. In the first six months of 1987 home foreclosures were running at an even higher rate than in 1986. There figures demonstrated that something was wrong with the market system in providing decent jobs and housing. But an exclusive focus on recent home ownership figures would produce a very restricted picture of what in fact has been a long-term affordable housing crisis for this free enterprise city. Houston's housing crisis preceded the oil-linked downturn in the 1980s—particularly the chronic crisis faced by many of its renters.[48]

Most of Houston's low-income citizens, white and nonwhite, have been renters. Prior to the 1950s this free enterprise city had substantial amounts of substandard housing without adequate plumbing, heating, and water lines. Although there is still substandard housing in the city, especially in some minority neighborhoods, several serious housing problems in the 1970s and 1980s have been of another character. In 1987 the Houston Housing Authority stated, "Today, low-income people in Houston and Harris County, Texas, face a housing crisis of *almost unprecedented portions.* High rent burdens, overcrowding, displacement and homelessness are becoming more commonplace among low-income persons."[49]

The housing authority's statement continues to note that very high housing costs confronted low-income Houstonians even during the prosperous years of the 1970s and early 1980s. Contrary to the arguments in *Resolving the Housing Crisis,* this entrepreneurial city and its business investors have not solved the housing crisis. Prior to the mid-1980s recession *half* of the city's white and Hispanic renters paid what federal standards suggest is an excessive amount of rent for housing, that is, more than 25 percent of their incomes. And the percentage was 61 percent for black Houstonians. Moreover, one in five renters was paying 50 percent or more of family income for housing. These renters statistics mirror those for the United States taken as a whole. But in other respects the city of Houston has a more severe housing problem than comparable cities. For example, the elderly and disabled face not only the shortage of affordable housing but also what some have called the "invisible jail." A recent study found that 70 percent of the disabled have no sidewalks, and 75 percent have no curb cuts. The absence of such basic public improvements makes it more difficult for them to traverse their neighborhoods. The free enterprise city has by no means solved the problem of affordable and accessible housing.[50]

In spite of the chronic burdens of high rents and overcrowding for low-income Houstonians the city's business and governmental leaders have never targeted these housing problems for major policy analysis and action. Since the beginning of the New Deal programs in the 1930s, Houston's leadership has resisted the construction of public housing and the introduction of other low-income programs. The modest number of public housing units constructed during the 1930s and 1940s was not augmented in subsequent decades with many additional units. In 1987, for example, the city had only 4,268 units of public housing, including the boarded-up units at Allen Parkway Village. This number can be compared to the 8,300 units in the much smaller city of San Antonio, the 7,110 units in Dallas, the 23,020 units in Philadelphia, and the 15,000 units in Atlanta. As the nation's fourth largest city, Houston ranked fifteenth in public housing units among the sixteen cities recently studied by the Houston Housing Authority.[51]

The situation was the same regarding other federally subsidized housing. Including the Section 8 rental housing vouchers program, in 1987 the Houston Housing Authority was involved in the subsidization of only 11,754 housing units, which placed the city thirteenth among these same U.S. cities, with far fewer units than Philadelphia, Baltimore, Ft. Worth, and Atlanta. By 1987 more than 13,000 people were on the Houston Housing Authority's waiting lists for all types of publicly subsidized housing. For decades this intentionally designed shortage of publicly subsidized low-income housing has helped to sustain the chronic housing crisis for Houstonians with modest incomes.

Furthermore, Houston has traditionally had few nonprofit housing corporations. In 1986, for example, the city had only two such organizations working to solve the city's housing crisis, in contrast to two hundred housing corporations in Boston and two hundred organizations in San Francisco. With growing community interest in these vehicles for housing action, the number in Houston had grown to five by 1988. The weakness in nonprofit housing organizations parallels the traditional lack of community organizations in Houston, the topic for discussion in the next chapter.[52]

Conclusion: Deficient Services for Low-Income Houstonians

The boomtown development of Houston brought prosperity to many Houstonians, especially big and little entrepreneurs and affluent white workers. But this prosperity was uneven, and the accompanying development entailed substantial social costs. Poor and minority communities paid a disproportionate share of the social costs of both development and decline, in part because of the central city areas where they largely reside. The free enterprise city, with its moderate taxes and modest services, provides a context in which the less affluent residents face serious everyday problems even in times of prosperity, when their main benefit is a low-wage job. These everyday problems are aggravated not only by periods of economic recession and depression but also by Houston's long history of racial discrimination and oppression.

The city's business leadership has had little appreciation of the depth and extent of the social costs created by freewheeling and unrestricted development and even less appreciation of the severe impact of discrimination and neglect on the city's minority communities. The roots of the city's wealth lie deep in the plantation slavery and subsequent semislavery of the region. And the majority of the city's white leaders and many white workers still maintain the "badges and vestiges" of that slavery—in the forms of subemployment, segregated housing patterns, and discriminatory public services.

In addition, the city's leaders have not discussed or developed public policies to alleviate the poverty, hunger, homelessness, high rents, and overcrowding faced for many decades by the many thousands of low-income and unemployed citizens in this free enterprise city. Contrary to views of conservative analysts, the free enterprise city has not purged itself of either its slums or its poor. And it has not resolved the chronic housing crisis faced by its low-income citizens.

10

The World Market, the State, and

the Social Costs of Growth

in the Free Enterprise City

A spring 1987 issue of *Time* magazine contained a sixteen-page advertising section from the Houston business community boldly proclaiming the message that Houston is still the best place in the world for business:

> Poised on the edge of the Gulf of Mexico sits Houston—a city that seems destined for prosperity. Out of the oil boom came new skyscrapers that pushed the city on to new heights. . . . Then the oil crisis hit, but the city endured and is still a vital place to do business.[1]

The text of the advertising supplement proceeds from this opening quote, nestled at the bottom of photos of office towers, to present a detailed portrait of the exciting business opportunities in the city and a discussion of what the business community regards as the city's main assets and features.

Boosterism in the 1980s: Advertising Houston in Adversity

In the late 1980s Houston's growth-oriented business leadership remained active in selling the city to corporate executives seeking a place to locate their productive enterprises. Growth in a free enterprise context is a major idea throughout the basic text and the specific ads printed in this lengthy advertising supplement. This supplement provides a useful window for looking into the perspectives and actions of the Houston business community in the late 1980s and therefore furnishes useful material to summarize themes accented in this book.

The International Context of
Houston's Development

One important aspect of the advertising supplement is its emphasis on the international trade and world market context of Houston. There are photos of the Port of Houston and of the international airport, a section on international trade, and a separate advertisement by the Port of Houston Authority. The discussions in the international trade section and also in the separate ad of the Port Authority proclaim Houston as the second largest United States port in foreign commerce and the gateway to the world market. The text notes the 200 steamship lines and fifty-seven foreign consulates in the city and proudly comments about a Houston firm's recent design of the tallest steel-structured building, an office tower, in China. The advantages of Houston's multi-dimensional access to the world market for capitalistic entrepreneurs are predominant.

The advertising supplement accurately portrays Houston's capitalistic economy as heavily dependent on international trade and business networks. Throughout this book I have accentuated the conceptual point that an understanding of the development, decline, and spatial character of a city can be illumined by a serious consideration of the city's international context. Too much social science analysis has dissected social phenomena, including metropolitan growth and decline, within a regional or nation-state context.

The evidence I reviewed in Chapters 3 and 4, together with the bits of information in the advertising supplement, underscore the weakness of a parochial nation-state approach. From the 1830s to the 1980s the Houston citizenry experienced several economic and population growth eras. In the first period, one of agricultural commerce, the city's significant context was the southwestern region, but by the 1860s the relationship of the national economy to the area's evolution was consequential. During the last decades of the nineteenth century the Houston metropolitan area became a major cotton marketing center, increasingly linked to a national railroad network and an international trading market. Houston became linked to the global economic system; for example, ties to British cities came early in its history. Moreover, the railroad and banking infrastructure created by the cotton commerce became the underpinning for oil development. Raw materials production was expanded with the development of the oil industry. By the 1920s and 1930s oil companies moving into international operations came to dominate, along with the agricultural marketing firms, the Houston economy. World events had an impact on situating Houston in the global matrix during the late 1930s and 1940s. Because of United States' war with Japan, raw materials imports from the Pacific ceased, generating massive state aid for new petrochemical industries on the Gulf Coast. In addition, during this era indispensable trading linkages to Mexico and South America were established, including ties to the international flow of Third World labor for Gulf Coast entrepreneurs.

Metropolitan Houston became a global oil tools and services center after World War II; oil tools, engineering, and other service contracts intimately connected Houston oil companies and the oil fields from Malaysia to the North Sea. Houston's dramatic longterm development has involved the import of domestic and overseas capital, construction materials, and labor—and the export of oil-related products, agricultural goods, and capital. In Chapter 7 I demonstrated the flow of capital from many parts of the global capitalistic economy into Houston's secondary circuit of real estate land and construction.

My discussion of this expansion of Houston's linkages to the world economy suggests several important methodological and conceptual points. In regard to methodology I note that in urban research historical data are critical for a deep understanding of city evolution; such empirical materials enable us to examine the underpinning of changing economic bases and translocal ties over time. There are a number of conceptual points to note as well. First, the international context is important to city development; not only does it elevate the general level of trade and expand linkages between dominant industry firms (for example, oil and gas) inside and outside the city, but it also builds a complex and sophisticated infrastructure of support companies, such as international law firms and banks.

Second, the economic situation in one historical period often lays the foundation for development in the next period; this can clearly be seen in the role of agricultural marketing in Houston in the nineteenth century. By tracing the translocal linkages of a particular city through historical periods, one may well discover that the urban economic rhythms become as closely tied to events in the global market as to those in the national economic system. International cotton marketing brought service companies in the form of railroads, law firms, and banks; this business support system enabled the Houston economy to attract the oil industry while competing with other Gulf Coast cities. Moreover, the internationally oriented oil business laid yet another foundation for worldwide expansion of the petrochemical industry in a later period, for the Port of Houston had developed extensively in response to the oil exporting trade.

The palimpsest of economic layers in the Houston case is impressive, and each layer builds on the previous one. Whether the Houston case is distinctive in this regard remains to be seen. Other cases in the social science literature, such as the work on Pittsburgh and Detroit, suggest that earlier economic stages can become barriers to later economic development. This may eventually be so in the Houston case, when oil and gas reserves in Texas and the rest of the central United States are finally depleted.

Third, given the global setting of urban development, cities in the world system tend to specialize in certain types of economic activities. Cities like Houston, Detroit, and New York have disproportionate concentrations of certain kinds of economic activities. In some cases the concentration is one of corporate headquarters; in others it is a concentration of operational activities in one major industry. Why specialization occurs is interesting to consider. A partial answer lies in the geographical position, resource features, and historical political-economic development of cities, and during this period of late capitalism in the needs of the world's dominant corporations. For some time a worldwide network of large corporations linked physically by a global net of cities has characterized capitalism. Major organizational units in this web of capitalism are the large international banks and transnational corporations. Yet another aspect of urban specialization is that it usually creates the problem of inadequate diversification. Thus, in the mid-1980s Houston was so well integrated into the world oil and agricultural markets that its apparently localized economic troubles were in reality rooted in global crises.

The Persisting Role of the State in the Free Enterprise City

Another important feature of the *Time* advertising supplement is an emphasis on the role of free enterprise and entrepreneurial activity in making the city great. The do-it-yourself bootstrap approach of Houston's business community is accented several times in the ad copy. The text does not explicitly feature the central role of governments in the city's development. The text promotes Houston as a truly free enterprise city whose "good business climate" is primarily responsible for its past and presumably future prosperity. Yet a closer reading of the supplement makes clear that this free enterprise city image is mythological. Even this business advertising cannot hide the reality of large-scale governmental intervention. A section on conventions and tourism notes the near completion of the George Brown Convention Center, without of course noting that local government used millions of dollars in governmental bonds for construction. Brief acknowledgment is made of the cooperative attitude of local government in insuring the good business climate. Mayor Kathy Whitmire is quoted: "We are proud of the public and private sector cooperation on the many projects that benefit the entire community. We work closely together to ensure a favorable business climate for existing businesses and future growth."[2] This is, of course, an understatement.

The ad copy emphasizes the city's low taxes, especially the absence of a corporate or personal income tax. A section features space-tech firms and the role of "dozens of entrepreneurs" in creating this prosperous industry. But no discussion mentions these companies as public-private corporations heavily dependent on federal expenditures. Nor is there even a hint of the political negotiations with the federal government by Houston's business elite that were required to secure the Lyndon B. Johnson Space Center for the city. Another section features Houston's Texas Medical Center, mentioning its joint ventures with private industry and the $110 million in research; yet there is no mention that this research facility has received substantial research and some construction funding from the federal government. In addition, the advertising supplement has two specific ads by local government authorities. The Port of Houston Authority ad highlights its world-class facilities and transport connections. And the M E T R O authority advertises its multimillion dollar expenditures to improve transportation within the metropolitan area, particularly the bus systems to speed commuters from the suburbs to downtown. Of course, both governmental authorities use various governmental funds to operate. Although free enterprise is the principal explicit theme of this advertising supplement, a heavy state presence is just behind the scenes in much concrete discussion of city history and facilities. Without local, state, and federal government intervention there would be no city poised for a new round of prosperity.

These examples from the advertising supplement illustrate a second theme of this book: the development and structuring of free enterprise cities like Houston heavily depend on decisions of governmental officials working for, or in cooperation with, the business elite. The chapters in this book demonstrate that Houston's history is replete with examples of the business elite using governmental agencies and public capital to facilitate private sector objectives. In a certain sense, Houston is an extreme example of Miliband's instrumentalist theory where business leaders run local government with little or no real opposition. All but one or two mayors and most council members since the 1830s have been business people, and many have had real estate development interests. I examined the actions and interests of these business leaders and found a three-part relationship between the business enterprise elites and various levels of the state: (1) business control over and participation in the government itself; (2) subsidization in the form of social capital expenditures for business needs; and (3) the structuring of governmental regulation to facilitate capital accumulation.

From Houston's earliest days government has assisted and subsidized private profit making. The Allen brothers relied on the local and Texas governments to ease profit making in land speculation. Since then, a broad range of

local and federal government subsidization of infrastructure has ranged from
dredging the ship channel for waterborne commerce, to federal capital for the
petrochemical industry, to subsidies for the extensive Houston highway system, to local government financing of the Houston Economic Development
Council. There have been tax and regulatory benefits for the business community as well, including the oil depletion allowance and the federal and state of
Texas regulations and enforcement intervention which helped organize the
competitive chaos in the East Texas oil field. In other cases, the business elite
has allowed relatively little real estate development regulation; indeed, Houston
has become famous as the city with weak planning and no zoning.

Some Theoretical Issues

In assessing the role of the state in Houston's history I have suggested the need
for more work on the local state. Too much existing literature on the state
focuses on the national or regional levels. The conceptualization of the state in
the literature discussed in Chapter 2 can be sharpened by some attention to the
points I have developed in looking at the data on Houston. James O'Connor
distinguishes between social investment expenditures, social consumption expenditures, and social expenses. I have found these distinctions useful, but I
would suggest the addition of regulatory expenditures and intervention as
other important categories of state action. In the Houston case both Texas and
federal regulation to rationalize excessive competition in the oil industry and
the use of local and Texas regulations to create Municipal Utility Districts are
important examples of state intervention. These regulations support capitalistic endeavors by cost reductions rather than by direct subsidies.

Another conceptual contribution is the demonstration that there is a greater
range of possibilities of urban political and economic relations than the Swanstrom and Dear and Clark discussions of the local state suggest. Swanstrom
usefully distinguishes between liberal and conservative growth policies, as-
suming a detached or semi-independent local government. His study of the
early period of Cleveland's development found that its economic boom entailed a conservative growth ideology that prescribed a minimal role for local
government, and low taxes; the conservative industrial elite generally ignored
local government. But as we have seen in the Houston case there is yet another
possibility; the government may in effect be controlled by the business elite, a
perspective often termed instrumentalist in discussions of the nation state.

The business community has by no means ignored government in Houston.
This attitude is interesting to speculate upon. Perhaps the business community's dominance stems from the relative weakness of unions and citizen orga-

nizations in the last half-century of the city's development (a point to which I will return). Or perhaps the city's southern tradition, disenfranchising its minority and moderate-income populations in the form of poll taxes and at-large elections, is a contributing factor. It is interesting that the two classics in the community power structure tradition—Robert Dahl's *Who Governs?* (on New Haven) and Floyd Hunter's *Community Power Structure* (on Atlanta)—disagree on the concentration of power in business elite hands; Hunter's study of a Deep South city shows the greatest concentration of business power.[3] It seems important to study the continuum of political power concentration in cities in terms of northern and southern historical and cultural traditions, including the role of racism and anti-union activities. In any event, future theoretical work on cities and the role of business elites needs to develop a continuum of cities in regard to the role of business elites in public and private decision making—one ranging from cities like Houston with extensive business elite control to cities like Liverpool, England, with more extensive working-class input or control.

As I discussed earlier, Dear and Clark have done some of the better conceptual work on the local state. They distinguish among the state apparatus, sub-apparatus, and the para-apparatus. In the Houston case I have shown an example of this latter category, the Houston Economic Development Council (H E D C). Generated by the private sector as a response to major economic troubles, the H E D C fits loosely into the para-apparatus category, as a privately-created independent organization carrying out local state functions and funded by tax revenues. Indeed, the case of the H E D C suggests the need to amplify the typology by separating the para-apparatus category into two types: (1) independent agencies created and funded by the state, and (2) independent agencies created by the private sector and funded by the state. Future work should also be directed to extending this typology of concrete state-related bureaucratic realities.

Quality of Life in the Free Enterprise City

The *Time* advertising supplement emphasizes the good quality of life in the city of Houston. In the aforementioned quote Mayor Whitmire comments upon the "low tax burden" and "improved quality of life" in what she terms the "liveable city." And the headline of a concluding segment of text is "quality living." This section accents the low cost of single-family homes, the strong school system, the mild climate, and the theater facilities. This discussion is inaccurate. Houston does not have a mild climate, nor is the struggling and underfunded school system one to brag about. In the late 1980s single-family homes cost less because of the city's severe economic recession, and the city has a shortage of good quality low-rent housing. Neither are the city's dramatic environmental and social costs mentioned, nor is there any hint that the low tax burden praised in the text is the culprit in the unmentioned infrastructural problems.

The materials on Houston's quality of life can be interpreted in regard to a third theme underscored in this book: privatized urban development without intelligent planning in the larger public interest can create huge social costs for city residents and communities. The concept of a capitalistic system creating costs in an urban setting generated by rapid investment and population growth fits Houston well. Velocity is an important factor. Houston is famous as a free enterprise city where for decades hundreds of individual firms have calculated advantage in terms of profits and market power. Yet free enterprise Houston has many problems, all of which have been either generated by or aggravated by the creation of low-tax, business-oriented government and a good business climate. Among these are major poverty, homelessness, minority displacement, subsidence, flooding, water pollution, toxic waste, sewage, and street maintenance problems. Houstonians have paid a price for the low taxes and laissez-faire government associated with the good business climate.

The data and discussion of Houston's social costs can help us sharpen some conceptual points, particularly in regard to mainstream ecological theories and the conservative view of planning. Houston is indeed the unplanned (in the public sense) city that many scholarly and popular writers have described, but that unplanned character, coupled with the starved public infrastructure and low taxation, has brought particularly massive social costs to the city's residents, with the poorest Houstonians often bearing the heaviest burden. In the 1970s and early 1980s Houston became a much discussed subject in the mass media of European countries, in scholarly books on urban issues, and even among politicians. Certain British books critical of urban planning, such as *The Omega File* by Butler, Pirie, and Young, assert the mistaken argument that the market in cities like Houston does not produce "chaos" or a multiplication of nuisances such as noise, water, and air pollution.[4] Houston is held up as a premier example of what is right about the free enterprise approach to solving the ills of British cities. This rosy image of Houston is mythical. Even at its peak prosperity Houston may well have ranked among the most troubled cities in the United States. Thus, the free market assumptions of the mainstream ecologists and other urbanists in the United States can also be demonstrated as naive in the extreme. The market does not know best, and a theory grounded in that notion will miss much of the full-textured and contradictory reality of the metropolitan scene.

The work of the late Karl Kapp is a useful conceptual starting point for digging deeper into the character and cause of these social costs of urban evolution and development. Social costs have been defined by Kapp and a few other European economists following in his tradition as the negative consequences of for-profit capitalistic production; in other words, these costs, created by capitalistic production, are not paid for by corporations but are shifted onto other individuals and communities. When costs are calculated at the level of the individual firm in terms of its profits or share of the market, there is a tendency to ignore costs of economic growth that can be displaced onto third parties. From this perspective, then, many problems confronting urbanites in capitalistic cities are created or aggravated by the fact that corporate decision making allows little or no democratic input. The data on Houston underscore several points about these social costs: (1) the importance of the physical context; (2) the velocity of capital flows into and out of cities; (3) the character and power of the large corporations; and (4) the willingness of the local state to provide the planning and infrastructure necessary to accommodate the growth. Thus, the physical environment has its own regularities, such as water pools, rainfall, and soil characteristics. When such natural features are neglected, the consequences of corporate decisions may well be negative, as in the case of Houston's subsidence. In addition, the velocity of capital investment can overwhelm the planning and infrastructure provision systems. The importance of corporate scale and business power are demonstrated in the Houston case, as are the consequences of a weak public-interest planning system.

Class and Community Struggles: Rebuilding the City from the Bottom Up

The Importance of Urban Actors

A general argument made throughout this book is that economic, political, and other social structures and institutions both shape and are shaped by individual actors. I have suggested a weakness in the work of the mainstream ecologists, as well as in the writings of David Harvey and in the earlier analyses of Manuel Castells: they neglect those particular actors whose actions drive and mold city development every day. The economic and state forms characteristic of cities in a particular period do not develop inevitably out of structural necessity; they develop contingently as the result of conscious moves made by urban actors, either singly or in concert, as members of various classes and racial groups, under particular historical and structural circumstances. Throughout this book I have noted the role of specific urban actors in the drama of Houston's formation and evolution. Chapter 5 focused in detail on the role of the most powerful individuals, especially the chief business leaders over a century and a half of the city's history. Much of my discussion has had a "top down" character because of the focus on the powerful business leaders and entrepreneurs at the peak of the economic and political pyramids.

However, we have not totally neglected the important, or potentially important, grass-roots actors in the general population. In *The City and the Grassroots* Castells has called for urban analysis that focuses on the historical struggle between antagonistic social actors and the social processes of urbanites reconstructing their lives within economic and political structures. On occasion, in our discussion we have touched on the actions of rank-and-file individuals or on the actions of citizen organizations. Some of this activity has had a reactionary character, attempting to turn the clock back; this can be seen in the Ku Klux Klan operations in the 1920s in Harris County. And there are attempts to forestall change, such as the white civic clubs of the 1950s which were created to forestall the movement of black families into formerly white areas. Rank-and-file white actors have sought to reinforce, with the aid and support of Houston's business elites, the structures of racism and racial discrimination.

But Houston has also seen progressive political and social movements aimed at liberating the citizenry from troubling or oppressive social conditions, including the many social costs of unrestrained growth under urban capitalism. Indeed, the United States has a history of reform movements in which people fight against the decisions of the dominant racial and class groups that are burdening them. Troubled U.S. society has provided fertile soil for the emergence of various people's groups. Progressive movements are typically small minorities of Americans, but their impact is greater than their numbers. Unions have forced wage and work place changes, and people's movements have forced business and governmental leaders to implement programs in an attempt to quell the protests. In many U.S. cities governmental programs reflect compromises between business elites and citizen's movements. Demands from organized citizens have forced the development of social service and educational programs, especially since the New Deal protests of the 1930s. Millions of urbanites have organized since that time to bring liberal reforms and more people-oriented governments to many cities.

Where does Houston fit into this picture of people struggling to overcome the burdens of their living environments? Fewer instances of urban protest movements appear than in other major cities; for example, there have been no ghetto riots comparable to those in the northern cities during the 1960s and early 1970s. The extensively repressive racial system in Houston may quell the rebellion. Still, black and Hispanic Houstonians have, on occasion, organized to change the city's racial and political structure. We have previously discussed the desegregation movements of the 1950s to 1970s period. Court suits and a few sit-in demonstrations directed against white-enforced segregation brought down barriers at the golf courses, public library, public schools, and restaurants. There were several demonstrations against police brutality by students at Texas Southern University and by Mexican Americans. In the 1970s the lawsuit brought by minority activists pressured the business leadership to accept a restructuring of the city council, with most of the seats representing specific districts; an improved representation of black and Hispanic views on the city council resulted. The activists directed these struggles against the problems of Houston's minority populations.

Early Class Struggles: Unions in Houston

Note also the cases of Houstonians struggling to overcome class-based and social-cost problems, both individually and in groups. For example, union struggles aimed at improving work place and community conditions. Clashes between working-class organizations and employers were characteristic of the Houston economy from 1897 to 1922, when workers conducted major strikes against the privately owned streetcar companies, railroads, and shipping firms. In 1889 the Houston Labor Council was formed, and by 1914 there were fifty unions in the city. About one-fifth of the white work force belonged to the unions, particularly in the building trades and transportation.[5]

This union organization contributed to a few successful working-class political campaigns in the late 1800s; in the 1880s business dominance was challenged. There was extensive organizing at the neighborhood level in that period of ward-based politics, and the business elite was forced to share power with skilled workers. After the business elite regained political control in the early 1890s, it faced yet another union-backed challenge from Samuel H. Brashear, who opposed the view of government as primary promoter of business. Brashear and his union supporters worked to improve the "collective consumption" situation in the city; they built a modern sanitation system serving neighborhoods, increased regulation of private utilities, and collected back taxes from the wealthy. Soon, however, the business community regained control of the local government; its control would persist into the late twentieth century.

Labor Organization in the 1920s and 1930s

The growth of the ship channel and port facilities in the 1920s and 1930s brought many workers to the Houston waterfront. Conditions were hard. In the mid-1920s laborers received thirty cents an hour for their back-breaking jobs. In the mid-1930s workers organized numerous strikes against the steamship lines. In the fall of 1935 during a major longshoremen's strike the steamship companies announced their intention to break the strike. Strike breakers from outside the city were brought in by employers, who also erected fences and recruited a private police force. Employer resistance to meaningful negotiation left fourteen men dead along the Texas and Louisiana waterfront.[6]

In this same period unionization came slowly to the Houston–Gulf Coast oil industry. One problem was the division between black and white workers. Black workers were given the dirtiest, lowest-paying jobs, thus leaving the better jobs for whites. The racial dividing line was a hard barrier for union organizers to cross. Anti-union attitudes were strong in the corporate offices of the Texas oil industry from the very beginning; the corporate elite could and did call on the state police or Texas Rangers to put down labor militancy. Some oil companies implemented paternalistic programs of benefits; sometimes executives improved pay and fringe benefits when worker protest surfaced, hoping to stave off more extensive organization.[7] In the 1930s the oil companies vigorously resisted the growing unionization movement. Local government authorities and newspapers attacked unions, particularly the militant CIO, as communist organizations. Union sympathizers were fired or harassed. Humble's Baytown refinery, Pratt notes, "resembled a large fortress, complete with an airfield for flying in men and supplies."[8] By the late 1930s and early 1940s the Oil Worker's Union of the CIO had become more successful in winning elections to represent workers in Gulf Coast refineries and other plants, largely because of new federal protection of free unions, especially the National Labor Relations Board.

More Recent Decades

There were other strikes and struggles in the late 1940s and 1950s, but the repression and anticommunism crusades made union organizing much more difficult; I will return to that point. Moreover, there was a gradual decline in union membership in the 1970s and 1980s. Between 1970 and 1978 the proportion of Houston's workforce in unions dropped from 14.4 percent to 11 percent, and the number of recorded work stoppages dropped from forty-one to twenty-four.[9] By 1980 the proportion of nonfarm workers in unions had dropped to only 11.4 percent in Texas, the third lowest figure in the country. Open shop and merit shop employers were increasing in numbers during the 1970s and 1980s.

Racial divisions have made collective, class-based coalitions hard to organize in Houston. Katznelson has demonstrated in his analysis of Manhattan in *City Trenches* that the presence of powerful nonclass divisions in communities, such as racial and ethnic divisions, make it more difficult to organize working people in large-scale, class-based coalitions. Both white workers and employers have accepted and perpetuated the racial prejudices and discrimination that have kept Houston's racial minorities "in their place." At the same time the racial divisions have hurt white workers by making it difficult to organize unions and other community struggles. David Moberg, senior editor of *In These Times,* suggests that, although the anti-union laws and atmosphere of Houston are major reasons for the low and declining union membership, another reason is that "labor hasn't tried hard enough." [10]

The A F L-C I O waited until October 1981 to begin a major organizing project in Houston, one modeled on a 1960 campaign in Los Angeles. This Houston Organizing Project involved twenty-nine international unions, thirty organizers and staff people, and a budget of $1 million. The local newspapers featured the A F L-C I O drive. The *Houston Business Journal* ran a frontpage story: "Labor Unions: Is Houston Target of Coming Organizational Blitz?" The business community was fearful of union organizing drives. For the first two years of the project the director claimed that 7,500 workers had been organized, but most of these were recruited into public employee unions that were forbidden by law to bargain with their governmental employers. Few blue-collar workers had been organized. The timing of the project was poor because the major recession hit two years after its inauguration. Layoffs enabled employers to defuse and frustrate organizing campaigns. Indeed, by 1985 the *Houston Post* ran a story headed: "Houston's unions poised to reverse membership woes." [11] The story recorded that local unions, no longer concerned with recruiting new members, were preoccupied with keeping existing members. They were portrayed as less likely to strike and more likely to concede. [12]

The 1980s: Labor Concessions in the Recession

The mid-1980s economic crisis weakened unions in Houston. Many unions made concessions, including wage reductions, to their employers. When a Crown Zellerbach box making plant, for example, offered its workers a wage freeze, they accepted. The plumbers and operating engineers took a 15 percent pay cut. Electrical workers made wage concessions, and many employers rewrote seniority and other work rules. Some companies refused to negotiate contracts with their unions. Many of Houston's union workers agreed with an out-of-work machinist who said: "What we need now is jobs." Those with jobs were afraid to strike because they might lose their jobs.

Reductions in labor force from 1983 to 1985 also hit the unions hard. The United Food and Commercial Workers union lost 1,500 members because of closing food stores in Houston. Oil industry cutbacks cost the Oil, Chemical, and Atomic Workers union 16 percent of its workers, down to 50,000 by the beginning of 1985. Craft workers in the building trades accepted wage freezes. The plumbers' union saw 40 percent of its members become unemployed, not only because of construction cutbacks but also because developers and contractors were trying to move away from using union workers. In the 1970s most large development projects were unionized; however, by 1983, 64 percent of Harris County projects used nonunion labor.[13] Scattered stories of union organizing in newspaper articles of late 1980s suggest the continuing attempts to increase the strength of local unions, particularly among white-collar workers and health care workers. Union organizing was by no means a lost cause in Houston, but it was nonetheless very difficult. Moreover, the weakness of unions may well account for the weak progressive *political* movements in the city. In some northern cities and in European cities strong unions often mean strong progressive political representation at the local level. For example, in Sweden the strength of the labor unions has allowed working-class power in the political sphere. Without that organized working-class strength in the economic sphere it is difficult to influence the government.

Other Citizens' Groups

Houstonians have repeatedly tried to deal with the city's many social and environmental problems. Many have struggled on an individual basis, and others have tried more or less successfully to organize collectively. Individual Houstonians, such as Jennifer Culberson, have fought for environmental causes; in 1982 she prepared 500 handbills calling for the creation of a small park where there was a beautiful spring-fed fishing lake in an old oak grove in west Houston. Not unexpectedly, an executive for the firm seeking to develop the site as a cemetery complained that "I just don't believe newspapers or TV are the right place to air our private property rights."[14] A number of relatively small environmental groups, including one or two supported by grants from chemical firms, have not as yet had much impact on the city's dramatic environmental problems. On the whole, one is impressed by the relative paucity of citizens' groups targeting the environmental costs of unrestrained growth. Most notably, there have never been *any* significant no-growth environmental groups in the city's history. Even a limited growth philosophy is considered too "radical" for local organizations.

Organizing the Poor

Organizing Houston's large moderate-income and minority populations has been very difficult, for reasons I will explore in detail later. For example, in 1982 two mothers and their children moved into unclaimed, abandoned houses in Houston and were being helped by the city's small A C O R N organization to "squat" illegally in the housing.[15] A C O R N, a national organization that has been very effective in some states in organizing the poor, had been in Houston since the 1970s, but it only had one paid organizer and was unsuccessful in developing much community support. By the mid-1980s A C O R N was gone from the Houston scene.

Perhaps the most successful poor people's organization in Houston, the Alinsky-influenced The Metropolitan Organization (T M O), came to the city in the late 1970s, at the peak of the prosperity boom. At first, it was vigorously attacked by the business community as a radical organization; local newspapers featured unfavorable stories on its organizers. As late as the fall of 1983, a group of city council members wrote a local Catholic bishop asking for an investigation of the participation of certain parishes in T M O and expressing concern about outsiders on the T M O staff. Yet T M O persisted. Its organizers have been effective in getting financial support from the Catholic Church and other church groups; in late 1987 fifty-five churches and five civic clubs were affiliated with T M O, most located in minority areas.

A major goal of the group is improving the inadequate infrastructural facilities in many poor neighborhoods. In the 1980s the organization succeeded in getting better police patrols for neighborhoods and a police crackdown on "drug houses." T M O secured a written promise from the mayor to meet regularly with T M O leaders, and its most impressive victory came in a campaign for a bond issue targeting, in part, essential infrastructural improvements for poor neighborhoods. T M O has also struggled, sometimes successfully, with the private electric utility company to reduce rates and provide a program to help the poor pay electric bills. But the organization's effectiveness has been limited when it struggled with developers and real estate interests. For example, T M O tried and failed in its attempt to block the development of the Hardy Toll Road, a road to speed the flow of white commuters into the city

from northern suburbs. The road would destroy moderate-income neighborhoods in its path. Thus, on the really big community issues T M O has lost.
With an annual budget of only $180,000, a handful of organizers, and, as I
will show, the persisting opposition of the business elite, T M O clearly has a
difficult struggle ahead.[16]

Controlling the Citizenry: The Business Community and Citizen Struggle

The beginning of the *Time* advertising supplement, in a section "Houston: what
businesses are looking for," refers to the fact that the average number of days
lost to strikes is less then half that for the country as a whole. The city's business
elite has traditionally been anti-union and anti-community-organizing. Indeed,
the Houston business elite and certain business organizations, including the
Chamber of Commerce, have maintained surveillance over potential and actual worker and citizen organizations that might protest against the unpleasant
realities of work and environment in Houston. For example, in the 1930s a
number of labor unions struck.

In 1939 the National Maritime Union (N M U) went on a long strike against
major oil and shipping companies on wage and unionization issues. N M U
picketing effectively slowed down the shipment of oil, and there were a number of violent conflicts between union members and the private "police" of
the employers, with the Houston police harassing strikers and their attorneys.
As the strike continued, a local chamber official expressed his concern publicly that "big industrialists" were reconsidering moves to Houston because
of the "labor situation."[17] The chamber became actively involved in the war
of words over the strike. Various business elites in Texas pressed for passage of anti-union laws in the state legislature. In 1947 the federal Taft-
Hartley Act permitted state legislatures to pass right-to-work laws; twenty
legislatures in the South, including Texas, and the Midwest implemented
right-to-work laws. This weakened labor's ability to organize. Meanwhile automation began to cut into union power by the 1950s and 1960s, as the number of workers grew more slowly than oil and petrochemical production.

Moreover, in the 1940s and the 1950s the Houston business elite and the
chamber became obsessed with "Communist menace." Business leaders
viewed most citizen organization as a threat to both their wealth and firm control of the local economy and politics. Interviewing wealthy Texans after
World War II, Theodore S. White concluded that "a sense of menace, of un-
ease, runs through their conversation as if the great wheel of fortune might
turn and suddenly deprive them of the wealth they have so lately won. And the

menace may be anywhere—in a neighbor's home, around the corner . . . certainly in Washington and New York."[18] Thus, encouraged by the national Chamber of Commerce, the Houston chamber launched a campaign in the 1940s to alert local citizens to the "threat" of labor unions, seen as examples of communism. The chamber's magazine, *Houston,* ran editorials warning of the threats of labor unions and the "Red" menace.

During the 1940s and 1950s, for the most part, the Suite 8F business leaders permitted or encouraged the persecution of local liberals, unions, and teachers. Important in legitimizing the red scare, Jesse Jones allowed his *Houston Chronicle* editor to stir up red scare attacks and encourage local right-wing activists. A *Chronicle* editorial went so far as to suggest that the federal government should arrest the 25,000 people alleged by the F B I to be members of the Communist party and imprison them at United States military bases. Local school teachers and administrators were harassed or fired because of their liberal views. A number of far-right groups sprang up in the city, hysterically alleging that communists were hiding in the city's political and educational institutions.[19]

Surveillance of Citizen Activity in the 1980s

After the demise of the Suite 8F group in the 1970s, the chamber persisted in agitating for the same conservative business ideology. The chamber and other business groups prepared materials for local public school use. In 1978 Houston Lighting and Power Co., a private firm and corporate member of the chamber, prepared a "free enterprise" economics course packaged by the chamber for use in the local school curriculum.[20] Moreover, like the Suite 8F crowd, the 1980s chamber has been actively monitoring citizen actions and movements.

The chamber's attempts to control or repress local citizen dissent can be seen in the section on "Civic Affairs" in the 1980–1981 "Action Plan" of the chamber. This plan expresses the general outlook of the business community: the prosperity of this period will bring many northern workers and organizers to the city with unconventional ideas; therefore, the plan urged the local "community forces," presumably including business leaders, to seek out and support "creditable leaders" among white and minority citizens.[21] Chamber officials were concerned about militant organizers changing unsophisticated local citizens into militant protesters. Preoccupation with citizen control is also apparent in a subsequent statement in the same action plan: "The Houston Chamber of Commerce has an opportunity to provide leadership and coordination to these activities." In line with the traditional business approach in the

city, the chamber leaders' objectives are provision of leadership and coordination of the activities of neighborhood groups.

There is one additional barrier. The American ideology of individualism is
very strong among rank-and-file Houstonians. Each breadwinner is expected
to work hard and to succeed in vigorous competition with other breadwinners.
Yet this does not mean that Houstonians are unconcerned about community or
public issues. But the growing feelings about necessary change are not easily
translated into organization. The Houston ideology of individualism, a variant
of the U.S. value system, is distinctively anti-organizing, perhaps because the
local business elite and the local media have portrayed progressive and militant organizing so unfavorably. Houston's religious institutions also support
this type of individualism. White and black Houstonians are for the most part
Protestant in orientation, and the dominant religious philosophy in many of
the city's hundreds of churches is inward and prayer-oriented, and therefore
individualistic.

Changing Economic Realities and
the Future of the City

Major Economic Restructuring?

By the mid-1980s Houston was changing dramatically. The long era of boomtown prosperity and growth appeared over. The good business climate was
replaced by high unemployment rates, record foreclosures and bankruptcies,
and the out-migration of many Houstonians. Although the precise conclusion
to the economic downturn was unclear, implications of the economic bust
were slowly penetrating the thinking of the more sensitive leaders and citizens. One thing seemed clear: the city's economy and its workforce would be
battered in the future by more of the negative swings in the capitalist business
cycle than in the past. Houston would no longer be protected by its energy
industry.

What the future holds in the way of specific cycles of boom and bust is
unclear. Some recovery in the price of oil had taken place by mid-1987. The
domestic wellhead price averaged $9 to $12 a barrel in 1986; this became $14
a barrel in April 1987. Spot market prices were higher. Oil futures contract
prices reached $16.60 in December 1987. Higher oil prices and a devalued
dollar increased the number of optimistic forecasts for the metropolitan economy. Both a Southern Methodist University study and a Rice Center report

predicted that the Houston economy had bottomed out early in 1987 and would gradually improve in subsequent years. Although recovery from the nadir of economic despair was underway in 1987, it was uneven. Demand increased for drilling rigs and other oil tools and services. The U.S. active rig count was moving upward to nearly 1,000 in mid-1987, but it was still far below the 4,521 active rigs in early 1982. The job losses of 1982–1986 were being replaced by slight increases by mid-1987, and the Rice Center was forecasting an increase in jobs by 1990. Unemployment decreased somewhat, but it still remained high by historical standards. Tonnage shipped through the Port of Houston was improving by mid-1987, perhaps because of the devalued dollar, but it, too, was still substantially below the early 1980s figures. Other parts of the metropolitan economy were reeling from the downturn; residential and other foreclosures were still setting records, and bank failures were commonplace.[22]

In addition, the price of oil late in 1987 was oscillating up and down, suggesting to some that the mid-1987 increase was perhaps a temporary respite. The only certainty about the oil price situation was the price volatility. The fact that the price of oil slumped late in 1987 even during the Iraq-Iran war in the Middle East, which involved attacks on oil tankers in the Persian Gulf, suggested a substantial international oil surplus; Houstonians might have to wait a long time before the price of oil would rise *and stabilize* at a price anywhere near that of the early 1980s. In 1987 a few observers were optimistically predicting further increases in the price of oil in the near future, and such a price recovery would reinvigorate the city's economy. But that recovery, if indeed it does occur, is likely to be followed by subsequent and perhaps more severe boom-bust oscillations than Houstonians have historically experienced. As I discussed in Chapter 4, the long-run problems for the Houston economy are major and difficult to overcome because of the global restructuring of the world's energy industry. The international restructuring of oil refining and petrochemical production will likely mean the loss of some better-paying manufacturing jobs, as well as the multiplier retail and service jobs, in the metropolitan economy. In addition, the underground oil reservoirs in Texas are being depleted, and, although there is a debate on timing and new oil discovery questions, the depletion will mean that Texas will not be a prosperous oil extraction region in the not-too-distant future.

In her book, *Profit Cycles, Oligopoly, and Regional Development,* Ann Markusen traces the spatial manifestations of the profit cycle for major industries. The last stage is one of industrial obsolescence and "negative profit." Markusen notes that resource extraction regions have the "greatest long-term adjustment problems" once the resource base is depleted and the dominant industry enters the negative-profit stage.[23] Without significant restructuring of the Houston economy a prediction of serious stagnation in the long run seems warranted. As Markusen and other analysts of regional development have noted, the profit cycle implies that regions with mature industries and extraction industries can survive economically only by diversifying or replacing the declining economic base. I have discussed the multimillion dollar efforts of the Chamber of Commerce and the H E D C to bring more diverse industries to the Houston metropolitan area, thereby developing a new economic base in the last decades of the twentieth century. The preferred new industries include computer, information, space-tech, and med-tech firms. Reinforced by the opening of the government-subsidized George Brown convention center, the Chamber of Commerce has emphasized the city as an important convention and leisure center. These diversification efforts are noteworthy because they signal the first time in many decades that local business leadership is on the defensive. Yet this effort comes at a time when the business elites and growth coalitions in many other economically troubled U.S. cities are attempting to attract similar firms.

In the past, cities have made the transition from one economic base to another, such as the shift of Houston from cotton to oil and the shift of Minneapolis from a timber-lumber economy to grain marketing and flour milling to computers and med-tech. But today such a transition has become more difficult because of the ease of investment flows in the world economy. Markusen notes that "profits from a region's local economy are no longer necessarily reinvested" there and that even Sunbelt areas in the United States are faced with "capital flight to yet cheaper regions." Other problems with southern areas, Markusen further notes, are the absence of excellent research universities and the deficient public service characteristics that attract the new innovative industrial (especially high-tech) sectors.[24]

The Prospects for the Future: Leadership in Free Enterprise Houston

Traditionally, Houston's leadership has had a strong commitment to a good business climate, which in practice has meant the weaknesses in many government services, as discussed in Chapters 8 and 9. The traditional promise of that leadership to rank-and-file Houstonians was that the good business climate would bring economic prosperity to the city. Although this contention was never true for all Houstonians, after several years of a major recession in the 1980s it had become clear even to adherents of the business-climate ideology that something was wrong. The economic future of the city no longer lay primarily in the energy industry. In some respects there was no longer a good business climate; some firms were going bankrupt, and many others were in trouble. Few new firms were considering a Houston location. The weakness of the public sector—a central feature of a low-tax, weak government, business-climate approach—means that in the long run a city may become unattractive to many prospective investors and firms, particularly in the innovative high-tech sectors. By the 1980s the neglect of the public infrastructure had created a negative image of Houston not only in the national media but also in the corporate boardrooms of many firms whose site location was eagerly sought by business organizations such as the H E D C.

I have already discussed the many problems of public services and infrastructure: sewage and toxic waste crises, air pollution, transportation and traffic dilemmas, flooding, water pollution and distribution problems, lacking parks and recreational space, and displaced minority communities. Even the Chamber of Commerce committees studying Houston's infrastructure and other service crises have estimated that *billions* of dollars must be spent to remedy the situation and make Houston a more attractive site for prospective investors and corporate entrants.

Among the most important of public services for the high-tech firms sought by the H E D C leadership is education. Yet in 1987 the education level of Houstonians was behind that of other major cities. And in 1987 accreditation status of the Houston public school system was downgraded by the Texas Education Agency because of multiple local problems. The economic future of the city may be determined in part by the willingness of the city's leadership to invest much more money in public education at all levels, an exhortation made to them by Massachusetts officials invited to a major gathering of Houston business leaders in the mid-1980s. Without building stronger area universities and research and development laboratories, in addition to those of local energy firms, and providing a better-educated workforce, the city will have difficulty competing with high-tech centers such as Boston and Minneapolis. Until the city's business leaders recognize the importance of first-rate public services, their calls for large-scale, high-tech diversification seem to be wishful thinking. And first-rate public services will undoubtedly require substantial tax increases, a requirement not now recognized by most of the city's leadership.

A comparison with Minneapolis is instructive. Minneapolis has been rated by the Urban Institute as the best American city in terms of quality of life. It has not only a leading national orchestra and first-rate art museums but also an acre of park land for every eight residents, little pollution, a low crime rate, an excellent array of health and welfare programs, many libraries, and public schools with extensive support and enhancement programs. Even a booklet for newcomers published by local *business* interests in Minneapolis explicitly notes that "Minnesota taxes tend to be higher than those in some parts of the country, because Minnesota offers a wide range of services to all of its citizens, with a special emphasis on meeting the needs of the disadvantaged." [25] A few optimistic observers of the Houston scene have argued that the business leadership there is moving in the direction of recognizing the need to abandon the old business mentality and to move toward the Minneapolis model of a high-service city with adequate public planning.

The People of Houston: A New Vision?

Houston can be viewed as the city that capital built, but it can also be viewed as the city that labor built. The toil and tears of millions of black, Hispanic, Asian, and white citizens over a century and a half have made the metropolis that is Houston. These rank-and-file Houstonians have periodically tried to improve their living conditions, although many attempts at citizen and community organization have usually been either short-lived ventures or failures. One major success is the aforementioned lawsuit that forced the city's leadership to accept single-member districts on the city council. Representation of black, Hispanic, *and* growth-control views on the city council improved. As a result of this political change, the business leadership has sometimes found it more difficult to implement its preferred goals. Although business influence still dominates on the council, the change in the council has insured more debate and more openness in local decision making. The trend may be in the direction of expanded political democracy. Moreover, the T M O organizational efforts hold out some hope for the city's huge poor populations, although the scale of that effort is relatively modest when examined against the size of the poverty and unemployment problems.

These organizations of poor and minority Houstonians suggest an alternative vision for Houston, one that places the aspirations and needs of ordinary Houstonians before the goals of unrestrained free enterprise. And the members of these organizations are not alone in their aspirations for a more liveable Houston. Thus the public opinion polls examined in Chapter 8 demonstrate that the majority of Houstonians are now critical of unrestrained growth. Only 28 percent of those interviewed thought that growth was unequivocally good for the city. In addition, the surveys of Houston residents found a majority was critical of air and water pollution and ready to support environmental action by government, even if such action meant higher taxes; in other words, a majority favored improvements in their living environment. There seems to be an attitudinal basis for renewed local community organization, perhaps with a populist or progressive cast. In *The Progressive City* Pierre Clavel has recently analyzed successful citizen movements in Hartford,

Burlington, Cleveland, Berkeley, and Santa Monica. Clavel concludes that these movements made a difference in the lives of ordinary urbanites, especially in the "shift away from a strict individual and corporate control" of local economic, land, and development issues toward public and collective sharing in control.[26]

Whether rank-and-file Houstonians can organize more effectively in the future to bring major changes through political representation in redefining Houston's quality of life and pressuring the business leadership to address the costs of the good business climate remains to be seen. In this book I have suggested several barriers to future social and political organization—the racial line between white and minority families, the individualistic ideology with its emphasis on the sacredness of private property, the surveillance of organizing by business elites and organizations, and the fear of militant organizing. Some of these obstacles have, on occasion, been overcome, but together they present formidable opposition to future community organizing. Nonetheless, the key to improvements in political democracy and in Houstonians' quality of life is likely to be effective citizen organization.

NOTES

1 Introduction: Houston, the Free Enterprise City

1   "Houston: A Historical Profile," *Houston* 31 (November 1960): 2.
2   Robert Jones, *Town and Country Chaos* (London: Adam Smith Institute, 1982), pp. 23–25; M. Bruce Johnson, ed., *Resolving the Housing Crisis* (San Francisco: Pacific Institute for Public Policy Research, 1982).
3   Michael J. McDonald and William B. Wheeler, *Knoxville, Tennessee* (Knoxville: University of Tennessee Press, 1983); Carol Hoffecker, *Corporate Capital* (Philadelphia: Temple University Press, 1983); Clarence N. Stone, *Economic Growth and Neighborhood Discontent: System Bias in the Urban Renewal Program of Atlanta* (Chapel Hill: University of North Carolina Press, 1976); Roger D. Olien and Diana D. Olien, *Oil Booms* (Lincoln: University of Nebraska Press, 1982); Susan Fainstein, Norman Fainstein, Michael Peter Smith, Dennis Judd, and Richard Child Hill, *Restructuring the City* (New York: Longman, 1983).
4   Janet L. Abu-Lughod, *Cairo* (Princeton, N.J.: Princeton University Press, 1971), p. v.
5   Kathleen C. Adams, Glenda K. Mill, and Ginger H. Hester, *Houston: A Profile of Its Business, Industry, and Port* (Houston: Pioneer Publications, 1982), p. 79.
6   Rice Center, "Houston Population and Employment Forecasts," *Research Summary* (Houston: Rice Center, 1984), pp. 1–4.
7   Rice Center, *1980 Population and Housing Census Results for Harris County: Research Summary* (Houston: Rice Center, 1981), pp. 1–4.
8   Rice Center, *Annexation and Houston: Research Summary* (Houston: Rice Center, 1979), pp. 1–3.

2 Theories of Urban Development

1   Robert E. Park and Ernest W. Burgess, *Introduction to the Science of Society* (Chicago: University of Chicago Press, 1924), p. 507.
2   Scott Greer, *The Emerging City* (New York: Free Press, 1962), p. 8.
3   William H. Form, "The Place of Social Structure in the Determination of Land Use: Some Implications for a Theory of Urban Ecology," *Social Forces* 32 (1954): 317–324.
4   Amos Hawley, *Human Ecology* (New York: Ronald Press, 1950), pp. 6–125; see also Otis D. Duncan, "Social Organization and the Ecosystem," in Robert Faris, ed., *Handbook of Modern Sociology* (Chicago: Rand-McNally, 1964), pp. 36–82.
5   Parker Frisbie and John Kasarda, "Spatial Processes," in N. Smelser and R. Burt, eds., *The Handbook of Modern Sociology* (Beverly Hills: Sage, forthcoming).

6   John Kasarda, "The Implications of Contemporary Redistribution Trends for National Urban Policy," *Social Science Quarterly* 61 (December 1980): 373–400.

7   Abu-Lughod, *Cairo*, p. 228.

8   Frisbie and Kasarda, "Spatial Processes."

9   John R. Logan and Harvey M. Molotch, *Urban Fortunes: The Political Economy of Place* (Berkeley: University of California Press, 1987).

10   Kasarda, "Implications of Contemporary Redistribution Trends," pp. 375–386; Amos Hawley, *Urban Society,* 2d ed. (New York: Wiley, 1981); Frisbie and Kasarda, "Spatial Processes."

11   Bradford Snell, *American Ground Transport,* a Committee Print of the Subcommittee on Antitrust and Monopoly of the Committee on the Judiciary, U.S. Senate, February 26, 1974; Glenn Yago, *The Decline of Transit* (Cambridge: Cambridge University Press, 1984); J. Allen Whitt, *Urban Elites and Mass Transportation* (Princeton, N.J.: Princeton University Press, 1982).

12   Ernest W. Burgess, "The Growth of the City," in Robert E. Park, Ernest W. Burgess, and R. D. McKenzie, eds., *The City* (Chicago: University of Chicago Press, 1925), pp. 47–62.

13   R. D. McKenzie, "The Scope of Human Ecology," in George A. Theodorson, ed., *Urban Patterns* (University Park, Pa.: Pennsylvania State University Press, 1982), p. 28.

14   Brian J. L. Berry and John Kasarda, *Contemporary Urban Ecology* (New York: Macmillan, 1977); Michael Micklin and Harvey M. Choldin, eds., *Sociological Human Ecology* (Boulder: Westview Press, 1984); Harvey M. Choldin, *Cities and Suburbs: An Introduction to Urban Sociology* (New York: McGraw-Hill, 1985); Frisbie and Kasarda, "Spatial Processes." See also the review of the ecological literature in Linda Stoneall, *Country Life, City Life* (New York: Praeger, 1983), pp. 68–99.

15   J. G. Williamson, "Regional Inequality and the Process of National Development: A Description of the Patterns," *Economic Development and Cultural Change* 13 (1965): 44.

16   Berry and Kasarda, *Contemporary Urban Ecology,* pp. 279–280.

17   Ibid., p. 282.

18   Rupert B. Vance and Sarah Smith, "Metropolitan Dominance and Integration," in Paul K. Hatt and Albert J. Reiss, eds., *Cities and Society* (New York: Free Press, 1957), p. 103.

19   Berry and Kasarda, *Contemporary Urban Ecology,* pp. 402, 353.

20   Hawley, *Urban Society,* pp. 228–229, 262–263; Micklin and Choldin, eds., *Sociological Human Ecology;* Choldin, *Cities and Suburbs: An Introduction to Urban Sociology;* Frisbie and Kasarda, "Spatial Processes."

21   President's Commission for a National Agenda for the Eighties, Panel on Policies and Prospects, *Urban America in the Eighties: Perspectives and Prospects* (Washington, D.C.: Government Printing Office, 1980).

22   Kasarda, "The Implications of Contemporary Redistribution Trends," p. 389.

23   Micklin and Choldin, eds., *Sociological Human Ecology.*

24   Manuel Castells, "Is There an Urban Sociology?" in C. G. Pickvance, ed., *Urban Sociology* (London: Tavistock, 1976), pp. 33–57; Manuel Castells, *The Urban*

Question (London: Edward Arnold, 1977); David Harvey, *Social Justice and the City* (Baltimore: Johns Hopkins University Press, 1973); Henri Lefebvre, *La révolution urbaine* (Paris: Gallimard, 1970).

25   David Harvey, *The Urbanization of Capital* (Baltimore: Johns Hopkins University Press, 1985); David Harvey, *Consciousness and the Urban Experience* (Baltimore: Johns Hopkins University Press, 1985).

26   Manuel Castells, *The City and the Grassroots* (Berkeley: University of California Press, 1983).

27   Michael Peter Smith, *The City and Social Theory* (New York: St. Martin's Press, 1979).

28   Mark Gottdiener, *The Social Production of Urban Space* (Austin: University of Texas Press, 1985).

29   Ibid., p. 199.

30   Harvey, *Consciousness and the Urban Experience*, p. 250.

31   Peter Hall, *World Cities* (New York: McGraw-Hill, 1977).

32   McKenzie, "The Scope of Human Ecology," p. 142.

33   Dudley Poston, "Regional Ecology," in Michael Micklin and Harvey M. Choldin, eds., *Sociological Human Ecology*, pp. 232–382.

34   Steven Hymer, *The Multinational Corporation* (Cambridge: Cambridge University Press, 1979); this paragraph draws on Joe R. Feagin and Michael P. Smith, "Cities and the New International Division of Labor," in Michael P. Smith and Joe R. Feagin, eds., *The Capitalist City* (London: Basil Blackwell, 1987), pp. 3–36.

35   Richard Child Hill, "Urban Political Economy," in Michael P. Smith, ed., *Cities in Transformation* (Beverly Hills, Calif.: Sage, 1984), pp. 123–138; Christopher Chase-Dunn, "The Systems of World Cities, 800 A.D.–1975," in Michael Timberlake, ed., *Urbanization in the World Economy* (New York: Academic Press, 1985), pp. 269–382.

36   Edward Soja, Rebecca Morales, and Goetz Wolff, "Urban Restructuring: Analysis of Social and Spatial Change in Los Angeles," *Economic Geography* 59 (1983): 195–230; on New York see Saskia Sassen-Koob, "The New Labor Demand in Global Cities," in Michael P. Smith, ed., *Cities in Transformation* (Beverly Hills, Calif.: Sage, 1984), pp. 139–172.

37   Ann Markusen, *Profit Cycles, Oligopoly, and Regional Development* (Cambridge: MIT Press, 1985).

38   Lefebvre, *La révolution urbaine*.

39   Ibid., pp. 211–212. The translation from French is by Gottdiener, *The Social Production of Urban Space*, pp. 184–185.

40   Gottdiener, *The Social Production of Urban Space*, pp. 184–194.

41   Harvey, *The Urbanization of Capital*, p. 25. For a critique of Harvey's analysis, see Gottdiener, *The Social Production of Urban Space*, p. 106ff.

42   Larry Sawers, "Urban Form and the Mode of Production," *The Review of Radical Political Economics* 7 (1975): 52.

43   Anna Lee Saxenian, "The Urban Contradictions of Silicon Valley," in William K. Tabb and Larry Sawers, eds., *Sunbelt/Snowbelt* (New York: Oxford, 1984), pp. 163–200.

44   Fainstein, et al., *Restructuring the City*.

45   An earlier version of this paradigm appeared in D. Claire McAdams and Joe R. Feagin, "A Power Conflict Approach of Urban Land Use" (Department of Sociology, University of Texas, 1980, typescript); see also Joe R. Feagin, *The Urban Real Estate Game* (Englewood Cliffs, N.J.: Prentice-Hall, 1983), pp. 13–15.

46   Sidney Willhelm, *Black in a White America* (Cambridge: Schenkman, 1983), p. 300 ff.

47   Harvey, *Consciousness and the Urban Experience*, p. 265; see also Jeffrey R. Lustig, *Corporate Liberalism* (Berkeley: University of California Press, 1982), p. 256.

48   Castells, *The City and the Grass Roots*, p. 318.

49   See Robert Dahl, *Who Governs?* (New Haven: Yale University Press, 1961). More recent mainstream assessments often assume a pluralism in internal city politics, even when they are analyzing cities more broadly as entities competing for corporations. See Paul Peterson, *City Limits* (Chicago: University of Chicago Press, 1981).

50   Ralph Miliband, *The State in Capitalist Society* (London: Weidenfeld and Nicolson, 1969); G. William Domhoff, *Who Rules America?* (Englewood Cliffs, N.J.: Prentice-Hall, 1967).

51   G. William Domhoff, "I am not an Instrumentalist," *Kapitalstate* 4 (1976): 223; Ralph Miliband, "State Power and Class Interests," *New Left Review* 138 (1983): 57–68; Whitt, *Urban Elites and Mass Transportation*, pp. 177–180.

52   Nicos Poulantzas, "The Problem of the Capitalist State," *New Left Review* 58 (1969): 67–78.

53   Castells, *The City and the Grassroots;* Nicos Poulantzas, *State, Power, Socialism* (London: New Left Books, 1980); Erik O. Wright, *Class, Crisis, and the State* (London: New Left Books, 1978).

54   Fred Block, "The Ruling Class Does Not Rule," *Socialist Revolution,* 7 (1977): 10, 13.

55   Margaret Weir and Theda Skocpol, "State Structures and the Possibilities for 'Keynesian' Responses to the Great Depression in Sweden, Britain, and the United States," in Peter B. Evans, Dietrich Rueschemeyer, and Theda Skocpol, eds., *Bringing the State Back In* (Cambridge: Cambridge University Press, 1985), pp. 107–168.

56   John Mollenkopf, *The Contested City* (Princeton: Princeton University Press, 1983), pp. 6, 9.

57   For data contradicting the Mollenkopf analysis see Susan Fainstein, Norman Fainstein, and P. Jefferson Armistead, "San Francisco: Urban Transformation and the Local State," in Fainstein, et al., *Restructuring the City*, pp. 202–240.

58   James O'Connor, *The Fiscal Crisis of the State* (New York: St. Martin's, 1973).

59   Gordon L. Clark and Michael Dear, *State Apparatus: Structures and Language of Legitimacy* (Boston: Allen and Unwin, 1984), pp. 131–145.

60   Harvey Molotch, "The City as a Growth Machine: Toward a Political Economy of Place," *American Journal of Sociology* 82 (1976): 309–333; G. William Domhoff, *Who Rules America Now?* (Englewood Cliffs, N.J.: Prentice-Hall, 1983), pp. 160–187.

61   Michael Dear and G. L. Clark, "Dimensions of Local State Economy," *Environment and Planning A* 13 (1981): 1278.

62   Todd Swanstrom, *The Crisis of Growth Politics: Cleveland, Kucinich, and the Challenge of Urban Populism* (Philadelphia: Temple University Press, 1985).

63   Henri Lefebvre, *Everyday Life in the Modern World* (New York: Harper and Row, 1971), p. 66.

64   Boston Federal Reserve Bank, *Introducing Economics* (Boston: Boston Federal Reserve Bank, 1984), p. 27.

65   Karl Kapp, *The Social Costs of Private Enterprise* (New York: Schocken Books, 1950), pp. 13–25.

66   Gottdiener, *Social Production of Urban Space*, p. 172.

67   Kapp, *Social Costs of Private Enterprise*, pp. xiv–xv.

68   Barry Bluestone and Bennett Harrison, *The Deindustrialization of America* (New York: Basic Books, 1982), p. 106.

69   Michael Peter Smith, Randy L. Ready, and Dennis R. Judd, "Capital Flight, Tax Incentives and the Marginalization of American States and Localities," in *Public Policy across States and Communities*, annual review (Greenwich, Conn.: J A I Press, 1985), pp. 181–201; David Smith, *The Public Balance Sheet* (Washington, D.C.: Conference on Alternative State and Local Policies, 1979), p. 3–5.

70   Christian Leipert, "The Other Economic Summit 1985" (Research Center draft, typescript, Berlin, Wissinschaftszeutrum), p. 13.

3   More Than Oil: Houston's Multisectored Economy

1   Sidney Willhelm, *Black in a White America* (Cambridge: Schenkman, 1983), p. 300 ff.

2   Susan MacManus, *Federal Aid to Houston* (Washington, D.C.: Brookings, 1983), p. 1.

3   "Houston: The International City," *Fortune* 61 (July 1980): 49.

4   Harold L. Platt, *City Building in the New South* (Philadelphia: Temple University Press, 1983), pp. 8–10.

5   R. D. Ernst, "Houston Owes Much to Cotton Industry," *Houston* 4 (June 1933): 5.

6   Platt, *City Building in the New South*, pp. 83–84; Walter L. Buenger and Joseph A. Pratt, *But Also Good Business* (College Station: Texas A & M University Press, 1987), pp. 20–21.

7   Buenger and Pratt, *But Also Good Business*, pp. 37–38.

8   Platt, *City Building in the New South*, pp. 29–92.

9   Joseph A. Pratt, *The Growth of a Refining Region* (Greenwich, Conn.: J A I Press, 1980), p. 27.

10   R. H. Montgomery, *The Brimstone Game* (Austin: privately published, 1949), pp. 29–61.

11   Harold F. Williamson, Ralph Andreano, Arnold Daum, and Gilbert Close,

The American Petroleum Industry: The Age of Energy, 1899–1950 (Evanstone, Ill.: Northwestern University Press, 1963), p. 22.

12   A. C. Laut, "Why Is Houston?" *Sunset* 29 (November 1912): 483–492; Platt, *City Building in the New South*, p. 79.

13   U.S. Bureau of the Census, *Historical Statistics of the United States* (Washington, D.C.: Government Printing Office, 1961), p. 462.

14   Quoted in Marvin Hurley, *Decisive Years for Houston* (Houston: Chamber of Commerce, 1966), p. 72.

15   Williamson, et al., *American Petroleum Industry*, p. 190; Gerald D. Nash, *United States Oil Policy, 1890–1964* (University of Pittsburgh Press, 1968), pp. 26–28.

16   Marilyn McAdams Sibley, *The Port of Houston* (Austin: University of Texas Press, 1968), pp. 133–135; David McComb, *Houston: A History* (Austin: University of Texas Press, 1981), pp. 65–67.

17   Sibley, *Port of Houston*, pp. 146–152.

18   Marquis James, *The Texaco Story* (New York: The Texas Company, 1953), pp. 60–73. I am indebted to Joseph Pratt for helping me clarify this point.

19   Henrietta M. Larson and Kenneth W. Porter, *History of Humble Oil and Refining Company* (New York: Harper and Brothers, 1959), pp. 72–104.

20   Platt, *City Building in the New South*, p. 75; Sibley, *Port of Houston*, p. 161.

21   McComb, *Houston*, pp. 80–81.

22   Nash, *United States Oil Policy*, pp. 71, 85–96.

23   M. de Barbieris, "The Wide World Is Houston's Cotton Market," *Houston* 5 (June 1934): 5; Thomas Kehoe, "Houston and Cotton—One Calls the Other to Mind," *Houston* 1 (June 1930): 12; McComb, *Houston*, pp. 82–83.

24   "Texas," *Fortune* 20 (December 1939): 87.

25   "They Still Want to 'Buy' Houston," *Houston* 4 (March 1933): 3.

26   James W. Lamare, *Texas Politics* (St. Paul: West, 1981), pp. 177–179; C. R. Wharton, "South Texas Is Resourceful," *Houston* 1 (June 1930): 9.

27   Pratt, *Growth of a Refining Region*, pp. 64–68; W. S. Farish, "Petroleum Industry Pays Millions to Texas," *Houston* 4 (February 1933): 5; J. K. Ridley, "Petroleum Refining," *Houston* 1 (June 1930): 18.

28   "Texas," *Fortune*, p. 81.

29   Hurley, *Decisive Years for Houston*, p. 56.

30   "Texas," *Fortune*, p. 87. Data in the paragraph are from the same source.

31   Ibid., p. 86.

32   Joe J. Fox, "Houston Reflects the Spirit of the New South," *Houston* 1 (June 1930): 4, 10; H. O. Clarke, "Houston's Industrial Life is Well Grounded," *Houston* 5 (June 1934): 22.

33   Writers Program, Works Progress Administration, *Houston: A History and Guide* (Houston: Anson Jones Press, 1942), pp. 119–121.

34   Nash, *United States Oil Policy*, pp. 118, 140–141; David Prindle, *Petroleum Politics and the Texas Railroad Commission* (Austin: University of Texas Press, 1981), pp. 36–160.

35   Royal Roussel, "Golden Band of the Gulf," *Houston* 15 (October 1940): 5; "Oil," *Houston* 17 (April 1945): 8.

36   Clarence H. Cramer, *American Enterprise* (Boston: Little, Brown, 1972), p. 179.

37   Pratt, *Growth of a Refining Region,* p. 94; Mollenkopf, *Contested City,* pp. 104–107; "$500,000 Plant for Houston," *Houston* 11 (August 1940): 43; James, *Texaco Story,* p. 78; Harris McAshan, "Houston Now Center of a Vast Chemical Empire," *Houston* 21 (February 1950): 17.

38   Jack Battle, "Chemical Resources and Their Trends," *Houston* 17 (November 1945): 6–7.

39   "Gulf Coast Looms Large," *Houston* 14 (April 1938): 66.

40   James, *Texaco Story,* p. 77; Larson and Porter, *History of Humble Oil and Refining Company,* pp. 566–587.

41   Mollenkopf, *Contested City,* p. 106.

42   "Houston Nation's 1st Cotton Exporting Port," *Houston* 18 (August 1946): 64.

43   "Proposed Arrivals and Departures of Vessels from Port Houston," *Houston* 18 (May 1946): 10.

44   Don Carleton, *Red Scare!* (Austin: Texas Monthly Press, 1985), p. 13.

45   Vance and Smith, "Metropolitan Dominance and Integration," in Hatt and Reiss, eds., *Cities and Society,* p. 103.

46   Ibid., pp. 113–115.

47   Hurley, *Decisive Years for Houston,* p. 183.

48   McComb, *Houston,* p. 120; Sibley, *Port of Houston,* pp. 200–205.

49   Ben F. Love, *People and Profits: A Bank Case Study* (Houston: Texas Commerce Bank, n.d. [c. 1978]), pp. 34–36.

4   The Houston Economy since the 1950s: Prosperity and Decline in a World Context

1   Bronwyn Brock, "Houston Less Vulnerable Than Dallas-Ft. Worth to Impact of Recession," *Voice* (October 1981): 1–2.

2   Thomas R. Plaut, "The Texas Economy," *Texas Business Review* (January–February 1983): 15–20.

3   Paul Burka, "The Year Everything Changed," *Texas Monthly,* 11 (February 1983): 109.

4   Bluestone and Harrison, *Deindustrialization of America,* p. 87; "2 Houston Suburbs Among Richest in U.S.," *Houston Post,* March 29, 1987, p. 7A.

5   Economic Division, Texas Commerce Bancshares, *Texas Facts and Figures* (Houston: Texas Commerce Bancshares, 1982), p. 14.

6   Ibid., p. 12; Mickey Wright, "Texas Industrial Wateruse Long-Term Projection. Draft Report" (Austin: Texas Department of Water Resources, 1982).

7   Nat Eisenberg, "Economic Newsletter," *Houston* 57 (August 1986): 5;

U.S. Department of Commerce, *Harris County Business Patterns* (1950, 1960, 1970, 1980).

8   Economic Division, *Texas Facts and Figures,* p. 42.

9   J. L. Taylor, Personal interview with economic development officer, Houston Chamber of Commerce, July 1983; Ed Shaffer, *The United States and the Control of World Oil* (New York: St. Martin's Press, 1983), pp. 189–229.

10   Brock, "Houston Less Vulnerable than Dallas-Ft. Worth," pp. 1–4.

11   Robert Sherrill, *The Oil Follies of 1970–1980* (Garden City, N.Y.: Anchor Press, 1983), pp. 61–65; Nash, *U.S. Oil Policy,* pp. 201–208.

12   Pratt, *Growth of a Refining Region,* pp. 189–219. Lamare, *Texas Politics,* pp. 179–181; the quote is from Lamare.

13   Hart Stillwell, "Texas: Owned by Oil and Interlocking Directorates," in Robert Allen, ed., *Our Sovereign State* (New York: Vanguard Press, 1949), p. 315.

14   Kenneth E. Gray, "A Report on the Politics of Houston" (Cambridge: Harvard/M I T Joint Center for Urban Studies, 1960, typescript), p. VI–31.

15   Hurley, *Decisive Years for Houston,* pp. 175–176.

16   McComb, *Houston,* pp. 187–189.

17   Bob Sablatura, "Clouds Cover City Convention Center," *Houston Business Journal,* September 15, 1987, p. 1A.

18   Anthony Sampson, *The Seven Sisters* (New York: Viking Press, 1975), pp. 10–11; J. L. Taylor, personal interview; "Shell's $25-million Trip to Houston," *Business Week,* September 19, 1970, p. 16.

19   Taylor, personal interview.

20   "Bayport Celebrates 20th Anniversary," *Port of Houston Magazine,* November 1984, pp. 4–5.

21   Edward J. Malecki, "Recent Trends in Location of Industrial Research and Development," in John Rees, Geoffrey Hewings, and Howard Stafford, eds., *Industrial Location and Regional Systems* (Brooklyn: J. F. Bergin, 1981), pp. 223–234.

22   "Petrochemicals and Petrochemical Feedstocks," *The Petroleum Situation Newsletter,* Chase Manhattan Bank, March, 1983, pp. 1–3.

23   Pratt, *Growth of a Refining Region,* p. 105.

24   Robert D. Anding, "Petrochemicals and Processing Industries," talk presented to the Houston Outlook Conference, Houston, January 20, 1983.

25   Larson and Porter, *History of Humble Oil and Refining Company,* p. 79.

26   Pratt, *Growth of a Refining Region,* p. 8.

27   Stillwell, "Texas: Owned by Oil and Interlocking Directorates," p. 315.

28   Burka, "The Year Everything Changed," p. 111.

29   S. H. Hymer, *The Multinational Corporation: A Radical Approach* (Cambridge: Cambridge University Press, 1979).

30   Taylor, personal interview.

In Chapter 3 I noted the debate over whether the oil industry is in fact concentrated. The data demonstrate that two dozen companies have controlled large shares of the major sectors of the oil industry for decades. Concentration of the oil industry declined after the breakup of Standard Oil in the early 1900s, but by 1938 the top twenty oil companies, still led by Standard Oil, controlled two-thirds of the total investment in the oil industry, more than half of the crude oil production, and most of the refining capacity. In the United States the control of just *eight* of the largest firms over net crude oil production increased from 39 percent in 1965 to 42.3 percent in 1970, then declined a little to 42.1 percent by the late 1970s. By the late 1970s just six of these vertically integrated companies (Exxon, Gulf, Shell, Conoco, Chevron, and Mobil) produced 37 percent of Texas crude oil (American Petroleum Institute, *Petroleum Industry Hearings before the Temporary National Economic Committee* [New York: American Petroleum Institute, 1942]), p. 12; Melvin de Chazeau and Alfred Kahn, *Integration and Competition in the Petroleum Industry* [New Haven: Yale University Press, 1959], pp. 13–14). There are medium-sized vertically integrated companies with headquarters in Texas, but they are smaller in assets and sales than the big multinational corporations.

31   Leading oil tools firms include Cameron Iron Works and Hughes Tool. ·

32   Lamare, *Texas Politics,* pp. 16–19; "Tenneco," in Milton Moskowitz, Michael Katz, and Robert Levering, eds., *Everybody's Business: An Almanac* (San Francisco: Harper and Row, 1980), pp. 848–850.

33   Daniel Benedict, "Houston Ranks in Top 10 of Two New Fortune 500 Rankings," *Houston Chronicle,* May 29, 1985, Sec. 3, p. 1. The 1983–1984 Fortune 500 data in this and the next paragraph are taken from two untitled brochures printed by the Economic Development Division, Houston Chamber of Commerce.

34   Benedict, "Houston Ranks in Top 10," Sec. 3, p. 1.

35   Taylor, personal interview.

36   Robert B. Cohen, "Multinational Corporations, International Finance, and the Sunbelt," in David Perry and Alfred Watkins, eds., *The Rise of the Sunbelt Cities* (Beverly Hills, Calif.: Sage, 1977), p. 221.

37   Burka, "The Year Everything Changed," p. 113.

38   Economics Division, *Texas Facts and Figures,* p. 35.

39   Corporate Data Exchange, *Banking and Finance: The Hidden Cost* (New York: Corporate Data Exchange, 1980), pp. 23–25; Alex Sheshunoff, *The Banks of Your State, 1980* (Austin: Sheshunoff, 1980).

40   "Port Booming Despite Decreased Volume," *Houston Business Journal,* Supplement, September 21, 1987, pp. 16–17.

41   Economic Division, *Texas Facts and Figures,* pp. 24–25; "Houston Leads U.S. Gulf Ports in Cotton Exports," *Port of Houston Magazine,* October 1986, pp. 4–6.

42   "Houston's Oil Firms Plunging into China," *Austin American Statesman,* December 10, 1973, p. B10; "Envoy Predicts Closer Houston-China Links," *Port of Houston Magazine,* June 1984, p. 34.

43   We do not have the space here to discuss changes in the laws on alcohol, which made Houston a more hospitable place for the convention business. See Burka, "The Year Everything Changed," p. 165.

44   Richard Child Hill and Joe R. Feagin, "Detroit and Houston: Two Cities in Global Perspective," in Michael P. Smith and Joe R. Feagin, eds., *The Capitalist City* (London: Basil Blackwell, 1987), pp. 155–177.

45   Ibid.; Economic Division, *Texas Facts and Figures,* p. 41.

46   Edward J. Malecki, "Public and Private Sector Interrelationships, Technological Change, and Regional Development, *Papers of the Regional Science Association* 47 (1981): 123–130; Edward J. Malecki, "Federal R and D Spending in the United States of America," *Regional Studies* 16 (1982): 27–32.

47   Rosanne Clark, "Part 2: High Tech on the Horizon," *Houston* 55 (May 1984): 34–35.

48   Ibid., pp. 37–38.

49   Ibid., pp. 37–38; Ray Berardinelli, "Houston Losing Ground in Venture Capital Game," *Houston Business Review,* November 5, 1984, pp. 1A, 20A.

50   First City Bancorporation, *Inside Texas 1983* (Houston: First City Bancorporation, 1983), p. 16; "Oil-field Supplies," *Business Week,* September 22, 1982, pp. 66–68.

51   Patrick Jankowski, "Houston's Top 100 Public Companies," *Houston* 54 (June 1983): 23–26; Patrick Jankowski, "Houston's Top 100 Public Companies," *Houston* 55 (June 1984): 20–25; Federal Reserve Bank of Dallas, "Texas Manufacturing Affected More by Dollar than by Oil Prices," *DallasFed,* September 1985, pp. 1–4.

52   Robert Reinhold, "Prosperity of Texas Begins to Fade as Prices for its Oil Treasure Fall," *New York Times,* March 20, 1983, pp. 1, 16; George Getschow, "The Dispossessed," *Wall Street Journal,* November 13, 1982, Sect. 1, p. 1.

53   Nat Eisenberg, "Economic Newsletter," *Houston* 57 (August 1986), p. 5.

54   Harold T. Gross and Bernard L. Weinstein, *Houston's Economic Development: Opportunities and Strategy* (Dallas: Southern Methodist University Center for Enterprising, 1985), p. 2; Plaut, "The Texas Economy," pp. 15–20; Gladys Ramirez, "Houston Travels Slow Road to Recovery," *Houston Post,* December 29, 1985, p. 1E.

55   Patrick Jankowski, "What's the Status of Texas' Reserves," *Houston* 57 (April 1986): 27–29.

56   Quoted in James Presley, *A Saga of Wealth: The Rise of the Texas Oilmen* (New York: G. P. Putnam's Sons, 1978), p. 391.

57   William Hoffman, personal interview, Texas Department of Water Resources, Planning and Development Division, 1983; Susan Sischoff, "Rippling Effects of Crude Oil Price Cuts Cause Anxiety Here," *Houston Chronicle,* October 21, 1984, Sec. 1, p. 1.

58   Patrick Jankowski, "Refining and the Challenge of Maturity," *Houston* 54 (July 1983): 19–20.

59   Patrick Jankowski, "Oil and Gas Companies Go Back to Basics," *Houston* 55 (August 1984): 45–49; "Fewer Corporate Faces in the Oil Patch Now," *Houston* 55 (December 1984): 9–13.

60   Thomas Petsinger, "In Houston Oil Employees Suffer," *Wall Street Journal,* November 29, 1984, pp. 1–2.

61   Taylor, personal interview.

62   Jankowski, "Refining and the Challenge of Maturity," pp. 19–21; John Tagliabue, "Oversupply in Petrochemicals," *New York Times,* April 2, 1983, p. 19Y.

63   A. Lewis Rhodes, "Oil Companies and the Environment in Ecological Per-

spective" (Tallahassee, Fla.: Florida State University, Department of Sociology, 1984, typescript); Barbara Shook, "New Saudi Refineries Will Not Increase Glut, O P E C Official Says," *Houston Chronicle,* November 9, 1984, Sec. 3, p. 1; Eileen O'Grady, "Big Growth for Chemicals in Houston," *Houston Post,* December 17, 1987, p. 1B.

64   Center for Economic and Demographic Forecasting, Rice Center, "Quarterly Update: Are We at the Bottom?" *Houston Profile,* Second Quarter, 1987, pp. 1–4; Ramirez, "Houston Travels Slow Road to Recovery," p. 1E; Susan Allen, "County Foreclosures Hit Record High," *Houston Business Journal,* April 13, 1987, p. 8.

65   Laurel Brubaker, "Local Bankruptcies Hit New High in '86," *Houston Business Journal,* March 16, 1987, p. 1A, 11A; Alison Cook and Peter Elkind, "Is This All There Is?" *Texas Monthly,* December 1984, p. 149; Carl Hooper, "2,500 Local Properties Repossessed," *Houston Post,* June 5, 1986, pp. 1F, 4F; Laurel Brubaker, "Houston Leads State in Business Bankruptcies," *Houston Business Journal,* May 29, 1984, p. 1A; "Cities Brace for Oil-slump Cutbacks," *Austin American-Statesman,* June 22, 1987, p. B4.

66   Eileen O'Grady, "Strong Medicine," *Houston Post,* January 5, 1987, p. 6F.

5   Who Runs Houston? The Succession of Business Elites

1   "Houston: The International City," *Fortune,* p. 49.

2   Ory M. Nergal, ed., *Houston: City of Destiny* (New York: Macmillan, 1980), p. 82.

3   McComb, *Houston,* p. 9.

4   Kathleen C. Abrams, Glenda K. Mill, and Ginger H. Hester, eds., *Houston: A Profile of Its Business, Industry and Port* (Woodlands, Tex.: Pioneer Publications, 1982), pp. 32–34; McComb, *Houston,* pp. 11–18.

5   Platt, *City Building in the New South,* pp. 9–19; Gail Rickey, "William M. Rice: Texas Merchant/Philanthropist," *Houston Business Journal,* November 4, 1985, pp. 1B, 4B–5B.

6   Platt, *City Building in the New South,* pp. 16–18.

7   Ibid., pp. 8, 18–22.

8   Ibid., pp. 144, 195. Buenger and Pratt, *But Also Good Business,* pp. 69–84; the quote is on p. 83.

9   Buenger and Pratt, *But Also Good Business,* pp. 81–82; John T. Maginnis, "Baker & Botts, 1866–1978," typescript.

10   Gail Rickey, "John H. Kirby," *Houston Business Journal,* June 3, 1985, pp. 1B, 10B; Mary Laswell, *John Henry Kirby: Prince of the Pines* (Austin: Encino Press, 1967), pp. 75–80.

11   Lasswell, *John Henry Kirby,* pp. 75–146.

12   Buenger and Pratt, *But Also Good Business,* pp. 51–53; Platt, *City Building in the New South,* pp. 185–187.

13   McComb, *Houston,* pp. 84–85; Platt, *City Building in the New South,* pp. 186–198.

14   Quoted in Platt, *City Building in the New South*, p. 176.
15   Ibid., pp. 86–132.
16   Ibid., pp. 137–140.
17   Ibid., pp. 170–179.
18   Ibid., p. 183.
19   Ibid., pp. 183–201.
20   The *New York Times* is quoted in *Progressive Houston* 1 (May 1909): 9. This was a publication of city government. The discussion of the channel draws on William D. Angel, "To Make a City," in David C. Perry and Alfred J. Watkins, eds., *The Rise of the Sunbelt Cities* (Beverly Hills: Sage, 1977), pp. 118–123; and Jerome H. Farber, "The Houston Chamber of Commerce," *National Municipal Review* 2 (January 1913): 104–107.
21   Joe J. Fox, "Houston Reflects the Spirit of the New South," *Houston* 1 (June 1930): 14, 25.
22   Don E. Carleton, *Red Scare* (Austin: Texas Monthly Press, 1985), pp. 65–71; Frank M. Stewart, "Mayor Oscar F. Holcombe of Houston," *National Municipal Review* (June 1928): 317–321.
23   "Texas," *Fortune*, p. 91.
24   Bascom H. Timmons, *Jesse H. Jones* (New York: Henry Holt, 1956), p. 83.
25   Ibid., pp. 30–80; Carleton, *Red Scare*, p. 66.
26   Ann Holmes, "Who was Alfred C. Finn?," *Houston Chronicle*, November 8, 1984, Section 4, pp. 1, 13.
27   Dana Blankenhorn, "Jesse Jones: The Financial Wizard Who Put Houston on the National Business Map," *Houston Business Journal*, September 10, 1984, pp. 1B, 4B–8B; Timmons, *Jesse H. Jones*, pp. 70–76.
28   Buenger and Pratt, *But Also Good Business*, pp. 102–105.
29   "Judge James A. Elkins, Sr.: For 50 Years 'The Judge' Ruled City," *Houston Business Journal*, September 24, 1984, pp. 1B, 4B–6B; Carleton, *Red Scare*, p. 70.
30   "The Brown Brothers: Houston's Contracting and Energy Giants," *Houston Business Journal*, October 1, 1984, pp. 1B, 6B–9B.
31   "Gus Wortham: Insurance Man Headed Houston Establishment," *Houston Business Journal*, October 8, 1984, pp. 1B, 4B–7B.
32   Gail Rickey, "'Mr. Jim' Abercrombie: A Giant in Oil Tools," *Houston Business Review*, July 1, 1985, pp. 14A–15A.
33   "Bob Smith: A Maverick Visionary with Very Keen Business Interests," *Houston Business Journal*, October 15, 1984, pp. 1B–8B; Scott Bennett, "Power," *Texas Business* (May 1980): 42.
34   "Will Clayton: Cotton Giant and Shaper of International Policy," *Houston Business Journal*, October 22, 1984, pp. 1B, 4B–7B; Gail Rickey, "M. D. Anderson: Catalyst Behind Major Med Center," *Houston Business Journal*, May 6, 1985, pp. 1B, 4B.
35   Gray, "A Report on the Politics of Houston," p. V-4.
36   Gail Rickey, "Glen H. McCarthy: A Legend Still Thriving in Oil and Real Estate," *Houston Business Journal*, November 5, 1984, pp. 1B, 6B; Dana Blankenhorn, "Hugh Roy Cullen: Oil Gifts Still Flow from King of the Texas Wildcatters,"

Houston Business Journal, September 17, 1984, pp. 1B, 13B–17B; Ed Kilman and Theon Wright, *Hugh Roy Cullen* (New York: Prentice-Hall, 1954).

37   Harry Hurt, "The Most Powerful Texans," *Texas Monthly* (April 1976): 73–123.

38   Phil Burch, personal communication, December 12, 1986; Stillwell, "Texas," p. 316.

39   Lee Jones, "Counsel to the Powerful," *Ft. Worth Star Telegram,* December 11, 1984, pp. 20–21; Ben Love, *People and Profits: A Bank Case Study* (Houston: Texas Commerce Bank, no date), pp. 26–41; Bennett, "Power," pp. 30–32.

40   Jones, "Counsel to the Powerful," pp. 20–21; Love, *People and Profits,* pp. 29–42; Bennett, "Power," p. 32.

41   "Eagle Lake Rod and Gun Club Year Book," Houston, Texas, February 1922.

42   *Houston Social Register* (Houston, 1963).

43   Anonymous, "Gus Wortham," pp. 4B–7B.

44   G. William Domhoff, "The Women's Page as a Window on the Ruling Class," in G. Tuchman, A. K. Daniels, and J. Benet, eds., *Hearth and Home* (New York: Oxford University Press, 1978), pp. 161–175. In this section I have used materials and tabulations kindly supplied by Bill Domhoff.

45   The original tabulations were supplied by Bill Domhoff.

46   Hurley, *Decisive Years for Houston,* p. 10.

47   "Wortham," p. 4B.

48   "Bob Smith," p. 6B.

49   "Carrying Houston's Industrial Message to the World," *Houston* 1 (May 1930): 25.

50   "Latin American Trade Up," *Houston* 12 (May 1941): 2.

51   McComb, *Houston,* pp. 174–185.

52   Blankenhorn, "Jesse Jones," pp. 5B–6B; Timmons, *Jesse H. Jones,* p. 136.

53   Anthony Champagne, *Congressman Sam Rayburn* (New Brunswick: Rutgers University Press, 1984), p. 153.

54   Robert A. Caro, *The Years of Lyndon Johnson: The Path to Power* (New York: Random House Vintage Books, 1983), pp. 371–372, 378–454.

55   Letters in author's files.

56   Letters in author's files.

57   Angel, "To Make a City," pp. 125–127.

58   Carleton, *Red Scare,* p. 67; "Judge James A. Elkins, Sr.," pp. 4B–6B.

59   Quoted in Griffin Smith, Jr., "Empires of Paper," in *Texas Monthly Political Reader* (Austin: Texas Monthly Press and Sterling Swift Publishing, 1978), p. 34.

60   Jones, "Counsel to the Powerful," pp. 20–21.

61   Lamare, *Texas Politics,* p. 81.

62   Bennett, "Power," p. 20.

63   Chandler Davidson, "Houston: The City Where the Business of Government is Business," in Wendell Bedichek and Neal Tannhill, eds., *Public Policy in Texas* (New York: Scott Foresman, 1982), p. 278.

64   Hurt, "The Most Powerful Texans," pp. 122–123.

65   Joe Hart, "The 'C' Club: Powerful Forces Lead Unusual P A C," *Houston Business Journal*, June 3, 1985, p. 1A.

66   For evidence on this point see Jesse H. Jones, *Fifty Billion Dollars: My Thirteen Years with the R F C* (New York: Macmillan, 1951).

6   "The Business of Government Is Business": Local Government and Privatized Planning

1   "Ex-Mayor Holcombe Dies," *Houston Post*, June 19, 1968, p. 1; see also McComb, *Houston*, pp. 96–98.

2   Ben Kaplan, "Houston Wins Manager Campaign," *National Municipal Review* 31 (October 1942): 481–484; "Houston Drops Out," *National Municipal Review* 36 (September 1947): 428–429; Gray, "A Report on the Politics of Houston," pp. II-1, II-30.

3   Lance Lalor, *City of Houston: Comprehensive Annual Financial Report* (Houston: Office of City Controller, 1985), pp. VII–IX.

4   See Carleton, *Red Scare*, p. 70; "Bob Smith: A Maverick Visionary with Very Keen Business Interests," *Houston Business Journal*, October 15, 1984, p. 6b; Gray, "A Report on the Politics of Houston," p. V-6.

5   Carleton, *Red Scare*, pp. 69–73; Gary, "A Report on the Politics of Houston," sections V and VI.

6   Louie Welch, "Forward," in Nergal, ed., *Houston*, p. i.

7   League of Women Voters, *Houston Handbook* (Houston: League of Women Voters, 1980); Gray, "A Report on the Politics of Houston," pp. IV-10, IV-13.

8   Nergal, *Houston: City of Destiny*, pp. 82–91.

9   Peter Elkind, "Mayor, Council Locked in a Bitter Struggle," *Texas Monthly*, February 1985, p. 122.

10   Dick Bryant, "City in the Red: Houston Feels the Heat of Fiscal Crisis," *Houston Business Journal*, March 21, 1983, Section A, p. 1; Brenda Sapino and Andrew Benson, "303 Layoffs in Whitmire's $1.29 Billion Budget," *Houston Post*, June 13, 1987, p. 1A; "Chamber Reviews City Budget," *At Work*, August 1987, p. 1. *At Work* is a newsletter of the Houston Chamber and replaced the magazine *Houston*, which ceased in the economic crisis of the 1980s.

11   Barry J. Kaplan, "Urban Development, Economic Growth, and Personal Liberty: The Rhetoric of the Houston Anti-Zoning Movements, 1947–1962," *Southwestern Historical Quarterly* 84 (October 1980): 133–141.

12   Ibid., pp. 154–155.

13   Ibid., pp. 153–158.

14   Neal R. Peirce, *The Megastates of America* (New York: Norton, 1972), p. 531.

15   Bernard H. Siegan, *Land Use without Planning* (Lexington: Heath-Lexington Books, 1972); Stephen Fox, "Planning in Houston: A Historic Overview," *Cite*, Fall 1985, p. 14.

16   Jones, "City Planning in Houston without Zoning," p. 6.

17   Robert Fisher, "'Be on the Lookout': Neighborhood Civic Clubs in Houston," *Houston Review* 6 (1984): 105–116.

18   Ibid., pp. 112–113.

19   Interview with Joe Chou, City Planning Department, Houston, Texas, May 6, 1981.

20   Fox, "Planning in Houston, p. 14.

21   City Planning Department, *1980 Annual Report* (Houston: City Planning Department, 1980), pp. 2–6.

22   Interview with Joe Chou.

23   Paul Burka, "Why is Houston Falling Apart?" *Texas Monthly,* November 1980, p. 190.

24   Ibid., pp. 190, 308–309.

25   Rice Center, *Annexation and Houston: Research Summary* (Houston: Rice Center, 1979), pp. 1–3; Virginia M. Perrenod, *Special Districts, Special Purposes* (College Station, Tex.: Texas A&M Press, 1984), pp. 3–31.

26   *Big Town, Big Money* (Houston: Cordovan Press, 1973), pp. 29–30.

27   Hurley, *Decisive Years for Houston,* p. 112.

28   *Big Town, Big Money,* pp. 29–30.

29   "Houston Chamber of Commerce: A History of Leadership" (Houston: Houston Chamber of Commerce, 1984).

30   Hurley, *Decisive Years for Houston,* p. 168; *Big Town, Big Money,* pp. 33–34.

31   See Susan S. Fainstein and Norman S. Fainstein, "Economic Change, National Policy and the System of Cities," in Fainstein, et al., *Restructuring the City,* pp. 1–26.

32   "City Leadership Presents Economic Development Plan," *Houston* 55 (July 1984): 9–13.

33   Eileen O'Grady, "Nearly $1 Million Pledged to H E D C," *Houston Post,* May 5, 1986, p. 1D; Eileen O'Grady, "H E D C Surpasses Goal, Raises $7.2 million," *Houston Post,* February 28, 1987, p. 1F.

34   Joe Hart, "Council Wins Fight to Fund H E D C," *Houston Business Journal,* March 24, 1986, p. 1A.

35   Ibid., p. 6A; John Gravois, "H E D C Weighs Strings Attached to Tax Dollars," *Houston Post,* April 14, 1986, p. 1A.

36   Rosanne Clark, "Development Council Maps Economic Strategy," *Houston* 56 (February 1985): 9–13.

37   Rosanne Clark, "What Can Houston Learn from Massachusetts?," *Houston* 57 (May 1986): 9–13.

38   Houston Economic Development Council (H E D C), "Strategic Priorities Agenda" (Houston: Houston Economic Development Council, 1986, typescript), p. 4.

39   Ibid., pp. 8–9.

40   Clark, "Development Council Maps Economic Strategy," pp. 12–13; Laurel Brubaker, "How Houston Really Landed Grumman," *Houston Business Journal,* October 13, 1986, p. 1.

41   Bob Sablatura, "The Many Roads to Economic Recovery: Other U.S. Cities Have Solved the Riddle of Economic Development," *Houston Business Journal,* October 6, 1986, p. 1.

42   H E D C, "Strategic Priorities Agenda," p. 14.

43   Dear, *State Apparatus,* pp. 131–151.

44   John Gravois, "Chamber of Commerce Backs Form of Zoning," *Houston Post,* September 8, 1986, p. 10A.

45   Phillip Lopate, "Pursuing the Unicorn: Public Space in Houston," *Cite,* Winter 1984, p. 18.

7   The Spatial Dimensions of Houston's Development: Investments in the Built Environment

1   McKenzie, "Scope of Human Ecology," in Theodorson, ed., *Urban Patterns,* p. 28.

2   Gottdiener, *Social Production of Urban Space,* pp. 239–252.

3   See Fainstein, et al, *Restructuring the City.*

4   Lopate, "Pursuing the Unicorn," p. 18. The discussion of areas draws on Robert H. McManus and Walter J. Addison, *Draft Environmental Impact Statement/ Alternatives Analysis: Southwest/Westpark Corridor* (Houston: Urban Mass Transit Administration and Harris County Metro Transit Authority, 1980), p. III-2.

5   Rosanne Clark, "Slow Industrial Market Means Bargains for Tenants and Buyers," *Houston* 57 (September 1986): 8–10.

6   Houston Independent School District, *A Compilation of General Statistical Information: August 1982* (Houston: Houston Independent School District, 1982), p. 26.

7   Kasarda, "The Implications of Contemporary Redistribution Trends," pp. 373–400; Hawley, *Urban Society.*

8   Helen Leavitt, *Superhighway-Superhoax* (Garden City, N.Y.: Doubleday, 1970), p. 40.

9   Quoted in Robert Goodman, *After the Planners* (New York: Simon and Schuster, 1971), p. 69.

10   "North By-Pass to be Built," *Houston* 13 (July 1942): 7.

11   Robert L. Bobbitt, "Texas Highways and National Defense," *Houston* 12 (March 1941): 15.

12   Fox, "Planning in Houston," p. 14.

13   "Huge Highway Program for Houston and Its Area, *Houston* 17 (October 1945): 34–35.

14   Robert D. Bullard, "Blacks in Heavenly Houston," Paper presented at Annual Meeting of the National Association of Black Social Workers, Chicago, Illinois, April 6–11, 1982, p. 32.

15   Bob Sablatura, "The Great Grand Parkway Experiment," *Houston Business Journal,* November 17, 1986, p. 1A.

16   Don E. Carleton and Thomas H. Kreneck, *Houston: Back Where We Started* (Houston: Houston City Magazine, 1979), p. 2.

17   Carleton and Kreneck, *Houston*, p. 21.

18   David Kaplan, "Suburbia Deserta," *Cite*, Winter 1986, pp. 18–19; Mark A. Hewitt, "The Stuff of Dreams: New Housing Outside the Loop," *Cite*, Summer 1985, p. 13.

19   The Woodlands Development Corporation, fact sheet in the author's files.

20   Rosanne Clark, "The Woodlands," *Houston* 57 (October 1986): 4W.

21   Interview with George Mitchell, originally published by Ginger Jester in *Houston North Magazine*, November 1980, revised and published as a brochure for The Woodlands, p. 5.

22   Ibid.

23   Mitchell Energy and Development Corporation, *Annual Report*, Houston, January 31, 1981, p. 43.

24   Kaplan, "Suburbia Deserta," p. 18; Susan Allen, "Owners Destroy 4,100 Houston Apartment Units," *Houston Business Journal*, November 30, 1987, pp. 1, 8.

25   Gordon Wittenberg, "The Environmental Impact of Tall Building," *Cite*, Spring-Summer 1984, pp. 14–16.

26   Francois Lamarche, "Property Development and the Economic Foundations of the Urban Question," in Chris Pickvance, ed., *Urban Sociology* (London: Tavistock, 1976), p. 98.

27   Stephen Fox, "Scraping the Houston Sky: 1894–1976," *Cite*, Spring-Summer 1984, pp. 10–12.

28   Urban Land Institute, *Development Review and Outlook 1983–1984* (Washington, D.C.: Urban Land Institute, 1983, p. 71.

29   Fox, "Scraping the Houston Sky," pp. 11–12.

30   "Houston Office Summary by Graphic Sectors," *Houston Business Journal*, February 11, 1985, pp. 28c–29c; "Office Space Survey," *Buildings*, 79 (January 1985): 72–73.

31   Robert E. Witherspoon, Jon P. Abbott, and Robert M. Gladstone, *Mixed-Use Developments: New Ways of Land Use* (Washington, D.C.: Urban Land Institute, 1976), pp. 6–44.

32   Quoted in Siegan, *Land Use without Zoning*, p. 70.

33   Speech by Texas Eastern Executive, July 17, 1981, p. 3, in the author's files.

34   Ibid., pp. 5–6.

35   Rice Center, "Downtown Area," *Research Brief 10*, January 1982, pp. 1–4.

36   Julie Hyland, "A Demand Analysis of the Houston Office Market" (Graduate seminar paper, Business School, University of Texas, 1985).

37   Gerald Hines Interests news release and brochures, in author's files.

38   J. Thomas Black, Donald O'Connell, and Michael Morina, *Downtown Office Growth and the Role of Public Transit* (Washington, D.C.: Urban Land Institute, 1982).

39   "The Master Builder," *Newsweek*, August 31, 1981, p. 45.

40   Century Development Corporation, Greenway Plaza brochures; interview with senior research official at the Rice Center, Greenway Plaza, May 1981.

41   Harvey, *Urbanization of Capital*.

42   Gottdiener, *Social Production of Urban Space*, pp. 94–101.

43   Interview with John Smith (Pseudonym), senior banking official, May 1985, Houston, Texas; Michael Moffitt, *The World's Money* (New York: Simon and Schuster, 1983).

44   Feagin, *Urban Real Estate Game,* pp. 48–55.

45   "Foreign Investors Buy Up Downtown Houston," *Austin American-Statesman,* August 23, 1987, p. G1. Warren, Gorham, and Lamont (investing firm), "The Mortgage and Real Estate Report," 15 (September 1982): 1–3; this a company newsletter.

46   Susan Allen, "Lenders Admit to a Lack of Caution, But Say Oversupply Not All Their Fault," *Houston Business Journal,* April 22, 1985, p. 2b.

47   "Forget the Gloom and Doom, Opportunities Still Abound," *Houston Business Journal,* February 11, 1985, p. 4c.

48   Ibid.

49   Mark Gottdiener, *Planned Sprawl* (Beverly Hills, Calif.: Sage, 1977), pp. 111–119.

50   "Forget the Gloom and Doom," p. 3c.

51   Peggy Roberts, "Office Space Survey Forecasts Market Trends," *Houston Business Journal,* July 30, 1984, p. 27c–29c; "Office Space Survey," *Buildings* 79 (January 1985): 72–73; "20 Tallest Buildings in Texas," *Houston Business Journal,* December 1, 1986, p. 20.

52   Hyland, "A Demand Analysis of the Houston Office Market."

53   Peggy Roberts, "Savvy Marketing Helps Developer Buck the Trend," *Houston Business Journal,* February 11, 1985, p. 26c–28c.

54   Deborah Fowler, "Real Estate Problems Worry Top Banks," *Houston Business Journal,* September 23, 1985, pp. 1a, 11a; Deborah Fowler, "Banks Take Another Beating in 1985," *Houston Business Journal,* February 3, 1986, pp. 1A, 14A.

55   Interview with W. L. Born, Assistant Research Economist, Texas Real Estate Research Center, Spring 1985.

56   Gerald D. Suttles, "The Cumulative Texture of Local Urban Culture," *American Journal of Sociology* 90 (September 1984): 282–304.

57   Roberts, "Office Space Survey," p. 27c.

58   J. A. F. Stoner, "A Comparison of Individual and Group Decisions Involving Risk" (Master's thesis, M I T Sloan School of Management, Cambridge, Mass., 1961).

59   David Harvey, *The Limits to Capital* (Chicago: University of Chicago Press, 1982), p. 395.

8   Problems in a Free Enterprise Paradise: The Social Costs of Good Business Climate

1   Karl Kapp, *The Social Costs of Private Enterprise* (New York: Schocken Books, 1950), pp. 13–25.

2   Francis X. Sutton, Seymour Harris, Karl Kaysen, and James Tobin, *The American Business Creed* (Cambridge: Harvard, 1956), p. 72.

3   Dan Luria and Jack Russell, *Rational Reindustrialization* (Detroit: Widge-tripper Press, 1981), pp. 30–34; David Smith, *The Public Balance Sheet* (Washington, D.C.: Conference on Alternative State and Local Policies, 1979), p. 3.

4   Bluestone and Harrison, *Deindustrialization of America*, p. 106.

5   Kapp, *Social Costs of Private Enterprise*, pp. xiv–xv.

6   For new work in the Kapp tradition see Leipert, "The Other Economic Summit 1985," p. 13.

7   Jerry Laws, "Houston Clearinghouse for Hazardous Materials," *Houston Post*, September 23, 1984, p. 1D.

8   Laurel Brubaker, "E P A Head Dumps on City's Waste," *Houston Business Journal*, October 8, 1984, p. 12A.

9   Bill Dawson, "Toxic Drums May Be at Sites Where Barbecue Pits Made," *Houston Chronicle*, March 8, 1985, Section 1, p. 1.

10   Harold Scarlett, "Residents Organizing to Fight Proposed P C B Storage," *Houston Post*, October 7, 1983, p. 6A.

11   Tom Curtis, "P C Bs Threaten Water in South Houston," *Dallas Times Herald Southwest Edition*, July 17, 1983, p. 29A; Peggy Roberts, "Toxic Waste Case Creeps into Court," *Houston Business Journal*, May 5, 1986, pp. 1A, 7A.

12   Peirce, *Megastates of America*, p. 533.

13   Bonnie Britt, "Pollution Far More than Abstract Term to Frustrated Deer Park Residents," *Houston Chronicle*, November 15, 1981, Section 7, p. 1.

14   Jimmie Woods, "Time Bomb Ticking Underneath the Hill," *Houston Post*, May 4, 1986, p. 13a.

15   Harold Scarlett, "Will River Oaks Sewage Still Go to Bayou?" *Houston Post*, July 5, 1984, p. 6D.

16   Harold Scarlett, "Additional Wastes Could Turn Buffalo Bayou in Giant Sewer," *Houston Post*, July 25, 1982, p. 1J; Harold Scarlett, "Buffalo Bayou: Mechanical Aeration Proposed for Stream," *Houston Post*, October 21, 1983, p. C5; Laurel Brubaker, "Houston Waste Sites," *Houston Business Journal*, March 10, 1986, p. 1A.

17   Allan C. Kimball and Leslie Loddeke, "West Side Subsidence Speeds Up," *Houston Post*, March 28, 1985, p. 1A.

18   Bill Coulter, "Subsidence Solution Outlined by Engineer," *Houston Post*, March 23, 1984, p. 5B; Rice Center, *Houston Initiatives: Phase One Report* (Houston: Rice Center, 1981), pp. 27–28; Leslie Loddeke, "Damages Estimated at 250 Homes," *Houston Post*, June 15, 1987, p. 1A.

19   Rice Center, *Houston Initiatives*, pp. 34–35.

20   Emily Yoffe, "Hate Thy Neighbor," *Texas Monthly*, June 1986, p. 117.

21   Geoffrey Leavenworth, "Houston: Will It Choke on Its Own Success?" *Texas Business*, December 1980, p. 31.

22   Harold Scarlett, "Public Cautioned to Avoid Polluted Sections of Lake Houston," *Houston Post*, October 20, 1983, Section A, p. 6.

23   Houston City Council, *Report of the City Council Committee on Lake Houston*, Houston, January 16, 1984, p. 6.

24   Harold Scarlett, "Buffalo Bayou: Mechanical Aeration Proposed for Stream," *Houston Post*, Section c, p. 5.

25   Ibid.

26   Gordon Wittenberg, "The Environmental Impact of Tall Building," *Cite,* Spring-Summer 1984, pp. 14–15.

27   Paul Sweeney, "Life—and Death—On the Job in Texas City," *Texas Observer,* November 6, 1981, pp. 1, 10–11.

28   Bonnie Britt, "Pollution Far More than an Abstract Term to Frustrated Deer Park Residents," *Houston Chronicle,* November 15, 1981, Section 7, p. 1.

29   *Ibid.,* p. 4; Guy Cantwell, "3,000 Flee Deadly Gas from Blaze at Ship Channel Sulfur Plant," *Houston Post,* May 25, 1986, pp. 1a, 26a.

30   Harold Scarlett, "Air Research Expanded: Experts Briefed on Study of Gulf Coast Pollutants," *Houston Post,* July 28, 1983, Section A, p. 8.

31   Jerry Laws, "Frantic Freeways Forecast for City," *Houston Post,* June 6, 1985, p. 1A; see also Bradford Snell, *American Ground Transport,* a Committee Print of the Subcommittee on Antitrust and Monopoly of the Committee on the Judiciary, United States Senate, February 26, 1974.

32   Rice Center, *Houston Initiatives,* p. 22.

33   Ibid.; Kim Cobb, "Katy Traffic Expected to Worsen for a While," *Houston Chronicle,* May 3, 1985, Section 1, p. 27.

34   Wayne King, "Unfriendly Driving Explodes into Violence on Texas Freeway," *New York Times,* December 16, 1983, Section A, p. 12.

35   Patricia Cronkright, "West University," *Houston Business Journal,* December 12, 1983, p. 1A.

36   Thomas H. Mayor and Richard Murray, *1983 Houston Metropolitan Area Survey* (Houston: Center for Public Policy, University of Houston, 1983), p. 5; Center for Public Policy, "Houston Metropolitan Area Survey" (University of Houston, University Park Campus, 1986).

37   Stephen L. Klineberg, "The Houston Area Survey—1985" (Report, Rice University, March 1985); Stephen L. Klineberg, "Public Perceptions of Environmental Quality in the Houston-Galveston Area" (Paper presented to General Assembly, Texas Environmental Coalition, Galveston, Texas, January 31, 1987), pp. 1–7.

38   Norma Henry Beard, ed., *The City Book of Houston,* (Houston: City Government, 1925); Burka, "Why is Houston Falling Apart?", p. 191.

39   Gray, "A Report on the Politics of Houston," p. VI–30.

40   Wittenberg, "The Environmental Impact of Tall Building," pp. 14–16; see also Patricia Cronkright, "Houston's Sewer Moratorium: Putting the Squeeze on Growth," *Houston Business Journal,* December 8, 1980, Section 1, p. 1.

41   Harold Scarlett and Andrew Benson, "Houston Fined $500,000," *Houston Post,* March 4, 1987, p. 1A.

42   Dick Bryant, "Inner City Ready to Grow as Sewer Moratorium Ends," *Houston Business Journal,* December 5, 1983, Section A, p. 1.

43   Patricia Cronkright, "Developers Use Detention Ponds to Fight Floods," *Houston Business Journal,* January 9, 1984, Section A, pp. 1, 12.

44   Bryant, "Inner City Ready to Grow as Sewer Moratorium Ends," Section A, p. 1.

45   Tom Kennedy, "Chamber Reveals Proposals for Flood Control, Waste Pick-up," *Houston Post*, September 21, 1983, Section A, p. 8.

46   Bonnie Britt, "West Houston is Slowly Sinking, but Solutions are Expensive," *Houston Chronicle*, May 29, 1983, Section 7, p. 8; Bill Coulter, "Subsidence Solution Outlined by Engineer," *Houston Post*, March 23, 1984, p. 5B.

47   Rice Center, *Houston Initiatives*, pp. 27–28.

48   Ibid., p. 34; see Britt, "Pollution Far More than an Abstract Term to Frustrated Deer Park Residents," Section 7, p. 1.

49   Cronkright, "Developers Use Detention Ponds," p. 1.

50   Geoffrey Leavenworth, "Houston: Will It Choke on Its Own Success?" *Texas Business*, December 1980, p. 31.

51   Houston City Council, *Report of the City Council Committee on Lake Houston*, Houston, January 16, 1984, p. 6.

52   Bill Dawson, "Haughton Passes Pollution Complaint to Air Control Board," *Houston Chronicle*, May 10, 1985, Section 1, p. 27.

53   Carlos Byars, "E P A Sanctions Could Ban Construction Along Ship Channel Unless Moves to Clear Air Taken," *Houston Chronicle*, February 2, 1983, Section 1, p. 10; Harold Scarlett, "Group Says Clean-air Bills Could Cost Houston," *Houston Post*, September 3, 1987, p. 3A.

54   Rice Center, *Houston Initiatives*, p. 50.

55   Robert Reinhold, "Houston Ponders Public Transit Plan," *New York Times*, September 28, 1982, Section Y, p. 11.

56   Wittenberg, "The Environmental Impact of Tall Building," pp. 14–16.

57   "City Jail Report Cites Poor Staffing, Safety," *Houston Chronicle*, January 18, 1983, Section 1, p. 1.

58   Mark Carreau, "Houston's Park System Could Be at Its Most Critical Juncture Ever," *Houston Post*, November 8, 1982: Section A, p. 1.

59   Lopate, "Pursuing the Unicorn," p. 18.

60   Burka, "Why is Houston Falling Apart?", p. 190; Mark Carreau, "Inspection Inadequacy Called Curb to Building," *Houston Post*, July 28, 1983, Section A, p. 8.

61   Margaret Downing, "Hiring Your Own Cop Pays Off," *Houston Post*, February 6, 1984, Section A, p. 3; Rice Center, *Houston Initiatives*, p. 53.

62   Dick Bryant, "City in the Red: Houston Feels the Heat of Fiscal Crisis," *Houston Business Journal*, March 21, 1983, Section A, p. 1; Sapino and Benson, "303 Layoffs in Whitmire's $1.29 Billion Budget," p. 1A.

63   Mike Snyder, "Lalor Says City Facing 'Retrenchment,'" *Houston Chronicle*, February 23, 1982, Section 1, p. 10.

64   Susan A. MacManus, *Federal Aid to Houston*, (Washington, D.C.: Brookings, 1983), p. 59.

65   Klineberg, "The Houston Area Survey—1985."

66   "Pro-Houston Wants to See Some Spirit Here," *Houston* 54 (January 1984), p. 35.

9   The Delivery of Services to Houston's Minority and Low-Income Communities

1   W. J. Cash, *The Mind of the South* (New York: Random House Vintage Books, 1960), pp. 4–34.

2   McComb, *Houston*, pp. 76–85; Cary D. Wintz, *Blacks in Houston* (Houston: Houston Center for the Humanities, 1982), pp. 10–14.

3   McComb, *Houston*, p. 108.

4   Tom Abernathy, "Houston's Little Harlem Thrives on Laughter," *Houston Press*, April 15, 1931, n.p.

5   Francis L. Lowenheim, "False Crescendo," *Texas Monthly*, January 1986, p. 168.

6   Robert Fisher, " 'Be on the Lookout': Neighborhood Civic Clubs in Houston," *Houston Review* 6 (1984): 105–113.

7   Wintz, *Blacks in Houston*, pp. 26–30.

8   Ibid., pp. 2–14.

9   City of Houston, Planning Department, *Third Ward: Community Development Area* (Houston: City Planning Department, 1979), pp. 1–7.

10   Urban Mass Transportation Administration, *Draft Environmental Impact Statement*, pp. III-30, III-32.

11   "City's Black Leaders Note Tortuous Road to Progress," *Houston Post*, June 16, 1985, p. 18A.

12   Platt, *City Building in the New South*, p. 211.

13   City of Houston, *Overall Economic Development Plan for the Economic Development Target Area* (Houston: City of Houston, 1978), p. 12.

14   Wintz, *Blacks in Houston*, p. 19.

15   Ibid., pp. 19–20.

16   Robert D. Bullard, "Blacks in Heavenly Houston" (Paper presented at Annual Meeting of the National Association of Black Social Workers, Chicago, Illinois, April 6–11, 1982), pp. 8–9.

17   Robert D. Bullard, "Solid Waste Sites and the Black Houston Community" (Paper presented at the Annual Meeting, Southwestern Sociological Association, March 17–20, 1982), pp. 6–14.

18   Ibid., p. 20.

19   City of Houston, Planning Department, *Montrose/4th Ward: Community Development Area* (Houston: City Planning Department, 1979), pp. 11–12; City of Houston, City Planning, *SouthPark/Foster Place/MacGregor: Community Development Area* (Houston: City Planning, Department, 1979), pp. 1–13.

20   Bullard, "Blacks in Heavenly Houston," p. 19; see also pp. 18–19.

21   Bill Minutaglio, "Houston's Baddest Street," *Houston Chronicle Magazine*, June 12, 1983, pp. 1–15.

22   Joel Garreau, *The Nine Nations of North America* (Boston: Houghton Mifflin, 1981), p. 138.

23   Bullard, "Blacks in Heavenly Houston," pp. 25–27; City of Houston, Planning Department, *Montrose/4th Ward*, pp. 1–10.

24   Kathy Collmer, "Fourth Ward," letter to the editor, *Houston Chronicle,* November 9, 1984, Section 2, p. 1.

25   Mark Carreau, "A C L U Brief Challenges Assessment of Allen Parkway," *Houston Chronicle,* October 4, 1984, Section 1, p. 20.

26   "Fourth Ward Update: Houston Proud," *Cite,* Winter, 1986, p. 4.

27   McComb, *Houston,* p. 112.

28   Leslie Linthicum, "Nightmare at T S U in '67 Still Spawns Controversy," *Houston Post,* May 11, 1987, p. 1A; McComb, *Houston,* p. 170.

29   Gray, "A Report on the Politics of Houston," p. VI-1.

30   McComb, *Houston,* pp. 166–168.

31   Platt, *City Building in the New South,* pp. 158–160.

32   Margarita Melville, *Mexicans in Houston* (Houston: Houston Center for the Humanities, 1982), pp. 1–6.

33   "City Ranks 7th as Hispanic Area," *Houston Post,* November 21, 1986, p. 6A; Nestor Rodriguez, "The Hispanic Communities" (University of Houston, Department of Sociology, 1986, typescript), pp. 18–20.

34   Interview with Leonel Castillo, Houston, Texas, October 3, 1984.

35   Chet Burchett, "Immigration Law Sparks Firings," *Houston Post,* March 1, 1987, p. 11a; Melville, *Mexicans in Houston,* pp. 19–20.

36   Urban Mass Transportation Administration, *Draft Environmental Impact Statement,* p. III-30, III-32.

37   Juan R. Palomo and Jim Simmon, "Houston Hispanics: Future Could Be Bright But Road Will Be Tough," *Houston Post,* March 1, 1987, pp. 1A, 16A.

38   City of Houston, City Planning Department, *Magnolia: Community Development Area* (Houston: City Planning Department, 1979), pp. 9–12.

39   Palomo and Simmon, "Houston Hispanics," pp. 1A, 16A.

40   Ibid., p. 16A.

41   Ibid.

42   Ibid. (emphasis in original).

43   Ibid.

44   Chandler Davidson, "Houston: The City where the Business of Government is Business," in Wendell Bedichek and Neal Tannhill, eds., *Public Policy in Texas* (New York: Scott Foresman, 1982), pp. 275–288.

45   Bonnie Britt and Nicholas C. Chriss, "More Go Hungry Despite All Efforts," *Houston Chronicle,* May 10, 1985, Section 1, p. 26; Lou Jakovac, "Thousands Stand in Food Lines for Salvation Army Handouts," *Houston Post,* February 25, 1987, p. 10A.

46   David Ellison, "Lack of Housing for Houston Homeless Decried," *Houston Post,* October 16, 1986, p. 16A.

47   M. Bruce Johnson, ed., *Resolving the Housing Crisis* (San Francisco: Pacific Institute for Public Policy Research, 1982).

48   Housing Authority of the City of Houston, "Assisted Housing in Houston—Harris County, Texas," Typescript statement, Houston, Texas, 1987.

49   Ibid., p. 1 (emphasis added). They probably meant to say "proportions."

50   These figures were supplied by John Gilderbloom, Department of Sociology, University of Houston; John Gilderbloom, Mark Rosentraub, and Robert Bullard,

"Designing, Locating and Financing Transportation services for Low Income, Elderly and Disabled Persons" University of Houston Center for Public Policy, Houston, Texas, July 23, 1987, typescript research report, pp. 21–28.

51   Ibid., pp. 2–3.

52   This paragraph draws on a telephone interview with the housing specialist John Gilderbloom, December 23, 1987.

10   The World Market, the State, and the Social Costs of Growth in the Free Enterprise City

1   "Houston," *Time,* Special advertising section, April 20, 1987, n.p.

2   Ibid.

3   Dahl, *Who Governs?;* Floyd Hunter, *Community Power Structure* (Chapel Hill: University of North Carolina, 1953).

4   E. Butler, M. Pirie, and P. Young, *The Omega File* (London: Adam Smith Institute, 1985), p. 368.

5   McComb, *Houston,* pp. 81–82.

6   Sibley, *Port of Houston,* pp. 177–179.

7   Platt, *City Building in the New South,* pp. 157–163.

8   Pratt, *Growth of a Refining Region,* p. 172; see also pp. 172–175.

9   Raymond Klempin, "Labor Unions: Is Houston Target of Coming Organizational Blitz?" *Houston Business Journal,* September 7, 1981, p. 1.

10   Ira Katznelson, *City Trenches,* (Chicago: University of Chicago Press, 1981); David Moberg, "Hard Organizing in Sunbelt City," *Progressive,* August 1983, pp. 34–36.

11   Patricia Manson, "Houston's Unions Poised to Reverse Membership Woes," *Houston Post,* April 28, 1985, p. 3E.

12   Moberg, "Hard Organizing in Sunbelt City," p. 36.

13   Raymond Klempin, "Houston Labor Unions Take Big Pay Cuts," *Houston Business Journal,* December 10, 1984, pp. 1A, 13A; Rodney Young, "Houston Labor Unions," *Houston Business Journal,* July 14, 1983, pp. 1A, 18A–20A.

14   Harold Scarlett, "Woman Launches Fight to Save Fishing Hole," *Houston Post,* October 7, 1982, p. 24A.

15   Diana Hunt, "'Squatter' in Protest against Housing Crunch," *Houston Chronicle,* April 16, 1982, Section 1, p. 14.

16   Jim Asker, "Funds for Change," *Houston Post,* October 22, 1983, p. 5F; "City Politicians and Houston's T M O," *The Texas Catholic Herald,* October 14, 1983, p. 1; Interview with Robert Rivera, T M O organizer, July 30, 1987.

17   Carleton, *Red Scare,* p. 25.

18   Quoted in ibid., p. 73.

19   Ibid., pp. 81–83.

20   Davidson, "Houston: The City Where the Business of Government is Business," in *Public Policy in Texas,* pp. 275–288.

21   Houston Chamber of Commerce, "1980–1981 Action Plan" (typescript, in author's files).

22   Center for Economic and Demographic Forecasting, Rice Center, "Quarterly Update: Are We at the Bottom?" *Houston. Profile,* Second Quarter, 1987, pp. 1–4.

23   Markusen, *Profit Cycles, Oligopoly, and Regional Development,* p. 288.

24   Ibid., p. 289.

25   Tomi J. Martella et al., *The Minneapolis New Resident Guide* (San Diego, Calif.: M A R C O A Publishing Inc., 1987), p. 42.

26   Pierre Clavel, *The Progressive City* (New Brunswick: Rutgers University Press, 1986), pp. 210–234.

INDEX